CONTENTS

PART I: GETTING STARTED WITH VISUAL BASIC 4

CHAPTER ONE

What's New in Visual Basic 4? **3**

CHAPTER NINE

The Visual Interface **105**

CHAPTER TEN

Graphics **123**

CHAPTER TWENTY-TWO

Project Development   **257**

CHAPTER TWENTY-THREE

Advanced Programming Techniques   **265**

CHAPTER TWENTY-FOUR

Miscellaneous Techniques   **291**

PART III   SAMPLE APPLICATIONS

CHAPTER TWENTY-FIVE

Graphics   **303**

CHAPTER TWENTY-SIX

Development Tools   **351**

CHAPTER TWENTY-SEVEN

Date and Time   **379**

CHAPTER TWENTY-EIGHT

Databases **425**

CHAPTER TWENTY-NINE

Utilities **455**

CHAPTER THIRTY

Advanced Techniques **479**

Microsoft®
Visual
Basic® 4.0
Developer's
Workshop
THIRD EDITION

John Clark Craig

***Microsoft* Press**

PUBLISHED BY
Microsoft Press
A Division of Microsoft Corporation
One Microsoft Way
Redmond, Washington 98052-6399

Copyright © 1996 by John Clark Craig

Library of Congress Cataloging-in-Publication Data
Craig, John Clark.
    Microsoft Visual Basic 4.0 developer's workshop / John Clark Craig.
        p.   cm.
    Includes index.
    ISBN 1-55615-664-2
    1. BASIC (Computer program language)   2. Microsoft Visual BASIC.
    I. Title.
    QA76.73.B3C717   1996
    005.265–dc20   95-51205
                                                            CIP

Printed and bound in the United States of America.

1 2 3 4 5 6 7 8 9   MLML   1 0 9 8 7 6

Distributed to the book trade in Canada by Macmillan of Canada, a division of Canada
Publishing Corporation.

A CIP catalogue record for this book is available from the British Library.

Microsoft Press books are available through booksellers and distributors worldwide. For further
information about international editions, contact your local Microsoft Corporation office. Or
contact Microsoft Press International directly at fax (206) 936-7329.

RoboHelp is a trademark of Blue Sky Software Corporation. Hyperterminal is a registered
trademark of Hilgraeve, Inc. Microsoft, Visual Basic, and Windows are registered trademarks
and Windows NT is a trademark of Microsoft Corporation. Unicode is a trademark of
Unicode, Inc.

Acquisitions Editors: Dean Holmes, Eric Stroo
Project Editor: Katherine A. Krause
Technical Editor: Jerry Joyce

ACKNOWLEDGMENTS

It just keeps getting better and better! The Basic language, that is. Microsoft once again has taken Visual Basic to new heights, providing us with a powerful tool for programming 32-bit applications for the popular Windows 95 operating system. I applaud Microsoft for a great product, and Bill Gates for his amazing vision for the future!

This book, and Visual Basic 4.0 itself, were a long time in development. I want to thank several of the fine people at Microsoft Press for their patience and understanding over the long haul. Dean Holmes provided much encouragement and insight at the beginning of the project, and Eric Stroo deserves a medal for jumping into the middle of all the chaos. Kathy Krause was very kind and patient while providing immense help with her editing advice. Jerry Joyce's technical expertise was valued more than he probably realizes. Many other unnamed people at Microsoft had a hand in this project, and I wish I could thank each of them individually. Thank you all for your help and expertise over the many months of this project.

On a more personal note, thanks go to my family and friends for hanging in there with me through it all. One person in particular deserves a big "Thank You!" Dakotah, you've brought much joy, love, hope, and stability to Grandpa during this project. When the going has gotten tough, all I've had to do is see the world through your eyes, and it's all fresh and new again. Thanks for being you!

INTRODUCTION

This book evolved from my previous editions of *Microsoft Visual Basic Workshop*. The contents and even the organization of the book have changed quite a bit, partly because of the many new features in Visual Basic 4, and partly because of the great response I've received from readers. I've taken note of several excellent suggestions for improvements to make this book more useful for the typical Visual Basic software developer.

Right up front you'll find a concise description of the new features in Visual Basic version 4. This will help you sift through all the hype to see just how Visual Basic 4 can help you become more efficient in the development of your projects. There have been some major changes to Visual Basic this time around, so be sure to at least skim this section to become familiar with the new capabilities.

Programming Style

I've also included information on standard programming style, as gleaned from experts at Microsoft and elsewhere. These suggestions are not intended to be too rigorous (indeed, programming shops that are too strict tend to be uncreative, boring, and unproductive), but rather to provide guidelines to help groups of developers more easily understand and share code. All of the source code presented in this book pretty much follows these guidelines.

What's Been Left Out

Introductory material on the history of Basic has been left out of this book, along with some very beginner-level instructions on using Visual Basic. This leaves more room for the good stuff! There's plenty of introductory material for beginners in the online tutorial that comes with Visual Basic, and also in several popular introductory books. I've found that most readers are already somewhat familiar with Visual Basic and are looking for new information to improve their skills and to add to their personal toolboxes of techniques.

How-To

In my presentations on Visual Basic, I've noticed that the majority of questions asked by the audience are of a "How do I..." nature. Visual Basic programmers have discovered a wealth of powerful, but sometimes not too well documented, tricks and techniques for getting things done. I've added a section of "Dear John, how do I..." questions to this book in Part II, in which I've either described solutions or pointed to pertinent descriptions in the example programs in Part III. Often Visual Basic 4 provides better solutions to these questions than previous versions of the language did, so the information in this section is more up-to-date than in many other books.

Sample Programs

The CD-ROM that accompanies this book differs from the disks of the previous editions in that I've dropped some programs and added many others in an attempt to provide more useful source code examples. Visual Basic is a rich, diversified development environment, and I've tried to provide useful, enlightening examples that cover all the major subject areas. This does impose limits on the depth of coverage possible in a single book, however. For example, I've provided a real, working example of a complete but relatively simple database program, but there's no way I can cover all aspects of the rich set of database programming features now built into Visual Basic. This book can provide a quick start in database programming with Visual Basic, but you might want to also refer to a book devoted entirely to the subject if this is your main area of interest.

Help Files

A lot of the emphasis in this book is on the complete Visual Basic application development cycle. For example, many books, including my earlier *Microsoft Visual Basic Workshop* titles, haven't covered the very important topic of integrating help files into an application. You'll find useful information and examples in this book that show several techniques for adding real help files to your projects.

Windows 95 and 32-Bit Programming

Visual Basic 4 now comes in both 16-bit and 32-bit flavors, and it is designed to run under the Windows 3.1, Windows 95, and Windows NT operating systems. It would probably triple the size of this book to duplicate all of the source code and examples in all possible combinations of these configurations. For this reason, I made the decision to simplify the presentation to the most interesting and most common configuration, a 32-bit version running on Windows 95.

Visual Basic 4 is one of the first application development systems for 32-bit programming, and Windows 95 is by far the most popular full 32-bit operating system around. This is where the new Visual Basic 4 shines, and that's why this book focuses on this timely and useful version of the language.

If you are developing for Windows NT, the book will still suit your needs well. Until Windows NT's user interface matches the new look and feel of Windows 95, some of the forms presented in this book will look different when they are running on a Windows NT computer. Some API system-level calls will need slight adjustments, but many of the programs and examples in this book will work just fine under Windows NT.

Likewise, if you are one of the unfortunate programmers required to develop applications for the 16-bit world, many of the programs and examples in this book will work well, but some will need adjustments. Several of the new Windows 95 custom controls will be unavailable to you, although there are a lot of commercial custom controls you can purchase to take their places.

Using the Companion CD

Bound into the back of this book is a Companion CD that contains all the projects, source code, forms, and associated files described in Part III of this book. The code is ready to be compiled into executable files, integrated into your own applications, or torn apart to see how it works.

You can load the project files directly into your Visual Basic environment from the CD or copy the files to your hard disk. You will need approximately 2 MB of free space on your hard disk to copy all the files from the CD. For additional information on using the CD and copying the files, see the Readme.txt file on the Companion CD.

PART I

GETTING STARTED WITH VISUAL BASIC 4

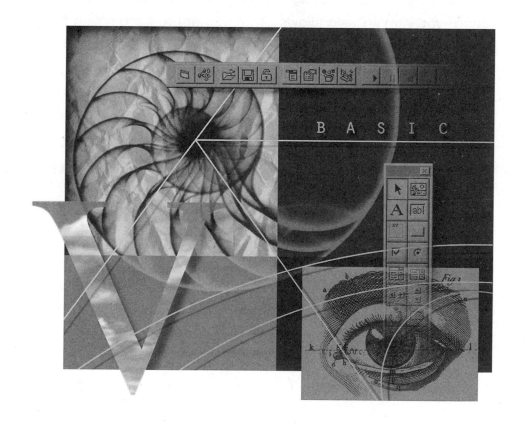

The Basic programming language, created in 1963, was the first language that let the programmer concentrate on the methods and algorithms for solving programming tasks rather than on the methods and algorithms that the computer hardware needed to build and debug programs. Visual Basic 4 has evolved far beyond the original design, but the underlying philosophy has remained consistent. Programming Windows using C or C++ is notoriously complicated, yet Visual Basic allows programmers to accomplish the same results with a much shorter learning curve. Visual Basic 4 is the ultimate high-productivity Windows development system for cost-effective and timely results.

In this chapter, you'll find short descriptions of many of the new features that make Visual Basic 4 the best Basic yet. For in-depth explanations of these features, Visual Basic's printed and online documentation can't be beat.

CHAPTER ONE

What's New in Visual Basic 4?

For the most part, Visual Basic 4 feels about the same to the programmer as previous versions of Visual Basic, even though Microsoft has made some major technical revisions to the language this time around. In the following paragraphs, I list many of the major changes, as well as some of the minor changes. Sometimes the little changes turn out to be important productivity enhancements.

This section provides "in a nutshell" descriptions of the new features of Visual Basic 4. For more detailed descriptions, see the online help or Visual Basic's printed documentation.

> NOTE: Most of the programs and demonstrations in this book will run just fine in either the Standard, the Professional, or the Enterprise Edition of Visual Basic 4. Instead of covering all the possible combinations of the 16-bit and 32-bit versions of these environments, I decided to simplify the book by focusing on a popular and powerful combination, which is the 32-bit Professional Edition running under Windows 95. If you are programming for previous editions of Windows using the 16-bit version of Visual Basic 4, you might need to rework some of my example code. Programming for the 32-bit Windows NT environment will probably require very few changes.

Object-Oriented Features

Visual Basic 4 provides several new features that will help you take advantage of object-oriented programming in your applications. The most significant of those features are listed in this section.

OLE

Perhaps the biggest change to Visual Basic is the full implementation of the OLE technology. Some of this change isn't readily apparent, but a lot is going on "under the hood" of the new Visual Basic. Much of Visual Basic's internal code was rewritten from the ground up, and many of the internal changes take advantage of OLE technology. OLE also plays a big part in the many obvious changes to Visual Basic. For instance, VBX custom controls are now out-of-date, and OLE-based OCX controls are the new standard. You can still use VBX modules if you are working with the 16-bit version of Visual Basic 4, but the new OCX controls replace, update, and enhance the way custom controls work. The OLE technology changes are for the better, and over time the advantages and capabilities will become more obvious.

OLE Automation

With OLE Automation, Visual Basic 4 allows you to programmatically interact with OLE-based objects exposed by other applications. This dynamic "gluing together" of code from a variety of sources is a powerful concept that will become ever more important as time goes on. In this book, you'll find examples of OLE Automation techniques for accessing the spell checking and word counting objects in Microsoft Word and for borrowing some of Microsoft Excel's advanced math functions.

Object Applications

Visual Basic 4 lets you create object applications that expose their objects for other applications to use. The exposed objects can be used by other Visual Basic applications or by applications written in other languages, such as Visual C++. A whole new approach to programming is at hand!

Objects and the Object Browser

Objects are everywhere in Visual Basic 4. An Object Browser is built into the development environment to help you find objects that your applications can use. And you aren't limited to Visual Basic objects—you can browse around and find objects exposed by other Windows applications, such as a spreadsheet object provided by Microsoft Excel or a document object in Word.

The syntax for accessing the properties and methods of objects is consistent and well thought out, although it can take some time to get used to the concepts. With a little practice, you'll quickly get the hang of the new terminology and this impressive new programming power will be yours. This book provides several working examples of object programming syntax.

Class Modules

A new type of programming module, the class module, is now available in Visual Basic 4. A *class module* lets you create the definition of an object, complete with properties and methods. You can then declare one or more instances of the object, and the object can be deleted from memory at runtime when it is no longer needed by your application. Even though this sounds a little like object-oriented C programming, you'll find yourself right at home with the straightforward and simpler terminology and implementation provided by Visual Basic for these class objects. A class module can be recognized by its filename extension, CLS.

Collections

Objects are often grouped into a containing object called a *collection*. For example, a database object might contain multiple TableDef objects. The collection of these TableDef objects is called TableDefs. (By convention, an object collection carries the same name as the individual objects but with an *s* added at the end, just like the plural ending in standard English.) Likewise, each TableDef object can have one or more Field objects, which are collectively called Fields. Later in this chapter, you'll find a description of the new *For Each–Next* syntax, which is a handy way to process all the member objects in these collections.

One interesting new feature of Visual Basic 4 is that it allows you to create your own collections of objects.

Property Procedures

Property procedures are used by class module objects to define properties that can be set or retrieved by your applications. You can use a public variable in a class module as a simple type of property, but if you want to perform any actions at the time a property is set or read, you should use the property procedures to get the flexibility you need. For example, imagine a case in which you want to build a property named TextColor. When you create a property procedure, your object can actually go out and change the color of some text in immediate response to the assignment of a color value to this property.

The Development Environment

This section describes some of the enhancements to the Visual Basic development environment that are new in Visual Basic 4.

32-Bit Capabilities

Another big change that has occurred with Visual Basic 4 is that the language now has 32-bit capabilities. Although you can still opt to create and work in the 16-bit Windows 3.*x* environment, Visual Basic 4 allows you to create 32-bit programs just as easily. This means that Visual Basic is one of the first products ready for Windows 95 and Windows NT operating system application development. Among the many advantages of 32-bit application development are relaxed memory limitations for arrays, strings, modules, and so on. Visual Basic 4 is an excellent development system for your Windows 95–based 32-bit applications.

Extendable Development Environment

You can now use Visual Basic 4 itself to create add-ins for the Visual Basic development environment. These tools patch themselves right into Visual Basic, creating new buttons or menu items so that the enhancements become one with the environment. We'll soon see creative new tools to enhance programming productivity—cross-referencers, object librarians, spell checkers, source code control systems, and so on—developed by third parties using Visual Basic instead of C!

Changes to the Editor

The source code editor has been enhanced. As in Visual Basic 3, you can still edit one procedure at a time in the edit window. Alternatively, a new option lets you display and work on all source code for a given module at once if you so desire. This gives the editing environment a new flexibility, and after you get used to the change, you'll find it a useful way to edit source code.

Several other details of the editing environment have also changed. For instance, the editor now lets you set your own font, toolbar buttons are more colorful, and built-in tooltips help you remember the purpose of each button. The overall look and feel of the development environment follows the standards for Windows 95. It's cool!

Conditional Compiling

One reason why the editor now allows you to display all of a module's code is to facilitate conditional compiling. The *#If, #ElseIf, #Else,* and *#End If* directives let you easily control which sections of your source code listing are processed and which parts are ignored by the Visual Basic compiler. A new type of conditional constant can also be declared, using the *#Const* directive, to work with the other conditional compiling directives. Conditional compiling is helpful for cross-platform project development, for which you might need different syntaxes for system-level API calls—for example, if you need to create versions of your program that can run on a 32-bit Windows 95 system, a 32-bit Windows NT system, and a 16-bit Windows 3.1 system.

Line Continuation Character

Visual Basic now lets you continue long statements on multiple lines. This much-requested feature is particularly useful for long *Declare* statements for API functions, but you'll find it useful for any complicated statements, especially when long variable names are frequently used.

There are actually two characters required for the line continuation: a space and an underscore. If the underscore is not preceded by a space, the line continuation won't work. This is one of those little gotchas that I struggled with at first, but you won't have that problem now that I've told you.

ToolTips

Can't remember which toolbox icon to click on to bring up the Common-Dialog control? Just run the mouse pointer over any of the icons or command buttons in the toolbar, wait a second or so, and presto, a little ToolTip box will pop up to tell you what the icon or button represents. This is a great help in today's button-and-icon-overloaded world.

Resource Files

With Visual Basic 4, you can now put strings, bitmaps, and other data in a single resource file. This technique is particularly valuable if you're planning to internationalize your applications. All strings can be stored in the resource file and assigned to captions, titles, prompts, and similar properties at runtime. To rebuild the application for a different language, simply change the contents of the resource file strings.

Resource files also offer an efficient way for you to ship bitmap images with your application while keeping the size of your main executable under control. If you store the bitmaps in your resource file, you don't have to ship individual BMP files with your application, and the images will actually load faster from the resource file than from individual BMP files. For more information, search the online help for details on the *LoadResData*, *LoadResPictures*, and *LoadResString* functions.

Improved Setup

The setup kit has been overhauled and greatly improved. It's no secret that in the past the setup kit has had a few unneeded "features" (bugs), but Microsoft has taken the time to iron out the kinks for this version. There is even a wizard to help you through the process. Try it, you'll like it!

Language Enhancements

Visual Basic 4 contains several language enhancements, the most significant of which are described in this section.

For Each–Next

The new *For Each–Next* programming construct is useful for object collections. The *For Each* command lets you loop through all members of a collection, even if you don't know how many members the object collection contains. This lets you process, for example, all the TableDef objects in a TableDefs collection, or all the Field objects in a Fields collection. See the online help for more details.

With–End With

Often you'll find that you need to set several properties of an object at the same time. The *With–End With* command structure provides an orderly and efficient way to set multiple properties of an object in one spot. For example, the following code sets several properties of a form:

```
'Straightforward setting of Form1's properties
Private Sub Form_Load()
    Form1.Caption = "Testing"
    Form1.Top = 1000
    Form1.Left = 2000
    Form1.Width = 3000
    Form1.Height = 4000
End Sub
```

Note how the following code uses *With–End With* to set the same Form1 properties in a more organized and structured way:

```
'Same result using With - End With
Private Sub Form_Load()
    With Form1
        .Caption = "Testing"
        .Top = 1000
        .left = 2000
        .Width = 3000
        .Height = 4000
    End With
End Sub
```

Built-In Constants

Because Visual Basic for Applications is now a part of Visual Basic 4, a full set of constants is built right into the language. In most cases, you don't have to declare constants for standard property settings and the like. For example, to set a form's mouse pointer to the standard hourglass image, use a variation of the following statement:

```
Form1.MousePointer = vbHourglass
```

Note that the constant vbHourglass is built in and requires no declaration on your part.

There are a couple of ways to find the available constants. Look in the Object Browser under Constants in the VBA library or under the specific class of constants in the VB library. Figure 1-1 on the following page shows the alignment constants from the VB library displayed in the Object Browser. You'll find a long alphabetized list of constants, which can be a good place to look if you just need the correct spelling.

If you're looking for constants for a specific command, look in the online help. The online help often turns out to be the best place to look for many built-in constants. From the *Contents* page, click on *Reference Information* and then *Miscellaneous Information*. Near the bottom of the list that appears, click on *Visual Basic Constants* or *Visual Basic for Applications Constants*. This will take you to categorized lists of constant types. None of these constants need to be declared in your applications; just use them instead of the numeric values they represent to make your applications more self-documenting and understandable.

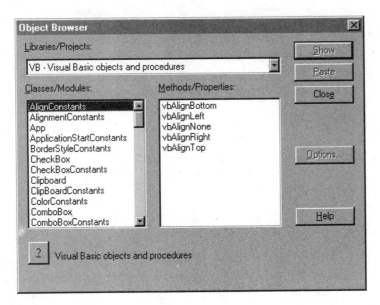

Figure 1-1.
The Object Browser displaying the Visual Basic constants list.

Public, Not Global

Variables are not global anymore—now they're public. The *Public* keyword replaces *Global*, although Visual Basic still recognizes the older term for backward compatibility. Public variables can be declared in any form, code, or class module, providing an improved, simpler, and easier to remember set of scoping rules.

Boolean Data Type

The new Boolean data type can be set only to *True* or *False*. Boolean variables are handy for flags and for assigning the results of logical evaluations.

Byte Data Type

You can now declare a variable to be of type Byte, which is a one-character, or one-byte, unsigned numeric value in the range 0 to 255. Byte arrays, instead of strings, are recommended for passing binary data to and from many API functions. They experience fewer complications with addressing issues, fewer complications arising from zero-byte values in strings, and fewer complications involving the new standard Unicode strings. In Chapter 11, I'll show you several examples of how to use these new byte arrays instead of strings.

Variant Data Type

Although variants are not new with Visual Basic 4, they're becoming increasingly important to the language, especially for certain types of parameter passing. A variant can hold any type of data, and special functions are provided to let you determine exactly what type of data a variant contains at the moment. The data type of a variant changes when any type of data is assigned to it. If you're not familiar with variants, I suggest you read the online help for further explanation. For now, be aware that unless they are explicitly declared otherwise, variables now default to type Variant instead of type Single (as in older versions of Basic).

3–D Look

The new *Appearance* property for forms and most controls defaults to 1 = 3D, providing the standard gray 3–D format that users of Windows are familiar with. Custom 3–D controls are also provided to enhance the effect (and to provide functionality beyond the standard controls).

Picture Object

The new Picture object lets you manipulate graphics images in memory, rather than limiting you to loading images only into the picture property of multiple forms, picture boxes, or image controls. An array of Picture objects, for example, provides an in-memory source of images with which you can quickly update your displayed graphics.

PaintPicture

BitBlt is the name of an API function frequently used to speed up graphics and to provide animation techniques. Visual Basic 4 now provides the same functionality in the new *PaintPicture* method, which lets you quickly copy and move rectangular regions of graphics pixels. *PaintPicture* is easier to use than *BitBlt* because it's a built-in part of Visual Basic. *PaintPicture* lets you speed up many types of animated images.

Custom Mouse Pointer

You can now use any icon file as a mouse pointer. Search the online help for the MouseIcon and MousePointer properties for information on how to set any icon file as the mouse pointer. Basically, you set the MousePointer property to *vbCustom* and use the *LoadPicture* function to load an icon image into the MouseIcon property. In Chapter 29 (Part III), the MousePtr application provides a working example of this useful technique.

Jet 2.5

Microsoft is serious about the database programming capabilities of Visual Basic. The latest and greatest database engine, Jet 2.5, is a powerful way to efficiently and flexibly interact with databases. Many new features of Jet 2.5 are available for database applications in Visual Basic 4.

More Bound Data Controls

Visual Basic 4 includes more database-capable controls for database programming, including a data-bound list box, a data-bound combo box, a data-bound grid control, and even the new OLE container control.

New Custom Controls

The new custom controls in Visual Basic 4 make it easy to add those professional touches to your applications—touches that in the past required a lot of fancy footwork. Although I describe the new controls only briefly here, I use each of them in a working example at least once in this book.

StatusBar Control

In previous versions of Visual Basic, you could create a pseudo–status bar by combining nested picture boxes on a form. Now you can simply add a Status-Bar control. Here's what it looks like:

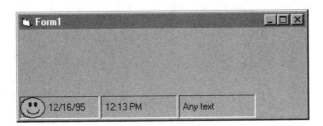

Slider Control

The new Slider control is similar to a scrollbar control in its properties, methods, and operation. Scrollbars are best suited to scrolling, and a slider is best suited to letting the user set a value from a range of allowable values. As shown on the facing page, a Slider control has an improved appearance that sets it apart from a scrollbar for these uses:

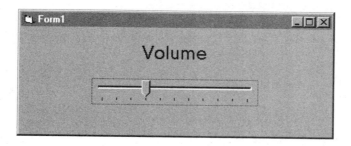

ImageList Control

The ImageList control stores a sequence of same-size graphics images, allowing your applications to gain fast access to images by providing an index into the list. As you can imagine, this control can enhance the ease and speed with which certain types of animation or other graphical data can be presented to the user.

ListView Control

A ListView window, shown below, displays a collection of items such as files or folders in a manner similar to the display in Windows Explorer. You can associate two ImageList controls with properties in a ListView control to provide small and large icons. This control helps you create applications with the right look and feel for Windows 95.

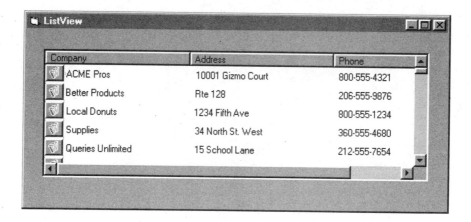

TreeView Control

A TreeView control displays a hierarchical list of nodes, such as the files and directories on a disk or the headings in a document. As with the ListView control, two associated ImageList controls provide small and large icons for tree elements. Here's what it looks like:

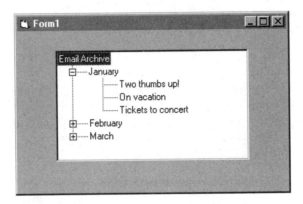

TabStrip Control

A TabStrip control lets you build tabbed dialog boxes, which have become the de facto standard for many types of Windows 95 dialog boxes. A TabStrip control contains a Tabs collection of Tab objects, each of which defines a page of a tabbed dialog box. An example is shown here:

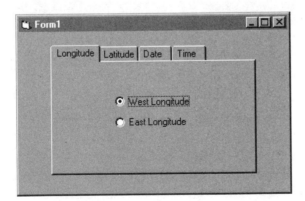

Toolbar Control

A Toolbar control, as shown below, lets you create a collection of buttons, complete with tooltips, for your applications. At runtime, you can opt to let the user customize the toolbar by enabling a dialog box that allows hiding, unhiding, or rearranging of the toolbar buttons.

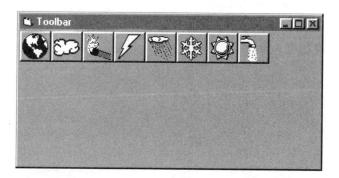

RichTextBox Control

The RichTextBox control, shown here, provides a full-blown, powerful editor window for your applications. The user can apply formatting, and the contents can be saved as an RTF (rich text format) file. This control can be bound to a database, allowing RTF data to be saved easily in database records.

15

ProgressBar Control

A ProgressBar control provides a visual indicator for the user during the time-consuming tasks performed by your applications. You've no doubt seen similar progress indicators, for example, during the installation and setup of Windows 95 or during the setup of applications such as Visual Basic itself. Here's what the ProgressBar control looks like:

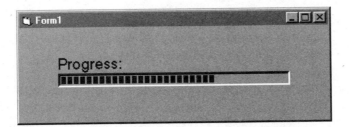

Programming Style Guidelines

Is the Basic programming language easy to read or hard to read? It depends on who you talk to, what your background is, and how clean your programming habits are. In the old days, line numbers and GOTO statements made it easy to create obscure spaghetti code. Fortunately, today's versions of Basic are much more structured and object oriented, although you can still mangle the readability of your code if you really want to!

Actually, with just a little care, Visual Basic source code can be easier to read and follow than just about any other programming language. A lot of suggestions for standard coding style have been floated over the past few years, some good and some not so useful. In my opinion, it's not worth getting uptight about. If you simply get into the habit of using a few relatively simple and standard techniques, you can gain a reputation for creating easy-to-read code. If you're part of a team programming effort, which often seems to be the case for Visual Basic programmers today, efforts at making code easier to read can greatly enhance productivity.

Control Prefixes

One of the easiest techniques to pick up is to name each control with a standard three-letter prefix that identifies references to the control in the source code. This really does improve the readability of your code. Consider, for example, an event-driven subprogram named Buffalo_Click. Does this refer to a command button? A picture? An option button? Until you figure out just what object on the form it refers to, you are pretty well buffaloed. However, cmdBuffalo_Click is easily recognized as belonging to a command button, picBuffalo_Click belongs to a picture control, and so on. A widely accepted list of standard prefixes has already been published in several places, and I'll repeat the same list here with some additions to help propagate the standard.

Object-Naming Prefix Conventions for Visual Basic

Prefix	Object
ani	Animation button
cbo	Combo box
chk	Check box
clp	Picture clip
ch3	3–D check box
cm3	3–D command button
cmd	Command button
com	Communications
ctr	Control (specific type is unknown)
dat	Data
db	ODBC database
dbc	Data-bound combo box
dbg	Data-bound grid
dbl	Data-bound list box
dir	Directory list box
dlg	Common dialog box
drv	Drive list box
ds	ODBC dynaset
fil	File list box
fra	Frame
fr3	3–D frame
frm	Form
gau	Gauge
gra	Graph
gpb	Group push button
grd	Grid
hsb	Horizontal scrollbar
img	Image
iml	Image list
key	Key status
lbl	Label
lin	Line
lst	List box

(continued)

Object-Naming Prefix Conventions for Visual Basic *continued*

Prefix	Object
lsv	ListView
med	Masked edit
mci	Multimedia MCI
mnu	Menu
mpm	MAPI message
mps	MAPI session
ole	OLE container
opt	Option button
op3	3–D option button
otl	Outline
pic	Picture box
pnl	3–D panel
prb	ProgressBar
rtb	RichTextBox
shp	Shape
sli	Slide
spn	Spin button
sst	SSTab dialog
stb	StatusBar
tbs	TabStrip
tmr	Timer
tlb	Toolbar
trv	TreeView
txt	Text box
vsb	Vertical scrollbar

Variable Names

Some people, particularly those coming from the world of C programming, suggest naming all variables with Hungarian Notation prefixes, similar to the control prefixes listed above. I have mixed feelings about this technique. On the one hand, it's nice to know what type of variable you're dealing with as you read it in the code, but on the other hand this can sometimes make for somewhat cluttered, less readable syntax.

Since day one, Microsoft Basic programmers have had the option of naming variables with a suffix to identify the variable type. For example, *X%* is an integer variable, *X!* is a single-precision floating-point number, and *X$* is a string. It's a matter of opinion whether these are better names than the Hungarian prefixes. I've even seen schemes for keeping track of the scope of variables using part of the prefix, which is an advantage of Hungarian Notation, but this much detail in the name of a variable might be overkill.

The following table lists the suffixes for various data types. It also lists the newer data types, which have no suffix, supporting my contention that Microsoft is heading away from the use of these suffixes.

Standard Suffixes for Variable Types

Suffix	Variable Type
%	2-byte signed integer
&	4-byte signed integer
@	8-byte currency
!	4-byte single-precision floating-point
#	8-byte double-precision floating-point
$	String
None	Boolean
None	Byte
None	Date
None	Object
None	Variant

You may feel that Hungarian Notation prefixes for all variable names are an absolute must, so I'll list the suggested Hungarian prefixes here. Note that some data types are indicated by more than one prefix type. This lets you keep track of the intended use of the variable. For example, the standard 16-bit signed integer data type can be called Boolean, Handle, Index, Integer, or Word, depending on how you want to look at a given variable.

Hungarian Notation Prefixes for Variable Types

Prefix	Variable Type
a	Array
b	Boolean
c	Currency
d	Double
f	Float/Single
h	Handle
i	Index
l	Long
n	Integer
s	String
u	Unsigned
ul	Unsigned Long
vnt	Variant
w	Word

Variable Declarations

A very important technique for keeping track of variable names is the use of the *Option Explicit* statement. You can choose to automatically add the *Option Explicit* statement whenever a new module is created, and I'd strongly recommend using this option. From the Tools menu, choose Options, select the Environment tab, and turn on the Require Variable Declaration check box.

The *Option Explicit* statement forces you to declare all variables before they are referenced. The *Dim* statement for each variable is an excellent place to explicitly declare the data type of the variable. This way, a variable name can be easy to read and easy to differentiate from the names of controls and other objects that do have prefixes, and its type can easily be determined by a quick glance at the block of *Dim* statements at the head of each module or routine. This is the technique I've chosen for the source code examples in this book, but feel free to use the standard Hungarian prefixes if this suits your style better.

WARNING: A very common and dangerous mistake, especially for those familiar with the C programming language, is to incorrectly combine the declarations of several variables of one data type into one statement. This won't cut the mustard! You must explicitly define the data type for each variable in a *Dim* statement. Read on!

The following explicit variable declarations are all OK, and you'll get what you expect:

```
Dim a As Integer, b As Single, c As Double
Dim a%, b!, c#
```

However, the following will create two Variant variables (*i* and *j*) and one Integer variable (*k*) instead of the expected Integers:

```
Dim i, j, k As Integer
```

Your program may or may not work as expected, and the reason for any unexpected behavior can be very hard to track down.

Menus

There are several schemes for naming menu items too. I've chosen to name all menu items with the now-standard *mnu* prefix. You might want to add letters to identify which parent pull-down menu a given menu item is associated with. For example, a menu item named mnuHelpAbout refers to the About item selected from the Help menu. I've chosen to keep things slightly simpler—I usually shorten the name to something like mnuAbout. When you see *mnu* as a prefix in the source code in this book, you'll know immediately that it's a menu item. It's usually quite simple to figure out where in the menu structure the item is positioned, so I don't confuse the issue with extra designators.

Other Objects

Occasionally other prefixes will be used to name objects. For example, a database object name is prefixed with *db*, whereas a dynaset object name is prefixed with *ds*. I've tried to use a consistent and fairly self-evident prefix scheme throughout this book for naming objects as they are declared.

More Information

You can find more information about standard naming schemes and programming style in the latest Microsoft Developer Network CD. If you're part of a large programming team and this is an important subject for you, I'd suggest this CD as a good reference for a standard set of techniques. Many corporations and programmers use this same set of standards, so there's no sense in setting off on a dead-end path with your own "standards."

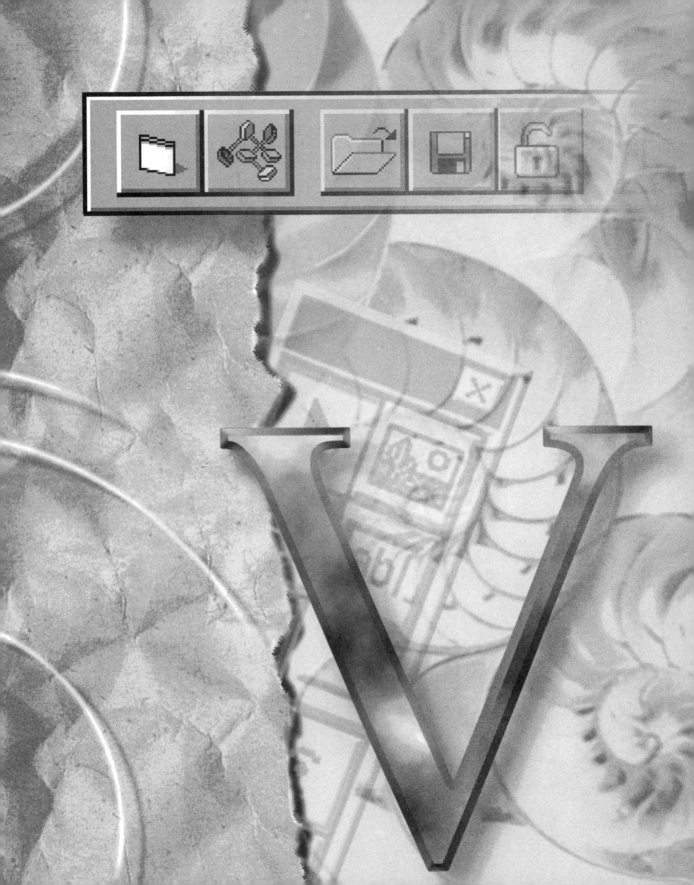

PART II

DEAR JOHN, HOW DO I...?

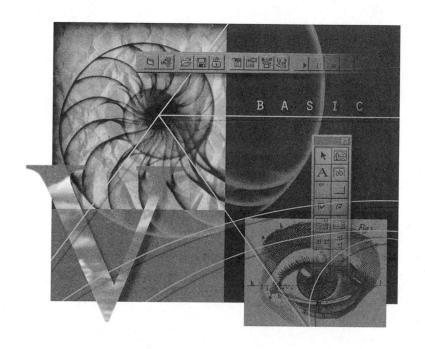

One of the great strengths of Visual Basic is its flexibility. If there's some programming goal you want to accomplish and Visual Basic doesn't provide a direct, built-in solution, you can invariably come up with a "trick" that uses application programming interface (API) function calls or that uses controls in creative ways that take them beyond what they were originally designed to do.

In this part of the book, I've collected some of my favorite "Dear John, how do I...?" questions and answers, and I've been careful to use the most up-to-date techniques. For example, although it is possible in Visual Basic 3 to create a custom mouse pointer by using a complicated set of API calls along with some smoke and mirrors, Visual Basic 4 provides a much simpler, more direct way to use any icon as a mouse pointer. Don't use the old technique—use Visual Basic 4's better way!

CHAPTER THREE

Variables

Visual Basic 4 supports all the data types that were supported in previous versions of Visual Basic and adds the following new types: Boolean variables, which take on the values *True* and *False*; Byte variables, which take on numeric values in the range 0 through 255; and Date variables, which hold dates and times.

This chapter covers the uses of these new variables and also discusses some new tricks for working with variables that are not new to this version of Visual Basic, such as Variants, which are playing an increasingly important role in Visual Basic 4. Also covered in this chapter are working with predefined constants and creating Type structures.

Dear John, How Do I...

Simulate Unsigned Integers?

Unfortunately, Visual Basic does not support unsigned 16-bit integers, a data type often encountered in API calls. But don't despair; there are ways to compensate for this.

Visual Basic's integer data types come in three flavors: Long, Integer, and the new Byte type. Long variables are 32-bit signed values that are in the range -2,147,483,648 through +2,147,483,647. The most frequently used of the three data types is Integer, which stores 16-bit signed integer values in the range -32,768 through +32,767. Byte variables hold unsigned 8-bit numeric values in the range 0 through 255. Notice that the only unsigned integer data type is Byte.

Unsigned 16-bit integers are useful in many API function calls. You can go ahead and pass signed integer variables to and from these functions instead, but you must develop a mechanism to deal with negative values when they show up. There are several approaches to simulating unsigned 16-bit integers, and I'll cover two of the best.

Transferring to and from Long Variables

In some cases, you can manipulate unsigned integers in the range 0 through 65,535 by storing them in long integers. When it comes time to assign the 16-bit values into a signed integer variable that will simulate an unsigned 16-bit variable, use this calculation and assignment:

```
iShort = (iLong And &H7FFF) - (iLong And &H8000)
```

where *iShort* is a signed Integer variable to be passed to the API and *iLong* is the Long variable containing the stored value to be passed. The calculation uses the logical And operator and hexadecimal-based bit masks to execute bitwise operations to convert the 32-bit value to a 16-bit unsigned value.

To store the value of a signed integer that has been used to simulate an unsigned 16-bit integer as a long integer (the inverse function to the calculation just shown), use this:

```
iLong = iShort And &HFFFF&
```

Be aware that the 16-bit unsigned value, while stored in a 16-bit signed integer variable, may be interpreted as a negative value if you print or calculate with it. Use these two calculations to convert the values just before and just after calling API functions that expect a 16-bit unsigned integer. Work with the long integer version of the unsigned integers in your code, and pass the Integer variable version of the value to API functions.

Packing Unsigned Byte Values Using Data Structures

Visual Basic doesn't have a Union construct as C does, but you can simulate the construct's functionality by copying bytes between user-defined data Type structures using the *LSet* statement. This makes it easy to pack and unpack unsigned Byte values into a signed integer. The following code fragments demonstrate this technique:

```
Option Explicit

Private Type UnsignedIntType
    lo As Byte
    hi As Byte
End Type

Private Type SignedIntType
    n As Integer
End Type
```

These two Type structures define storage for 2 bytes each. Although the memory allocation is not overlapping, as would be true in a C union, the binary contents can be shuffled between variables of these types, as the next block of code demonstrates.

```
Private Sub Form_Click()
    'Create variables of user-defined types
    Dim u As UnsignedIntType
    Dim s As SignedIntType

    'Assign high and low bytes to create integer
    u.hi = 231
    u.lo = 123

    'Copy binary data into the other structure
    LSet s = u
    Print s.n, u.hi; u.lo

    'Assign integer and extract high and low bytes
    s.n = s.n - 1   'Decrement integer for new value

    'Copy back into the other data structure
    LSet u = s
    Print s.n, u.hi; u.lo
End Sub
```

With these two code fragments in a form, when the form is clicked, the signed integer value (–6277) and the two Byte values (231 and 123) on which it is based are printed on the form. After conducting an operation on the integer—in this case subtracting 1—the result of the reverse operation is also printed: the new signed integer value (–6278) and the high and low bytes (231 and 122) of the integer. This is accomplished by first declaring two variables, *u* and *s*, using the declared Type structure definitions. The *u.hi* and *u.lo* bytes are used to assign values to the high and low bytes of the *u* variable, the binary contents of *u* are then copied into *s* using *LSet*, and the resulting signed integer is printed out. Finally, the integer value in *s* is decremented to provide a value different from the original, and *s* is copied back into *u* to show how a signed integer can be split into two unsigned Byte values.

By adding text boxes and labels to your form, it's easy to transform the code fragments into a working integer-byte calculator, as shown in Figure 3-1 on the following page.

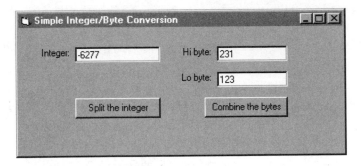

Figure 3-1.
A signed integer comprising two unsigned bytes.

Note that *LSet* can be used to copy any binary contents of one user-defined Type structure to another. This provides an efficient way to treat the binary contents of memory as different types of data.

> **WARNING:** In 32-bit Visual Basic 4, the elements in your Type structures might not line up in memory exactly as you expect. This is because each element is aligned on a 4-byte boundary, with extra padding bytes inserted to accomplish the alignment. When using *LSet* to move data from one Type structure to another, experiment to make sure that the bytes end up where you want them to go. Be careful!

 See Also...

- "Dear John, How Do I Use C to Create a DLL?" in Chapter 23 for information about creating a DLL using Visual C++. The C language is ideally suited to the packing and unpacking of bytes within integers.

Dear John, How Do I...

Use Boolean Variables?

The new Boolean data type stores either the value *True* or the value *False*, and nothing else. Typically, Boolean variables are used to store the results of comparisons or other logical tests. For example, the following block of code assigns the result of a logical comparison of two values to a Boolean variable named *TestResult* and then prints this variable to the display:

```
Private Sub Form_Click()
    Dim TestResult As Boolean
    TestResult = 123 < 246
    Print TestResult
End Sub
```

Notice that the displayed result appears as *True* in this case. When you print or display a Boolean variable, you print or display either *True* or *False*.

WARNING: Watch out for strange variable type coercions! Read on....

Visual Basic 4 now supports many types of automatic variable type coercions, which means you can assign just about anything to just about anything. For example, even though Boolean variables hold only the values *True* and *False*, you can assign a number or even a string to a Boolean variable. The results might not be what you'd expect, though, so be careful!

Here's one short example of this rather strange behavior. The following code will display *True*, *True*, and *False*, which implies that *a* equals *True* and *b* equals *True*, but that *a* does not equal *b*! The reason for the final result of *False* might not be obvious, but it results from the internal conversions of the unlike variables *a* and *b* to like data types during the test to see whether they equal each other.

```
Private Sub Form_Click()
    Dim a As Byte
    Dim b As Integer
    a = True
    b = True
    Print a = True
    Print b = True
    Print a = b
End Sub
```

Dear John, How Do I...

Use Byte Arrays?

One of the main reasons that Byte arrays were created was to allow the passing of binary buffers to and from the new 32-bit API functions. One of the differences to be aware of between 16-bit and 32-bit Visual Basic applications is that 32-bit version strings are assumed to contain Unicode characters, which require 2 bytes for each character. The system automatically converts Unicode 2-byte sequences to 1-byte ANSI characters, but if the string contains binary data the contents can become unintelligible. To prevent problems, you should get into the habit of passing only printable string data in strings, and passing binary data in Byte arrays.

Passing Byte Arrays Instead of Strings

Byte arrays contain only unsigned byte values in the range 0 through 255. Unlike the contents of strings, Byte array contents are guaranteed not to be preprocessed by the system. You can pass Byte arrays in place of strings in many API functions.

For example, the following code, which uses the *GetWindowsDirectory* API function to find the path to the Windows directory, demonstrates the changes you'll need to make to the function declarations and function parameters. The code is shown in two versions: the first passes a string for the API function to return the Windows directory in, and the second passes a Byte array instead. When you place either of these code examples in a form, run it, and click on the form, you'll see the path to your Windows directory, as shown in Figure 3-2.

Figure 3-2.
The API function returning the path to your Windows directory.

By carefully noting the differences in these two routines, you'll gain insight into the difference between string and Byte array parameters:

```
Option Explicit

Private Declare Function GetWindowsDirectory _
Lib "kernel32" _
Alias "GetWindowsDirectoryA" ( _
    ByVal lpBuffer As String, _
    ByVal nSize As Long _
) As Long

Private Sub Form_Click()
    Dim n As Integer
    Dim strA As String
    'Size the string variable
    strA = Space$(256)
```

(continued)

```
    n = GetWindowsDirectory(strA, 256)
    'Strip off extra characters
    strA = Left$(strA, n)
    Print strA
End Sub
```

In this first code example, the string parameter lpBuffer returns the path to the Windows directory. I presized the variable *strA* to 256 characters before calling the function, and I stripped off the extra characters upon returning from the function.

> **WARNING:** Before making the function call, always presize a string or a Byte array that an API function fills with data. Your program will probably crash if you forget to do this!

Here's the second routine:

```
Option Explicit

Private Declare Function GetWindowsDirectory _
Lib "kernel32" _
Alias "GetWindowsDirectoryA" ( _
    ByRef lpBuffer As Byte, _
    ByVal nSize As Long _
) As Long

Private Sub Form_Click()
    Dim n As Integer
    Dim Buffer() As Byte
    Dim strA As String
    'Size the Byte array
    Buffer = Space$(256)
    n = GetWindowsDirectory(Buffer(0), 256)
    strA = StrConv(Buffer, vbUnicode)
    'Strip off extra characters
    strA = Left$(strA, n)
    Print strA
End Sub
```

Take a close look at the function declaration for the *GetWindowsDirectory* API function in this second routine. I changed the declaration for the first parameter from a ByVal string to a ByRef Byte array. The original parameter declaration was

```
ByVal lpBuffer As String
```

I changed the *ByVal* keyword to *ByRef* and changed *String* to *Byte* in the new form of this declaration:

```
ByRef lpBuffer As Byte
```

A *ByVal* modifier is required for passing string buffers to API functions because the string variable actually identifies the place in memory where the address of the string contents is stored—in C terminology, a pointer to a pointer. *ByVal* causes the contents of the memory identified by the string name to be passed, which means that the value passed is a memory address to the actual string contents. Notice that in my function call I pass *Buffer(0)*, which, when passed using *ByRef*, is passed as the memory address for the contents of the first byte of the array. The end result is the same, and the *GetWindowsDirectory* API function will blindly load the addressed buffer memory with the path to the Windows directory in both cases.

Further along in the code is this important line that requires some explanation:

```
strA = StrConv(Buffer, vbUnicode)
```

This command converts the Byte array's binary data to a valid Visual Basic 4 string. Dynamic Byte arrays allow direct assignment to and from strings, which is accomplished like this:

```
Buffer = strA
strB = Buffer
```

When you assign a string to a dynamic Byte array, the number of bytes in the array will be twice the number of characters in the string. This is because Visual Basic 4 strings now use Unicode, and each Unicode character is actually 2 bytes in size. When ASCII characters are converted to a Byte array, every other byte in the array will be a zero. (The second byte is used to represent foreign characters and becomes important when internationalization of your applications is considered.) In the case of the *GetWindowsDirectory* API function, however, the returned buffer is not in Unicode format, and we must convert the byte buffer's binary contents to a Unicode string ourselves, using the *StrConv* function as shown. In the first code example, we let Visual Basic perform this housekeeping chore automatically as it filled our string parameter.

The conversion to Unicode converts each character in the buffer to 2 bytes and actually doubles the number of bytes stored in the resulting string. This isn't readily apparent when you consider that the function *Len(strA)* reports the same size as would *Ubound(Buffer)* in the above case. However, the new function *LenB(strA)* does report a number twice the size of the number reported by the *Len(strA)* function. This is because the *Len* function returns the number of characters in the string, whereas the *LenB* function returns the number of bytes in the string. The character length of a Unicode string (remember, this includes all 32-bit Visual Basic 4 strings) is only half the number of actual bytes in the string because each Unicode character is 2 bytes.

To summarize, when converting an API function parameter from a string buffer to the new Byte array type, change the *ByVal* keyword to *ByRef*, pass the first byte of the array instead of the string's name, and if the binary data is to be converted to a string, remember to use *StrConv* with the vbUnicode parameter.

Copying Between Byte Arrays and Strings

To simplify the transfer of data between Byte arrays and strings, the designers of Visual Basic 4 decided to allow a special case assignment between any dynamic Byte array and any string.

NOTE: You can assign a string to a Byte array only if the array is dynamic, not if it is fixed in size.

The easiest way to declare a dynamic byte array is to use empty parentheses in the Dim statement, like this:

```
Dim Buffer()
```

The following Dim statement creates a fixed-size byte array, which is useful for a lot of things but not for string assignment. It will, in fact, generate an error if you try to assign a string to it:

```
Dim Buffer(80)
```

Dear John, How Do I...

Work with Dates and Times?

Another new data type in Visual Basic 4 is Date. Internally, a Date variable is allocated 8 bytes of memory that contain packed bit patterns for not only a date but also an exact time. Magically, when you print a Date variable, you'll see a string designation for the month, year, day, hour, minute, and second that the 8-byte internal data represents. The exact format for the displayed or printed date and time is dependent on your system's country settings. For all the sample calculations that follow, I've assumed that date and time values are always stored in Date variables.

Loading a Date Variable

To load date and time values directly into a variable, enclose the information between two # characters. As you enter a program line with date values of this form, Visual Basic checks your syntax. If the date or time is illegal or non-existent, you'll immediately get an error. Here's an example in which a Date variable, *D*, is loaded with a specific date and time. We'll use this value of *D* throughout the following examples:

```
Dim D As Date
D = #11/17/96 6:19:20 PM#
```

Several functions convert date and time numbers to a Date type variable. *DateSerial* combines month, day, and year numbers into a Date value. In a similar way, *TimeSerial* combines hour, minute, and second numbers into a Date value:

```
D = DateSerial(1996, 11, 17)
D = TimeSerial(18, 19, 20)
```

To combine both a date and a time into a Date variable, simply add the results of the two functions:

```
D = DateSerial(1996, 11, 17) + TimeSerial(18, 19, 20)
```

To load a Date variable from a string representation of a date or time, use the *DateValue* and *TimeValue* functions:

```
D = DateValue("11/17/96")
D = TimeValue("18:19:20")
```

Again, to load both a date and a time at the same time, simply add the results of each of the functions:

```
D = DateValue("Nov-17-1996") + TimeValue("6:19:20 PM")
```

A wide variety of legal formats are recognized as valid date and time strings, but you do need to be aware of the expected format for the country setting on a given system. In some countries, for example, the month and day numbers might be expected in reverse order.

Displaying a Date or a Time

The *Format* function provides great flexibility for converting a Date variable to a printable or displayable string. The following block of code shows the predefined named formats for these conversions. Be aware that the results depend on your system's country settings. You should run this code to see whether your results differ from mine:

```
Print Format(D, "General Date")  ' 11/17/96 6:19:20 PM
Print Format(D, "Long Date")     ' Sunday, November 17, 1996
Print Format(D, "Medium Date")   ' 17-Nov-96
Print Format(D, "Short Date")    ' 11/17/96
Print Format(D, "Long Time")     ' 6:19:20 PM
Print Format(D, "Medium Time")   ' 06:19 PM
Print Format(D, "Short Time")    ' 18:19
```

In addition to the named formats, you can create your own user-defined formats for outputting date and time data. For example, the following line formats each part of the date and time in a unique way and stores the result in a string variable:

```
A$ = Format(D, "m/d/yyyy hh:mm AM/PM")  ' 11/17/1996 06:19 PM
```

These user-defined formats are extremely flexible. For another example, here's how you can generate the textual name of the month for a date:

```
MonthName$ = Format(D, "mmmm")   ' November
```

See the online help for the *Format* function for a detailed description of the many combinations of user-defined date and time formats you can use.

Extracting the Details

Several functions are available to extract parts of the Date variable. The following lines of code provide a quick reference to this group of related functions:

```
Print Month(D)     '11
Print Day(D)       '17
Print Year(D)      '1996
Print Hour(D)      '18
Print Minute(D)    '19
Print Second(D)    '20
Print WeekDay(D)   '1
```

A set of built-in constants is provided by Visual Basic for the *WeekDay* result; vbSunday is 1, vbMonday is 2, and so on through vbSaturday, which is 7.

Date and Time Calculations

Date variables can be directly manipulated in a mathematical sense if you keep in mind that the unit value is a day. For example, you can easily create an application to calculate your age in days, as shown in Figure 3-3 on the following page. To do so, simply subtract your date of birth (stored in a Date variable) from *Now*, the function that returns today's date.

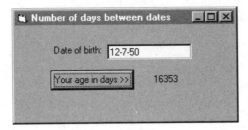

Figure 3-3.
Using Date variables to calculate the number of days between dates.

To calculate date values using hours, minutes, or seconds, you could multiply or divide the date value by 24, 60, and 60, but the *DateSerial* and *TimeSerial* functions provide a better way. Let's say, for instance, that you want to calculate the exact date and time 10,000 minutes from the current moment. Here's how to do this without getting tangled up in a lot of math:

```
D = Now + TimeSerial(0, 10000, 0)
```

The *TimeSerial* function returns a value representing no hours, 10,000 minutes, and no seconds. This value is added to *Now* to calculate a Date variable containing the desired date and time. If you print the value of *D*, you'll see a date and time that's roughly one hour short of exactly a week from now.

Date and Time Validity Checking

You can use an error trap when assigning a user-entered date or time string to a Date variable. If the date or time is not recognizable as a valid date or time, a "Type mismatch" error is generated by Visual Basic. Another approach to getting a valid date from the user is to use a calendar dialog box. This prevents errors by letting the user interactively select only a valid date from a one-month calendar page.

See Also...

- The VBCal application in Chapter 27 (Part III) for a date selection dialog box that you can plug into your own applications

Dear John, How Do I...

Work with Variants?

Variants are a relatively recent addition to Visual Basic, and they're playing an ever increasing role in the language. Variants are extremely flexible (some say too flexible), but they do allow for some clever new ways to structure and organize your data.

If not declared as something else, all variables default to Variant. You can store just about anything in a Variant variable, including arrays, objects, type structures, and other Variants. Arrays always contain like elements, which means you normally can't mix strings and numbers in the same array, for instance. But an array of Variants gets around this limitation. Consider the following code, which creates a Variant array and loads it with an integer, a string, and another Variant. To hint at the flexibility here, I've even stored a second Variant array in the third element of the primary Variant array. Remember, you can store just about anything in a Variant!

```
Option Explicit

Private Sub Form_Click()
    Dim i        'Notice that this defaults to Variant
    Dim varMain(1 To 3) As Variant
    Dim X As Integer
    Dim A As String
    Dim varAry(1 To 20) As Variant

    'Fill primary variables
    A = "This is a test"
    For i = 1 To 20
        varAry(i) = i ^ 2
    Next i

    'Store everything in main Variant array
    varMain(1) = X
    varMain(2) = A
    varMain(3) = varAry()
```

(continued)

```
      'Display sampling of main Variant's contents
      Print varMain(1)        ' 0
      Print varMain(2)        ' This is a test
      Print varMain(3)(17)    ' 289
End Sub
```

Notice, in the last line of the routine, how the Variant array element within another Variant array is accessed. *varMain(3)(17)* looks, and indeed acts, somewhat like a two-dimensional array, but the subscripting syntax is quite different. This technique effectively lets you create multidimensional arrays with differing dimensions and data types for all elements.

Flexible Parameter Passing

The Variant type is useful as a parameter type, especially for object properties for which you want to set any of several types of data in a single property. You can pass just about anything by assigning it to a Variant variable and then passing this data as a Variant parameter.

Variant-Related Functions

You should be aware of several useful functions for working with Variants. *TypeName* returns a string describing the current contents of a Variant. The family of *Is...* functions, such as *IsNumeric* and *IsObject*, provide fast logical checks on a Variant's contents. Do a search in the online help for more information on these and other, related, functions.

Empty and Null

Be careful of the difference between an *Empty* Variant and a *Null* one. A Variant is Empty until it's been assigned a value of any type. Null is a special indication that the Variant contains no valid data. A Null value can be assigned explicitly to a Variant, and a Null value propagates through all calculations. The Null value most often appears in database applications, where it indicates unknown or missing data.

Data Type Coercion

Variants are very flexible, but you need to be careful when dealing with the complexities of automatic data conversions. For example, some of the following program steps may surprise you:

```
Option Explicit

Private Sub Form_Click()
    Dim a, b
    a = "123"
    b = True
    Print a + b              ' 122
    Print a & b              ' 123True
    Print a And b = 0        ' 0
    Print b And a = 0        ' False
End Sub
```

The first Print statement treats the contents of the two Variants as numeric values, and the second statement treats them as strings. The last two Print statements produce considerably different results based on the operational hierarchy, which isn't at all obvious. The best advice I can provide is to be cautious and to carefully check out the results of your coding to make sure the results you get are what you expect.

Dear John, How Do I...

Work with Predefined Constants?

There are actually several types of constants in Visual Basic 4, including some predefined constants provided by the system.

Compiler Constants

If you need to develop your applications in both 16-bit and 32-bit versions, be sure to check out the constants Win16 and Win32. These constants indicate the current system in use during development of your Visual Basic applications and let you select appropriate blocks of code to suit the conditions.

These constants are used with the new *#If ... #ElseIf ... #Then ... #End If* directives to select or skip over sections of code during compilation.

Visual Basic Constants

A huge list of predefined constants is provided automatically by Visual Basic for virtually every need. To see what's available, click on the Object Browser button, select VBA or VB from the *Libraries/Projects* drop-down list, and click on *Constants* in the *Classes/Modules* list. A long list of constants, each identifiable by the "vb" prefix, is shown on the right side of the dialog box, as you can see in Figure 3-4 on the following page.

Note that many objects in the Libraries/Projects list also provide constants, and this is the place to locate them when you need them.

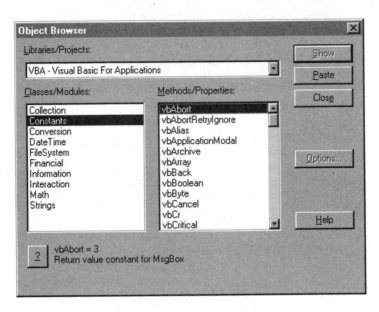

Figure 3-4.
Built-in constants, as shown in the Object Browser.

You'll find that there are predefined constants for almost every control and function parameter imaginable. For example, there's *vbModal* and *vbModeless* for the form *Show* command; *vbRed*, *vbBlue*, and *vbGreen* for color constants used in most graphics methods; and even *vbCr*, *vbLf*, and *vbTab* for common text characters. The following code shows the new way to insert a carriage return/linefeed into a string:

```
a$ = "Line one" & vbCrLf & "Line two"
```

Anytime you find yourself starting to type a numeric value for a command or a method parameter, you should stop yourself and check to see whether there is already a constant defined by the system that you could use instead. This can help make your programs self-documenting, easier to read, and easier to maintain.

User-Defined Constants

As in previous versions of Visual Basic, you can define your own constants in your programs, using the *Const* keyword. You can also create conditional compiler constants using the similar, but actually quite different, *#Const* directive. Constants created by *#Const* are to be used only with the *#If ... #ElseIf ... #Then ... #End If* directives I described earlier. Conversely, user-defined constants created with the *Const* keyword are not to be used as conditional compiler constants.

Some of the new predefined constants are extremely helpful for building complex string constants. For example, the following code prints one constant to display digits in a column on a form. This same formatting was impossible without extra coding in prior versions of Visual Basic. Now you can do all this formatting at design time. Note that only one executable statement is executed in the following routine at runtime:

```
Option Explicit

Private Sub Form_Click()

    Const DIGITS = _
        "1" & vbCrLf & _
        "2" & vbCrLf & _
        "3" & vbCrLf & _
        "4" & vbCrLf & _
        "5" & vbCrLf & _
        "6" & vbCrLf & _
        "7" & vbCrLf & _
        "8" & vbCrLf & _
        "9" & vbCrLf

    Print DIGITS

End Sub
```

Use the *Private* and *Public* keywords for constants declared at the module level to define their scope. If declared *Private*, the constants will be local to the module only, whereas *Public* constants are available project-wide. These keywords cannot be used for defining constants inside procedures. A constant declared within a procedure is always local to that procedure.

Dear John, How Do I...
Create Type Structures?

The *Type* keyword is used to declare the framework of a Type data structure. Notice that the *Type* command doesn't actually create a data structure; it only provides a detailed definition of the structure. You use a *Dim* statement to actually create variables of the new type.

You can declare a Type structure only at the module level. Unlike Visual Basic 3, Visual Basic 4 allows you to put the Type definition in any module, even in a Form. The only limitation is that in a form or a class module you must declare the Type structure as *Private* to its module. Type structures are getting more and more flexible with each release of Visual Basic. When combined with Variants, amazingly dynamic and adjustable data structures can result. The following code example demonstrates a few of these details:

```
Option Explicit

Private Type typX
    a() As Integer
    b As String
    c As Variant
End Type

Private Sub Form_Click()
    'Create some variables
    Dim X As typX
    'Resize the dynamic array within the structure
    ReDim X.a(22 To 33)
    'Assign values into the structure
    X.a(27) = 29
    X.b = "abc"
    'Insert an entire array into the structure
    Dim y(100) As Double
    y(33) = 4 * Atn(1)
    X.c = y()
    'Verify a few elements of the structure
    Print X.a(27)    ' 29
    Print X.b        ' abc
    Print X.c(33)    ' 3.14159265358979
End Sub
```

Notice the third element of the typX data structure, which is declared as a Variant. Recall that we can store just about anything in a Variant, which means that at runtime we can create an array and insert it into the Type data structure by assigning the array to the Variant.

Memory Alignment

32-bit Visual Basic, in its attempt to mesh well with 32-bit operating system standards, now performs alignment of Type structure elements on 4-byte boundaries in memory (DWORD alignment). This means that the amount of memory your Type structures actually use is probably more than you'd expect. More important, it means that the old trick of using *LSet* to transfer binary data from one Type structure to another might not work as you expect it to.

Again, your best bet is to experiment carefully and remain aware of this potential trouble spot. It could cause the kind of bugs that are hard to track down unless you're lucidly aware of the potential for trouble ahead of time.

Parameters

Now that Visual Basic 4 incorporates Visual Basic for Applications, there are several new twists to parameter passing in Visual Basic. In this chapter, we'll take a look at these new techniques.

Dear John, How Do I...

Use Named Parameters?

The most common way to pass parameters in Visual Basic, and indeed, in almost every programming language, is by position in a comma-delimited list. So, for instance, if you create a subprogram that expects the parameters *(Red, Green, Blue)*, you always pass three values to the routine, and it's understood that the first parameter will always represent Red, the second Green, and the last Blue.

Now take a look at the following subprogram and the code that calls it. I've used the explicit parameter naming feature of Visual Basic 4 to pass the three parameters, but in reverse order!

```
Option Explicit

Private Sub FormColor(Red, Green, Blue)
    BackColor = RGB(Red * 256, Green * 256, Blue * 256)
End Sub

Private Sub Form_Click()
    FormColor Blue:=0, Green:=0.5, Red:=1      'Brown
End Sub
```

The real value of named parameters isn't so much in their ability to be passed in any order but in their ability to clearly pass a subset of parameters to a routine that expects any of a large number of parameters. To take full advantage of named parameters in your applications, you need to make some or all of your parameters optional, which takes us right into the next question.

Dear John, How Do I...

Use Optional Parameters?

Optional parameters are especially useful when you have a relatively long list of named parameters for a function or a subprogram. Here's a simple modification of the previous example to show you how this works:

```
Option Explicit

Private Sub FormColor(Optional Red, Optional Green, Optional Blue)
Dim r, g, b
    If IsMissing(Red) Then r = 0 Else r = Red
    If IsMissing(Green) Then g = 0 Else g = Green
    If IsMissing(Blue) Then b = 0 Else b = Blue
    BackColor = RGB(r * 256, g * 256, b * 256)
End Sub

Private Sub Form_Click()
    FormColor Green:=0.5      'Medium green
End Sub
```

I've added the keyword *Optional* to the parameter declarations in the subprogram, which allows you to pass any or all of the parameters using named arguments to clearly indicate which parameters are passed. In this example, I've passed only the Green argument, knowing that the subprogram will default to the value 0 for the optional arguments I didn't pass.

You can add the *Optional* modifier only if a parameter is a Variant, as are all three parameters in the example above. The other rule to be aware of is that once a parameter is defined with the *Optional* modifier, all remaining parameters in the argument list must also be declared as optional.

See Also...

- The Metric application in Chapter 26 (Part III) for a demonstration of the use of optional parameters

Dear John, How Do I...

Pass Parameter Arrays?

If you declare the last parameter in the argument list of a routine as a Variant array with the *ParamArray* keyword, you can pass a flexible number of parameters. The following sample code demonstrates this by converting any number of parameters passed into a vertically formatted string list of all items:

```
Option Explicit

Private Function MakeVerticalList(ParamArray N()) As String
    Dim A$, i
    For i = LBound(N) To UBound(N)
        A$ = A$ + vbCrLf + CStr(N(i))
    Next i
    MakeVerticalList = A$
End Function

Private Sub Form_Click()
    Dim A As Integer
    Dim B As Single
    Dim C As String
    A = 123
    B = 3.1416
    C = "This is a test"
    Print MakeVerticalList(A, B, C)
    Print
    Print MakeVerticalList("This", "time", "we'll", "pass five", _
"string parameters.")
End Sub
```

Notice that I called *MakeVerticalList* twice, the first time with a variety of types of parameters—three in all—and the second time with five string parameters. Figure 4-1 shows the results displayed when you click on the form.

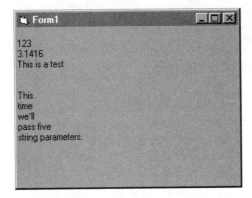

Figure 4-1.
Results of passing first three and then five parameters to the
MakeVerticalList *function.*

Dear John, How Do I...

Pass Any Type of Data in a Parameter?

Remember that Variant variables can contain just about any kind of data imaginable. This opens the door to passing any type of data you want to a parameter as long as the parameter has been declared as Variant.

For example, in this code sample I've passed an integer, a string, and an array to a small subprogram:

```
Option Explicit

Private Sub varTest(V)
    Print TypeName(V)
End Sub

Private Sub Form_Click()
    Dim A(3, 4, 5, 6, 7) As Double
    varTest 123
    varTest "This is a test string"
    varTest A
End Sub
```

The Variant V, defined as the only parameter in the varTest subprogram, accepts whatever you want to pass it. The *TypeName* function is then used to display the type of data that was passed. Figure 4-2 shows the results of running this sample code.

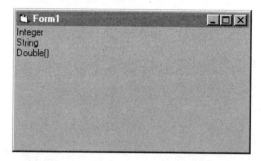

Figure 4-2.

Results of a routine that uses a Variant parameter.

Object-Oriented Programming

Perhaps the most important new features in Visual Basic 4 are those that allow you to do true object-oriented programming. This is a huge topic, and indeed many pages of Microsoft's manuals deal with this important subject in great detail. Instead of repeating all these details, in this chapter I'll highlight the main concepts, provide simple code examples, and give you a foundation from which to further your studies of this subject.

Object-oriented programming in Visual Basic is a fascinating subject. Class modules let you structure your applications in ways that you never could before. You'll also find yourself able to grasp the organization of much bigger projects and keep this structure clearly in mind as you work on all the pieces. Team programming and single programmer projects alike are made easier by this object-oriented approach.

OLE server applications let you combine the objects you've created into an application that can provide these objects to other applications through OLE Automation. OLE servers modularize your applications by providing a source of programmable objects that is external to your application.

But for me, the moment of enlightenment came when I suddenly realized that creating objects is actually a lot of fun! In this chapter, we'll create a sample class module object and a sample OLE server.

Dear John, How Do I...

Create a New Object?

The short answer is: create a class module. These modules are new to Visual Basic version 4, and they open the door to some powerful new ways of structuring programs. The printed manuals and online help are the best resources to study for all the intricacies of class modules and the objects you can create with them. Here I'll present a simple example, just enough to whet your appetite and provide a framework for learning. Throughout this book, you'll find many working examples of class modules because they provide a great way to create structured code and I like using them.

Loan—A Class Module Example

To demonstrate many of the most important features of class module objects, I've built a relatively simple class module that lets you create Loan objects. The Loan object is used to calculate the payment schedule over the life of a loan. You could easily add more methods and properties to this class or restructure the way it works, but I kept it fairly simple on purpose, to provide a working model for you to study.

To create a class module, start a new project and, from the Insert menu, choose Class Module. After adding the following code, save the module as Loan.cls. Here's the code for the Loan class, followed by explanations of the different parts of the code.

```
'Loan.cls - This is a class module that provides a
'           blueprint for creating Loan objects
'
Option Explicit

'These variables are public properties of Loan object
Public Principal As Currency
Public AnnualInterestRate As Single

'These variables are known only within this class module
Private Mo As Integer      'Number of months of loan
Private Ba() As Currency   'Amortized balance array

'This lets user assign a value to Months property
Property Let Months(M)
    Mo = M
End Property

'This gets current value of Months property for user
Property Get Months()
    Months = Mo
End Property

'This lets user assign a value to Years property
Property Let Years(Y)
    Mo = Y * 12
End Property
```

(continued)

```
'This gets current value of Years property for user
Property Get Years()
    Years = Mo / 12
End Property

'This gets calculated Payment property for user
Property Get Payment()
    Dim MonthlyInterestRate As Single
    'Verify that all properties are loaded
    If Principal = 0 Or AnnualInterestRate = 0 Or Mo = 0 Then
        Payment = 0
    Else
        MonthlyInterestRate = AnnualInterestRate / 1200
        Payment = (-MonthlyInterestRate * Principal) / _
            ((MonthlyInterestRate + 1) ^ (-Mo) - 1)
    End If
End Property

'This is a method to fill amortized balance array
Public Sub Amortize()
    Dim i
    Dim Balance As Currency
    Dim Paid As Currency
    ReDim Ba(0)
    Ba(0) = Principal
    Paid = CCur(Payment / 100) * 100       'Rounds to nearest penny
    Do Until Ba(i) <= 0
        i = i + 1
        ReDim Preserve Ba(i)
        Ba(i) = Ba(i - 1) * (1 + AnnualInterestRate / 1200)
        Ba(i) = Ba(i) - Paid
        Ba(i) = CCur(Ba(i) / 100) * 100
    Loop
End Sub

'This gets balance of loan after N months for user
Property Get Balance(N)
    If N > UBound(Ba) Or N < 1 Then
        Balance = 0
    Else
        Balance = Ba(N)
    End If
End Property
```

The Loan objects we create in our main program will have properties and methods, just like other objects. The simplest way to create a property is to declare Public variables. Principal and AnnualInterestRate, shown on the following page, are two such properties.

```
Public Principal As Currency
Public AnnualInterestRate As Single
```

Two variables, *Mo* and *Ba()*, are declared Private (as shown below) so that the outside world will be unaware of their existence. Within the Loan object, we can be assured that the values contained in these variables are always under direct control of the object's internal code.

```
Private Mo As Integer      'Number of months of loan
Private Ba() As Currency   'Amortized balance array
```

Mo stores the number of months of the loan. I could have made this a simple Public variable, but I've designed the Loan object with two related Public properties, Years and Months, either of which can be set by the user to define the length of the loan. These properties then internally set the value of *Mo*. Read on to see how these two properties are set up to do this.

The *Property Let* statement provides a way to create a property in your object that can take action when the user assigns a value to it. Simple properties, such as Principal, described above, just sit there and accept whatever value the user assigns. The Months property, on the other hand, is defined in such a way that you can add code that will be executed whenever a value is assigned to the property. In this case, the code is a simple assignment of the number of months to the local *Mo* variable for safekeeping:

```
Property Let Months(M)
    Mo = M
End Property
```

The *Property Let* and *Property Get* statements work hand in hand to build a readable and writable property of an object. Here the *Property Get Months* statement provides a way for the user to access the current contents of the Months property:

```
Property Get Months()
    Months = Mo
End Property
```

If you don't add a corresponding *Property Get* statement to go along with a *Property Let*, the defined property will be write-only. Conversely, a *Property Get* without a corresponding *Property Let* results in a read-only property. For some properties, this can be a good thing. This is true for the Payment property, which is described later on.

The Years property, shown at the top of the next page, provides a second, alternative, property that the user can set to define the length of the loan. Notice that the value set into the Years property is multiplied by 12 internally to convert it to months. This detail is hidden from the user.

```
Property Let Years(Y)
    Mo = Y * 12
End Property

Property Get Years()
    Years = Mo / 12
End Property
```

Compare the Years and Months property routines to see why I created the local variable *Mo* to store the actual length of the loan separately from the properties used to set this value.

When the user accesses the value of the Loan object's Payment property, shown below, a complicated calculation is triggered, and the payment amount is computed from the current value of the other property settings. This is a clear example that shows why *Property Get* statements add useful capabilities beyond those provided by properties that are created by simply declaring a public variable in a class module.

```
Property Get Payment()
    Dim MonthlyInterestRate As Single
    If Principal = 0 Or AnnualInterestRate = 0 Or Mo = 0 Then
        Payment = 0
    Else
        MonthlyInterestRate = AnnualInterestRate / 1200
        Payment = (-MonthlyInterestRate * Principal) / _
            ((MonthlyInterestRate + 1) ^ (-Mo) - 1)
    End If
End Property
```

The Amortize subprogram, shown below, defines a *method* of the Loan object. When the user calls this method, the Loan object expands and fills the local dynamic array *Ba()* with monthly balances until the balance goes to zero. This array is filled just once, when this method is called, and values are returned one at a time by the Balance property, which follows.

```
Public Sub Amortize()
    Dim i
    Dim Balance As Currency
    Dim Paid As Currency
    ReDim Ba(0)
    Ba(0) = Principal
    Paid = CCur(Payment / 100) * 100        'Rounds to nearest penny
    Do Until Ba(i) <= 0
        i = i + 1
        ReDim Preserve Ba(i)
```

(continued)

```
        Ba(i) = Ba(i - 1) * (1 + AnnualInterestRate / 1200)
        Ba(i) = Ba(i) - Paid
        Ba(i) = CCur(Ba(i) / 100) * 100
    Loop
End Sub
```

Finally, the Balance property, which is set up as a read-only property because we define it only in a *Property Get* statement with no corresponding *Property Let*, returns a precalculated value from the monthly balances array. Here is the code for the Balance property:

```
Property Get Balance(N)
    If N > UBound(Ba) Or N < 1 Then
        Balance = 0
    Else
        Balance = Ba(N)
    End If
End Property
```

If anything goes wrong here—if the month number is out of range, or if the user hasn't called the *Amortize* method first, for example—the property will return the value 0. This is a simplified way to handle potential errors. My intent is not to cover the best ways to handle all potential errors but simply to show you an example class object in a simplified, straightforward manner.

See Also...

- The next topic, "Dear John, How Do I Use My New Objects?"

Dear John, How Do I...

Use My New Objects?

The Loan class module doesn't actually create an object; it just creates a blueprint that lets your program stamp out one or more real Loan objects as needed. Let's complete the example by adding the Loan.cls module to a simple project and doing something with it.

Start with a fresh project containing just a single Form1 module. Add the Loan class module to your project. Notice that this class module shows only three properties in the Properties window: Instancing, Name, and Public. These are all important properties, and you should set them as follows:

- Instancing should be set to *2 - Creatable MultiUse*. This lets you create as many copies of the Loan object as you want in your application.

■ Name should be set to *Loan*. This is the name of the object as used in the *Dim* statement to create new Loan objects.

■ Public should be set to *False*. This indicates that the objects can be created only within the current application or project. You would set Public to *True*, for instance, when creating an OLE server application that provides programmable objects for other applications to use.

To try out the Loan object, add the following lines of code to your main form's click event routine. Following the code listing are explanations of the different parts of this code.

```
Private Sub Form_Click()
Dim L As New Loan
Dim Mon As Integer
Dim Bal As Currency

' Set loan parameters
    L.Principal = 1000
    L.Months = 12
    L.AnnualInterestRate = 9.6

' Display parameters used
    Print "Principal: ", , Format(L.Principal, "Currency")
    Print "No. Months:", , L.Months
    Print "Interest Rate:", , Format(L.AnnualInterestRate / 100, _
        "Percent")
    Print "Monthly Payment: ", Format(L.Payment, "Currency")
    Print
    L.Amortize
' Display payment schedule
    Do
        Mon = Mon + 1
        Bal = L.Balance(Mon)
        If Bal <= 0 Then Exit Do
        Print "Month: "; Mon,
        Print "Balance: "; Format(Bal, "Currency")
    Loop
End Sub
```

A new Loan object named L is created in the code shown below. It will be destroyed automatically, just like any other local variable, when it goes out of scope.

```
Dim L As New Loan
```

The following three lines assign values to three of the properties we've created for the Loan object. Review the Loan class code to see how the Months property is built differently from the other two.

```
L.Principal = 1000
L.Months = 12
L.AnnualInterestRate = 9.6
```

As we output results, various properties of the Loan object are accessed as required. (See the following code.) In most cases, the Loan object simply hands back each value as it is currently stored in the object. In the case of the L.Payment property, however, a complex calculation is triggered. The calling code is blissfully unaware of when, where, and how the calculations are performed.

```
Print "Principal: ", , Format(L.Principal, "Currency")
Print "No. Months:", , L.Months
Print "Interest Rate:", , Format(L.AnnualInterestRate / 100, _
    "Percent")
Print "Monthly Payment: ", Format(L.Payment, "Currency")
Print
```

The *Amortize* method, shown here, tells the Loan object to go ahead and internally prepare a table of loan balances, in preparation for accessing each month's balance in the next few lines of the program.

```
L.Amortize
```

The last few lines of our sample program display an amortized table of the loan's balance at the end of each month of the loan:

```
Do
    Mon = Mon + 1
    Bal = L.Balance(Mon)
    If Bal <= 0 Then Exit Do
    Print "Month: "; Mon,
    Print "Balance: "; Format(Bal, "Currency")
Loop
```

When the end of the Form_Click routine is reached, all variables declared in the routine are automatically destroyed by the system. This includes the Loan object, with all its code and data.

Figure 5-1 shows the displayed results of running this program. Notice that you could greatly improve and expand upon this simple program without ever having to touch the contents of the Loan class module.

A carefully designed object, in the form of a class module, lets you extend Visual Basic by adding some new programmable objects to your bag of tricks.

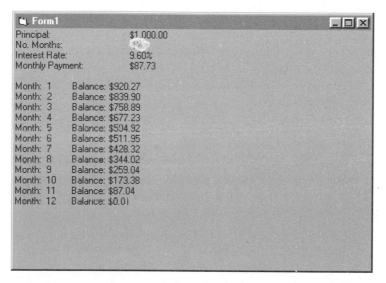

Figure 5-1.
Output generated by using a Loan object.

Once you get an object the way you want it, all you need to document for future reference and use is the object's properties and methods. The internal workings and implementation of the object can be mentally "black-boxed" and ignored. That demonstrates the true power and beauty of object-oriented programming!

The Loan class was simply added as another module to our sample application. This is a great way to use class modules, but you can also combine one or more class modules into a complete, "stand-alone," OLE server. This is the subject of the next topic.

See Also...

- The Lottery application in Chapter 25 (Part III) for a demonstration of the use of objects

Dear John, How Do I...

Create and Use an OLE Server?

An OLE server application makes OLE objects available for use by external applications. Visual Basic 4 now allows the creation of OLE servers, opening the door to a powerful new way to organize and modularize reusable code.

The Gravity example shipped with Visual Basic 4 is a good working example of an OLE server application, but I want to take a closer look at the steps required to create and use such applications. After you walk through the following example, you'll have a solid background from which to begin further exploration of the diverse and powerful features of OLE server development.

Overview

In this example, we'll create a very simple OLE server containing the definition for one type of object. Or, to use the correct terminology, we'll create one *class*. The class can then function as a template to produce copies of the object. Once the object application is up and running and registered with the system, we'll create a second, more conventional, Visual Basic application that will create a couple of these objects on the fly, and properties and methods of these objects will be manipulated to get the desired results.

We'll create an object named Dice in an OLE server named Chance-Server. Even though I've named the object Dice, I've provided properties that let the calling application set the number of sides so that each die can act more like a coin (if it has two sides), a dodecahedron-shaped die (if the number of sides is set to 12), and so on.

Dice.cls

Let's jump right in and build the OLE server first. Start a new project, and choose Class Module from the Insert menu. Save the module as Dice.cls and the project as Chance.vbp. (A class module is automatically given the filename extension CLS when saved on disk, and the project file's extension is VBP.) Add the following lines of code to the DICE class module:

```
Option Explicit

'Declare properties that define the range of possible values
Public Smallest As Integer
Public Largest As Integer

'Declare a read-only property
'and define its value as a roll of the die
Public Property Get Value()
    Value = Int(Rnd * (Largest - Smallest + 1)) + Smallest
End Property
```

(continued)

```
'Use a method to shuffle the random sequence
Public Sub Shuffle()
    Randomize
End Sub
```

This class code defines three properties and one method for the Dice object. Smallest and Largest are two properties that I've declared as public variables so that the client application (which is created a little later on) can set the range of returned values, or in this case the number of sides of the die. Properties of objects are often simply declared as public variables in this way.

Value is another property of the Dice object, but in this case we want to do a little calculation before handing a number back to the client application. The *Property Get* statement provides the mechanism for performing any extra steps we want to have done when the property's value is requested. In this case, a random number is generated to simulate the roll of the die, and this number is returned as the value of the property. (For the mathematical purists among us, the number is not truly random, but it's close enough for our needs.) The Value property is read-only by the client application because the *Property Get* statement was used but there is no corresponding *Property Let* statement. Adding a *Property Let* statement would enable the client application to write a new value to the Value property. In this example, we just want to return a random roll of the die, so we have no need to let the client application set a value for this property.

Shuffle is a simple method I've added so that the object will have at least one method to show for itself. When this method is invoked, the object will randomize the random number generator to effectively shuffle the outcome of rolls of the die.

Notice, as shown in Figure 5-2 on the following page, that this class module has only three property settings: Instancing, Name, and Public. Set Instancing to *2 - Creatable MultiUse* to allow a client application to create new instances or objects of this class or type of object. Set Name to *Dice*. Each object in an OLE server is defined in its own CLS module, and the Name property of the module is the object's name as it is known to the outside world. Finally, set the Public property to *True* to make this object available to the outside world. (It's quite feasible in certain circumstances to create objects that are not public so that they can be created and manipulated only from within the object application itself. The Loan class in the previous topic is a good example of this.) The Properties settings should now look like those in Figure 5-2.

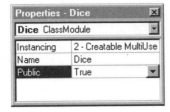

Figure 5-2.
The Chance class module's three properties.

Chance.bas

An OLE server's executable file must have a starting point. This can be either a form or, as is often the case, a Sub Main() procedure. Let's add this starting point to our object application. Add a new module to the project by choosing Module from the Insert menu, and name it Chance when you save the project. The BAS extension will be added automatically by Visual Basic. Add the following code to this module:

```
Option Explicit

Sub Main()
    Randomize
End Sub
```

The Main() procedure is the place to add initialization code for your OLE server. In this case, I've added a *Randomize* statement to produce a new seed value for the random number generator, so even if the client application doesn't invoke the *Shuffle* method, the dice sequences should be unique.

Application-Level Settings

We've now completed the creation of the code and class modules for our new OLE server. An important last step is to set the properties of the project as a whole. Choose Options from the Tools menu, and, on the Project tab of the Options dialog box, select Sub Main as the Startup form, set the Project name to ChanceServer, select the OLE Server option for the StartMode, and set the Application Description to Dice, Coins, Or Similar Objects. The dialog box should now look like the one shown in Figure 5-3. These are the critical entries; later on you will probably want to learn about and experiment with the other fields.

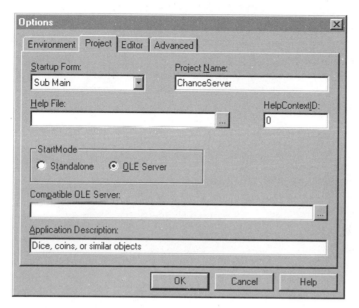

Figure 5-3.
Setting project options to create an OLE server.

Once these options are set, the ChanceServer OLE server application is ready to run. You can create an EXE and run it, or you can simply run the application from the environment, which works great during the normal development cycle. Even though this program doesn't actually do anything noticeable by itself, you need to run it to have it register its objects with the system. Otherwise, external client applications will know nothing about the objects your application provides. For debugging purposes, I suggest running it in the environment. Run it now, leave it running, and minimize the whole Visual Basic environment to an icon in preparation for the next step. Be sure to select Run With Full Compile from the Run menu to ensure that the application is finalized and registered correctly.

The OLE Client Application

Let's create a simple controlling application, or OLE client, to access the new Dice object. Start up a second instance of Visual Basic while still leaving the ChanceServer object application running and minimized. (This is a slick new feature of Visual Basic 4, by the way—the ability to run multiple instances of Visual Basic itself.) On a new form, add two command buttons, and name them cmdCoin and cmdDie. Add the code on the following page to the click events of these buttons.

```
Option Explicit

Private Sub cmdCoin_Click()
    'Create new object
    Dim Coin As New Dice
    'Set properties to define range
    Coin.Smallest = 0
    Coin.Largest = 1
    'Call a method of the object
    Coin.Shuffle
    'Access a property
    If Coin.Value = 1 Then
        Print "Heads"
    Else
        Print "Tails"
    End If
    'Remove object from memory
    Set Coin = Nothing
End Sub

Private Sub cmdDie_Click()
    'Create new object
    Dim Dodecahedron As New Dice
    'Set properties to define range
    Dodecahedron.Smallest = 1
    Dodecahedron.Largest = 12
    'Call a method of the object
    Dodecahedron.Shuffle
    'Access a property
    Print Dodecahedron.Value
    'Remove object from memory
    Set Dodecahedron = Nothing
End Sub
```

When you started the OLE server, it registered itself with the system. Now, to have the current client application refer to the registered objects, you must add Dice, Coins, Or Similar Objects to the current client application's list of external references. Choose References from the Tools menu, and check the Dice, Coins, Or Similar Objects entry in the Available References list. (See Figure 5-4.) Click OK to close the References dialog box.

Now press F2 to open the Object Browser, and select ChanceServer from the Libraries/Projects drop-down list to verify the availability of the objects in the object application. Figure 5-5 shows the Dice class and its four methods and properties as listed in the Object Browser. Remember, use the References tool to select and enable an available object application, and then make sure the application's objects are available for use by checking in the Object Browser.

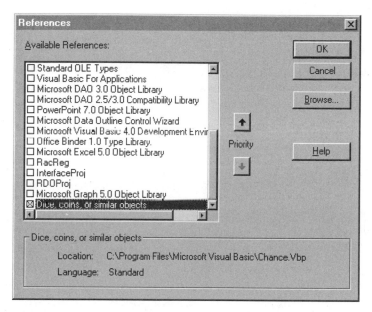

Figure 5-4.
Enabling the OLE server's objects for reference by the current application.

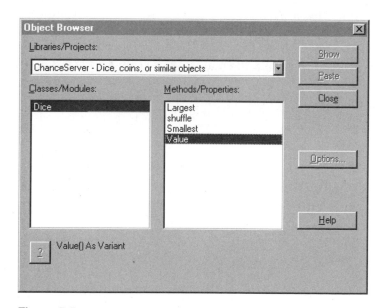

Figure 5-5.
The Object Browser, showing available objects, methods, and properties in the selected OLE server.

Click on the Close button to close the Object Browser dialog box. Run the sample controlling application, and click on the Coin and Die buttons. Two slightly different instances of the Dice object are created, one to simulate a coin and the other to simulate a dodecahedron-shaped die. As shown in Figure 5-6, with each click of one of these buttons a randomly generated value for the given Dice object is returned and the result is displayed.

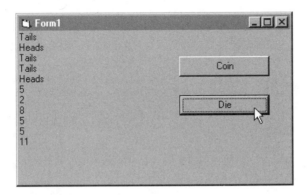

Figure 5-6.
Two Dice objects created in a client application.

When everything's working right, create an EXE file from the Chance-Server object application and run it once outside the Visual Basic environment. When the EXE file has registered in the system, any external client application is free to refer to it to create and use the objects it defines.

API Functions

A powerful feature of Visual Basic is its ability to call functions that reside in dynamic link library (DLL) files, including all the API functions that are provided—and used—by Windows. The API functions and their syntax are described in the Windows SDK Help file that is included with Visual Basic 4. Access to the hundreds of API functions, as well as other functions contained in DLLs, extends the capabilities of Visual Basic far beyond those of many other languages.

In this chapter, I show you a way to declare these functions in an easy to read format using Visual Basic's new line continuation character, and I demonstrate a few useful functions to give you a head start in using these API calls. I also describe a few simple details and potential gotchas that seem to trip up most of us once or twice as we begin to experiment with API function calling.

Dear John, How Do I...

Call API Functions?

To use API functions, simply declare them in your source code and then call them just like you would any other function in Visual Basic. Let's take a look at these two steps in more detail.

Declarations

Because API functions are not internal to Visual Basic, you must explicitly declare them before you can use them. The online help covers the exact syntax for the *Declare* statement, but there are a few tricks I've discovered—using some new features of Visual Basic 4—that you will probably find useful.

Some API function declarations are quite long. In the past, either you lived with a long declaration or you somehow condensed the declaration so that it would all fit comfortably on one line. For example, the following code shows the standard declaration for the API function *GetTempFileName*. Note that in previous versions of Visual Basic this entire declaration was entered on one line in the source code file.

```
Private Declare Function GetTempFileName Lib "kernel32" Alias
"GetTempFileNameA" (ByVal lpszPath As String, ByVal lpPrefixString
As String, ByVal wUnique As Long, ByVal lpTempFileName As String)
As Long
```

Here's a shortened version of this declaration also entered on one line, which makes the declaration more manageable but somewhat less readable:

```
Declare Function GetTempFileName& Lib "kernel32" Alias
"GetTempFileNameA" (ByVal Pth$, ByVal Prf$, ByVal Unq&, ByVal Fnm$)
```

Visual Basic 4 lets you format these declarations in a new way, keeping the longer, more readable parameter keywords but using much shorter lines that are visible in a normal-size edit window. The new line continuation character is the key to this improved format. The following code shows the same declaration in a style that I find easy to read. (Feel free to modify the layout to suit your own style.)

```
Private Declare Function GetTempFileName _
Lib "kernel32" Alias "GetTempFileNameA" ( _
    ByVal lpszPath As String, _
    ByVal lpPrefixString As String, _
    ByVal wUnique As Long, _
    ByVal lpTempFileName As String _
) As Long
```

You'll find this style used throughout this book wherever I declare API functions.

32-Bit Function Declarations

Notice in the previous example that the *GetTempFileName* function name is actually aliased to a function named *GetTempFileNameA*. In Windows 95, 32-bit function declarations involving string parameters have been renamed from their 16-bit predecessors because they've been rebuilt using 32-bit coding specifications, although they still use ANSI strings internally (hence the *A*).

NOTE: A third set of functions has been defined for 32-bit Windows NT development, in which strings are internally manipulated in the system DLLs as Unicode strings. In this case the original function names now have the suffix *W* (for *Wide* characters).

To make sure you get the properly formatted function declaration, you can access the Visual Basic 4 API function declarations in the file Win32-api.txt, which you'll find in the Winapi folder in your Microsoft Visual Basic folder. There are several ways to get the function declarations from this file into your application. You can load the file into WordPad and copy the desired declarations into your Visual Basic applications by hand, making the editing changes mentioned above. Or you might prefer to use the API Viewer application, which comes with Visual Basic, to automate this process. You can start the API Viewer by choosing it from the Visual Basic folder on the Windows Start menu or by running the program Apilod32 from the Winapi folder on your CD-ROM disc. In Part III (Chapter 26), I'll show you how to create an add-in to the Visual Basic environment that helps you insert API function declarations.

Strings

There are a couple of gotchas to watch out for when you are passing strings as parameters to API functions. One is that API functions will not create any string space for you. You must create a string long enough to handle the longest possible string that could be returned before you pass the string to the function. For example, the code shown on the following page declares the API function *GetWindowsDirectory*, which returns the path to the Windows folder. The documentation for this function states that the string buffer for the path should be no less than 144 bytes in length. Before the function is called, the string variable *WinPath* is built to be 144 bytes in length using the *Space$* function, as shown. Failure to build a string parameter to a sufficient length is a recipe for disaster because an API function will take as much string space as it needs and will write over unknown memory locations if the allocated string space is not adequate.

If you incorporate the following code fragment into a program, the Windows directory path, as returned by the *GetWindowsDirectory* API function, is displayed when the form is clicked. The result is shown in Figure 6-1.

```
Option Explicit

Private Declare Function GetWindowsDirectory _
Lib "kernel32" Alias "GetWindowsDirectoryA" ( _
    ByVal lpBuffer As String, _
    ByVal nSize As Long _
) As Long

Private Sub Form_Click()
    Dim WinPath As String
    Dim Rtn As Integer
    Const MAXWINPATH = 144
    WinPath = Space$(MAXWINPATH)
    Rtn = GetWindowsDirectory(WinPath, MAXWINPATH)
    WinPath = Left$(WinPath, Rtn) 'Truncate at the 0 byte
    Print WinPath
End Sub
```

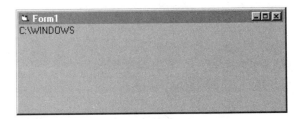

Figure 6-1.
The Windows directory path as returned by GetWindowsDirectory.

Also, note that returned strings are terminated by a byte of value 0. In the sample code above, the function returns the length of the string, but in many cases when you use API functions you won't know the actual length of the string data unless you look for the first 0 byte. If the API function doesn't return the length of the returned string, here's a way to lop off those extra 0 bytes on the string:

```
WinPath = Left$(WinPath, InStr(WinPath, Chr$(0)) - 1)
```

See Also...

- The APIAddin application in Chapter 26 (Part III) for a demonstration of how to select, copy, and paste API declarations to your source code using the new format

Dear John, How Do I...

Understand *ByVal*, *ByRef*, and As Any in an API Function Declaration?

This question is not so important in 32-bit Visual Basic programming, because most of the As Any declarations have been replaced with explicit parameter data types. Nonetheless, I'll go ahead and describe a specific case—the 16-bit version of the *WinHelp* API function—for which this is a concern. Note, however, that the 32-bit version of this function has no As Any parameter declarations.

Many 16-bit API function declarations (and a few 32-bit ones) have one or more parameters declared As Any instead of as a specific data type such as Integer or String. This is so that these parameters can be used to pass a variety of data types, depending on the intended use of the function. For example, in the following code, which uses the 16-bit version of the *WinHelp* API function to display the Visual Basic help file, consider the *WinHelp* function's fourth parameter, which is declared As Any. (This function, in its 32-bit version, will be demonstrated in more detail in Chapter 13.) Depending on the value of *wCommand*, the last parameter can be used to pass a long integer or a pointer to a string.

```
Option Explicit

Private Declare Function WinHelp Lib "User" ( _
    ByVal hWnd As Integer, _
    ByVal lpHelpFile As String, _
    ByVal wCommand As Integer, _
    ByRef dwData As Any _
) As Integer

Private Sub Form_Click()
    Dim x%, y&
    x% = WinHelp(Form1.hWnd, "VB.HLP", vbHelpContents, _
        ByVal y&)
End Sub
```

By convention, all As Any parameters in API functions are declared by reference. (I've added the *ByRef* keyword to my form of the declarations to explicitly declare them as such, but *ByRef* is the default when you don't see either *ByVal* or *ByRef* in a parameter declaration.) You'll also usually find the

ByVal keyword stuck in front of the variable that is passed for the As Any parameter *at the place where the function is called.* This means that you must pay special attention to how you treat these parameters at the place in your application where the function is actually called. In fact, incorrect use of the *ByRef* and *ByVal* keywords can cause your application to crash. Take a close look at the sample call to *WinHelp* in the code. In this case, the long integer *y&* is passed as the fourth parameter using the *ByVal* modifier, which ensures that a long integer value of 0 is passed.

Dear John, How Do I...

Easily Add API Declarations?

The Visual Basic 4 package includes the handy API Viewer utility (Apilod32) for browsing and inserting the long list of API constants, associated Type structures, and function declarations. As an alternative, I've created an add-in utility application named APIAddin that I like even better. I've reformatted the declarations using the new line continuation character, and I've made the list accessible directly from Visual Basic's editing environment. I've also prefixed the declarations with the *Private* keyword, which makes it easier to add them to any form, class, or code module in which you want to use the functions.

See Also...

- The APIAddin application in Chapter 26 (Part III) for a better alternative to the Apilod32 utility included with Visual Basic 4

Dear John, How Do I...

Use API Calls to Get System Information?

You can use API functions to readily access a lot of information that Windows normally keeps hidden from Visual Basic applications. In the previous topics, I gave a general introduction to setting up API function calls in your applications. Let's explore some techniques and API functions that can be used to access system information. The following functions and techniques show how to use standard API calls to access just a few of the many types of data available from the system.

Determining the Version of the Operating System

The API function *GetVersionEx* returns a data structure that contains the major and minor version numbers of the operating system, among other things. The following code shows how to declare the *GetVersionEx* function and extract the version numbers. To try this code, enter it as code for a new form, run the application, and click anywhere on the form.

```
Option Explicit

Private Type OSVERSIONINFO
    dwOSVersionInfoSize As Long
    dwMajorVersion As long
    dwMinorVersion As Long
    dwBuildNumber As Long
    dwPlatformId As Long
    szCSDVersion As String * 128
End Type

Private Declare Function GetVersionEx _
Lib "kernel32" Alias "GetVersionExA" ( _
    ByRef lpVersionInformation As OSVERSIONINFO _
) As Long

Private Sub Form_Click()
    Dim Ver As OSVERSIONINFO
    Dim x As Long
    Ver.dwOSVersionInfoSize = Len(Ver)
    Caption = GetVersionEx(Ver)
    Print "Major version number:", Ver.dwMajorVersion
    Print "Minor version number:", Ver.dwMinorVersion
End Sub
```

Determining System Colors

The *GetSysColor* API function returns an RGB color for window items such as captions, menus, borders, and the like. You can get color information on any of 31 window components by passing the appropriate constant to the *GetSysColor* function. Some of these components are available only in specific versions of Windows—the constants from COLOR_3DDKSHADOW to the end of the list are for Windows 95, for example. The code on the following pages lists these constants and demonstrates the *GetSysColor* function by setting the main form's background color to match the current color inside the scrollbars when you click anywhere on the form.

I've also provided a handy function to extract the red, green, and blue values from the RGB color value returned by these functions. You might find this function useful for other graphics calculations. It's the inverse function of Visual Basic's *RGB* function, which returns a long RGB integer formed by combining red, green, and blue color values, each in the range 0 through 255.

```
Option Explicit

Private Const COLOR_SCROLLBAR = 0
Private Const COLOR_BACKGROUND = 1
Private Const COLOR_ACTIVECAPTION = 2
Private Const COLOR_INACTIVECAPTION = 3
Private Const COLOR_MENU = 4
Private Const COLOR_WINDOW = 5
Private Const COLOR_WINDOWFRAME = 6
Private Const COLOR_MENUTEXT = 7
Private Const COLOR_WINDOWTEXT = 8
Private Const COLOR_CAPTIONTEXT = 9
Private Const COLOR_ACTIVEBORDER = 10
Private Const COLOR_INACTIVEBORDER = 11
Private Const COLOR_APPWORKSPACE = 12
Private Const COLOR_HIGHLIGHT = 13
Private Const COLOR_HIGHLIGHTTEXT = 14
Private Const COLOR_BTNFACE = 15
Private Const COLOR_BTNSHADOW = 16
Private Const COLOR_GRAYTEXT = 17
Private Const COLOR_BTNTEXT = 18
Private Const COLOR_INACTIVECAPTIONTEXT = 19
Private Const COLOR_BTNHIGHLIGHT = 20
Private Const COLOR_3DDKSHADOW = 21
Private Const COLOR_3DLIGHT = 22
Private Const COLOR_INFOTEXT = 23
Private Const COLOR_INFOBK = 24
Private Const COLOR_DESKTOP = COLOR_BACKGROUND
Private Const COLOR_3DFACE = COLOR_BTNFACE
Private Const COLOR_3DSHADOW = COLOR_BTNSHADOW
Private Const COLOR_3DHIGHLIGHT = COLOR_BTNHIGHLIGHT
Private Const COLOR_3DHILIGHT = COLOR_3DHIGHLIGHT
Private Const COLOR_BTNHILIGHT = COLOR_BTNHIGHLIGHT

Private Declare Function GetSysColor _
Lib "user32" ( _
    ByVal nIndex As Long _
) As Long
```

(continued)

```
Private Sub Form_Click()
    Dim SystemColor As Long
    Dim Red As Integer, Green As Integer, Blue As Integer
    'Get color of scrollbars
    SystemColor = GetSysColor(COLOR_SCROLLBAR)
    'Set form's background color same as scrollbars
    BackColor = SystemColor
    'Split this color into its components
    ColorSplit SystemColor, Red, Green, Blue
    Print "R,G,B = "; Red, Green, Blue
End Sub

Function ColorSplit(RGBMix As Long, R%, G%, B%)
'Extract R, G, and B values from an RGB color
    R% = RGBMix And &HFF
    G% = (RGBMix \ &H100) And &HFF
    B% = (RGBMix \ &H10000) And &HFF
End Function
```

See Chapter 10 if you're interested in another approach to coordinated color schemes.

Determining CPU Type

The following code uses the *GetSystemInfo* API function to determine the type of CPU in the system. By inspecting the SYSTEM_INFO type structure, you'll find that this function returns several other useful bits of information about the system. In anticipation of more advanced systems that will be arriving in the near future, this data structure even returns the number of processors on the current system.

```
Option Explicit

Private Type SYSTEM_INFO
    dwOemID As Long
    dwPageSize As Long
    lpMinimumApplicationAddress As Long
    lpMaximumApplicationAddress As Long
    dwActiveProcessorMask As Long
    dwNumberOfProcessors As Long
    dwProcessorType As Long
    dwAllocationGranularity As Long
    dwReserved As Long
End Type
```

(continued)

77

```
Private Declare Sub GetSystemInfo _
Lib "kernel32" ( _
    lpSystemInfo As SYSTEM_INFO _
)

Private Sub Form_Click()
    Dim Sys As SYSTEM_INFO
    GetSystemInfo Sys
    Print "Processor type: "; Sys.dwProcessorType
End Sub
```

Determining Elapsed Time

The *GetTickCount* API function returns the number of milliseconds that have elapsed since Windows was started. Depending on your system, this function returns a value with greater precision than that of Visual Basic's *Timer* function. The *Timer* function returns the number of seconds since midnight and includes fractions of seconds that provide the illusion of millisecond accuracy, but Visual Basic actually updates the value returned by *Timer* only 18.2 times per second. On my 486 system, the value returned by *GetTickCount* is updated almost 100 times each second, as shown in the data displayed in Figure 6-2.

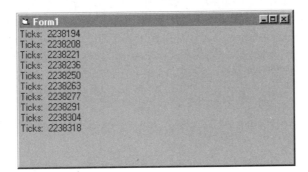

Figure 6-2.
Time elapsed since Windows started, as reported by GetTickCount.

Another advantage of *GetTickCount* over the *Timer* function is that crossing the midnight boundary causes no problems. The *Timer* value returns to 0 at midnight, whereas the *GetTickCount* value returns to 0 only after about 49 days of continuous computer operation. In the following code, when the form is clicked the *GetTickCount* API function is called and the time since Windows was started, in milliseconds, is printed on the form. This API call is repeated nine more times to show how often this API can return its value.

```
Option Explicit

Private Declare Function GetTickCount _
Lib "kernel32" ( _
) As Long

Private Sub Form_Click()
    Dim i, j, k
    For i = 1 To 10
        j = GetTickCount
        Do While j = GetTickCount
        Loop
        Print "Ticks: "; j
    Next i
End Sub
```

Determining Drive Types

It's easy to determine whether the user's computer has one or two floppy drives or one or more hard drives or is connected to any remote drives. As the following code demonstrates, this is accomplished by calling the *GetDriveType* API function. You might want to use this function in a program that searches all available drives for a specific data file, for instance. In the following code, the function is used to detect all drives that are present on the system.

```
Option Explicit

' GetDriveType return values
Private Const DRIVE_REMOVABLE = 2
Private Const DRIVE_FIXED = 3
Private Const DRIVE_REMOTE = 4
Private Const DRIVE_CDROM = 5
Private Const DRIVE_RAMDISK = 6

Private Declare Function GetDriveType _
Lib "kernel32" Alias "GetDriveTypeA" ( _
    ByVal nDrive As String _
) As Long
```

(continued)

```
Private Sub Form_Click()
    Dim i, Drv, D$
    For i = 0 To 25  'All possible drives A to Z
        D$ = Chr$(i + 65) & ":"
        Drv = GetDriveType(D$)
        Select Case Drv
        Case DRIVE_REMOVABLE
            Print "Drive " & D$ & " is removable."
        Case DRIVE_FIXED
            Print "Drive " & D$ & " is fixed."
        Case DRIVE_REMOTE
            Print "Drive " & D$ & " is remote."
        Case DRIVE_CDROM
            Print "Drive " & D$ & " is CD-ROM."
        Case DRIVE_RAMDISK
            Print "Drive " & D$ & " is RAM disk."
        Case Else
        End Select
    Next i
End Sub
```

The list of drives is displayed when the form is clicked, as shown in Figure 6-3.

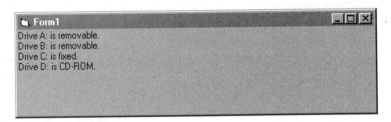

Figure 6-3.
GetDriveType *returning the types of drives on a system.*

CHAPTER SEVEN

Multimedia

In this chapter, I show you two ways to add sound files and video clips to your applications. To try the code examples, you need to have a sound board and the appropriate multimedia drivers installed. You also need a sample WAV file to play sound and a sample AVI file to play a video clip.

> NOTE: You can find many sample sound and video files on your Windows 95 CD-ROM. Right-click on the Start button and choose Find to search for *.WAV and *.AVI files on your CD-ROM drive.

Dear John, How Do I...

Play a Sound (WAV) File?

There are several ways to play a sound file. Here we take a look at two very straightforward methods, one using the *mciExecute* API function supplied by Windows 3.1 and later, and the other using the Multimedia MCI (Media Control Interface) custom control.

mciExecute

The following code shows how to declare the *mciExecute* API function and then use it to play a WAV file. To try this example, add the code to a blank form in a new project, run the application, and click anywhere on the form.

```
Option Explicit

Private Declare Function mciExecute _
Lib "winmm.dll" ( _
    ByVal lpstrCommand As String _
) As Long

Private Sub Form_Click()
    Dim x
```

(continued)

```
     x = mciExecute("Play C:\Windows\Media\Tada.wav")
     'Change filename to name of your sample WAV file
End Sub
```

This same function can be used to send other multimedia commands. For example, we'll soon see how to play a video clip with it.

The Multimedia MCI Custom Control

Visual Basic 4's Multimedia MCI control is an excellent tool for playing sound files. With minor modifications to the code, you can also use this control to play Video for Windows (AVI) files and multimedia movie (MMM) files and to control multimedia hardware. Here we concentrate on playing a sound file.

For the example that follows, draw a Multimedia MCI control on the blank form of a new project. If the Multimedia MCI control (whose Class Name, and thus its ToolTip name, is MMControl) is not in your Toolbox, add it by choosing Custom Controls from the Tools menu and turning on the Microsoft Multimedia Control check box in the Custom Controls dialog box. Name this control mciTest, and set its Visible property to *False*. This example demonstrates how to use an invisible control behind the scenes at runtime, which provides complete programmatic control. For a description of all the buttons on the control and an explanation of how the user can interact with them in the visible mode, refer to the documentation and online help.

I've set up the following example to play the sample sound file Tada.wav when you click anywhere on the form. You can add this code to any event-driven routine you want, such as an error-trapping subroutine or any other event for which you want to give audible notification to the user.

```
Private Sub Form_Click()
    With mciTest
        .FileName = "C:\Windows\Media\Tada.wav"
        'Change filename to name of your sample WAV file
        .Command = "Sound"
    End With
End Sub
```

Dear John, How Do I...

Play a Video (AVI) File?

It's surprisingly easy to play an AVI file on a system configured for playing Video for Windows files. You can use the *mciExecute* API function supplied by Windows or the Visual Basic Multimedia MCI custom control.

mciExecute

The code below shows how to declare the *mciExecute* API function and then use it to play a sample video file. To try this example, add the code to a blank form in a new project, run the application, and click anywhere on the form. I've assumed you have a Windows 95 CD-ROM in your D drive and will use one of its AVI files as your sample video file. Notice that this code is almost identical to the code for playing a sound (WAV) file. Figure 7-1 shows this form and the video window in action.

Artwork courtesy of Bill Plympton

Figure 7-1.
A video demonstration initiated by a click on the form.

```
Option Explicit

Private Declare Function mciExecute _
Lib "winmm.dll" ( _
    ByVal lpstrCommand As String _
) As Long

Private Sub Form_Click()
    Dim x
```

(continued)

```
        x = mciExecute("Play D:\Funstuff\Videos\Welcome1.avi")
        'Change filename to name of your sample AVI file
End Sub
```

The Multimedia MCI Custom Control

Visual Basic 4's Multimedia MCI control works well for playing video files. The documentation covers the user's interaction with the visible buttons, but I'll show you a simple way to use the control in an "invisible" mode to programmatically play a video.

> NOTE: Because of an internal conflict, the MCI control's Done event does not fire as expected if the control's Visible property is set to *False*. The workaround, as shown here, is to leave the control visible and simply move it off the screen.

To try this example, draw a Multimedia MCI control on the blank form of a new project and name it mciTest. Add the following code, run the application, and click anywhere on the form. You'll need to change the FileName property setting to the name of an AVI file you have on your hard disk.

```
Option Explicit

Private Sub Form_Click()
    With mciTest
        .FileName = "D:\Funstuff\Videos\Welcome1.avi"
        .Command = "Open"
        .Command = "Play"
    End With
End Sub

Private Sub Form_Load()
    'Move control out of sight
    mciTest.Left = -32000
End Sub

Private Sub mciTest_Done(NotifyCode As Integer)
    mciTest.Command = "Close"
End Sub
```

Originally, I tried to put the *Close* command immediately after the *Play* command. This didn't work—the video would quit as soon as it started. I solved this problem by putting *Close* in the Done event code, as shown. The system tells us automatically when the video is finished, at which time it's safe to do the *Close*.

CHAPTER EIGHT

Dialog Boxes, Windows, and Other Forms

In this chapter, I provide several helpful hints and tips for working with forms. Some of these techniques are simple, such as centering a form on the screen, and some are fairly complex, such as creating a tabbed dialog box. I've found each of these tips to be a useful addition to my bag of tricks.

Dear John, How Do I...

Add a Standard About Dialog Box?

One of the standard elements of full-featured Windows applications is the About dialog box. Usually, the user activates an About dialog box by choosing About from the Help menu. Check out the Help menu of almost any Windows application, and you'll find About there.

You can easily add your own About dialog box to your applications. It doesn't have to be very fancy; in fact, you can use the *MsgBox* function to create a simple About dialog box. For a display with a more professional appearance, you can create your own About dialog box using a complete form module.

I've created a form called About.frm (with the Name property *About*) that can easily be loaded into a project. When the form is called, it will look something like Figure 8-1 on the following page, depending on what text strings are passed to the About form.

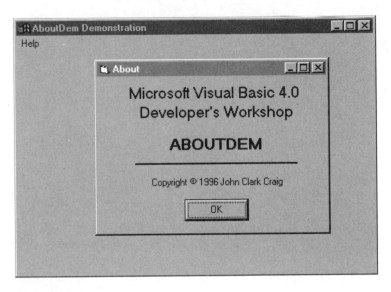

Figure 8-1.
A standard About dialog box.

Here is the code for the About form:

```
Option Explicit

Private Sub cmdOK_Click()
    'Cancel About form
    Unload About
End Sub

Private Sub Form_Load()
    'Center this form
    Left = (Screen.Width - Width) \ 2
    Top = (Screen.Height - Height) \ 2
    'Set defaults
    lblApplication.Caption = "- Application -"
    lblHeading.Caption = "- Heading -"
    lblCopyright.Caption = "- Copyright -"
End Sub

Public Sub Display()
    'Display self as modal
    Me.Show vbModal
End Sub
```

(continued)

```
Property Let Application(Application As String)
    'Define string property for Application
    lblApplication.Caption = Application
End Property

Property Let Heading(Heading As String)
    'Define string property for Heading
    lblHeading.Caption = Heading
End Property

Property Let Copyright(Copyright As String)
    'Build complete Copyright string property
    lblCopyright.Caption = "Copyright © " & Copyright
End Property
```

Notice that in the code I've used Property Let procedures to define the Heading, Application, and Copyright properties as properties of the form instead of properties of different controls on the form. By using these property procedures, available for the first time in Visual Basic 4, your calling application can set these properties to whatever strings you like without worrying about public variables or directly referencing properties of controls on an external form. For example, to have the calling application assign the string "We do it all" to the heading caption in the form by setting the property of the control, the code would be

```
frmAbout.lblHeading.Caption= "We do it all"
```

By treating the form as an object and using the property procedures, the call would be much easier:

```
About.Heading= "We do it all"
```

Another advantage of using property procedures is that other actions can be initiated by the object when a property is assigned. For example, the string assigned to the Copyright property is concatenated to a standard copyright notice before it's displayed. Setting a label's caption property directly would not have allowed the form to do this.

The About form code also uses one public method, *Display*, which I've substituted for the standard *Show* method. I've added the *Display* method so that you don't have to include the vbModal constant as the style argument in the *Show* method. This value for the style argument sets the form as being modal and requires the user to respond to the form before interaction with other forms in an application is allowed. Having the form set as modal is the standard state in which to display the About dialog box. If you use the *Display* method, which is part of the About form module, you don't need to address the issue of modal or nonmodal state when you show the form. You could also add code to the *Display* method procedure to enhance the display. For example, you could use a timer control to display the About dialog box for a specific period and then hide it from view. As a general rule, object-oriented programming transfers the responsibility of taking actions to the objects themselves, and this *Display* method follows this rule.

If you want a different style of generic About box, feel free to modify the About form to your heart's content. Be sure to change the default string property settings to something appropriate for your purposes. Look in the Form_Load procedure to see where these default strings are set.

I've used this About dialog box in many of the demonstration applications in Part III of this book. It was easy to add this form to each project: I added an About menu item to the standard Help menu and added a few lines of code to activate the About form when this menu item is selected.

To use this code, you need to create an application and add the About.frm file to the project. For a simple example, which creates an About dialog box similar to the one shown in Figure 8-1, create a startup form with a menu to call the About form, and add the following code:

```
Option Explicit

Private Sub cmdAbout_Click()
    'Set properties
    About.Application = "ABOUTDEM"
    About.Heading = "Microsoft Visual Basic 4.0 Developer's Workshop"
    About.Copyright = "1996 John Clark Craig"
    'Call a method
    About.Display
End Sub
```

You will also need to place three label controls (lblHeading, lblApplication, and lblCopyright) on the About form and add any graphics you may want.

See Also...

- The Dialogs application in Chapter 30 (Part III) for a demonstration of the use of an About dialog box

Dear John, How Do I...

Automatically Center a Form on the Screen?

The best place to put code to center a form is in the form's Load procedure. This positions the form before it actually appears on the screen. Simply add two lines to the form's Load event procedure that calculates and specifies the location of the upper-left corner of your form, as shown in the following code:

```
Private Sub Form_Load()
    'Center this form
    Left = (Screen.Width - Width) \ 2
    Top - (Screen.Height - Height) \ 2
End Sub
```

Notice that the backslash character (\) is used to execute integer division by 2. Integer division is faster than floating-point division, and in many situations (such as when you're centering a form) the result is to be rounded to the nearest integer value anyway. Use \ instead of / whenever it will work just as well. Figure 8-2 shows a centered form.

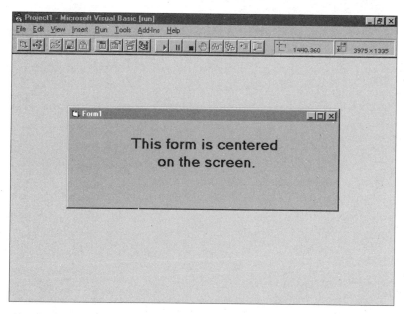

Figure 8-2.
Sample form centered on the screen.

89

Sometimes you might want to position a form somewhere else on the screen. For example, no matter what the screen resolution is, the following code will position the center of your form a quarter of the way in from the left and one-third of the way down from the top:

```
Private Sub Form_Load()
    'Position this form
    Left = 0.25 * Screen.Width - Width \ 2
    Top = 0.333 * Screen.Height - Height \ 2
End Sub
```

You can change the values 0.25 and 0.333 to position the form relative to any desired percentage of the screen's dimensions.

See Also...

- The Dialogs application in Chapter 30 (Part III) for a demonstration of this form-centering technique

Dear John, How Do I...

Create a Floating Window?

This is a rather loaded question because you can create a form that is modal, floating, or topmost, and the form will stay visible in front of other forms and windows. Let's look at techniques for controlling a form in each of these ways.

Modal

Forms are displayed programmatically using the *Show* method. If you include the constant vbModal as the value for the optional argument in the *Show* method of a form, the user must attend to the form before any other parts of the application will recognize keystrokes or mouse activity. In a sense, you might call this behavior *application modal*. Here's a code line that demonstrates this use of the *Show* method:

```
frmTest.Show vbModal
```

Note that your modal form must have some way of hiding or unloading itself, directly or indirectly, so that the application can go on from there.

Floating

I consider the floating mode a little different from the topmost mode, which we'll get to next, although the two terms are often used interchangeably. You might think of a floating window as continually bobbing back to the surface. This type of form is created using the technique I'll now describe.

Add a timer control to your form, and set its Interval property to the speed at which you want the form to come floating back up. An interval of 500 milliseconds (0.5 second), for instance, is a reasonable value to try. Add the following lines to your Timer_Timer routine to force the form to the top using the *ZOrder* method:

```
Private Sub Timer1_Timer()
    ZOrder
End Sub
```

Topmost

You can use the Windows API function *SetWindowPos* to make a form stay on top. This creates a better effect than the bobbing motion just described and lets Windows do all the dirty work. Your form will stay on top of all other forms and windows until you close it. Add the following lines to your topmost form's code:

```
Option Explicit

' SetWindowPos Flags
Private Const SWP_NOSIZE = &H1
Private Const SWP_NOMOVE = &H2
Private Const SWP_NOZORDER = &H4
Private Const SWP_NOREDRAW = &H8
Private Const SWP_NOACTIVATE = &H10
Private Const SWP_FRAMECHANGED = &H20
Private Const SWP_SHOWWINDOW = &H40
Private Const SWP_HIDEWINDOW = &H80
Private Const SWP_NOCOPYBITS = &H100
Private Const SWP_NOOWNERZORDER = &H200
Private Const SWP_DRAWFRAME = SWP_FRAMECHANGED
Private Const SWP_NOREPOSITION = SWP_NOOWNERZORDER
```

(continued)

```
' SetWindowPos() hwndInsertAfter values
Private Const HWND_TOP = 0
Private Const HWND_BOTTOM = 1
Private Const HWND_TOPMOST = -1
Private Const HWND_NOTOPMOST = -2

Private Declare Function SetWindowPos _
Lib "user32" ( _
    ByVal hwnd As Long, _
    ByVal hWndInsertAfter As Long, _
    ByVal x As Long, _
    ByVal y As Long, _
    ByVal cx As Long, _
    ByVal cy As Long, _
    ByVal wFlags As Long _
) As Long

Private Sub Form_Load()
    'Set this form as topmost
    SetWindowPos hwnd, HWND_TOPMOST, _
        0, 0, 0, 0, SWP_NOMOVE Or SWP_NOSIZE
End Sub

Private Sub Form_Unload(Cancel As Integer)
    'Remove topmost setting from this form
    SetWindowPos hwnd, HWND_NOTOPMOST, _
        0, 0, 0, 0, SWP_NOMOVE Or SWP_NOSIZE
End Sub
```

I've put the code to remove the topmost flags in the Form_Unload routine, but you can clear the topmost setting from anywhere in your application. For instance, you could set up the code so that you can toggle the form into and out of the topmost state at will.

You don't actually need to add all of the above constants to your code. I included all relevant constants for handy reference. If you feel brave, you may want to experiment with some of these other constants by combining them in various ways using an Or operation and then using the resulting integer value in the call in which the wFlags parameter is passed.

Dear John, How Do I...

Create a Splash (Logo) Screen?

Often a large application will take several seconds to get up and running, its loading time varying according to both the amount of initialization needed and the speed of the user's system. One of the best ways to use the screen during this delay is to display a logo, a trademark, or what some have come to call a *splash screen*. Here's a straightforward way to accomplish this:

```
Private Sub Form_Load()
    'Show this form
    Show
    'Show splash window
    Splash.Show
    DoEvents
    'Perform time-consuming initializations...
    Initialize
    'Erase splash window
    Unload Splash
End Sub
```

The code in this procedure should be inserted into the Load event procedure for the application's startup form. Usually, the startup form is the main form that will remain active as long as the application is running. Everything for the splash screen can be done right here in the form's Load event procedure because Visual Basic gives us some control over the order of events. The first *Show* method forces Windows to draw the main form on the screen. (Normally this doesn't take place until after the form's Form_Load routine is finished.) The next *Show* method displays the splash screen, which is any form of your own design. I've followed this *Show* method with a *DoEvents* function to ensure that all elements of the splash form are completely drawn right away. The *DoEvents* function causes Visual Basic to yield control to the operating system until all pending operations are completed. The Initialize subprogram represents the time-consuming tasks that your application performs at startup, such as loading data from files, loading resources from a resource file, loading forms into memory, and so on. Once the initialization is complete, the splash form is unloaded and everything's ready to go.

Figure 8-3 on the following page shows an example of a splash display centered on the application's main form.

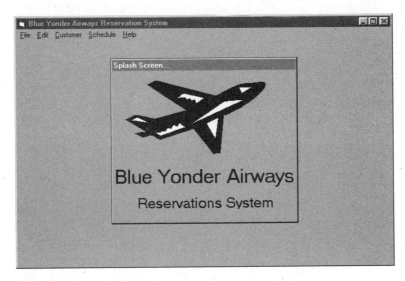

Figure 8-3.
Imaginary application's splash screen in action.

See Also...

- The Jot application in Chapter 28 (Part III) for a demonstration of the incorporation of a splash screen

Dear John, How Do I...

Create a Tabbed Control?

There are actually at least three solutions to this programming task. Visual Basic 4 now ships with a TabStrip control (in the 32-bit version only) and an SSTab control (in the 16-bit and 32-bit versions), both created by Sheridan Software. I'll provide a short demonstration of the use of these controls so you can compare them with another method I'll show you. I'm including this "homegrown" technique because it's a good example of the flexibility and adaptability of Visual Basic.

A Homegrown Technique

If you prefer to roll your own tabbed dialog box, here's a relatively simple but effective technique that combines several PictureBox controls into a simulation of a tabbed control. Figure 8-4 shows the first box (card) of a triple-tabbed collection of picture boxes. The result is not as 3–D looking as the other custom controls, but the advantage is that you can modify and customize this code in whatever way you want.

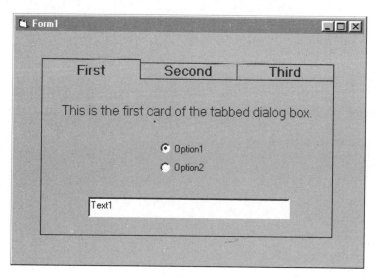

Figure 8-4.
The first of three picture boxes that have been combined to simulate a tabbed control.

There are quite a few lines of code in the following listing, but you'll find it easy to modify this code for your own set of tab labels.

```
Option Explicit

'Label count must match PictureBox control count
Const TABLABEL$ = "First Second Third"

Private mX As Integer, mY As Integer
Private MaxTab As Integer, Twide As Integer

Private Sub Form_Load()
    Dim i As Integer
    'Determine number of tabs
    Do
        If i Then MaxTab = MaxTab + 1
```

(continued)

```
            i = InStr(i + 1, TABLABEL$, Space$(1))
    Loop While i
    'Move all picture boxes to same spot on form
    For i = 0 To MaxTab
        picTab(i).Move 500, 500
    Next i
    'Create the tabs on each picture box
    DrawTabs
End Sub

Private Sub picTab_Click(Index As Integer)
    'Show a picture box based on mouse location
    If mY < picTab(Index).TextHeight(TABLABEL$) Then
        picTab(mX \ Twide).ZOrder
    End If
End Sub

Private Sub picTab_MouseMove(Index As Integer, _
Button As Integer, Shift As Integer, X As Single, Y As Single)
    'Keep track of mouse position
    mX = X
    mY = Y
End Sub

Private Sub DrawTabs()
    Dim i As Integer, j As Integer
    Dim p1 As Integer, p2 As Integer
    Dim RightEdge As Integer
    Dim Tmp$, Alabel$
    'Get working copy of tab label's string
    Tmp$ = TABLABEL$ & Space$(1)
    'Process each picture control
    For i = 0 To MaxTab
        'Adjust picture control properties here
        With picTab(i)
            .AutoRedraw = True
            .BorderStyle = 0
            .ScaleMode = vbPixels
            .FontSize = 12
            .FontBold = True
        End With
        'Draw pseudo border coordinated with tab outlines
        picTab(i).Line (0, picTab(i).TextHeight(Alabel$)) _
            -(0, picTab(i).ScaleHeight - 1)
```

(continued)

96

```
        picTab(i).Line -(picTab(i).ScaleWidth - 1, _
            picTab(i).ScaleHeight - 1)
        picTab(i).Line -(picTab(i).ScaleWidth - 1, _
            picTab(i).TextHeight(Alabel$))
        p2 = 0
        For j = 0 To MaxTab
            'Isolate each tab label
            p1 = p2 + 1
            p2 = InStr(p1, Tmp$, " ")
            Alabel$ = Mid$(Tmp$, p1, p2 - p1)
            'Calculate width of each tab
            Twide = picTab(0).ScaleWidth / (MaxTab + 1)
            'Calculate position for sticking label on tab
            picTab(i).CurrentX = (j + 0.5) * Twide - _
                picTab(i).TextWidth(Alabel$) / 2
            picTab(i).CurrentY = 0.2 *_
                picTab(i).TextHeight(Alabel$)
            'Center label on each tab
            picTab(i).Print Alabel$
            'Perform special calculation for right edge of last tab
            If j = MaxTab Then
                RightEdge = picTab(i).ScaleWidth - 1
            Else
                RightEdge = (j + 1) * Twide
            End If
            'Draw box around all labels but one
            If i <> j Then
                picTab(i).Line (j * Twide, _
                    picTab(i).TextHeight(Tmp$) * 0.2) _
                    -(RightEdge, picTab(i).TextHeight(Tmp$) *_
                    1.2), , B
            'Draw partial box around the one
            Else
                picTab(i).Line (j * Twide, _
                    picTab(i).TextHeight(Tmp$) * 1.2) _
                    -(j * Twide, 0)
                picTab(i).Line -(RightEdge, 0)
                picTab(i).Line -(RightEdge, _
                    picTab(i).TextHeight(Tmp$) * 1.2)
            End If
        Next j
    Next i
End Sub
```

Most of the heavy-duty work is performed just once, when the form loads. The routine modifies each picture box by printing the tab labels along the top edge and drawing lines for the tab outlines. Several properties of the picture box, such as TextHeight and ScaleWidth, are useful in the calculations for drawing the tabs. Notice that if you change the font size of the tabs, the lines will adjust automatically.

The *ZOrder* method brings one of the multiple picture boxes to the surface when you click on a tab. The picTab_Click routine does the calculations to determine whether the mouse was on a tab when it was clicked. The picTab_MouseMove routine keeps track of the current mouse location, and the variables *mX* and *mY* are continually updated as the mouse moves across the surface of any of the picture boxes.

You need to follow a few simple guidelines when you are setting up a group of picture boxes to work with this code: Create an array of PictureBox controls named picTab, with the Index property ranging from 0 to *N*, where *N* is 1 less than the number of tabs. Each picture box should be the same size, but each can contain any arrangement of controls—just leave enough room at the top of the picture boxes for the tabs. I found it easiest to stack the picture boxes most of the way off the edge of the form during development, and from that position I could drag them one at a time onto the form to edit the controls.

Modifying the code for different sets of tabs is the easiest part. Simply change the constant TABLABEL$, near the top of the listing, for the set of tab labels you want. This string should contain one-word labels, each label separated from the next by a space. The spaces are counted to determine the number of tabs to draw, so be careful to separate each tab label from the next with a single space.

It's important that the number of picture boxes and the number of labels in TABLABEL$ match. You'll get an error if there are fewer picture boxes than labels.

The TabStrip Control

For a standard Windows 95 tabbed control appearance, use the TabStrip control. (This control is not available in the 16-bit version of Visual Basic 4.) Figure 8-5 shows a sample of this control at runtime. After you have drawn a TabStrip control on a form, be sure to select Custom from the Properties list. I found that using this tabbed dialog box was a much easier way to set appropriate properties than to use a hit-or-miss method with the individual property settings, especially while I was learning how to use this control. The online help is an excellent source of information about this control.

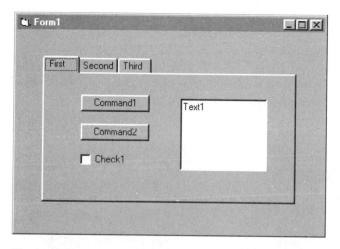

Figure 8-5.
A Windows 95 TabStrip control in operation.

You should be aware that clicking on a tab at runtime does not automatically bring the controls on the indicated card to the front. In fact, the TabStrip control is not a container at all, so you need to organize your controls onto controls that are containers, such as picture boxes and frames. The following code snippet demonstrates what you need to do to bring a given picture box (here named picTab) to the front:

```
Private Sub TabStrip1_Click()
    picTab(TabStrip1.SelectedItem.Index - 1).ZOrder 0
End Sub
```

This code assumes that you've set up an array of picture controls named picTab(), all of which are the same size and all of which are located, one on top of the other, on the TabStrip control. Any control you've drawn on each of these picture controls will appear when its parent picture control pops to the top in response to the *ZOrder* command.

The SSTab Control

Use the SSTab control instead of the TabStrip control if you need to write your application in 16-bit only or both 16-bit and 32-bit versions of Visual Basic, because it comes in both flavors. Again, be sure to double-click the Custom entry in the Properties list to set the properties. This control is also easier to work with than the TabStrip control, but you give up built-in ToolTips and Windows 95 standard appearance (although the resemblance is still pretty close). I've created a third sample form displaying this type of tabbed dialog

99

box so that you can compare the results with those of the other two techniques. Figure 8-6 shows the results, with the same three tabs but with a random selection of controls to flesh out the face of the first card.

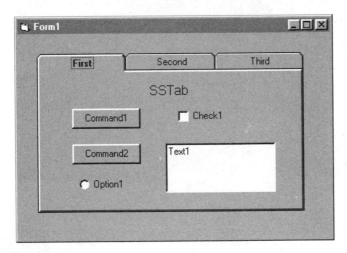

Figure 8-6.
The SSTab control in action.

Dear John, How Do I...

Flash a Form to Get the User's Attention?

There's an API function, *FlashWindow*, you can use to toggle, or flash, a window. This might be useful for critical conditions that demand user attention. To try this technique, create two forms, Form1 and frmFlash. Command buttons on Form1 are used to turn on or off the flashing of the frmFlash form. Add a Timer control to the frmFlash form, and name it tmrFlash. Add the following code to the frmFlash form:

```
Option Explicit

Private Declare Function FlashWindow _
Lib "user32" ( _
    ByVal hwnd As Long, _
    ByVal bInvert As Long _
```

(continued)

```
) As Long

Private Sub Form_Load()
    tmrFlash.Enabled = False
End Sub

Private Sub tmrFlash_Timer()
    Dim Rtn As Long
    Rtn - FlashWindow(hwnd, CLng(True))
End Sub

Property Let Rate(PerSecond As Integer)
    tmrFlash.Interval = 1000 / PerSecond
End Property

Property Let Flash(State As Boolean)
    tmrFlash.Enabled = State
End Property
```

Add the following code to Form1 to control the flashing rate.

```
Option Explicit

Private Sub cmdFast_Click()
    frmFlash.Rate = 5
    frmFlash.Flash = True
End Sub

Private Sub cmdStop_Click()
    frmFlash.Flash = False
End Sub

Private Sub cmdSlow_Click()
    frmFlash.Rate = 1
    frmFlash.Flash = True
End Sub

Private Sub Form_Load()
    frmFlash.Show
 End Sub
```

Note that you'll need to add three command buttons to this form (*cmdFast*, *cmdSlow*, and *cmdStop*) to control the flashing. Change the captions of these command buttons appropriately. Figure 8-7 on the following page shows this pair of forms in action.

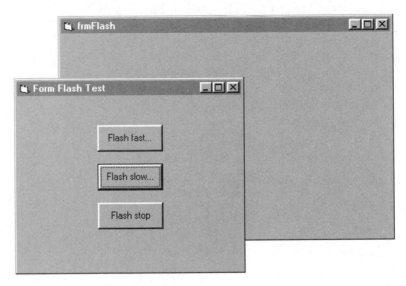

Figure 8-7.
Form1 controlling the flashing of frmFlash.

In Figure 8-7, Form1 (the form with the Form Flash Test caption) has the focus, but frmFlash is flashing. Notice that in Windows 95, if the task bar is visible, the task bar icon for frmFlash flashes right along with the caption of the form itself. The user will see items flashing on the task bar even if the flashing form is covered up with other windows.

I've set up Rate and Flash as properties of the flashing form itself, in keeping with the spirit of standard object-oriented programming techniques. From anywhere in your application, you simply set the flash rate (in flashes per second) by assigning a value to the form's Rate property and set the Flash property to *True* or *False* to activate or deactivate the flashing effect. Take a look at Form1's command buttons to see how these properties are set to control frmFlash's flashing state.

See Also...

- The Messages application in Chapter 30 (Part III) to see how a flashing form can be used in an application to get the user's attention

Dear John, How Do I...

Move a Control to a New Container?

This is a slick new capability of Visual Basic 4 that could open the door to some creative programming techniques. Controls can be drawn within Container controls, which currently include picture boxes and frames. The Container property of most controls is readable and writable, which means that you can make a control jump to a different container!

To see how this works, draw two Frame controls, named *Frame1* and *Frame2*, on a blank form. Draw a command button named *Command1* in the middle of Frame1. Figure 8-8 shows the general layout of this form. Add the following lines of code to the form:

```
Option Explicit

Private Sub Command1_Click()
    Set Command1.Container = Frame2
End Sub
```

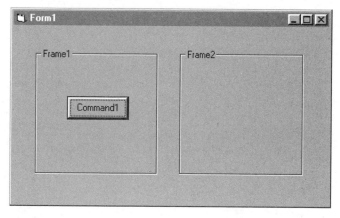

Figure 8-8.
A demonstration of the Container property, which lets controls move into new objects at runtime.

When you run this program, click on the button and watch it jump to the center of the other frame. This simple demonstration hints at the new flexibility in Visual Basic 4. Objects are much more dynamic and under the control of your program than they used to be.

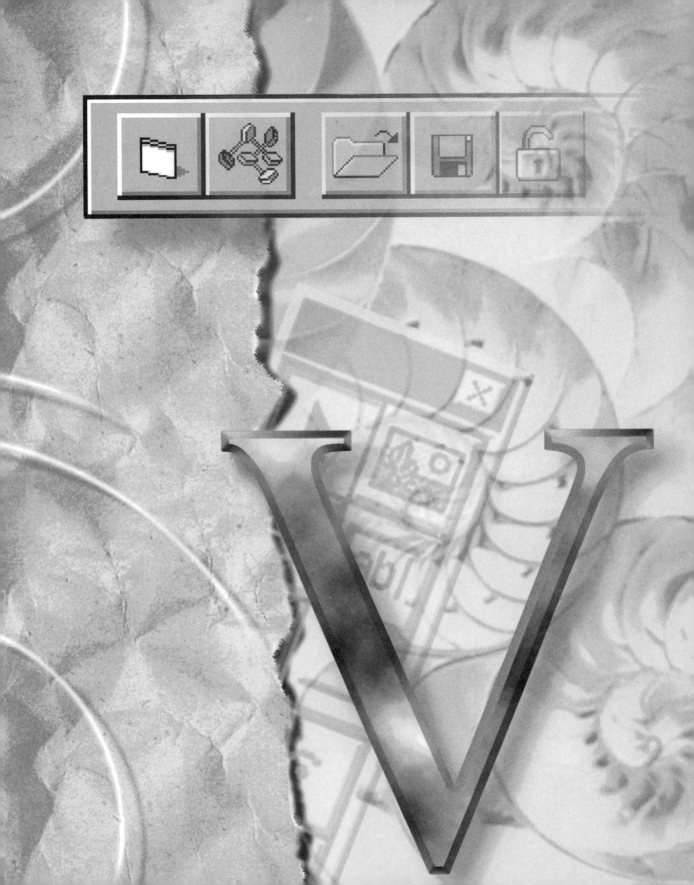

CHAPTER NINE

The Visual Interface

One of the significant changes to the Basic programming language occurred when Microsoft added the word "Visual" to the name. At the very heart of Visual Basic's success has been the enhanced and easy-to-use visual interface that your programs present to the user. This chapter explains and demonstrates some techniques for enhancing your program's interface by using new features of Visual Basic 4 and Windows 95, and some creative programming techniques as well.

Dear John, How Do I...

Add a Status Bar to My Application?

For 32-bit programming for Windows 95, I suggest you use the new StatusBar custom control to add a status bar to your program. A StatusBar control creates a window, usually across the bottom of your form, containing up to 16 Panel objects. Panel objects have a number of properties that let you display any text or predefined data, such as an automatically updated time and date. You can combine pictures with your text in each panel too. The easiest way to set up the number of panels and their properties is by clicking on the Custom property in the Properties window and completing the information on the different tabs of the StatusBar Control Properties dialog box.

Figure 9-1 on the following page shows a sample form with three Status-Bar controls added, one with its alignment set to the bottom, and two set to align on the form at the top. The online help provides a good reference for the many properties of the StatusBar control and its associated Panel objects.

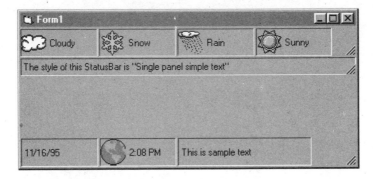

Figure 9-1.
Three sample StatusBar controls in action.

It's also fairly easy to create your own status bars. This can be handy if you are programming for 16 bits, or if you want to customize your status bar to do something a little out of the ordinary. Here's one way I've discovered to create my own status bar.

Add a PictureBox control to a form. Set its Align property to *2 - Align Bottom,* and add one or more Label controls inside this picture box. Setting the Align property to *Align Bottom* causes the picture box to stretch itself across the bottom edge of the containing form at runtime, which is the desired position for a status bar. Draw one or more labels on this picture box. At runtime, change the label captions to display status line messages.

From this starting point, you can make several simple improvements to make your status bar more professional looking. You'll probably want to change the BackColor properties of both the PictureBox and the Label controls to light gray. You can also try changing the BorderStyle properties to improve the appearance.

For an even better-looking status bar, start by loading the Sheridan 3D custom controls into your development environment. (Choose Custom Controls from the Tools menu, turn on the Sheridan 3D Controls check box in the Available Controls list, and click on OK.) The SSPanel control provides a slick way to add a nice-looking status bar to your application. The SSPanel control has an Align property that works just like the PictureBox control's Align property. Set the property to *2 - Align Bottom.* Draw a second SSPanel control inside the main one to display status information. The BevelInner, BevelOuter, and BevelWidth properties let you fine-tune the appearance of the status bar and the text panels it contains. Figure 9-2 shows a status bar of this design.

Figure 9-2.

A status bar created with Sheridan 3D SSPanel controls.

See Also...

- "Dear John, How Do I Create a Toolbar?" later in this chapter
- The Dialogs application in Chapter 30 (Part III) for an example of the use of Sheridan 3D SSPanel controls to display a status bar

Dear John, How Do I...

Add a Horizontal Scrollbar to a List Box?

Sometimes it's hard to predict the width of text that will appear in a list box. The *SendMessage* API function provides an easy way to tell a list box to add a horizontal scrollbar to itself if the text lines are too long. The following demonstration code shows a working example of this technique.

Start a new project, and add a ListBox control and a command button to the form. I've named the controls lstTest and cmdShrinkList, respectively. Draw the list box so that it is fairly wide on the form—the command button will shrink it during the demonstration.

Add the required declaration to your module for the *SendMessage* API function, as follows:

```
Private Declare Function SendMessage _
Lib "user32" Alias "SendMessageA" ( _
    ByVal hwnd As Long, _
    ByVal wMsg As Long, _
    ByVal wParam As Integer, _
    ByVal lParam As Long _
) As Long
```

Here's the code for the command button. Its purpose is to shrink the list box width by 10 percent each time the button is clicked. When the list box is so narrow that the text doesn't fit, a horizontal scrollbar will automatically appear at the bottom edge of the list box.

```
Private Sub cmdShrinkList_Click()
    lstTest.Width = lstTest.Width * 9 \ 10
End Sub
```

The horizontal scrollbar capability is added to the list box when the form loads. The following code loads a fairly long string into the list box and then adds the scrollbar by calling the *SendMessage* function. The third parameter in the function call determines the scrollbar's scale. By setting the form's ScaleMode property to *vbPixels*, we set the threshold width for the appearance of the scrollbar to the pixel width of the string using the *TextWidth* function.

```
Private Sub Form_Load()
Dim Longest$, Rtn As Long
    'Set ScaleMode to Pixels
    ScaleMode = vbPixels
    'Place text in list
    Longest$ = "This is a list of months of the year "
    lstTest.AddItem Longest$
    lstTest.AddItem "January"
    lstTest.AddItem "February"
    lstTest.AddItem "March"
    lstTest.AddItem "April"
    lstTest.AddItem "May"
    lstTest.AddItem "June"
    lstTest.AddItem "July"
    lstTest.AddItem "August"
    lstTest.AddItem "September"
    lstTest.AddItem "October"
    lstTest.AddItem "November"
    lstTest.AddItem "December"
    'Set form's font properties to match list box
    Form1.Font.Size = lstTest.Font.Size
    'Set list box scrollbar threshold width
    Rtn = SendMessage(lstTest.hwnd, &H415, _
        Form1.TextWidth(Longest$), ByVal 0&)
End Sub
```

When you run the program, if the list box in its first appearance is wide enough to display the entire string, you'll need to click on the Shrink List command button one or more times before the scrollbar will appear. With each click, the list box width is reduced to 90 percent of its previous width. Figures 9-3 and 9-4 show the list box with and without the scrollbar.

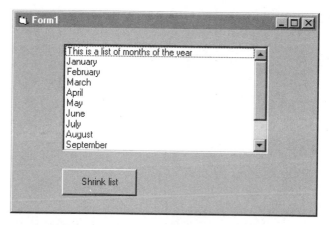

Figure 9-3.
A list box that is wide enough to display the longest string (scrollbar doesn't appear).

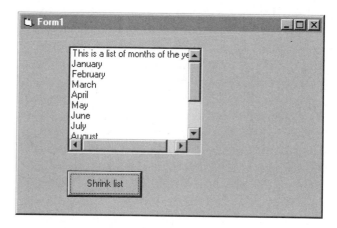

Figure 9-4.
A list box that is too narrow to display the longest string (horizontal scrollbar appears).

Notice that the third parameter in the *SendMessage* call is the threshold width of the list box in pixels. The scrollbar will appear when the width is less than this value. The *TextWidth* method returns the width of a string, but this method doesn't apply to list boxes. To work around this limitation, and to automatically allow for variations in the list box's font size, I copied the value of the Size property of the list box Font object to the Size property of the form's

Font object just before using the form's *TextWidth* method to determine and set the threshold width at which the list box scrollbar will appear. If other properties of the list box's Font object are altered, you should also copy these properties to the form's Font object properties.

Dear John, How Do I...

Add ToolTips to My Buttons?

If you're programming with the 32-bit version of Visual Basic 4, the TabStrip and Toolbar custom controls have ToolTip properties built into them. See the following topic for more information about using the new Toolbar control. Here I present a do-it-yourself object-oriented technique that lets you add ToolTips to any control that supports the MouseMove event. One advantage of this technique is that the online help lists 17 objects that support the MouseMove event, whereas the new ToolTip properties are built into only the Toolbar and TabStrip controls.

The behavior of the ToolTips created here is very similar to that of the ToolTips in the Visual Basic 4 development environment—if you pause the mouse over a ToolTip-enabled object, the ToolTip pops up in less than a second and remains until the mouse is moved off the object.

Creating the ToolTip form is a one-time chore, and it actually isn't very complicated, considering the complex actions it takes. Modifying a button to be ToolTip-enabled in your applications turns out to be extremely easy. Let's build the tool first, and then I'll show an example of the ToolTips in action.

Create a form and set its Name property to *frmToolTip*. To this form, add a PictureBox control and name it picToolTip, and add a timer and name it tmrToolTip. The size and placement of these controls are not important because they'll be adjusted automatically at runtime. Change the PictureBox control's BackColor property to white or light yellow, the Appearance property to *0 - Flat*, and the BorderStyle property to *0 - None* to match the standard ToolTip appearance. Set the timer's Interval property to 700 milliseconds (the amount of time that will pass between the moment the mouse pointer is paused over a control and the moment the ToolTip pops up). The ToolTip form is displayed to allow us to create the ToolTip label, but we don't want the title bar, the border, or the control buttons to appear. You can eliminate all these components by setting the BorderStyle property to *0 - None*. Figure 9-5 shows this form just before we add code to it.

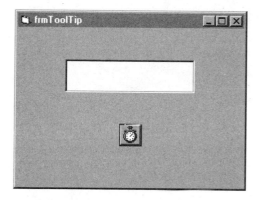

Figure 9-5.
The ToolTip form during development.

Add the following code to the ToolTip form:

```
'--------------
'ToolTips
'--------------
Option Explicit

Private Type POINTAPI
    x As Long
    y As Long
End Type

Private Declare Function GetCursorPos _
Lib "user32" ( _
    lpPoint As POINTAPI _
) As Long

Private Cap$

Public Property Let Label(C$)
    tmrToolTip.Enabled = False
    If C$ = "" Then
        Hide
    Else
        Cap$ = C$
        tmrToolTip.Enabled = True
    End If
End Property
```

(continued)

```
Private Sub tmrToolTip_Timer()
    Dim Papi As POINTAPI
    Dim Wrk$
    Wrk$ = Space$(1) & Trim$(Cap$) & Space$(2)
    picToolTip.Move 0, 0, picToolTip.TextWidth(Wrk$), _
        picToolTip.TextHeight(Wrk$) * 1.1
    GetCursorPos Papi
    Move Papi.x * Screen.TwipsPerPixelX _
        - picToolTip.Width * 0.4, _
        Papi.y * Screen.TwipsPerPixelY _
        + picToolTip.Height * 1.3, _
        picToolTip.Width, picToolTip.Height
    Show
    DoEvents
    picToolTip.Cls
    picToolTip.Print Wrk$
    picToolTip.Line (0, 0)-( _
        picToolTip.ScaleWidth - Screen.TwipsPerPixelX, _
        picToolTip.ScaleHeight - Screen.TwipsPerPixelY), , B
End Sub
```

The *GetCursorPos* API function is used to determine the exact location of the mouse pointer so that we can pop up the ToolTip label at the correct location. POINTAPI is a user-defined Type structure filled in by the *GetCursorPos* function. The string variable *Cap$* stores the text that is to appear in the Tool-Tip. Your application doesn't touch this variable. (In fact, it's declared Private so that you won't be able to call it from outside this form.) I've created a public property named frmToolTip.Label that you interface with. As you'll see, this is the only property that the outside world needs to work with. I'll say a little more about that property in a minute.

Most of the work takes place when the Timer event occurs. The form and its PictureBox control are sized, placed, and shown to the user with the indicated label. Figure 9-6 shows the appearance of a ToolTip label assigned to an image.

Now for the surprisingly easy part—adding ToolTip labels to buttons, images, pictures, or other controls. To complete the example shown here, create a startup form that contains a command button, an Image control, and a PictureBox control. Load any desired icons or pictures (I've loaded an icon and a Windows metafile supplied with Visual Basic), and add the following lines to the various MouseMove event routines:

```
Option Explicit

Private Sub Command1_MouseMove(Button As Integer, _
Shift As Integer, x As Single, y As Single)
    frmToolTip.Label = "Command1"
End Sub

Private Sub Image1_MouseMove(Button As Integer,
Shift As Integer, x As Single, y As Single)
    frmToolTip.Label = "An airplane"
End Sub

Private Sub Picture1_MouseMove(Button As Integer, _
Shift As Integer, x As Single, y As Single)
    frmToolTip.Label = "Calendar"
End Sub

Private Sub Form_MouseMove(Button As Integer, _
Shift As Integer, x As Single, y As Single)
    frmToolTip.Label = ""
End Sub
```

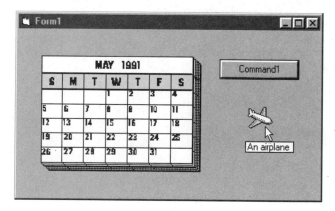

Figure 9-6.
Testing the ToolTips assigned to three controls.

To add ToolTip capability to any control, follow two simple rules: First, in the control's MouseMove event procedure, assign the desired label to the frmToolTip.Label property. Second, assign an empty string to this property from the MouseMove event routine for the form or containing control. This way, as soon as the mouse pointer moves off the control, the ToolTip will disappear as the label is erased.

See Also...

- The Jot application in Chapter 28 (Part III) for a demonstration of using an SSPanel control for button information, as an alternative to ToolTips

Dear John, How Do I...

Create a Toolbar?

Once again, for 32-bit programming I suggest using the new Toolbar custom control that now ships with Visual Basic 4. To put a series of picture buttons on one of these Toolbars, you'll also need to add an ImageList control to your form. In both cases, choose Custom from the properties list to add images and set properties in the easiest way possible. Figure 9-7 shows a Toolbar with images from an associated image list running in Windows 95.

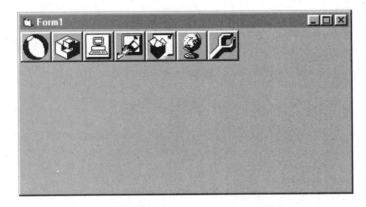

Figure 9-7.
A Toolbar custom control in action.

For maximum flexibility, or to create a Toolbar for the 16-bit version of Visual Basic 4, you can simulate a toolbar by using a combination of Picture-Box, Image, and perhaps the SSPanel controls. This approach is very similar to creating a status bar. Add a PictureBox control to a form, set its Align property to *1 - Align Top*, and add command buttons inside this picture box. The *Align Top* setting causes the picture box to stretch itself across the top edge of the containing form at runtime, even if the form is resized by the user.

You'll probably want to set the BackColor property of the picture box to light gray if it is not already that color. You can also try changing the Border-Style properties to enhance its appearance. To improve the effect, also consider adding ToolTip capability to these buttons, as described in the previous topic.

For an even better-looking toolbar, use the Sheridan 3D custom controls, as described in the first topic in this chapter. Draw your command buttons (or images containing icons) directly on the SSPanel control—it won't work if you simply move these controls onto the SSPanel. Figure 9-8 shows a toolbar of this design. Notice that the "buttons" on this toolbar are actually SSCommand controls. SSCommand is another 3–D control in the Sheridan suite. It is an excellent choice for creating sculptured toolbar buttons.

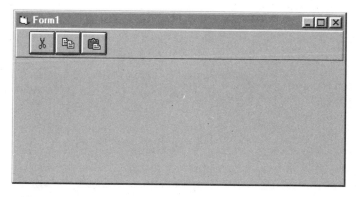

Figure 9-8.
A toolbar created with a Sheridan 3D SSPanel control.

See Also...

- "Dear John, How Do I Add a Status Bar to My Application?" earlier in this chapter

- "Dear John, How Do I Add ToolTips to My Buttons?" earlier in this chapter

- The Dialogs application in Chapter 30 (Part III) for an example of the use of Sheridan 3D SSPanel controls to display a toolbar

Dear John, How Do I...

Dynamically Change the Appearance of a Form?

In Chapter 8, I showed how multiple picture boxes can be stacked to form what looks like a tabbed control. When ZOrder is toggled, each picture box, along with all the contained controls drawn on its surface, is brought to the front. That's one useful technique for dynamically changing a form's appearance, but there are others worth knowing about, such as the one described here.

At runtime, you can set a control's Top or Left property to move the control off the visible surface of the containing form or control. A safe way to do this is to move the control to twice the width or height of the containing control or form. If you save the original position in the control's Tag property, you have an easy way to later move it back to its starting position. For example, the following code hides the command button cmdButton when you click the button and redisplays it when the form is clicked:

```
Private Sub cmdButton_Click()
cmdButton.Tag = cmdButton.Left
    cmdButton.Left = Screen.Width * 2
End Sub

Private Sub Form_Click()
    cmdButton.Left = cmdButton.Tag
End Sub
```

You can position and size controls using Width and Height properties in conjunction with the ScaleWidth and ScaleHeight properties of the containing form or control. This technique can accommodate a sizeable form and keep controls proportionally spaced as the user changes the form's size or shape. Add code in the form's Resize event to accomplish this.

See Also...

- "Dear John, How Do I Automatically Center a Form on the Screen?" in Chapter 8 for a detailed example of the positioning and sizing of controls

- "Dear John, How Do I Create a Tabbed Control?" in Chapter 8

Dear John, How Do I...

Dynamically Customize the Menus?

With Visual Basic 4, you can now edit menu objects in the Properties Window, just as you can edit the properties of the other controls in your application. This new feature is easily overlooked, yet it makes the editing of menus a much more manageable task. (Note that you still need to create menu objects by using the Menu Editor.) To get to the menu properties, pull down the list of objects at the top of the Properties Window and select one of your menus.

Another useful technique for working with menus is to use menu arrays, which offer a powerful way to expand and shrink your menus. This subject is covered well in the Visual Basic 4 documentation.

There's another simple trick that isn't too well known that I'd like to present here, one that provides an easy-to-understand and easy-to-use technique for creating multiple sets of menus. If you set a menu's Visible property to *False*, the menu and all of its submenus will be hidden, both at runtime and in the development environment. So, to create two unique File menus, for instance, name the topmost menu item mnuFile1 for the first File menu and mnuFile2 for the second File menu. They can both have the same Caption property (*File*, in this case), but they must have unique Name properties. The menu items for each File menu can be entirely unique, or they can share some of the same captions. Just remember to keep each menu item's Name property unique.

Either in the development environment or at runtime, toggle the Visible properties of these two top-level menu items to make one visible and the other hidden. You can set up three or more File menus this way, again by toggling the Visible properties so that only one is visible at a time. Note that you don't need to toggle the Visible property for the items on each File menu because they all effectively become invisible when the top-level menu object is made invisible.

You can simply extend this concept to all the menus to get full use of this technique. You can set up multiple Edit menus or have menu items that come and go depending on the state of the application. You can easily swap out entire sets of menus with replacement sets by using this technique. Figures 9-9 and 9-10 show two unique sets of menus on the same form, one before and one after the New Menus command button has been clicked.

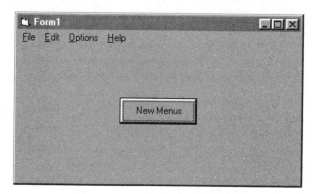

Figure 9-9.
A form showing the first of two unique sets of menus.

Figure 9-10.
The same form showing the second set of menus.

Dear John, How Do I...

Remove the Title Bar from a Form?

The first step to remove a title bar from a form is to eliminate all menu objects. Then you can use one of two methods. Using the first method, if you set the ControlBox, MaxButton, and MinButton properties to *False*, delete any text from the Caption property, and set the BorderStyle to *1 - Fixed Single*, the form will have a single border and no title bar. For the other method, you set the BorderStyle property to *0 - None*. The form will have no border and no title bar, even if any of the ControlBox, MaxButton, and MinButton properties are set to *True* or you have text in the Caption property. If you want a border around the form, you can draw it yourself.

See Also...

- "Dear John, How Do I Add ToolTips to My Buttons?" earlier in this chapter for an example of this technique

Dear John, How Do I...

Create a Progress Indicator?

The easiest way to learn how to use the new ProgressBar control is to create a simple application and put it through its paces. The following short application creates a 3-minute timer, suitable for timing the boiling of eggs as well as demonstrating the ProgressBar control.

On a new form, add a command button named cmdStart, a label named lblDone, a timer named tmrTest, and a ProgressBar control named pbrEgg. Set the label's caption to "Ready to start," and set its font size as desired. Set the Timer's Enabled property to *False* and its Interval property to 1000 milliseconds. I've left the ProgressBar control's properties set to their defaults. Figure 9-11 shows the form at runtime, with my egg about two-thirds done.

Figure 9-11.
Using a progress bar as a 3-minute egg timer.

Add the following code to the form to control the action:

```
Option Explicit

Private Sub cmdStart_Click()
    pbrEgg.Value = 0
    tmrTest.Enabled = True
End Sub

Private Sub tmrTest_Timer()
    Static StartTime As Single
    Dim Percent
    If StartTime = 0! Then
        StartTime = Timer
    End If
    Percent = 100 * (Timer - StartTime) / 180
    If Percent < 100 Then
        pbrEgg.Value = Percent
        lblDone.Caption = "Cooking..."
    Else
        lblDone.Caption = "Done!"
        Beep
        tmrTest.Enabled = False
    End If
End Sub
```

You might want to temporarily change the value of the divisor 180 (the number of seconds in 3 minutes) to something much smaller to test this program. A value of 10, for instance, will cause the ProgressBar control to fill out in 10 seconds instead of 3 minutes. However, I wouldn't advise you to eat an egg cooked for this length of time.

You can learn a lot about the ProgressBar control by experimenting with this program. For instance, the number of "chunks" inside the bar is adjusted by changing the height of the bar, an effect that's easier to understand if you try it for yourself rather than just reading about it.

Rolling Your Own Progress Indicator

The ProgressBar control is yet another of those great new 32-bit controls that can be used in programs for Windows 95 and Windows NT. But don't despair if you're still stuck in the 16-bit programming world. It's easy to create your own progress bar by using a pair of nested picture box controls.

To see how similar this is to the previous example using the ProgressBar control, make the following changes to the example. Replace the Progress-Bar control with a PictureBox control named picProgress. Draw a second PictureBox control inside the first, and name it picFill. Set the Backcolor properties of these two controls as desired. I used dark blue for picFill and white for picProgress, but you can use any color. If you change the picProgress control's ScaleWidth property to 100 and its ScaleHeight to 1, very little of the program code will require change. Here's the new code, which has only a few modifications:

```
Option Explicit

Private Sub cmdStart_Click()
    tmrTest.Enabled = True
End Sub

Private Sub Form_Load()
    picFill.Move 0, 0, 0, 0
End Sub

Private Sub tmrTest_Timer()
    Static StartTime As Single
    Dim Percent
    If StartTime = 0! Then
        StartTime = Timer
    End If
    Percent = 100 * (Timer - StartTime) / 180
```

(continued)

```
    If Percent < 100 Then
        picFill.Move 0, 0, Percent, 1
        lblDone.Caption = "Cooking..."
    Else
        lblDone.Caption = "Done!"
        Beep
        tmrTest.Enabled = False
    End If
End Sub
```

This type of progress indicator fills with a solid color instead of using the new "chunky" fill style, but the action and appearance are otherwise very similar. Figure 9-12 shows the egg-timer program in action, again at about the soft-boiled stage.

Figure 9-12.
A homegrown progress indicator in action.

Dear John, How Do I...

Use the New Slider Control?

The new 32-bit-only Slider control is similar to a scrollbar control except that it has some enhancements that make it a better choice for allowing the user to input numeric values selected from a range. You might think of the scrollbar as a qualitative approach to selecting from a range (it provides visual feedback of an approximate nature) and of the slider as more of a quantitative control (it provides an exact value or range of values from the range of choices).

An interesting and unique feature of the Slider control is its ability to select either a single value or a range of values. You select a range by setting the SelectRange property to *True* and manipulating the SelStart and SelLength properties to define the range. Microsoft suggests that you programmatically set the range properties when the user holds down the Shift key and moves the slider. The Visual Basic online help provides a good working example of this technique.

Figure 9-13 shows an imaginary database filtering application in which the user, from a large list of all major cities, can select cities located in a range of latitudes. The Slider control simplifies this type of range selection, but it can also be used to select a single value from a range, as in setting the volume control of a multimedia device. The online help system is the best source of information for the properties and methods of the Slider control.

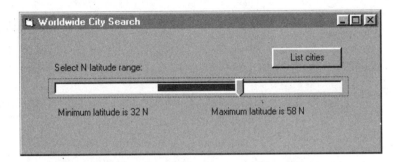

Figure 9-13.
A Slider control being used to select a range of values.

Graphics

Visual Basic 4 provides a rich set of graphics tools, including the new *Paint-Picture* method, which is a user-friendly wrapper around the popular *BitBlt* API function. You'll find *PaintPicture* used several places in this chapter—it's a real workhorse for efficient manipulation of graphics images. You'll also find that I've used *BitBlt* directly, which is the fastest way to create animation. Several other useful API functions are also demonstrated in this chapter, such as those that allow you to create a rubber band selection rectangle, draw polygons efficiently, and perform other graphics magic.

Dear John, How Do I...

Calculate a Color Constant from RGB or HSV Values?

In Visual Basic, a color is indicated by a single number, the RGB color value. The bit pattern in this number is composed of three values corresponding to color intensity levels: one for red, one for green, and one for blue, each ranging from 0 through 255. The *RGB* function lets you combine the three intensity levels into the desired color number, but there are no built-in functions for extracting the three intensity levels from a given RGB color value. The following function performs this task for you, extracting values for *R* (red), *G* (green), and *B* (blue) from the combined color value *C*:

```
Sub Shades(C, R, G, B)
    R = C And &hff
    G = (C \ &h100) And &hff
    B = (C \ &h10000) And &hff
End Sub
```

In addition to the RGB color specification, another common way to classify colors is by hue, saturation, and value, or HSV. For some people the

HSV scheme is more intuitive, and for some types of graphics these values are definitely easier to work with. For instance, the colors required for a sunset scene might be easier to describe as a group of red colors that vary in value but remain constant in hue and saturation. Hue represents the relative position of a color in the spectrum and, in the HSV system, corresponds to the angle of the color in a color wheel. The range for the hue values is 0 through 360 (360 degrees forming a complete circle). Saturation specifies the purity of the color. The saturation value is a percentage, ranging from 0 (no color) through 100 (the pure color, as specified by the hue value). Value specifies the brightness of the color and is also a percentage, ranging from 0 (black) through 100 (white). Here is a useful function for converting RGB values to HSV values:

```
Public Sub RgbToHsv(R, G, B, H, S, V)
    'Convert RGB to HSV values
    Dim vRed, vGreen, vBlue
    Dim Mx, Mn, Va, Sa, rc, gc, bc

    vRed = R / 255
    vGreen = G / 255
    vBlue = B / 255

    Mx = vRed
    If vGreen > Mx Then Mx = vGreen
    If vBlue > Mx Then Mx = vBlue

    Mn = vRed
    If vGreen < Mn Then Mn = vGreen
    If vBlue < Mn Then Mn = vBlue

    Va = Mx
    If Mx Then
        Sa = (Mx - Mn) / Mx
    Else
        Sa = 0
    End If
    If Sa = 0 Then
        H = 0
    Else
        rc = (Mx - vRed) / (Mx - Mn)
        gc = (Mx - vGreen) / (Mx - Mn)
        bc = (Mx - vBlue) / (Mx - Mn)
        Select Case Mx
        Case vRed
            H = bc - gc
```

(continued)

```
        Case vGreen
            H = 2 + rc - bc
        Case vBlue
            H = 4 + gc - rc
        End Select
        H = H * 60
        If H < 0 Then H = H + 360
    End If

    S = Sa * 100
    V = Va * 100
End Sub
```

The following subprogram converts from HSV values back to RGB values.

```
Public Sub HsvToRgb(H, S, V, R, G, B)
    'Convert HSV to RGB values
    Dim Sa, Va, Hue, i, f, p, q, t

    Sa = S / 100
    Va = V / 100
    If S = 0 Then
        R = Va
        G = Va
        B = Va
    Else
        Hue = H / 60
        If Hue = 6 Then Hue = 0
        i = Int(Hue)
        f = Hue - i
        p = Va * (1 - Sa)
        q = Va * (1 - (Sa * f))
        t = Va * (1 - (Sa * (1 - f)))
        Select Case i
        Case 0
            R = Va
            G = t
            B = p
        Case 1
            R = q
            G = Va
            B = p
        Case 2
            R = p
            G = Va
            B = t
```

(continued)

```
        Case 3
            R = p
            G = q
            B = Va
        Case 4
            R = t
            G = p
            B = Va
        Case 5
            R = Va
            G = p
            B = q
        End Select
    End If

    R = Int(255.9999 * R)
    G = Int(255.9999 * G)
    B = Int(255.9999 * B)
End Sub
```

To see a similar color scheme in action, take a look at the colors available in Microsoft Windows 95. In the Control Panel, double-click on the Display icon and select the Appearance tab of the Display Properties dialog box. Open the drop-down list of colors next to the Item list and click on Other. The resulting dialog box lets you choose any color of the rainbow and shows integer values for RGB and HSL (hue, saturation, and luminosity). The HSL color system is similar to the HSV system, although the HSL system uses only integer values ranging from 0 through 255, and the conversion algorithm is slightly different. Conceptually and functionally, the two systems are quite similar.

See Also...

- The RGBHSV application in Chapter 25 (Part III) to see these two functions in action

Dear John, How Do I...

Convert Between Twips, Pixels, Centimeters, Inches, Points, Characters, and Millimeters?

A form, picture box, or printer object can be scaled using the ScaleMode property. You can scale these objects by custom units or by a close representation of twips, points, pixels, characters, inches, millimeters, or centimeters.

I say "close representation" because for many systems Windows can only guess what the real dimensions of your display are. When used with the printer object, these dimensional units are usually much more accurate because the size of a sheet of paper is very predictable. The following shows the relationships between some of these units of measure:

1440 twips per inch
567 twips per centimeter
72 points per inch
2.54 centimeters per inch
10 millimeters per centimeter

The character unit is special in that it has one measurement in the horizontal direction and a different one in the vertical:

120 twips per character in the x direction
240 twips per character in the y direction

Two very useful Visual Basic properties help you determine the number of twips per pixel. This value can vary widely based on the actual pixel resolution of your display. Again, the number of pixels in the horizontal direction may not be the same as in the vertical, so there are two similar functions for the two directions.

Property	Return Value
TwipsPerPixelX	Twips per pixel in the horizontal direction
TwipsPerPixelY	Twips per pixel in the vertical direction

By combining these properties and the relationships defined above, you can easily convert between any of the various units of measurement.

Dear John, How Do I...

Create One of Those
Backgrounds That Fade from Blue to Black?

The following code paints a form's background with 16 shades of blue, from bright blue to black. The trickiest part is getting a continuous and smooth fade effect at the edges where regions abut. (The difficulty is due to round-off errors in the integer math.) To correct for this, the following routine changes the DrawStyle property to *5 - Transparent* and the scaling mode of the form to vbPixels. The *Transparent* DrawStyle property value prevents a border from being drawn around each blue box. Although the border would have the same specified color as the fill of the box, the border line would appear different from the fill area of the box on the screen. The vbPixels scale mode lets us calculate exact dimensions for each box with no round-off errors; this prevents overlap or blank spaces between the boxes.

```
Private Sub Form_Paint()
    Dim i
    ScaleMode = vbPixels
    DrawStyle = 5 'Transparent
    DrawWidth = 1
    For i = 0 To ScaleHeight Step ScaleHeight \ 16
        Line (-1, i - 1)-(ScaleWidth, i + ScaleHeight \ 16), _
            RGB(0, 0, 255 - i * 255 \ ScaleHeight), BF
    Next i
End Sub
```

This routine fills the form with shades of blue, no matter what size the form is. To create a dramatic full-screen backdrop, set the form's BorderStyle to *0 - None* and its WindowState to *2 - Maximized.*

There's a lot of room for you to experiment with this routine. The *RGB* function can be modified to produce shades of red instead of blue, for instance. Or you might consider reversing the colors so that bright blue is at the bottom and black is at the top. Figure 10-1 demonstrates the fading effect.

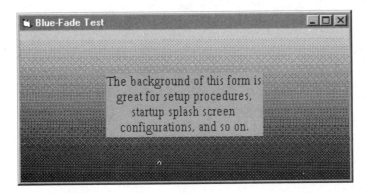

Figure 10-1.
A form that fades from blue to black.

See Also...

- The Dialogs application in Chapter 30 (Part III) for a demonstration of a fading screen

Dear John, How Do I...

Create a Rubber Band Selection Rectangle?

The *DrawFocusRect* API function is great for drawing a rubber band selection rectangle. The following code demonstrates its use. Create a new form, add a picture box named picSample, and add these lines of code to try it out. When you run the program, a selection rectangle is created as you hold down the left mouse button and drag the mouse. When you release the button, the selection rectangle is replaced by a permanent red rectangle to indicate the final selection area. Figure 10-2 on page 131 shows the program in action.

```
Option Explicit


Private Type RECT
    rLeft As Long
    rTop As Long
    rRight As Long
    rBottom As Long
End Type

Private Declare Function DrawFocusRect _
Lib "user32" ( _
    ByVal hdc As Long, _
    lpRect As RECT _
) As Long

Private FocusRec As RECT
Private X1, Y1
Private X2, Y2

Private Sub Form_Load()
    'Use units expected by the API function
    picSample.ScaleMode = vbPixels
End Sub
```

(continued)

```
Private Sub picSample_MouseDown(Button As Integer, _
Shift As Integer, X As Single, Y As Single)
    'Be sure left mouse button is used
    If (Button And vbLeftButton) = 0 Then Exit Sub
    'Set starting corner of box
    X1 = X
    Y1 = Y
End Sub

Private Sub picSample_MouseMove(Button As Integer, _
Shift As Integer, X As Single, Y As Single)
    'Be sure left mouse button is depressed
    If (Button And vbLeftButton) = 0 Then Exit Sub
    'Erase focus rectangle if it exists
    If (X2 <> 0) Or (Y2 <> 0) Then
        DrawFocusRect picSample.hdc, FocusRec
    End If
    'Update coordinates
    X2 = X
    Y2 = Y
    'Update rectangle
    FocusRec.rLeft = X1
    FocusRec.rTop = Y1
    FocusRec.rRight = X2
    FocusRec.rBottom = Y2
    'Adjust rectangle if reversed
    If Y2 < Y1 Then Swap FocusRec.rTop, FocusRec.rBottom
    If X2 < X1 Then Swap FocusRec.rLeft, FocusRec.rRight
    'Draw focus rectangle
    DrawFocusRect picSample.hdc, FocusRec
    picSample.Refresh
End Sub

Private Sub picSample_MouseUp(Button As Integer, _
Shift As Integer, X As Single, Y As Single)
    Dim Ret%
    'Be sure left mouse button is used
    If (Button And vbLeftButton) = 0 Then Exit Sub
    'Erase focus rectangle if it exists
    If FocusRec.rRight Or FocusRec.rBottom Then
        DrawFocusRect picSample.hdc, FocusRec
    End If
    'Draw indicated rectangle in red
    picSample.Line (X1, Y1)-(X2, Y2), QBColor(12), B
    'Zero the rectangle coordinates
```

(continued)

```
        X1 = 0
        Y1 = 0
        X2 = 0
        Y2 = 0
End Sub

Private Sub Swap(A, B)
    Dim T
    T = A
    A = B
    B = T
  End Sub
```

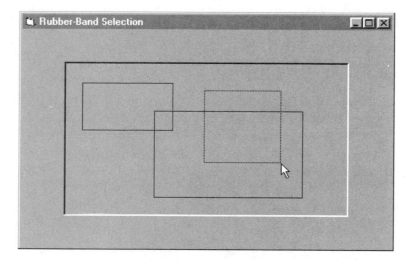

Figure 10-2.
An interactive rubber band selection rectangle in action.

The *DrawFocusRect* API function draws a dotted selection rectangle using an Xor drawing mode. As the mouse is dragged, your code must erase each selection rectangle before the next is drawn. Fortunately, the built-in Xor action of the *DrawFocusRect* API function makes this easy to do. In the Mouse-Move routine above, you can see that the *DrawFocusRect* function is called twice, once to erase the previous rectangle and once to draw the next.

Mouse actions are separated into down, up, and move events by Visual Basic. For this reason, the program uses all three event-driven routines. MouseDown indicates the start of a rectangle selection, MouseMove indicates the sizing of the rectangle while the mouse button is held down, and Mouse-Up indicates the completion of the selection.

In this example, only mouse actions in a picture box named picSample can create a selection rectangle. You can change picSample to the name of any picture box or form in which you want a selection rectangle. The preceding code will give you a good start on integrating rubber band selection rectangle capabilities into your own applications.

See Also...

- The MousePtr application in Chapter 29 (Part III) for a demonstration of rubber band selection

Dear John, How Do I...

Create Graphics Hot Spots?

The Image control is an efficient tool with which to add rectangular hot spot regions to your graphics images. Let's walk through an example to see how it's done. Figure 10-3 shows a simple graphic of the earth, with four hot spots.

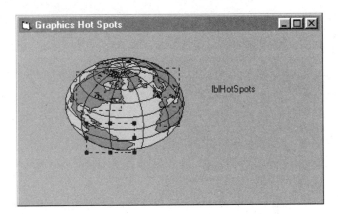

Figure 10-3.
Hot spots shown during application development.

I first loaded a graphic named World.bmp into an Image control named imgWorld, and then I carefully drew four more Image controls on top of the image of the world. I named these imgNAmerica, imgSAmerica, imgEurope, and imgAfrica. Each rectangle covers the appropriate part of the world. I then added a label named lblHotSpots to the form. The following code completes the demonstration by displaying a label for each hot spot when the hot spot is clicked.

```
Option Explicit

Private Sub imgAfrica_Click()
    lblHotSpots.Caption = "Africa"
End Sub

Private Sub imgEurope_Click()
    lblHotSpots.Caption = "Europe"
End Sub

Private Sub imgNAmerica_Click()
    lblHotSpots.Caption = "North America"
End Sub

Private Sub imgSAmerica_Click()
    lblHotSpots.Caption = "South America"
End Sub

Private Sub imgWorld_Click()
    lblHotSpots.Caption = "The World"
End Sub
```

Figure 10-4 shows the result when the South America hot spot rectangle is clicked.

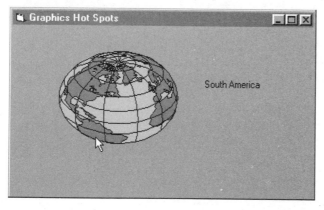

Figure 10-4.
A hot spot activated with a click.

The Image control outlines are visible during development but invisible at runtime. Because these hot spot Image controls are drawn on top of a larger image, click events are acted upon by the hot spots rather than by the underlying image.

See Also...

- The VBClock application in Chapter 27 (Part III) for a demonstration of graphics hot spots

Dear John, How Do I...

Draw a Polygon Quickly?

You can use the *Line* method to connect a sequence of points with straight lines and return to the starting point to draw a closed polygon. But the API function *Polygon* is faster, and it has the advantage of being able to efficiently fill the interior of the polygon with a color. The following code, when added to a new form, creates a demonstration program that uses the *Polygon* API function to create a 17-point polygon and fill it with color when you click on the form.

```
Option Explicit

Private Type POINTAPI
    x As Long
    y As Long
End Type

Private Declare Function Polygon _
Lib "gdi32" (_
    ByVal hdc As Long, _
    lpPoint As POINTAPI, _
    ByVal nCount As Long _
) As Long

Const POINTS = 17

Private Sub Form_Click()
    Dim i As Integer, Rtn As Integer
    Dim P(1 To POINTS) As POINTAPI
    'Clear form with each click
    Cls
```

(continued)

```
          'Create unique polygon each time
          Randomize
          'Use units expected by the API function
          ScaleMode = vbPixels
          FillStyle = vbSolid
          'Build array of random coordinates
          For i = 1 To POINTS
              P(i).x = Rnd * ScaleWidth
              P(i).y = Rnd * ScaleHeight
          Next i
          'Create unique fill color each time
          FillColor = RGB(Rnd * 256, Rnd * 256, Rnd * 256)
          'Draw polygon, filling the interior
          Rtn = Polygon(hDC, P(1), UBound(P))
End Sub
```

The first and last points in your array of polygon vertices don't have to be the same. The *Polygon* function will automatically connect the first and last points to close the shape. Figure 10-5 shows a 17-point polygon created with this demonstration program. The "inside" part of the polygon is a function of the number of times the edges of the polygon cross over each other.

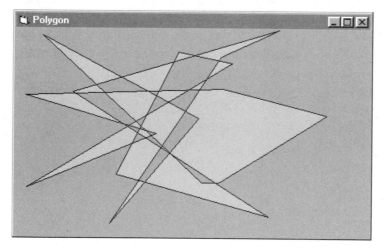

Figure 10-5.
A multipointed polygon drawn with one API function call.

Notice that I dimensioned the array of coordinates from 1 to the constant POINTS instead of the default of 0 to POINTS, and I passed P(1) instead of P(0) to the *Polygon* function. This creates a polygon with the intended number of vertices. If I had dimensioned the array from 0 to POINTS and passed P(0) to the function call, the polygon would have ended up with an extra corner.

Like most API graphics functions, *Polygon* expects coordinates to be in pixel units. This function is unaware of the current scale mode and will interpret the array of coordinates as pixels regardless of the size of the numbers in it. For this reason, always set the ScaleMode property for the form, picture, or printer object to *vbPixels* before you draw polygons.

See Also...

- "Dear John, How Do I Fill an Irregularly Shaped Area with a Color?" below

Dear John, How Do I...

Fill an Irregularly Shaped Area with a Color?

The *Polygon* API function described in the previous topic is great for filling an area with a color if you know the boundary coordinates of the area. Sometimes, however, you don't know the boundary coordinates but you do know the boundary color, and you can use this information to fill the area. To simulate the old *Paint* command found in earlier versions of Microsoft Basic, which floods an area bounded by a color, the *FloodFill* API function is the one to use.

The following code demonstrates the use of this function to fill a triangle with color. Each time you click on the form, the triangle is flooded with a random color.

```
Option Explicit

Private Declare Function FloodFill _
Lib "gdi32" (_
    ByVal hdc As Long, _
    ByVal x As Long, _
    ByVal x As Long, _
    ByVal y As Long, _
    ByVal crColor As Long _
) As Long

Private Sub Form_Click()
    Dim Rtn As Integer
    'Clear form with each click
    Cls
```

(continued)

```
Randomize
'Use units expected by the API function
ScaleMode = vbPixels
FillStyle = vbSolid
'Draw a triangle on the form
Line (ScaleWidth * 0.1, ScaleHeight * 0.1)- _
    (ScaleWidth * 0.8, ScaleHeight * 0.5)
Line -(ScaleWidth * 0.4, ScaleHeight * 0.8)
Line -(ScaleWidth * 0.1, ScaleHeight * 0.1)
'Create unique fill color each time
FillColor = RGB(Rnd * 256, Rnd * 256, Rnd * 256)
'Set function to start painting at center of form
Rtn = FloodFill(hDC, ScaleWidth * 0.5, _
    ScaleHeight * 0.5, ForeColor)
End Sub
```

Figure 10-6 shows the filled triangle that this program creates.

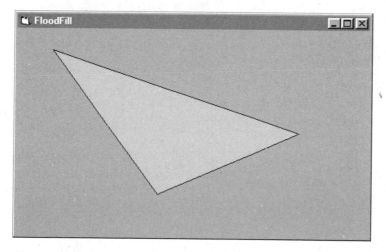

Figure 10-6.
Triangular area painted using the API FloodFill *function.*

In this example, the color that is used as the boundary of the color flood is returned from the form's ForeColor property. If you draw the boundary by using a color that is different from the ForeColor value, you must explicitly pass the color value to the API function.

See Also...

- "Dear John, How Do I Draw a Polygon Quickly?" earlier in this chapter

Dear John, How Do I...

Rotate a Bitmap?

There is a new 32-bit function, *PlgBlt*, that is designed to help you do a generalized polygon transformation of a picture. Even though it's been documented in Windows 95, it has not yet been implemented. I get an error 120 message when I try to call this function, which means it's still just a stub function, to be implemented later. Stay tuned—this function should be much more efficient than the technique I'll show you here.

The code below will rotate a picture 90 degrees while copying it, pixel by pixel, from one picture box to another. It's slow, so you probably would want to use this code to rotate individual images while you are building a set of images for an application, instead of using it in an application to rotate the images when the application is running.

The *Point* and *Pset* methods are used to read and write the pixels, and this short demonstration provides a good example of their use. Be sure to set the ScaleMode to *vbPixels*, as shown here, before using these functions on graphics images.

To try this technique, start a new project and add the following code to the form. On the form, create two picture boxes, picOne and picTwo. Assign a bitmap picture to the Picture property of picOne, and size picOne to display the bitmap. Only the part of the bitmap that is displayed in the picture box will be copied. Don't worry about sizing picTwo—this will be taken care of by the program. When you run the program, click on the form to start the rotating and copying process.

```
Option Explicit

Private Sub Form_Click()
    Dim x As Integer, y As Integer
    'Set all scale modes to pixels
    ScaleMode = vbPixels
    picOne.ScaleMode = vbPixels
    picTwo.ScaleMode = vbPixels
    'Size destination picture
    picTwo.Width = picOne.Height
    picTwo.Height = picOne.Width
    'Rotate picture 90 degrees
    For x = 0 To picOne.ScaleWidth
        For y = 0 To picOne.ScaleHeight
            picTwo.PSet (y, x), picOne.Point(picOne.ScaleWidth x, y)
        Next y
    Next x
End Sub
```

You might want to use the *SavePicture* statement to save the rotated image as a bitmap file. Figure 10-7 shows the demonstration program during development, and Figure 10-8 shows the picture after rotation.

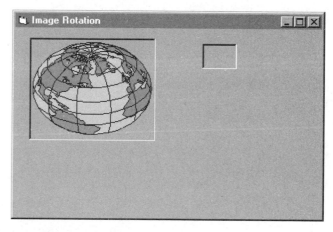

Figure 10-7.
A picture of the earth before rotation.

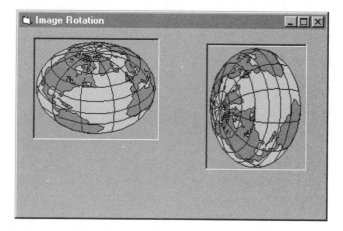

Figure 10-8.
A picture of the earth plus a copy rotated 90 degrees.

Dear John, How Do I...
Scroll a Graphics Image?

Visual Basic's new *PaintPicture* method simplifies many graphics manipulation techniques. In the following code, for instance, I use it to display a small window on a larger bitmap, with scrollbars to let the user smoothly scroll the image. As shown in Figure 10-9, an entire butterfly image appears in the first full-size picture box, and a small window on a second copy of the image appears in the second, smaller, picture box.

```
Option Explicit

Private Sub Form_Load()
    hsbScroll.Max = picOne.ScaleWidth - picTwo.ScaleWidth
    hsbScroll.LargeChange = hsbScroll.Max \ 10
    vsbScroll.Max = picOne.ScaleHeight - picTwo.ScaleHeight
    vsbScroll.LargeChange = vsbScroll.Max \ 10
End Sub

Private Sub hsbScroll_Change()
    UpdatePicTwo
End Sub

Private Sub hsbScroll_Scroll()
    hsbScroll_Change
End Sub

Private Sub vsbScroll_Change()
    UpdatePicTwo
End Sub

Private Sub vsbScroll_Scroll()
    vsbScroll_Change
End Sub

Private Sub UpdatePicTwo()
    picTwo.PaintPicture picOne.Picture, _
        -hsbScroll.Value, -vsbScroll.Value
End Sub
```

Note that the full-size image need not be visible for this program to work. During the development process, you can load the source picture box with a large bitmap and then set its Visible property to *False*. The small picture box will still display the picture.

Figure 10-9.
Scrolling a large image in a smaller picture box.

To try this program, add two different-size picture boxes to a new form. Name the larger one picOne and the smaller one picTwo. Add a vertical scrollbar named vsbScroll and a horizontal scrollbar named hsbScroll to the form, as shown in Figure 10-9. Position these two scrollbar controls close to picTwo since they will control the contents of this picture box. Load any bitmap file into the Picture property of picOne, and size the picture box—only the part of the bitmap displayed in the picOne picture box can be displayed in the picTwo picture box. The program scrolls this image in picTwo by copying a rectangular region from picOne using the *PaintPicture* method.

Notice that the program triggers scrollbar Change events from within each scrollbar's Scroll event. This lets you grab the scrollbar box and smoothly slide the image in real time.

Dear John, How Do I...
Use *BitBlt* to Create Animation?

Visual Basic's new *PaintPicture* method is a convenient and fairly fast method for moving irregularly shaped graphics objects around on the screen without disturbing the background. *PaintPicture* is Visual Basic's equivalent of the *BitBlt* API function. (Actually, after *PaintPicture* performs error checking and scaling from the current graphics units, it calls *BitBlt*.) The only drawback to

PaintPicture is its slowness. By calling *BitBlt* directly, you avoid the overhead of the calculations that *PaintPicture* must perform before it in turn calls *BitBlt*. The result is an animated sequence created with *BitBlt* that is considerably faster, with smoother action. That's why this demonstration calls *BitBlt* directly.

The *BitBlt* API function quickly moves a rectangular block of pixels from a picture box or form to another picture box or form, or to the printer object. *BitBlt* requires an hDC (handle to a device context) for both the source and the destination of the image transfer. The PictureBox, Form, and Printer objects all provide an hDC property. Note, however, that with the Auto-Redraw property set to *True*, the hDC property of a picture box points to the control's Image property, not to its Picture property. The image is a behind-the-scenes copy of what you see on the screen. It's where the actual work is performed as you draw or use the *BitBlt* API function to manipulate the contents of a PictureBox control when AutoRedraw is *True*. The results are transferred from the image to the picture only when the system refreshes a picture box. This works well for our purposes, avoiding flicker and other problems.

The following code animates an image of a red ball, moving it across a 3–D checkerboard background without disturbing the background image. This action requires three picture boxes: one containing the ball's image, the second containing a mask to prepare the background for the ball's image, and the third to temporarily hold the background that will be restored when the ball moves on. Much more complicated objects can be animated using the same technique; I chose a ball shape to keep the explanation simple.

```
Option Explicit

Private Declare Function BitBlt _
Lib "gdi32" ( _
    ByVal hDestDC As Long, _
    ByVal x As Long, ByVal y As Long, _
    ByVal nWidth As Long, ByVal nHeight As Long, _
    ByVal hSrcDC As Long, _
    ByVal xSrc As Long, ByVal ySrc As Long, _
    ByVal dwRop As Long _
) As Long

  Private Sub cmdAnimate_Click()
    Static x As Long, y As Long
    Static w As Long, h As Long
    Static BackSavedFlag As Boolean
    Dim Rtn As Long, dx As Long
    'Provide starting state
    x = 5
```

(continued)

```
            y = 60
            dx = 1
            'Save sizes in local variables once for speed
            w = picBall.ScaleWidth
            h = picBall.ScaleHeight
            'Loop to animate the ball
            Do
                'Restore background unless this is first time object is drawn
                If BackSavedFlag = True Then
                    Rtn = BitBlt(picFloor.hDC, x, y, w, h, _
                        picBack.hDC, 0, 0, vbSrcCopy)
                    'Stop ball's motion when it gets to the edges
                    If x > 350 Then
                        BackSavedFlag = False
                        picFloor.Refresh
                        Exit Do
                    End If
                End If
                'Move ball to a new location
                x = x + dx
                'Save background at new location
                Rtn = BitBlt(picBack.hDC, 0, 0, w, h, _
                    picFloor.hDC, x, y, vbSrcCopy)
                BackSavedFlag = True
                'Apply mask
                Rtn = BitBlt(picFloor.hDC, x, y, w, h, _
                    picBallMask.hDC, 0, 0, vbSrcAnd)
                'Draw ball
                Rtn = BitBlt(picFloor.hDC, x, y, w, h, _
                    picBall.hDC, 0, 0, vbSrcPaint)
                picFloor.Refresh
            Loop
        End Sub
```

To try out this code, start a new project and add a command button and four PictureBox controls to the form. Name them cmdAnimate, picFloor, picBall, picBallMask, and picBack, respectively. Now you need three bitmaps: one large bitmap of the checkerboard "floor" (or any other background image), one of the ball, and one of the mask. (I created these bitmaps with Windows Paint.) Set the picFloor Picture property to a bitmap of the floor or other background image, and set the AutoRedraw property to *True*. For the other three PictureBox controls, set the picBall Picture property to the ball bitmap, set the picBallMask Picture property to the mask bitmap, and set the picBack Picture property to the ball bitmap. Size these three controls so that these three pictures are the same size, and position them on the form so that none of the four picture boxes will overlap when the program is run. For all four of the PictureBox controls, set the AutoSize property to *True* and the Scale-Mode property to *3 - Pixel*. Figure 10-10 shows the form during the development phase.

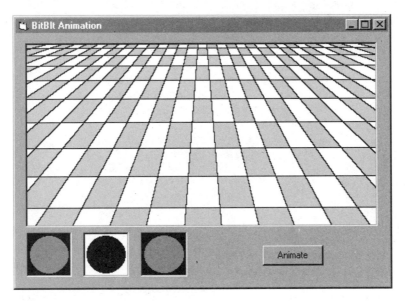

Figure 10-10.
The animation example during development.

The ball and mask bitmaps must be created in a special way. The ball image in this example consists of a red ball against a black background. You can use any color except black for an object that is to appear in front of the background. In this case, all the red pixels that make up the ball will show. Wherever there are black pixels in an image, however, the background will appear in the animated version. For example, if you want to change the ball into a donut, draw a solid black circle in the center of the red ball.

The mask image is created using the following rule: wherever there are black pixels in the first bitmap, make them white in the mask; and wherever there are pixels of any color other than black in the first bitmap, make those pixels black in the mask. The mask is a type of negative image of the primary bitmap and should contain only black and white pixels.

Here's how these bitmaps work to create the animation. First the saved background is restored to erase the ball at its current location. (Note that this step is skipped the first time the ball is drawn.) The background at the ball's next location is saved in the third picture box. This will be used to restore the background when the ball moves again. At the new location, the mask image is placed on the background image using a Boolean And operation on a pixel-by-pixel basis. The last parameter in the *PaintPicture* method determines this logical bit-mixing operation. An And operation results in the display of black pixels wherever the applied mask is black, and undisturbed background pixels wherever the mask is white. A solid black dot will be on the form at this point, but it will go away with the next step before you witness it.

The final step in updating the ball image to a new location is to apply the primary ball bitmap (the first picture box) using an Or bitwise operation. The nonblack pixels in the ball appear where the background is blacked out, and the black pixels leave the background undisturbed. The result is a solid red ball that appears to hover in front of the background scene.

The action is repeated using a loop, causing the ball to "roll" across the form from left to right. The ball is shown in mid-roll in Figure 10-11.

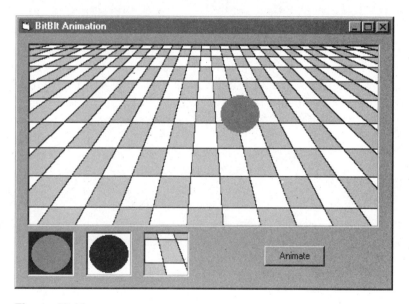

Figure 10-11.
The animation program in progress, showing the ball as it "rolls" across the background.

 See Also...

- The Lottery application in Chapter 25 (Part III) for a demonstration of animation

Dear John, How Do I...

Use Picture Objects for Animation?

Picture properties have been included in all previous versions of Visual Basic, and now Visual Basic 4 provides a companion Picture object, which greatly enhances the options you have for manipulating images. A Picture object is an independent entity you can use to load and store images so that you no longer have to use a PictureBox or an Image control. When it's time to access the pictures, it's easy to copy them from Picture objects to visible controls.

> NOTE: In addition to the new Picture object, Visual Basic 4 provides a new ImageList control and allows you to load multiple images from a resource file. You might want to try these techniques to improve the speed and efficiency of your graphics displays.

Here's some example code for you to experiment with. This routine creates an array of Picture objects and loads a sequence of images into each one when the form loads. A timer, named tmrAnimate, is set to the minimum interval of 1 millisecond, the rate at which it will assign the Picture objects sequentially to a PictureBox control named picTest. The result is a smooth, flicker-free animation of whatever images you've created in the sequence of bitmap files.

I used Paint to create 15 images, each exactly 100 by 100 pixels in size, and named them Frame1, Frame2, and so on, through Frame15. I drew concentric circles to create an expanding and collapsing tunnel effect when the animation runs. You might want to create a rotating object, or a stick figure walking, or some other clever scene. The picTest PictureBox control should be sized to 100 by 100 pixels too, so that the frames of the animation fit well. Figure 10-12 shows the animation frozen at about the middle of the sequence of frames I created.

```
Option Explicit

Const NUMFRAMES = 15
Dim p(1 To NUMFRAMES) As Picture

Private Sub Form_Load()
    Dim Fil$, i
    For i = 1 To NUMFRAMES
        Fil$ = "C:\Graphics\Frame" & _
```

(continued)

```
                Format$(i) & ".Bmp"
            Set p(i) = LoadPicture(Fil$)
        Next i
    End Sub

    Private Sub tmrAnimate_Timer()
        Static n As Integer
        n = (n Mod NUMFRAMES) + 1
        picTest.Picture = p(n)
    End Sub
```

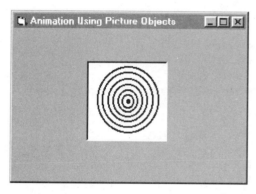

Figure 10-12.
Simple animation sequence created using an array of picture objects.

Dear John, How Do I...

Position Text at an Exact Location in a Picture Box?

One advantage a picture box has over a text box or a label is that a picture box allows you to print text at any location, with a mix of fonts, in a variety of colors, and intermixed with graphics. You can change the font characteristics using standard properties of the picture box, and you can place the text for printing at any location in the picture box using a combination of the Scale-Width, ScaleHeight, TextWidth, and TextHeight properties of the picture box. The following code demonstrates how to center a string at a point and how to place a string so that it prints right up against the lower-right corner of the picture box. Figure 10-13 on the following page shows the result of this code. To try it, add a picture box named picTest to a new form, add the following code, run the application, and click on the picture box.

```
Option Explicit

Private Sub picTest_Click()
    Dim X, Y, A$
    'Determine center of picture box
    X = picTest.ScaleWidth \ 2
    Y = picTest.ScaleHeight \ 2
    'Draw circle at center for reference
    picTest.Circle (X, Y), 700
    'Print string centered in picture box
    A$ = "CENTER"
    picTest.CurrentX = X - picTest.TextWidth(A$) \ 2
    picTest.CurrentY = Y - picTest.TextHeight(A$) \ 2
    picTest.Print A$
    'Determine lower-right corner of picture box
    X = picTest.ScaleWidth
    Y = picTest.ScaleHeight
    'Print string at lower-right corner
    A$ = "Lower-right corner..."
    picTest.CurrentX = X - picTest.TextWidth(A$)
    picTest.CurrentY = Y - picTest.TextHeight(A$)
    picTest.Print A$
End Sub
```

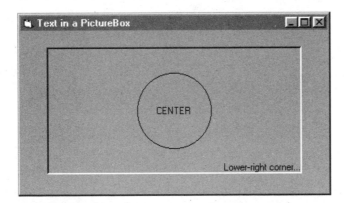

Figure 10-13.
Printing text at exact locations in a picture box.

Notice that the *TextWidth* function returns the effective length of the entire string, taking into account the current font settings, the number of characters in the string, and the proportional spacing for those characters.

For this reason, always pass the exact string to be printed to this function just before printing and after any font properties have been set.

The above example shows the general technique for exact text placement. By extrapolating from this example, you can print superscript characters, label graph axes, and perform similar tasks.

Dear John, How Do I...

Use Multiple Fonts in a Picture Box?

The PictureBox control has a full set of properties for font characteristics. Unlike the TextBox and Label controls, the PictureBox control lets you change these properties on the fly, without affecting any text already drawn in the picture box. Simply reset the font properties, print the text, and then move on to print other text using any other combination of these properties. Figure 10-14 shows a few different types of fonts all drawn in one picture box.

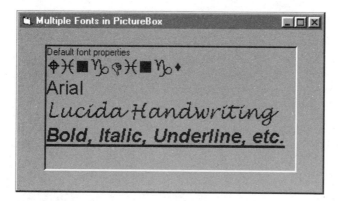

Figure 10-14.
A creative combination of text styles in one picture box.

Picture boxes support the previous font properties, such as FontName and FontSize, for backward compatibility with previous editions of Visual Basic, but the new Font property is an object in itself, and it now provides a set of its own properties. Look at the sample code I used to create Figure 10-14, and notice how I set these properties by using the new Font object. Keep in mind that you can actually create a Font object as an independent entity and assign the whole set of its properties to any object having a Font property in one command. For more details, see the online help for Font objects.

```
Option Explicit

Private Sub picTest_Click()
    '
    picTest.Print "Default font properties"
    '
    picTest.Font.Name = "WingDings"
    picTest.Font.Size = 18
    picTest.Print "WingDings"
    '
    picTest.Font.Name = "Arial"
    picTest.Print "Arial"
    '
    picTest.Font.Name = "Lucida Handwriting"
    picTest.Print "Lucida Handwriting"
    '
    picTest.Font.Bold = True
    picTest.Font.Italic = True
    picTest.Font.Underline = True
    picTest.Font.Name = "Arial"
    picTest.Print "Bold, Italic, Underline, etc."

End Sub
```

To run this code, start a new project and add a PictureBox control named picText to the form. Add the code to the form, and when you run the program, click on the picture box to have the different formats of text printed in the picture box.

> NOTE: For some purposes, Visual Basic's new RichTextBox control also provides excellent multifont capabilities. Although the ability to position text at an exact location is not part of the RichTextBox control's properties and methods, you can align text left, right, and centered; and you can use multiple fonts within the same control. Check it out.

CHAPTER ELEVEN

File I/O

Visual Basic provides several efficient techniques you can use to read and write files. This chapter describes some of the most useful techniques for file I/O (input/output), along with several functions that people overlook when they are preparing to delete, rename, or copy files.

Dear John, How Do I...

Rename, Delete, or Copy a File Efficiently?

Visual Basic has three statements that were specifically designed for renaming, deleting, and copying files. Use the *Kill* statement to delete a file, the *Name* statement to rename a file, and the *FileCopy* statement to copy a file. The following block of code demonstrates all three of these important file manipulation statements better than words can describe. When you click on the form, this program creates a simple text file named File-A, renames it as File-B, copies File-B to create File-C, displays the contents of File-C, and then deletes both File-B and File-C.

```
Option Explicit

Private Sub Form_Click()
    Dim A$, FilNum As Integer
    'Create a small file
    FilNum = FreeFile
    Open "File-A" For Output As #FilNum
    Print #FilNum, "This is a test..."
    Close #FilNum
    'Rename file
    Name "File-A" As "File-B"
    'Copy file
    FileCopy "File-B", "File-C"
    'Read and display resulting file
    Open "File-C" For Input As #FilNum
```

(continued)

```
        Line Input #FilNum, A$
        Close #FilNum
        MsgBox A$, vbOKOnly, "Contents of the Renamed and Copied File..."
        'Delete files
        Kill "File-B"
        Kill "File-C"
End Sub
```

As shown in Figure 11-1, the contents of the copied file are displayed in a message box, verifying the correct operation of the demonstrated functions. When you click on OK, all the files will be deleted.

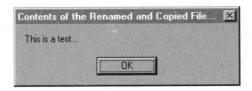

Figure 11-1.
Contents of a renamed and copied file.

Dear John, How Do I...

Work with Directories and Paths?

Visual Basic 4 has several statements that mimic their equivalent MS-DOS commands but don't require your program to shell out to MS-DOS or do any other fancy gymnastics.

MkDir, ChDir, and *RmDir*

The *MkDir* statement creates a new directory, *ChDir* lets you change the current working directory, and *RmDir* deletes a directory. If you know how to use the commands of the same name at the MS-DOS prompt, you're all set to use them in your Visual Basic applications. Read the online help for more details about these statements.

CurDir and App.Path

Your application can determine the current working directory for any drive by using the *CurDir* function. Often, however, it's more useful to know the directory that the application itself resides in, rather than the current directory. The Path property of the App object provides this information. For example, with the following lines of code, your application can determine the current working directory and can determine a good location at which to read and write application-specific data files:

```
CurDirectory$ = CurDir
IniDirectory$ = App.Path
```

Dir

The *Dir* function is a powerful means of locating files or directories on any drive. The online help describes this function in detail, but I do want to point out that if you use the *Dir* function with parameters to specify the path or filename pattern and then use the *Dir* function again without parameters, the function will return the next file that matches the previously specified parameters from the directory currently specified to be searched. This makes possible the sequential collection of all the files in a directory. The following code demonstrates this important feature. This code lists all normal files (hidden, system, and directory files are not included) in all directories on the C drive to a file named Filetree. Add these two subprograms to a new form, and run the program to create Filetree in the current working directory. The program will automatically unload when it is through.

```
Option Explicit

Sub RecurseTree(CurrentPath$)
    Dim i, n
    Dim FileName$, DirectoryList$()
    'First list all normal files in this directory
    FileName$ = Dir(CurrentPath$)
    Do While FileName$ <> ""
        Print #1, CurrentPath$ & FileName$
        FileName$ = Dir
    Loop
    'Next build temporary list of subdirectories
    FileName$ = Dir(CurrentPath$, vbDirectory)
    Do While FileName$ <> ""
        'Ignore current and parent directories
        If FileName$ <> "." And FileName$ <> ".." Then
            'Ignore non-directories
            If GetAttr(CurrentPath$ & FileName$) _
                    And vbDirectory Then
                n = n + 1
                ReDim Preserve DirectoryList$(n)
                DirectoryList$(n) = CurrentPath$ & FileName$
            End If
        End If
```

(continued)

```
        FileName$ = Dir
    Loop
    'Recursively process each directory
    For i = 1 To n
        RecurseTree DirectoryList$(i) & "\"
    Next i
End Sub

Private Sub Form_Load()
    Dim StartPath$
    Me.Show
    Print "Working..."
    StartPath$ = "C:\"
    Open "Filetree" For Output As #1
    RecurseTree StartPath$
    Close #1
    Unload Me
End Sub
```

This program also illustrates the use of recursive routines in Visual Basic. In this example, the nesting depth of the recursive calls to *RecurseTree* is determined by the nested depth of your subdirectories.

You might wonder why *RecurseTree* builds a dynamically allocated array of subdirectory names instead of just calling itself each time a subdirectory is encountered. It turns out that the *Dir* function call, when passed with no parameters, keeps track of the file and path it has most recently found in preparation for the next time *Dir* is called, regardless of where the function call originated. When it returns from a nested, recursive call, the *Dir* function will have lost track of its position in the current directory. The string array list of subdirectories, however, is updated accurately with each nested call because at each level a new, local copy of the string array variable is built. This is one of those annoying software details that will drive you up the wall until it suddenly makes sense!

After you have run this short program, look for a new file named Filetree that contains a list of all files in all subdirectories on your C drive. (Be patient—the program might take a while to finish.)

Dear John, How Do I...

Do Fast File I/O?

The best way to increase the speed of your file I/O operations is to use binary file access whenever possible. You can open any file for binary access, even if it's a text file.

Also, to increase file processing speed, remember to use the *FileCopy* command whenever it's appropriate, instead of reading and writing from one file to another.

See Also...

- "Dear John, How Do I Work with Binary Files?" below
- "Dear John, How Do I Rename, Delete, or Copy a File Efficiently?" earlier in this chapter

Dear John, How Do I...

Work with Binary Files?

Binary file operations in Visual Basic are fast. Whenever possible, I prefer to read and write files using the binary file *Get* and *Put* statements. Even if this requires extra processing of the data once the data is loaded into variables, the whole process is usually still faster than using the older *Input, Output,* and other such functions that have been around since the earliest versions of Microsoft Basic. Today, with Type data structures and very large strings (such as those in 32-bit operating systems), binary file access makes more sense than ever. Let's take a look at a few examples.

Type Data Structures

Type data structures are read and written to binary files in one fell swoop. For example, the following code loops to read personnel data records from an existing data file named Test until it gets to the end of the file:

```
Option Explicit

Private Type Employee
    FirstName As String * 20
    MiddleInitial As String * 1
    LastName As String * 20
    Age As Byte
    Retired As Boolean
    Street As String * 30
    City As String * 20
    State As String * 2
    Comments As String * 200
End Type
```

(continued)

```
Private Sub Form_Click()
    Dim Emp(1 To 10) As Employee
    Dim i As Integer
    Open "C:\Test" For Binary As #1
    For i = 1 To 10
        Get #1, , Emp(i)
        Print Emp(i).FirstName
    Next i
    Close #1
End Sub
```

Notice that the file is accessed only 10 times in this sample routine, to read in 10 data records, but that this procedure actually reads 2960 bytes from the file. Each record in the Employee Type data structure contains 296 bytes of data, so the entire structure is read from the file each time the *Get* statement is executed.

> WARNING: As a general rule, you should always read binary file data by using the same Type data structure that was used to write the data. Starting with Visual Basic 4, data layout in memory and in binary files became very tricky and unpredictable because of internal changes necessary for the global programming goals of Unicode, and because of the need to make 32-bit applications run faster.
>
> The 32-bit version of Visual Basic 4 internally manipulates all string data, even within Type structures, as 2-byte-per-character Unicode data. When performing file I/O, Visual Basic 4 converts all Unicode strings to 1-byte-per-character ANSI strings, which completely changes the overall size of Type data structures that contain strings.
>
> Type structure data items are also double word–aligned to achieve the most efficient I/O throughput possible in 32-bit operating systems. This extra padding also changes the exact layout of the data within a Type data structure.
>
> Be careful!

Strings

A fast and flexible method of inputting a chunk of data from a file to your program is to open the data file in binary mode and use the *Get* statement to place the entire chunk of data in a string variable. To input a given number of bytes from a file, first set the size of the string. The *Get* statement will read bytes until the string is filled, so if the string is one character long, 1 byte will be read from the file. Similarly, if the string is 10,000 bytes long, 10,000 bytes from the file will be loaded. The following lines demonstrate this technique:

```
Option Explicit

Private Sub Form_Click()
    Dim A As String * 1
    Open "C:\Test" For Binary As #1
    Get #1, , A
    Print A
    Close #1
End Sub

Private Sub Text1_Click
    Dim B$
    Open "C:\Test" For Binary As #1
    B$ = Space$(LOF(1))
    Get #1, , B$
    Text1.Text - B$
    Close #1
    End Sub
```

In the Form_Click subprogram code, a fixed-length string of 1 byte is used to get 1 byte from the test file. In the Text1_Click subprogram code, the string *B$* is filled with spaces to set the size of the variable to the size of the file. The *Get* statement is then used with the *B$* variable to input a chunk of data from the Test data file that is equal in length to the string variable *B$*. This results in the variable *B$* being assigned the entire contents of the file.

> NOTE: This isn't supposed to work! Microsoft warns us that Unicode character conversions "might" cause binary file data loaded into strings to become corrupted. However, testing the above technique with files containing all 256 possible byte values revealed nothing unexpected. Each byte of the file is assumed to be an ANSI character, and when it is loaded into a string, each byte is padded with a binary byte value of 0 to make it a Unicode character. Everything works as it has in previous versions of Visual Basic, but in future versions everything might not work that way. The solution is to start using binary arrays now for this type of work instead of strings. Read on!

Note that strings are limited to approximately 65,400 bytes in size in earlier, 16-bit, versions of Windows, and to approximately 2 billion bytes in 32-bit versions of Windows NT and Windows 95. This means, in most cases, that you can load the entire file into a single string using one *Get* statement. Just be sure to size the string to the file's size before doing the *Get* by using the *LOF* function, as shown above.

See Also...

- The Secret application in Chapter 30 (Part III) for a demonstration of binary file I/O

Byte Arrays

One way to process each byte of a file is to load the file into a string (see above) and then use the *ASC* function to convert each character of the string to its ASCII numeric value. However, with the introduction of Visual Basic's new Byte variable type, byte processing can now be accomplished much more efficiently.

In the following code, I've created a dynamic Byte array that can be dimensioned to match a file's size. You can load the entire file into the array by passing the Byte array variable to the *Get* statement, as shown.

```
Option Explicit

Private Sub Form_Click()
    Dim i
    Open "C:\Test" For Binary As #1
    ReDim Buf(1 To LOF(1)) As Byte
    Get #1, , Buf()
    For i = LBound(Buf) To UBound(Buf)
        Print Chr$(Buf(i));
    Next i
    Close #1
End Sub
```

The Connection Between Strings and Byte Arrays

The preceding example hints at the connection between strings and Byte arrays. But there's much more to this duality, and I'll describe some of the details you'll need to know to work effectively with the new Byte array type.

Byte arrays should be used more and more for the kinds of byte manipulations we've accomplished with strings in the past. To ease this transition, you can plop a Byte array into the middle of many commands and functions that, in the past, would only work with string parameters. For example, as shown in the following code, you can assign a string to a Byte array and a Byte array to a string:

```
Option Explicit

Private Sub Form_Click()
    Dim i As Integer
    Dim a$, c$
```

(continued)

```
    Dim b() As Byte
    a$ = "ABC"
    b() = a$
    ' This displays 65 0 66 0 67 0
    For i = LBound(b) To UBound(b)
        Print b(i);
    Next I
    Print
    c$ = b()
    ' This displays ABC
    Print c$
    ' Notice actual size of string
    Print a$, Len(a$), LenB(a$)
End Sub
```

Notice that I've declared the Byte array b() as a dynamic array. In general, you should always declare your Byte arrays as dynamic when assigning strings to them. Visual Basic will then be able to automatically expand or collapse the size of the array to match the length of the string, just as it does for dynamic strings.

I suggest you take the time to run the preceding code and study its output carefully. It will help you understand how string variables are maintained in memory as Unicode characters. The 3-byte string "ABC" is shuffled from the string *a$* into the Byte array b(), and then all the bytes in b() are printed out. Instead of the expected three byte values of 65, 66, and 67 (ASCII representations of "A", "B", and "C"), we find that the Byte array actually contains six byte values. This is because the three-character string is maintained in memory in a 6-byte Unicode format, and the contents of this string are shuffled straight across, with no translation back to its 3-byte ANSI string representation upon assignment to the Byte array. Understanding this can help you clearly visualize how Unicode strings are manipulated in memory by Visual Basic 4.

The 6-byte array is then assigned to a second string, *c$*. Toward the end of the code listing, I added a print command to display *c$*, its length in number of characters, and its length in actual byte count. *Len* and *LenB*, respectively, provide this information.

The *StrConv* Function

There's a handy new conversion function that lets you control the conversion of string data to and from Unicode representation. The code snippet on the following page demonstrates the *StrConv* function as it forces a 3-byte string to transfer its ANSI characters to a 3-byte array, and then it shows how you can use it to transfer a 3-byte array into a string.

NOTE: What happens if you assign a Byte array to a string when the array bytes are not padded with extra 0 bytes, so as to be in proper internal Unicode format? They transfer into the string, but Visual Basic 4 doesn't know what the heck to do with those strange characters when you try to print the string. You'll get a question mark instead of whatever you might be expecting.

```
Option Explicit

Private Sub Form_Click()
    Dim i As Integer
    Dim a$
    Dim b() As Byte
    a$ = "ABC"
    b() = StrConv(a$, vbFromUnicode)
    ' This displays 65 66 67
    For i = LBound(b) To UBound(b)
        Print b(i);
    Next I
    Print
    a$ = b()
    ' This displays a question mark
    Print a$
    a$ = StrConv(b(), vbUnicode)
    ' This displays ABC 3 6
    Print a$, Len(a$), LenB(a$)
End Sub
```

The constants vbFromUnicode and vbUnicode are just two of several constants defined for the *StrConv* function. Check the online help for more information about other handy uses for this versatile function.

By understanding the ways in which Byte arrays work hand in hand with strings, and how you can control the ANSI/Unicode conversions by using the *StrConv* function, you will gain mastery of the efficient and fast capabilities of binary file I/O.

CHAPTER TWELVE

The Registry

In 32-bit Windows 95 and Windows NT, the *Registry* replaces the initialization (INI) files used by most 16-bit Windows-based applications to keep track of information between sessions. The Registry is a systemwide file designed to let all 32-bit applications keep track of application-specific data between runs of the application. The transition from using INI files to using the Registry is easy because Visual Basic 4 provides a handful of functions that simplify the reading and writing of the Registry. Typical information stored in the Registry includes user preferences for colors, fonts, window positions, and the like. This chapter explains and demonstrates these new Registry functions.

Dear John, How Do I...
Read and Write to the Registry?

There are four new functions that are used for reading and writing to the Registry: *SaveSetting, GetSetting, DeleteSetting,* and *GetAllSettings.* The first three are, in my opinion, the most important.

As indicated by their names, these functions get or save (read or write) string data (settings) from or to the Registry and delete any settings no longer used. *GetAllSettings* is a special function that lets you get all settings from a section in one call. This is an extension of the *GetSetting* function, so I'll leave it up to you to read the online help for more information on this particular function.

To demonstrate the first three functions, I've created a small application that lets you save and get settings in the Registry. The three Registry functions refer to a setting stored in the Registry at a specific *Appname, Section,* and *Key* location. Notice that I've assigned the App.Title property of the App object to the *Appname$* string, and I've hardwired a *Section$* string, "Testing". Look in the Form_Load event to see how I've set these two strings. You can, of course, change these strings as desired.

To run this program, create a form with three command buttons named cmdDelete, cmdGet, and cmdSave. Also add two text boxes named txtSetting and txtKey. The form at design time, with labels added to identify the text boxes, is shown in Figure 12-1. At runtime, you should type a string into the Key field. To save a setting for your Key, type a string into the Setting field and click on Save Setting. To access a previously stored setting, enter a Key string and click on Get Setting. Click Delete Setting to erase the entry for the given Key from the Registry.

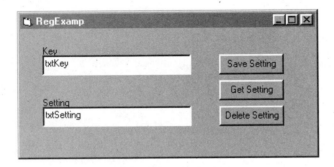

Figure 12-1.
The RegExamp form at design time.

Here's the code:

```
Option Explicit

Dim Appname$, Section$, Key$, Setting$

Private Sub cmdDelete_Click()
    'Removes a setting from Registry
    Key$ = txtKey.Text
    DeleteSetting Appname$, Section$, Key$
    txtSetting.Text = ""
End Sub

Private Sub cmdGet_Click()
    'Retrieves a setting from Registry
    Key$ = txtKey.Text
    Setting$ = GetSetting(Appname$, Section$, Key$)
    txtSetting.Text = Setting$
End Sub
```

(continued)

```
Private Sub cmdSave_Click()
    'Saves a setting in Registry
    Key$ = txtKey.Text
    Setting$ = txtSetting.Text
    SaveSetting Appname$, Section$, Key$, Setting$
End Sub

Private Sub Form_Load()
    Appname$ = App.Title     'RegExamp
    Section$ = "Testing"
End Sub
```

A couple of notes about these functions are in order. The GetSetting function has an optional *Default$* parameter that I chose not to use. If you provide a string for this parameter, the string is returned by the function if the indicated setting is not found in the Registry. If you don't provide a *Default$*, an empty string is returned if nothing is found, and this scenario works just fine for my example. Also, note that these functions are suitable for use with named parameters, which you might prefer to use for readability. For example, these two SaveSetting statements are identical except for the use of named parameters in the second case:

```
SaveSetting Appname$, Section$, Key$, Setting$

SaveSetting Appname:=Appname$, Section:=Section$, _
    Key:=Key$, Setting:=Setting$
```

Figure 12-2 shows RegExamp at runtime. An entry of Peaches at the Key location has just been saved in the Registry.

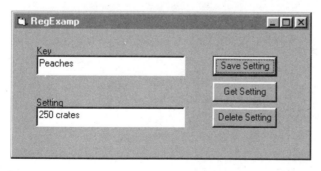

Figure 12-2.
The RegExamp application at runtime.

The best way to see exactly how the Registry is modified as you save and get settings is to run the Regedit application provided by Windows 95. From the Start button on the Windows task bar choose Run, type *Regedit*, and click OK. As shown in Figure 12-3, these Visual Basic functions always save and get settings from the HKEY_CURRENT_USER\Software\VB and VBA Program Settings section of the Registry, and this is where you should always look for them. Notice that the *Appname* and *Section* strings further define the location of saved settings. In this example, the *Appname* is RegExamp, and the *Section* is Testing. These show up as part of the tree structure on the left side of Regedit's display. On the right side of the display you'll find the specific *Key* and *Setting* strings. As shown in Figure 12-3, I entered settings for the three keys Apples, Oranges, and Peaches. While you are experimenting with the RegExamp sample application, be sure to refresh Regedit's display after you save or delete settings, either by pressing F5 or by selecting Refresh from the View menu.

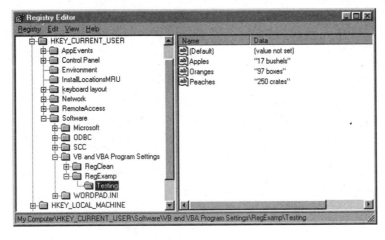

Figure 12-3.
The contents of the Registry as displayed by the Regedit application.

See Also...

- The Ssaver application in Chapter 25 and the VBClock application in Chapter 27 (both in Part III) for a demonstration of the use of the Registry

Dear John, How Do I...

Remember the State of an Application?

The answer to this question is really just an extension of the previous topic. Use *SaveSetting* to save the current state of your application, and use *GetSetting* to recall the state. An excellent place to put this code is in the Form_Unload and Form_Load event routines. With this arrangement, when the form is loaded, but before it is actually drawn onto the screen, the previous size, shape, location, color, and any other detail of the state of the application can be restored. Similarly, immediately before the form is unloaded, the current state can be written for the next time the application is run.

See Also...

- "Dear John, How Do I Read and Write to the Registry?" earlier in this chapter

- The Ssaver application in Chapter 25 and VBClock application in Chapter 27 (both in Part III) for a demonstration of the use of the Registry to save and restore an application's state

CHAPTER THIRTEEN

Help Files

A help file is an important part of any full-featured Windows-based application. You can create your own help files using any of several good help-file development tools on the market today, such as RoboHelp or HelpBreeze. There's even a shareware program named VBHelp, which was written in Visual Basic. Of course, you could create the text and text coding for your help file using any word processor that supports RTF (Rich Text Format) output, but you'll probably find that the commercial tools are much easier to use for this specific task.

One tool that you must have is the Microsoft Help Compiler, which converts your help-file source into a working help program. Some help-file development tools include a copy of this compiler, and some don't. Fortunately, the help compiler is included in the Professional and Enterprise editions of Visual Basic 4.

It is beyond the scope of this book to describe the actual creation of a help file using the tools mentioned above. Instead, this chapter describes the many ways in which your Visual Basic 4 application can access its help file. These techniques have never been gathered together in one place—until now, that is!

Most of the demonstration applications in Part III of this book share a common help file. I've used all of the techniques described here to activate this help file in various locations throughout these applications.

Dear John, How Do I...

Use the *WinHelp* API Function to Add Help Files to My Projects?

You can activate a help file using a direct Windows API call, which is the tried and true, old-fashioned way to access help. The function is named *WinHelp*, and you have to add a declaration for it in your application, as shown in the following example. In this sample code, the Contents topic of Visual Basic's main help file pops up when the form is clicked:

```
Option Explicit

Private Declare Function WinHelp _
Lib "user32" Alias "WinHelpA" ( _
    ByVal hWnd As Long, _
    ByVal lpHelpFile As String, _
    ByVal wCommand As Long, _
    ByVal dwData As Long _
) As Long

Private Sub Form_Click()
    Dim x
    x = WinHelp(hWnd, "vb.hlp", cdlHelpContents, 0)
End Sub
```

The hWnd parameter is set to the hWnd property of your application's form. The lpHelpFile parameter is a string that contains the name of the help file to be activated. The wCommand parameter is one of the predefined constants for controlling this function. (These constants are listed under the MSComDlg entry of the Object Browser, in the online help under Help Constants, and at the end of this discussion.) The dwData parameter can take on several types of values, depending on the value of wCommand. In particular, if wCommand is set to cdlHelpContext, dwData's value determines the help file topic to pop up.

To demonstrate how this works, the following form of the *WinHelp* function activates the help file created for the applications in Part III of this book, activating the specific topic for the Lottery application. (You will probably need to edit the path to the location of Mvbdw.hlp on your computer.)

```
Private Sub Form_Click()
    Dim x
    x = WinHelp(hWnd, _
        "D:\Help\Mvbdw.hlp", _
        cdlHelpContext, LOTTERY)
End Sub
```

The Lottery topic will display as the help file starts because I've set the wCommand parameter to the cdlHelpContext constant and the dwData parameter to the Lottery topic number constant I defined. (Some help building tools, such as RoboHelp, automate the creation of a BAS file that contains constants for all topics—this is a great time-saver.)

There are several other variations on the function call that you might find useful. Each of the constants listed in the following table, when passed in the wCommand parameter, causes a specific action to be carried out by the *WinHelp* function. (These constants are defined by Visual Basic 4 for the Common Dialog custom control, hence the *cdl* prefixes.) For example, to display help information on how to use the help system itself, use the constant cdlHelpHelpOnHelp.

Constant	Value	Description
cdlHelpContext	1	Displays help for a particular topic
cdlHelpQuit	2	Closes the specified help file
cdlHelpIndex	3	Displays the index of the specified help file
cdlHelpContents	3	Displays the Contents topic in the current help file
cdlHelpHelpOnHelp	4	Displays help for using the help application itself
cdlHelpSetIndex	5	Sets the current index for multi-index help
cdlHelpSetContents	5	Designates a specific topic as the Contents topic
cdlHelpContextPopup	8	Displays a topic identified by a context number
cdlHelpForceFile	9	Creates a help file that displays text in only one font
cdlHelpKey	257	Displays help for a particular keyword
cdlHelpCommandHelp	258	Displays help for a particular command
cdlHelpPartialKey	261	Calls the search engine in Windows help

These constants are predefined for the Common Dialog. You can copy them into your code by using the Object Browser. They are also discussed in the description of the HelpCommand property in Visual Basic's online help.

See Also...

- The Lottery application in Chapter 25 (Part III) for a demonstration of the *WinHelp* function

Dear John, How Do I...

Add Context-Sensitive F1 Help to My Projects?

Forms, menu items, and most controls have a HelpContextID property that provides a context-sensitive jump to a specific help topic when the F1 key is pressed. The HelpFile property of the App object sets the path and name of the help file for the entire application, and the control with the focus determines which help topic is activated when F1 is pressed. If a control's HelpContextID is set to *0* (the default), the containing control or form is checked for a nonzero HelpContextID value. Finally, if the form's HelpContextID is *0*, the help file's Contents topic is activated as the default.

This scheme works well for accessing context-sensitive help, which is activated when the F1 key is pressed, but how can we activate the help file programmatically without actually pressing the F1 key? Well, here's a slick trick that makes the HelpContextID property much more valuable. Simply code your program to send an F1 keypress to your application using the *SendKeys* command. The *SendKeys* statement tells Windows to send keypresses to the window that currently has the focus, so the program responds as though the F1 key had been pressed.

The following code fragments demonstrate this technique.

```
Private Sub Form_Load()
    App.HelpFile = "vbdwhelp.hlp"
End Sub

Private Sub cmdHelp_Click()
    cmdHelp.HelpContextID = LOTTERY
    SendKeys "{F1}"
End Sub
```

The help file to be accessed is set in the Form_Load routine, but you can change the path and filename at any point in your program if you want to access multiple help files. In the cmdHelp_Click routine, you activate a specific topic in the help file by setting the HelpContextID property to the context number of the desired topic and then sending the F1 keypress using the *SendKeys* command. These HelpFile and HelpContextID properties can be set at runtime, as shown above, or you can set them at design time.

Menu items also have a HelpContextID property, but the designated topic in the help file will be activated only if the highlight is moved to the menu item and the F1 key is manually pressed. If you click on the menu item and set up a *SendKeys* command in the menu event routine, as shown in the following code,

```
Private Sub mnuHelp_Click()
    SendKeys "{F1}"
End Sub
```

the topic that will be activated will not be determined by the menu item's HelpContextID value but by the HelpContextID value for whatever control currently has the focus. This happens because the menu goes away as soon as it is clicked on and the focus is returned to the control before the *SendKeys* command has time to send the F1 keypress. Using a menu command to get context-sensitive help for a control works well, but the behavior seems a little strange until you figure out the sequence of events.

Dear John, How Do I...

Use the CommonDialog Control to Add Help Files to My Projects?

The CommonDialog control provides a powerful and flexible way to access help files. Add a CommonDialog control to your form, set its relevant help-file properties, and use the new *ShowHelp* method to activate the help system. It's that easy—you don't even need to use the control to show a dialog box. For example, the following code activates the Contents topic in our help file when the cmdHelpContents command button is clicked.

```
Private Sub cmdHelpContents_Click()
    dlgCommon.HelpFile = " vbdwhelp.hlp"
    dlgCommon.HelpCommand = cdlHelpContents
    dlgCommon.ShowHelp
End Sub
```

Here's an example that shows the activation of a specific help-file topic when a menu item is clicked:

```
Private Sub mnuHelpLottery_Click()
    dlgCommon.HelpFile = " vbdwhelp.hlp"
    dlgCommon.HelpCommand = cdlHelpContext
    dlgCommon.HelpContext = LOTTERY
    dlgCommon.ShowHelp
End Sub
```

Dear John, How Do I...

Add WhatsThisHelp to a Form?

Windows 95 provides a few new twists to the way help files work. One of the nice new features is called WhatsThisHelp. A form that has this feature displays a question-mark box on the title bar that, when clicked, changes the mouse pointer to a special question-mark symbol. Clicking on a control on the form with this special pointer then activates a pop-up topic specific to the object clicked.

It's easy to add WhatsThisHelp to your Visual Basic 4 form and its controls. Start by setting the form's WhatsThisButton and WhatsThisHelp properties to *True*. The form's BorderStyle property must also be changed from its default setting before you'll see the question-mark box on the title bar. Set BorderStyle to either *1 - Fixed Single* or *3 - Fixed Dialog*. Figure 13-1 shows a form with the question-mark title bar button.

Figure 13-1.
A form showing the question-mark button that activates WhatsThisHelp.

To determine exactly which help file will be activated, you must set the HelpFile property of the App object to the path and name of the help file. You can do this either at design time or at runtime. At design time, from the Tools menu choose Options, select the Project tab of the Options dialog box, and complete the Help File box with the appropriate Help file, including the full path to the file. At runtime, assign the pathname and filename to the App.HelpFile property.

Finally, to define the topic in the help file that will pop up when a given control is clicked on, set that control's WhatsThisHelpID property to the topic's number.

WhatsThisMode

There's one other way you can use WhatsThisHelp popups. You can program-matically activate the special question-mark mouse pointer by using the *WhatsThisMode* method of the form. This is a useful technique when you want to add the WhatsThisHelp feature to a form that has the BorderStyle set to *2 - Sizeable*. Figure 13-2 shows a form set up to activate WhatsThisHelp when the Get Help command button is clicked.

Figure 13-2.
A form showing how WhatsThisHelp can be activated using the WhatsThisMode method.

When the Get Help button is clicked, the mouse pointer changes to the special question mark, and the WhatsThisHelp state operates in exactly the same way as when the title bar question-mark button is clicked in the previous example. To use this WhatsThisHelp technique, all I had to do was set the form's WhatsThisHelp property to *True* and add one line to the command button's click event. Here's the code:

```
Private Sub cmdGetHelp_Click()
    WhatsThisMode
End Sub
```

CHAPTER FOURTEEN

Security

Legal issues around software development and software rights can get thorny. One simple device used to prove authorship of an application is a hidden credits dialog box, sometimes referred to as an *Easter egg*. Another handy technique is to embed ciphered messages that declare authorship. Both of these techniques are described in this chapter.

Passwords are an integral part of many applications for which security is an issue. It's easy to create a password entry dialog box in Visual Basic 4, as I describe here.

Dear John, How Do I...

Add a Hidden Credits Screen?

Sometimes they're called Easter eggs; sometimes they're not called anything at all. Many applications have a hidden, undocumented feature whereby the authors can put on an impressive little show. Creatively designed Easter eggs can be a lot of fun, as shown in Figure 14-1 on the following page.

Another purpose of these Easter eggs is to provide some legal protection for the author. If there's ever a disagreement as to who is the original creator of a piece of software, the real author can duly impress everyone by clicking here or there to pop up a dialog box that will prove authorship. Wouldn't that be fun to do in a court of law someday?

A straightforward approach is to create a special-purpose form to display whatever information you want on your hidden credits screen. The real trick is in deciding how such a form will be activated. I can offer general concepts and a specific example, but there's a lot of room for creativity in determining exactly how to activate your Easter egg.

Figure 14-1.
A sample Easter egg (semisecret hidden credits screen).

It's easy to detect where the mouse is clicked on a form or control. The MouseDown and MouseUp events provide X and Y parameters that tell you exactly where the mouse pointer is located when the mouse is clicked. Likewise, it's easy to determine the state of the shift keys (Shift, Ctrl, and Alt) and which mouse button or buttons are depressed. All of this information is passed as parameters to your MouseUp or MouseDown event–driven subprogram. So, for example, your application can check the status of the shift keys and the mouse and then activate the Easter egg only if the right mouse button is pressed while the Shift key is depressed and while the mouse pointer is located within 1 centimeter of the upper-right corner of a specific picture box.

Alternatively, by using static variables in your MouseUp or MouseDown routine, you can detect a specific sequence of left and right button clicks or watch for something like five clicks in less than 2 seconds.

In a similar way, you can secretly monitor a sequence of specific keystrokes by setting the form's KeyPreview property to *True* and using static variables to keep track of recent keypresses detected in the Form_KeyDown routine. Let's look at some sample code to see how you might secretly detect the keypress sequence *EGG*.

```
Option Explicit

Sub Form_Load()
    KeyPreview = True
End Sub

Sub Form_KeyDown(KeyCode As Integer, Shift As Integer)
    Static K$
```

(continued)

```
    Select Case KeyCode
        Case vbKeyE: K$ = K$ & "E"
        Case vbKeyG: K$ = K$ & "G"
        Case Else: K$ = ""
    End Select
    If Len(K$) > 3 Then K$ = Right$(K$, 3)
    If K$ = "EGG" Then EasterEgg
End Sub

Sub EasterEgg()
    MsgBox "JCC was here"
End Sub
```

The Form_Load routine sets the form's KeyPreview property to *True* so that all keypresses can be checked, no matter which control on the form has the focus. The EasterEgg routine in this example displays a simple message box. You'll want to enhance this routine for your own use.

The Form_KeyDown routine is activated whenever the form, or any control on the form, has the focus and a key is pressed. The static variable *K$* accumulates the three most recent keypresses, and only if the pattern *EGG* is detected is the EasterEgg routine called.

See Also...

- The Dialogs application in Chapter 30 (Part III) for a hidden credits screen that shows more detail and provides a working example of the activation of an Easter egg by a pattern of mouse clicks

Dear John, How Do I...

Create a Password Dialog Box?

In the earliest versions of Visual Basic, you had to jump through hoops and get out the smoke and mirrors to create a password dialog box, but with Visual Basic 4 this is an easy task.

The goal is to create a dialog box that displays asterisks, or some other chosen character, when the user types in the secret password. The asterisks provide visual feedback about the number of characters typed, without giving away the actual password to anyone lurking within eyesight of the screen. The program must keep track of the actual characters typed in by the user, of course, so that the password can be verified. A typical password dialog box is shown in Figure 14-2 on the following page.

177

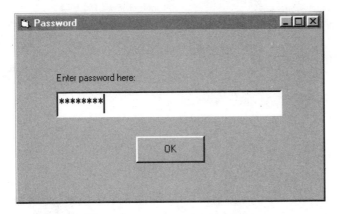

Figure 14-2.
A typical password dialog box.

A Text Box control is usually set up so that the user can enter text from the keyboard. Beginning with Visual Basic 3, the Text Box control has a property named PasswordChar. Set this property to the character that you want to use to hide the password as it is entered. Notice that the Text property will contain the actual characters entered, even though they won't be displayed.

The following lines of code illustrate the basic technique. Add a text box named txtPassword and a command button named cmdOK to a form. The cmdOK_Click routine shown here checks for a password match on *sesame*, but you can modify the code to check for matches with any string you want.

```
Option Explicit

Private Sub cmdOK_Click()
    If txtPassword.Text <> "sesame" Then
        MsgBox "Incorrect password", vbCritical
    Else
        MsgBox "Okay!...Correct password"
    End If
End Sub

Private Sub Form_Load()
    txtPassword.PasswordChar = "*"
    txtPassword.Text=""
End Sub
```

See Also...

- The Secret application in Chapter 30 (Part III) for a more complete demonstration of this topic

Dear John, How Do I...

Encipher a Password or Other Text?

Cipher techniques range from simplistic to extremely complex and secure. In most cases, you don't need or really want the level of security required by the National Security Agency; you just don't want the user to scan through your EXE file or a data file to discover copyright strings or other sensitive information. In fact, you've got to be careful about powerful ciphers, especially if there's any chance that your software will be shipped to foreign locations. The same laws that cover the shipping of munitions overseas apply to the exportation of strong ciphers! The following technique provides an ASCII-to-ASCII cipher suitable for hiding sensitive information from 99.9 percent of the curious people out there. It's not secure enough to keep out the most determined hacker, though.

In this subprogram, you use a simple algorithm to encipher your text and later use the same algorithm to decipher the text. To increase the level of security, you can change the algorithm's startup parameters each time you use it and you can produce customized keys that are required for deciphering the text.

Theory of the Cipher Algorithm

If you don't care about the theory of my simple cipher technique, feel free to skip the next few paragraphs. You can use the algorithm just as well without knowing how it works.

The cipher is based on a sequence of X pseudorandom integers where X is an exact power of 2. You create these integers by using a multiplier, M, and an add-on term, N, where $M = 4 \times A + 1$, $N = 2 \times B + 1$, and A and B are any reasonable integer constants. The value for each number in the sequence is based on the value of the previous number in the sequence, created by multiplying the previous value by M and adding N. The result of the calculation is then constrained to remain less than or equal to your maximum value by using Mod X. In other words, each number is calculated using the formula $R_{i+1} = (R_i \times M + N)$ Mod X, where R_i is a number in the sequence and R_{i+1} is the next number in the sequence. The sequence will cycle through all X values.

A concrete example will help to pin this down. Let's say that we want to create a pseudorandom sequence of the integers from 0 through 32,767. This will give us 32,768 unique values, 32,768 being an exact power of 2. To pick the multiplier, take any reasonable integer, multiply it by 4, and add 1. I'll choose $A = 17$, which provides a multiplier value (M) of $4 \times 17 + 1 = 69$. Likewise, the add-on term is formed by picking any reasonable integer, say $B = 23$, multiplying it by 2, and adding 1, which gives us in this case a value of $N = 47$. Each term is formed from the previous term by multiplying by 69, adding 47, and then using the Mod operator to keep the result of the calculation in the range 0 through 32,767.

Starting with 0, the first few numbers of our sample sequence are 0, 47, 3290, 30449, 3876, 5347, and so on. This sequence won't repeat until all 32,768 unique integers have been used. This longest-possible sequence always works when the multiplier and add-on terms are chosen by the formulas given above.

Putting Cipher to Work

The Cipher subprogram uses the algorithm described above to provide a sequence of random-looking integers. These integers interact bitwise with the bits in a string of bytes through Xor operations to make the string unintelligible. To decipher the string, you execute the Xor operations on the same bytes with the same sequence of bits from the pseudorandom integers a second time. This effectively extracts the original byte stream. I've modified the technique to affect only the bytes in the range of printable characters, which avoids a lot of hassles with the display and printing of ciphered strings but still makes the strings unreadable. Figure 14-3 shows a copyright string in clear text and ciphered versions.

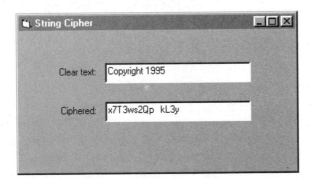

Figure 14-3.
Clear text and ciphered versions of a copyright string.

A thorough example of this algorithm is provided in the Secret application in Part III of this book. The following should provide you with enough code to implement ciphering in your own applications:

```
Sub Cipher(Txt$, Optional Rvalue, Optional A, Optional B)
    Static R As Long
    Static M As Long
    Static N As Long
    'Period of pseudorandom numbers (power of 2)
    Const BigNum As Long = 32768
    Dim i As Integer, c As Integer, d As Integer
    'Optional starting-point random number
    If IsMissing(Rvalue) = False Then
        R = Rvalue
    End If
    'Optional multiplier initializer value
    If IsMissing(A) Then
        If M = 0 Then M = 69
    Else
        M = (A * 4 + 1) Mod BigNum
    End If
    'Optional additive initializer value
    If IsMissing(B) Then
        If N = 0 Then N = 47
    Else
        N = (B * 2 + 1) Mod BigNum
    End If
    'Process the string
    For i = 1 To Len(Txt$)
        c = Asc(Mid$(Txt$, i, 1))
        'Modify only a subset of printable characters
        Select Case c
        Case 48 To 57
            d = c - 48
        Case 63 To 90
            d = c - 53
        Case 97 To 122
            d = c - 59
        Case Else
            d = -1
        End Select
        'Get ready to encipher one character
        If d >= 0 Then
            'Generate next pseudorandom number
            R = (R * M + N) Mod BigNum
            'Xor character and pseudorandom bits
            d = (R And 63) Xor d
            'Put character back into printable range
            Select Case d
```

(continued)

181

```
                    Case 0 To 9
                        c = d + 48
                    Case 10 To 37
                        c = d + 53
                    Case 38 To 63
                        c = d + 59
                    End Select
                    'Replace original character with result
                    Mid$(Txt$, i, 1) = Chr$(c)
            End If
        Next i
End Sub
```

Notice the use of optional parameters for the Cipher subprogram—another new feature of Visual Basic 4. You should always pass at least a string parameter to Cipher, but you now also have the option of passing a new starting point in the pseudorandom sequence (*Rvalue*) and new values that determine the multiplier (*A*) and additive (*B*) terms. This gives you better control of the pseudorandom sequence if you want it.

To use this routine in your own applications, be sure to reset the pseudorandom sequence to the same starting point for enciphering and deciphering. For example, before enciphering a block of strings, you can pass a dummy string and a starting *Rvalue* with a call like this:

```
Cipher "", 1234
```

The enciphering can then proceed from this starting point:

```
Cipher A$
Cipher B$
```

The same sequence of calls is used to decipher the block of strings, starting with setting the *Rvalue* as above. If the pseudorandom sequence is not initialized to the same starting point, the deciphering will fail. Likewise, if you pass the optional *A* and *B* parameters before enciphering begins, be sure to pass these same values before deciphering the same set of strings.

Because the 64 ASCII characters in a selected subset are the only bytes that can be modified by this algorithm, the ciphered version of a string can still be printed, displayed, or written to a file using standard file I/O. These ciphered strings also work well for sending data over a modem because no hidden escape code sequences or control codes will mess up the communication. You won't have to use any complicated binary transfer method.

Registry Data

Finally, here's an idea for making demonstration software secure. You can keep track of the installation date and number of runs of an application by enciphering a string and storing it in the Registry entry for the application. Consider writing the ciphered version of an ASCII representation of an *Rvalue* number to one key in the Registry and a string containing the date and runs information, plus another copy of the *Rvalue*, to a second key in the Registry. Your program can then load the *Rvalue* string, decipher it with a fixed *Rvalue*, and use this result as the *Rvalue* to decipher the date and runs string of information. Your program can easily detect whether either string has been tampered with and then take appropriate action.

There's room for creative variations on this theme, but the important concept to note is that strings ciphered with the algorithm presented here are compatible with standard printable and displayable text strings. You can read and write them with no problem.

See Also...

- The Secret application in Chapter 30 (Part III) for a thorough demonstration of the cipher algorithm

The Mouse

Visual Basic 4 provides 16 standard mouse pointers and also lets you define your own mouse pointer. This chapter explains the manipulation of these pointers and shows you how to easily create custom mouse pointers to use in your applications.

Dear John, How Do I...

Change the Mouse Pointer?

Each form and visible control has a property named MousePointer that allows you to control the appearance of the mouse pointer when it is displayed in front of the form or control. This property is usually set programmatically at runtime because the appropriate mouse pointer might vary according to what the program is executing. (For example, while a time-consuming task is being performed it is usually best to set the mouse pointer to an hourglass shape.) The MousePointer property remains set as *vbDefault* in the development environment.

Visual Basic 4 provides a handy collection of constant declarations for setting the MousePointer property. You don't have to load a special file into your project—the following constants are readily available in Visual Basic 4 whenever you need to use them in your program. You can see a full list of constants and paste the appropriate constant directly into your code by opening the Object Viewer, choosing MousePointer Constants from the Classes/Modules list for the VB library, selecting the constant, and clicking on Paste. The following table lists these constants and describes the appearance of the mouse pointer when the constant is applied to the MousePointer property.

Constant	Value	Mouse Pointer Description
vbDefault	0	Default: shape is determined by the object
vbArrow	1	Arrow
vbCrosshair	2	Cross (crosshair pointer)
vbIbeam	3	I-beam
vbIconPointer	4	Icon
vbSizePointer	5	Size: four-headed arrow
vbSizeNESW	6	Size: double-headed arrow
vbSizeNS	7	Size: double-headed arrow
vbSizeNWSE	8	Size: double-headed arrow
vbSizeWE	9	Size: double-headed arrow
vbUpArrow	10	Up arrow
vbHourglass	11	Hourglass
vbNoDrop	12	No drop
vbArrowHourglass	13	Arrow and hourglass (32-bit Visual Basic 4 only)
vbArrowQuestion	14	Arrow and question mark (32-bit Visual Basic 4 only)
vbSizeAll	15	Size all (32-bit Visual Basic 4 only)
vbCustom	99	Custom icon specified by the MouseIcon property

Notice that there are four different double-headed arrows for sizing. Each one of these arrows points in a different direction. The pointing direction is referenced as if your screen were a map, with up as north, down as south, left as west, and right as east. For example, the mouse pointer set with the vbSizeNS constant is a two-headed arrow pointing up and down, and the vbSizeWE constant specifies a double-headed arrow that points left and right. The other two double-headed arrows point diagonally toward the corners of the screen.

One common use of the MousePointer property is that of changing the mouse pointer shape to an hourglass while your program is busy. This pointer lets the user know that something is going on and encourages the user to wait patiently. Figure 15-1 shows the hourglass mouse pointer in action. Be sure to change the pointer back to its previous state when the program has finished its time-consuming task.

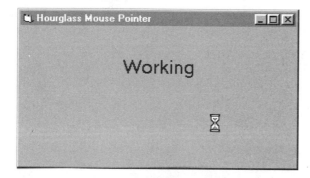

Figure 15-1.
The hourglass mouse pointer that appears while the application is busy.

The following lines of code illustrate this technique; the MousePtr application in Part III provides a more thorough example.

```
frmMain.MousePointer = vbHourglass
ReturnValue = TimeConsumingFunction()
frmMain.MousePointer = vbDefault
```

Notice also that the fairly common "hand" pointer is missing from the list of standard mouse pointers. Visual Basic 4 now allows you to create your own mouse pointer shapes. The MousePtr application presented later in this book demonstrates the creation and display of the hand pointer.

See Also...

- "Dear John, How Do I Create a Custom Mouse Pointer?" below for more information on creating and using custom mouse pointers

- The MousePtr application in Chapter 29 (Part III) for an opportunity to experiment with the mouse pointers and see what they look like

Dear John, How Do I...

Create a Custom Mouse Pointer?

You can use any icon or cursor file as a custom mouse pointer. To do this, set the MousePointer property to *vbCustom* and set the MouseIcon property to the name of the icon (ICO) or cursor (CUR) file. That's all there is to it! You can quickly switch between any of the standard mouse pointers and the custom pointer by resetting the MousePointer property. If you want to change to a second custom pointer, you'll have to assign a different icon to the MouseIcon property. Figure 15-2 shows a left-pointing hand icon loaded from the icons that are part of the Visual Basic 4 package.

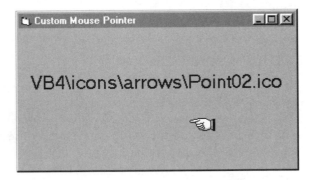

Figure 15-2.
A custom mouse pointer using an icon file.

> NOTE: Animated cursors are not yet supported by Visual Basic's MouseIcon property.

Note that you can create an array of Picture objects, load icon files into these at design time, and assign the Picture properties one at a time to the MouseIcon property to quickly flip through a set of custom mouse pointers.

Dear John, How Do I...

Determine Where the Mouse Pointer Is?

The MouseMove, MouseUp, and MouseDown events can provide you with several useful parameters when they are activated. Search Visual Basic's online help for these events to get a full explanation of their parameters. Note that these events all provide x and y values that tell your application exactly where the mouse pointer is located at the time the event occurs. In most cases, you'll need to copy these x and y values to more permanent variables to keep track of them, depending on what you're trying to accomplish.

A simple example demonstrates this technique clearly. The following code draws lines on your form: one endpoint appears where the mouse button is depressed, and the other endpoint appears where the mouse button is released. Notice that the location of the mouse pointer at the MouseDown event is stored in the module-level variables *X1* and *Y1* so that these values are available to the MouseUp event procedure. When the MouseUp event occurs, the *X1* and *Y1* module-level variables are used with the *X* and *Y* local variables as the starting and ending coordinates for the line. Figure 15-3 shows this simple line-drawing code in action.

```
Option Explicit

Private X1, Y1

Private Sub Form_MouseDown(Button As Integer, Shift As Integer, _
X As Single, Y As Single)
    X1 = X
    Y1 = Y
End Sub

Private Sub Form_MouseUp(Button As Integer, Shift As Integer, _
X As Single, Y As Single)
    Line (X1, Y1)-(X, Y)
End Sub
```

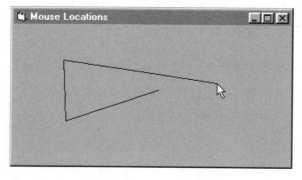

Figure 15-3.
Using the MouseUp and MouseDown events to draw straight line segments.

 See Also...

- The MousePtr application in Chapter 29 (Part III) for a demonstration of mouse pointer location

CHAPTER SIXTEEN

The Keyboard

Here are a few useful ideas for handling user keypresses from within a running Visual Basic application. This chapter covers a few techniques that you might otherwise have overlooked and that you might want to add to your bag of tricks.

Dear John, How Do I...

Change the Behavior of the Enter Key?

Although it's not standard Windows programming practice, you might occasionally want to have the Enter key act like a Tab key when the focus is on a particular control. That is, you might want a press of the Enter key to move the focus to the next control instead of having it cause any other action. The following code does the trick for a text box and can be modified to work on any other control that provides a KeyPress event. (This won't work with the command button because no KeyPress event is available.)

```
Private Sub txtText1_KeyPress(KeyAscii As Integer)
    If KeyAscii = vbKeyReturn Then
        SendKeys "{tab}"
        KeyAscii = 0
    End If
End Sub
```

The ASCII code for the pressed key is handed to the KeyPress event in the KeyAscii parameter. The ASCII value of the Enter key is 13, which is the value of the built-in constant vbKeyReturn. *SendKeys* lets your Visual Basic application send any keypress to the window that currently has the focus. (This is a very handy statement because it lets your application send keystrokes to other Windows-based applications just as easily as to itself.) The string {tab} shows how *SendKeys* sends a Tab keypress, which will be processed exactly as if the Tab key had really been pressed. To override the default action of the Enter key, set the KeyAscii value to *0*. If you don't do this, you'll get a beep from the control.

If you want to ignore all Enter keypresses when the focus is on a particular control, you can easily set this up: simply assign *0* to KeyAscii to ignore the Enter key, as above, and don't use *SendKeys* to substitute any other keypress.

Dear John, How Do I...

Determine the State of the Shift Keys?

The KeyPress event does not directly detect the state of the Shift, Ctrl, and Alt keys (collectively known as the shift keys) at the time of a keypress, but the Shift key state does modify the character (by making it an uppercase or lowercase letter, for example) that is detected. To directly detect the state of these shift keys, you can use the closely related KeyDown and KeyUp event routines. You can act on the state of these keys directly in the KeyDown and KeyUp events, or you can keep track of their states in module-level variables. I prefer the second technique in many cases because it lets me act on the shift keys' states from within the KeyPress event routine or from any other code in the module.

The following code immediately updates the state of one of three Boolean variables whenever any of the shift keys is depressed or released. I've used the Visual Basic constants vbShiftMask, vbCtrlMask, and vbAltMask to test for each of the shift states and return a Boolean value. To enable this code for the entire form, be sure to set the form's KeyPreview property to *True*. Then, regardless of which control is active, your code can instantaneously check the state of the three shift keys simply by referring to the current value of these variables.

```
Option Explicit

Private ShiftState As Boolean
Private CtrlState As Boolean
Private AltState As Boolean

Private Sub Form_KeyDown(KeyCode As Integer, Shift As Integer)
    ShiftState = (Shift And vbShiftMask)
    CtrlState = (Shift And vbCtrlMask)
    AltState = (Shift And vbAltMask)
End Sub
```

(continued)

```
Private Sub Form_KeyUp(KeyCode As Integer, Shift As Integer)
    ShiftState = (Shift And vbShiftMask)
    CtrlState = (Shift And vbCtrlMask)
    AltState = (Shift And vbAltMask)
End Sub
Private Sub tmrTest_Timer()
    Cls
    Print "Shift = "; ShiftState
    Print "Ctrl  = "; CtrlState
    Print "Alt   = "; AltState
End Sub
```

To see how this code works, create a new form, add the code to the form, and add a timer named tmrTest. Set the timer's Interval property to *100* to sample the state of the keys every 0.1 second. The preceding code will then display the state of the shift keys as you press them. Try holding down combinations of the Shift, Ctrl, and Alt keys to see how all three state variables are updated independently. Figure 16-1 shows the form as it appears when the Ctrl and Alt keys are simultaneously held down.

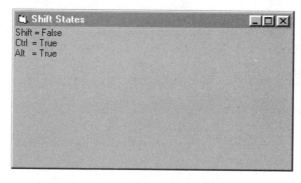

Figure 16-1.
Real-time display of the status of the shift keys.

Dear John, How Do I...

Create Hot Keys?

The KeyPreview property for Visual Basic forms provides an excellent way to set up hot keys. This property lets your application act on any combination of keypresses, such as function keys, shifted function keys, or numeric keypad keys. Here's the general technique: First set your form's KeyPreview property to *True*, and then add code to the form's KeyDown event to check for and act on any desired keypresses. In the following code, I check for F1, F2, and any of the shift keys in combination with the F3 key. I use the Visual Basic constants vbKeyF1, vbKeyF2, and vbKeyF3 to identify the key that is pressed. Note that this type of procedure works well to test only one or just a few keys, but the technique in the previous topic would help simplify the key tests if we needed to check several function keys for the current shift keys' states.

```
Private Sub Form_KeyDown(KeyCode As Integer, Shift As Integer)
    Select Case KeyCode
    Case vbKeyF1
        Print "F1"
    Case vbKeyF2
        Print "F2"
    Case vbKeyF3
        If (Shift And vbShiftMask) Then
            Print "Shift-F3"
        ElseIf (Shift And vbCtrlMask) Then
            Print "Ctrl-F3"
        ElseIf (Shift And vbAltMask) Then
            Print "Alt-F3"
        Else
            Print "F3"
        End If
    End Select
End Sub
```

Figure 16-2 shows the result of running this code and pressing a few of the function keys. Note that the form intercepts the keypresses before the Command1 button receives them, even though Command1 has the focus.

Figure 16-2.
A demonstration of the hot key code.

See Also...

- "Dear John, How Do I Determine the State of the Shift Keys?" earlier in this chapter

- The Jot application in Chapter 28 (Part III) for a demonstration of this hot key setup

Text Box and Rich Text Box Tricks

One of the most powerful and useful new controls in Visual Basic 4 is the RichTextBox control. With just a few simple changes to the control's property settings, a rich text box can become a decent editor, with capabilities similar to those of Windows' WordPad utility. This chapter shows you how to accomplish this and also explains a few other techniques that take your TextBox and RichTextBox control capabilities to new heights.

Dear John, How Do I...

Display a File?

You can set up either a text box or a rich text box as a convenient way to display the contents of a file. The following code loads the Autoexec.bat file and displays its contents in a scrollable window, as shown in Figure 17-1 on the following page. To try this example, draw one of these controls on a new form and name it either txtTest (if you're using a text box) or rtfTest (if you're using a rich text box). You'll need to set a couple of the control's properties: set MultiLine to *True* and ScrollBars to *3 - Both*. If you want to view a file other than Autoexec.bat, change the filename in the Open statement. In the following example, I've used a RichTextBox control to display my Autoexec.bat file, but you can easily substitute a TextBox control if desired.

```
Option Explicit

Private Sub Form_Load()
Dim F$
    'Load a file into a string
    Open "C:\Autoexec.bat" For Binary As #1
```

(continued)

```
      F$ = Space$(LOF(1))
      Get #1, , F$
      Close #1
      'Display file in rich text box
      rtfTest.Text = F$
End Sub
```

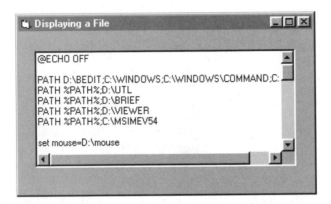

Figure 17-1.
The contents of Autoexec.bat displayed in a scrollable rich text box.

In the above example, the entire Autoexec.bat file is read into a single string using binary file input. Binary file input is a useful technique because it reads every byte from the file regardless of the content of the byte. This means that when a file with multiple lines is read into a single string, the linefeeds and carriage returns are included in the string. (Chapter 11, "File I/O," goes into greater detail about binary file input/output techniques.)

There's another technique that you should know about for building a multiline string. You can concatenate strings (tack them together end to end), but you must insert a carriage return and a linefeed at the end of each string. The following code demonstrates this. This example performs the same action as in the previous example, except that in this case Autoexec.bat is loaded from the file one line at a time to build up the string for the text box. Compare this code with the previous listing.

```
Option Explicit

Private Sub Form_Load()
Dim A$, F$
    'Load a file into a string
    Open "C:\Autoexec.bat" For Input As #1
```

(continued)

```
    Do Until EOF(1)
        Line Input #1, A$
        F$ = F$ & A$ & vbCrLf
    Loop
    Close #1
    'Display file in rich text box
    rtfTest.Text = F$
End Sub
```

NOTE: In previous versions of Visual Basic, you had to create a string of carriage return and linefeed characters yourself. Visual Basic 4 now provides the built-in constant vbCrLf, as shown in the example above.

In the past, I have used a TextBox control in both of these examples, but even in 32-bit Visual Basic 4 the TextBox control has a maximum limit of roughly 64,000 characters. For smaller files, such as Autoexec.bat shown above, a TextBox control will work just fine, but I suggest using the new Rich-TextBox control because of its greater flexibility.

See Also...

- "Dear John, How Do I Fit More than 64 KB of Text into a Text Box?" later in this chapter

Dear John, How Do I...

Create a Simple Text Editor?

If you need a full-featured word processor window in your application, consider using OLE capabilities to embed a Microsoft Word document object. But if you just want a simple text editor along the lines of the Windows Note-Pad or WordPad utility, a TextBox or RichTextBox control is probably all you need. Let's see how you can do this by building a simple editor on a form. The following code shows how to build the text editor, and Figure 17-2 on page 201 shows the completed text editor in action.

```
Option Explicit

Private Sub cmdCut_Click()
    'Cut selected text to clipboard
    Dim Work$
```

(continued)

199

```
        Dim Wstart, Wlength

        'Keep focus on rich text box
        rtfEdit.SetFocus

        'Get working parameters
        Work$ = rtfEdit.Text
        Wstart = rtfEdit.SelStart
        Wlength = rtfEdit.SelLength

        'Copy cut text to clipboard
        Clipboard.SetText Mid$(Work$, Wstart + 1, Wlength)

        'Cut out text
        Work$ = Left$(Work$, Wstart) + _
            Mid$(Work$, Wstart + Wlength + 1)
        rtfEdit.Text = Work$

        'Position edit cursor
        rtfEdit.SelStart = Wstart
End Sub

Private Sub cmdCopy_Click()
        'Copy selected text to clipboard
        'Keep focus on edit box
        rtfEdit.SetFocus
        Clipboard.SetText rtfEdit.SelText
End Sub

Private Sub cmdPaste_Click()
        'Paste text from clipboard
        Dim Work$, Clip$
        Dim Wstart, Wlength

        'Keep focus on rich text box
        rtfEdit.SetFocus

        'Get working parameters
        Work$ = rtfEdit.Text
        Wstart = rtfEdit.SelStart
        Wlength = rtfEdit.SelLength

        'Cut out text, if any, and insert clipboard text
        Clip$ = Clipboard.GetText()
        Work$ = Left$(Work$, Wstart) + Clip$ + _
            Mid$(Work$, Wstart + Wlength + 1)
```

(continued)

```
        rtfEdit.Text = Work$

        'Position edit cursor
        rtfEdit.SelStart = Wstart + Len(Clip$)
End Sub
```

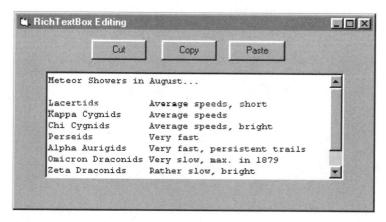

Figure 17-2.
A rich text box editor in action.

In this case, the RichTextBox control is named rtfEdit. Be sure to set its MultiLine property to *True*, and set the ScrollBars property as desired. If you think that the user might type more text than will fit into the window, set the ScrollBars property to *2 - Vertical.* If the horizontal scrollbar is not present, text will wrap automatically as the user types past the right edge of the text box. If the horizontal scrollbar is present, however, the user must press the Enter key to proceed to the next line. Try it both ways to see the difference and to determine which setting best suits your requirements.

The form contains three command buttons: cmdCut, cmdCopy, and cmdPaste. You don't really need these buttons if you want to rely on the Ctrl-X, Ctrl-C, and Ctrl-V shortcut keys because these keys are automatically processed by the control to cut, copy, and paste without any additional coding on your part. The code I've added for these command buttons allows them to mimic the action of the control keys and provides more flexibility in your programming. You might, for example, want to add a standard Edit menu to the form, and this code is the only convenient way to process menu events. Simply copy the code to the corresponding menu item Click event to set up your own menu-driven cut, copy, and paste routines.

So when would you want to use a TextBox control instead of a RichTextBox control? Even in 32-bit Visual Basic 4, there's a limit of roughly 64,000 characters for the Text property of a TextBox control. The new 32-bit RichTextBox control removes this restriction and allows for extremely large pieces of text. However, if you're programming for 16-bit applications, the text box is the only option you have. Virtually anything a text box can do a rich text box can do better. I haven't even touched on the multiple fonts and the rich set of embedded RTF (rich text format) commands, or the many methods and properties of the RichTextBox control that make it much more powerful and adaptable than the TextBox control. See the online help and printed documentation for more information on all these details.

See Also...

- The Jot application in Chapter 28 (Part III) for a demonstration of the use of a rich text box as a text editor

Dear John, How Do I...

Detect Changed Text?

The Change event is a text box/rich text box event, and you would think that this would make it easy to detect whether a control's contents are edited by the user while a form is displayed. But it gets a little tricky. Usually the initial or default text is loaded into the Text property when the control's form loads. This causes the control's Change event to occur, even though the text has not yet been changed by the user, which is what we're really trying to detect.

The following code solves this problem for a RichTextBox control by manipulating two Boolean flags, but the same method can be used with a TextBox control. The *NotFirstFlag* variable is set to *True* after the first Change event takes place. The *TextChangeFlag* is set to *True* only if the *NotFirstFlag* is *True*. This happens the second time the control's Change event occurs, which is when the user makes the first change to the text in the rtfEditBox text box. *TextChangeFlag*'s scope is the entire form, so it's easy to check the value of the flag in the form's Unload event routine. In the sample code here, the unloading of the form is disabled if the contents have been changed by the user. When you use this technique in your applications, you might want to perform some other action beyond this simple example. To try this example, place a rich text box named rtfEdit on a form. When you run the program, change the text in the rich text box and then try to unload the form by pressing the Alt-F4 key combination to close the form.

```
Option Explicit

Private TextChangeFlag As Boolean

Private Sub Form_Load()
    rtfEdit.Text = "Edit this string..."
    TextChangeFlag = False
End Sub

Private Sub Form_Unload(Cancel As Integer)
    If TextChangeFlag = True Then
        Cancel = True
        MsgBox "Save changes first", 0, _
            "(Testing the Change event...)"
    End If
End Sub

Private Sub rtfEdit_Change()
    Static NotFirstFlag As Boolean
    TextChangeFlag = NotFirstFlag
    NotFirstFlag = True
End Sub
```

Dear John, How Do I...

Fit More than 64 KB of Text into a Text Box?

In 16-bit Visual Basic 4 applications, the Text property for a text box is limited to less than 64 KB of text. (Actually, depending on how you are using string space, the limit might be around 32 KB.) In the 32-bit version of Visual Basic 4, you can use the RichTextBox control instead of a text box to bypass this limitation. This book is focused on 32-bit programming for Windows 95, so I considered not addressing this topic. However, the techniques shown here, such as using the *Preserve* modifier with the *ReDim* statement, are quite useful for other programming tasks, so I decided to include this topic in the book. If you are doing 16-bit programming, you'll find it immediately useful. If you are doing 32-bit programming, read on anyway, because the techniques presented here are useful additions to your bag of tricks.

You can work around the text box string size limitation by placing the text in an array and then assigning an element of the array to the Text property of a TextBox control. With this method, the individual array elements are limited to less than 64 KB, but because arrays can be huge even in 16-bit Visual Basic 4, a very large amount of text can be contained in the array and subsequently displayed in the text box. In the example shown here, the text box will contain only a handful of lines, but these lines will be quickly updated from a huge dynamic string array that contains more than 64 KB of text. Figure 17-3 shows the result of using this technique to display a text file containing 105,824 bytes in a text box.

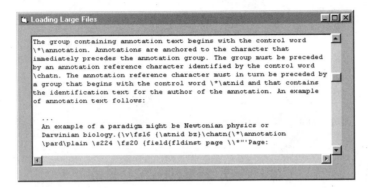

Figure 17-3.
Displaying a large text file in a text box.

To re-create this example, add a text box named txtTest and a vertical scrollbar named vsbTest to a new form. Set the text box's MultiLine property to *True* and its ScrollBars property to *1 - Horizontal*. The vertical scrollbar takes the place of the text box's built-in scrollbar, so move it to the right edge of the text box so that it appears to be attached to it. Add the following code to the form, and change the name of the file in the *Open* statement to the name of a file on your disk.

```
Option Explicit

Private Const LINES = 15
Private A$()

Private Sub Form_Load()
    Dim n
    'Load dynamic string array from large text file
    Open "D:\Txt\Rtf-spec.txt" For Input As #1 Len = 1024
    Do Until EOF(1)
        n = n + 1
        ReDim Preserve A$(n + LINES)
        Line Input #1, A$(n)
    Loop
    Close #1
    'Set scrollbar properties
```

(continued)

```
        With vsbTest
            .Min = 1
            .Max = n
            .SmallChange = 1
            .LargeChange = n \ 10
        End With
    End Sub

    Private Sub vsbTest_Change()
    Dim i As Integer
    Dim Tmp$
        'Create display string from array elements
        For i = vsbTest.Value To vsbTest.Value + LINES
            Tmp$ = Tmp$ + A$(i) + vbCrLf
        Next i
        txtTest.Text = Tmp$
    End Sub
```

At form load time, the entire large text file is read into a dynamically allocated string array. This can take a few seconds, so in a real application you might want to load the file while other things are going on so that the user doesn't become anxious. For this demonstration, you can use any text file greater than 64 KB in size, but be prepared to wait if the file is very large.

Once the file is loaded into memory, the string array dimensions are used to set the vertical scrollbar's properties. The text box contents are updated whenever the vertical scrollbar's value changes. A block of strings from the string array are concatenated, with carriage return and linefeed characters inserted at the end of each line, and the resulting temporary string is copied into the text box's Text property.

This demonstration only displays the file's contents and doesn't attempt to keep track of changes made by the user. If you want to turn this text box into a text editor, you'll have to add code to update the string array when there are changes to the text box's contents.

Dear John, How Do I...

Allow the User to Select a Font for a Text Box or a Rich Text Box?

The CommonDialog control provides the most convenient and foolproof way to let the user select a font at runtime. (It's also the best tool for allowing the user to select files, choose colors, set up a printer, and so on.) To experiment with this technique, add a text box named txtTest, a command button named cmdFont, and a CommonDialog control named dlgFonts to a new form. Add the following code to complete the demonstration:

```
Option Explicit

Private Sub cmdFont_Click()
    dlgFonts.Flags = cdlCFScreenFonts
    dlgFonts.ShowFont
    With txtTest.Font
        .Name = dlgFonts.FontName
        .Bold = dlgFonts.FontBold
        .Italic = dlgFonts.FontItalic
        .Size = dlgFonts.FontSize
    End With
End Sub

Private Sub Form_Load()
    txtTest.Text = "ABCDEF abcdef 0123456789"
End Sub
```

The Form_Load routine simply loads the text box with some sample text so that the font changes can be seen. The cmdFont_Click routine does the interesting stuff. It first sets the CommonDialog control's Flag property to display the system's screen fonts (see the online help for other Flag options), then it activates the *ShowFont* method to activate the dialog box, and then it sets the text box font properties according to the user's selections. Figures 17-4 and 17-5 show the text box before and after font selection, and Figure 17-6 shows the font selection dialog box itself.

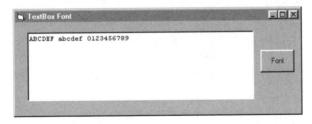

Figure 17-4.
Text box showing font properties at their default settings.

Figure 17-5.
Text box font set to user's font choice.

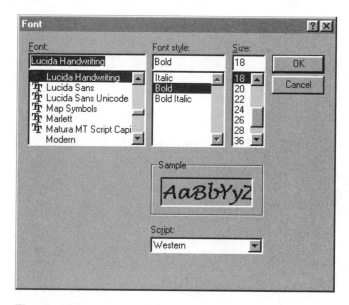

Figure 17-6.
The font selection dialog box in action.

NOTE: The TextBox control allows just one font at a time to be in use for the entire control, but the RichTextBox control allows fonts to vary throughout its text contents. Refer to the rich text box properties that start with "Sel" (there are a lot of them) in the Visual Basic online help for a detailed explanation of how to manipulate character fonts within the RichTextBox control.

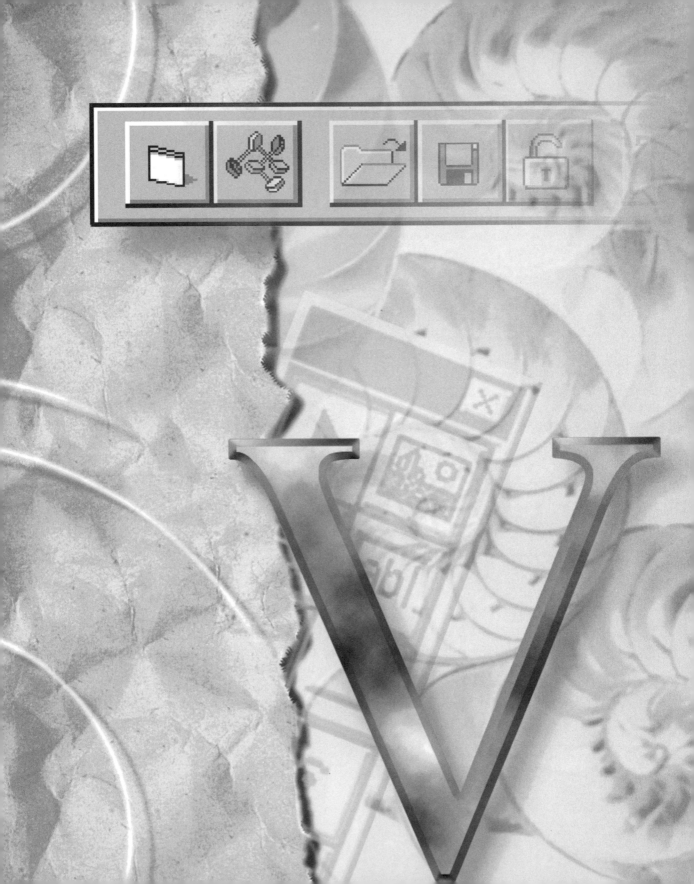

CHAPTER EIGHTEEN

Multiple-Document Interface

With each new version of Visual Basic, the multiple-document interface (MDI) capabilities get better. For a lot of applications, the MDI metaphor provides an ideal framework for structuring the user interface, but some of the tricky nuances of this interface have prevented many of us from taking full advantage of it. This chapter highlights some of the main concepts behind creating an MDI application and provides a solid background upon which to expand your expertise.

Dear John, How Do I...

Create an MDI Application?

This topic provides concise coverage of the basic concepts of creating an MDI application. For more details, refer to the Visual Basic 4 online help or the printed documentation.

When I first started working with MDI forms, I had trouble integrating all the relevant information in such a way that it made sense to me. The following discussion should give you a better foothold than I had.

The MDI Form

A Visual Basic project can have only one MDI form. The MDI form is the container for all the individual child forms. To add an MDI form to your project, open the Insert menu in the Visual Basic development environment and click on MDI Form. You'll notice that this form has a shorter list of properties than a standard form. The MDI form doesn't have to be the startup form for your application, but you can make it so by selecting Options from the Tools menu and, in the Project tab of the dialog box that appears, selecting the MDI form from the Startup Form drop-down list box.

MDI Child Forms

Your project can have any number of child forms contained in an MDI form. (And it can have any number of independent, nonchild, forms too.) To create a child form, set a standard form's MDIChild property to *True*. The form becomes a child of the MDI form in your project. At runtime, the program code is responsible for loading these child forms and showing, hiding, or unloading them as desired. Notice that, at design time, child forms look and act just like standard forms. The big difference in their behavior shows up at runtime.

Figure 18-1 shows a running MDI application with an assortment of child forms. I've minimized some of the child forms and displayed others.

Figure 18-1.
A sample MDI form with an assortment of child forms.

The ActiveForm and ActiveControl Properties

When used together, the ActiveForm and ActiveControl properties let your MDI form refer to controls on the child form that currently has the focus. For example, your MDI application might have identical text controls on several child forms. When text is highlighted in a text box in one of these child forms, and when a Copy menu item is clicked, the ActiveForm.ActiveControl.SelText property refers to the text selected in the currently active text box on the currently active child form.

The *Me* Keyword

The *Me* keyword functions like a variable, referring to the identity of the active child window. When multiple instances of a child form are created, *Me* provides a way for the code that was designed for the original form to operate on the specific instance of that form that currently has the focus.

The Tag Property

The Tag property provides a handy way to uniquely identify exact copies of child forms. As each new copy is created, have a number or string placed into its Tag property. This creates an index, somewhat like an array index, that keeps track of forms that are otherwise identical copies of one another.

Fundamental MDI Features

The MDI form is unique when compared to other forms. The following features of the MDI form should be kept in mind when you are designing and coding MDI applications:

- Child forms always appear in the MDI form and never appear elsewhere. Even when minimized, the child form icons appear only in the MDI form. They ride along with the MDI form—for instance, when the MDI form is minimized you'll see nothing of the child forms it contains.

- If a child form has a menu, that menu shows up on the MDI form when that child form has the focus. At runtime, you'll never see menus on any child forms; they instantly migrate to the parent MDI form.

- You can add a menu to the MDI form at design time, but the only controls that can be added are those with an Align property. (There is a way to work around this, though—simply draw a picture box on the MDI form and draw your controls inside this box.) When a control is placed on the MDI form, child windows cannot overlap any part of the control.

- You can create multiple instances of a single child form at runtime using the *Dim As New* statement. In many MDI applications, this is an extremely important feature. As mentioned above, the Active-Form, ActiveControl, and Tag properties and the *Me* keyword are very useful for working with multiple copies of child forms. Take a look at the online help for more information.

■ A new MDIForm property, Picture, now lets you install a bitmap or other graphic images onto the backdrop of the MDI form. This is handy for displaying graphics such as company logos.

See Also...

- The Jot application in Chapter 28 (Part III) to see how a single child edit form is mass-produced to let the user edit in multiple windows

Dear John, How Do I...

Add a Logo (Splash Screen) to an MDI Form?

It's tricky to place an image in the center of an MDI form. The new Picture property always plops an image in the upper-left corner, and only aligned controls can be placed on an MDI form. But an MDI form makes a good backdrop for an entire application, and it's nice to be able to put your company logo right in the middle of things. Here's a workaround that displays a logo (or any image) in the middle of your MDI form. With this technique, the logo stays there even if the form is resized. Figure 18-2 shows an imaginary application at startup. In this application, the MDI form is set as the startup form and the company logo appears centered on the form.

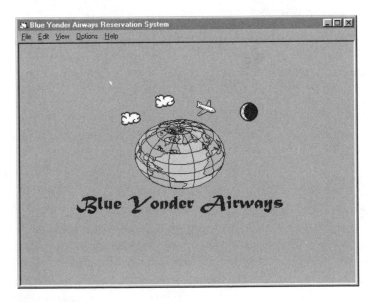

Figure 18-2.
An MDI form displaying a centered logo.

To try this example, create a new project containing an MDI form and one child form named frmLogo. Add an image control named imgLogo to the child form. You can't add the image control directly to the MDI form, and if you use a picture box to contain the image control (or to directly display the logo), you won't be able to center the logo if the MDI form is resized. By placing the image control on the child window, you can always center the child form and thus center the logo. So the trick here is to size frmLogo to the size of the image, remove frmLogo's borders and title bar, and then keep frmLogo centered on the MDI form. Set frmLogo's MDIChild property to *True* and the BorderStyle property to *0 - None*. Load a bitmap logo file into imgLogo. Don't worry about the placement of this image on frmLogo—the runtime code shown below will take care of these details. Add this code to the MDI form and give it a try:

```
Option Explicit

Private Sub MDIForm_Resize()
    'Move logo to upper-left corner of Image control
    frmLogo.imgLogo.Move 0, 0
    'Size form to size of image it contains
    frmLogo.Width = frmLogo.imgLogo.Width
    frmLogo.Height = frmLogo.imgLogo.Height
    'Center logo form on MDI form
    frmLogo.Left = (ScaleWidth - frmLogo.Width) \ 2
    frmLogo.Top = (ScaleHeight - frmLogo.Height) \ 2
    'Show logo
    frmLogo.Show
End Sub
```

The image is moved to the upper-left corner of its containing form. The form is then resized to match the image size and is relocated to the center of the MDI form. I've put this code in the MDIForm_Resize event so that the logo will always shift to the center of the form if the form is resized.

Database Access

Microsoft's evolving approach to data access has been increasingly evident in recent versions of Visual Basic. Visual Basic 4 has many new features that make it an ideal language for all of your database programming requirements. Although a full discussion of database programming is beyond the scope of this book, this chapter provides a short introduction to give you a feel for this important subject. For more in-depth information, see Visual Basic's printed documentation and online help. Excellent coverage is also provided in the Microsoft Office Developer's Kit (ODK).

This chapter covers the two different ways to connect a Visual Basic application to a database. The first technique uses the Data control and is a simple and straightforward approach that requires very little programming; and the second uses data access objects, which provide flexible, complete control of a database.

Dear John, How Do I...

Use the Data Control to Connect an Application to a Database?

Let's put together a very simple database using a Data control. You must take two basic steps to accomplish this: create a database and then create the user interface.

Create a Database

You can programmatically create a database, which we'll do in the next topic, or you can create a database using the add-in Data Manager tool. When I am working with a Data control, I prefer to use the Data Manager for this one-time task. This utility lets you create a database by defining its tables and fields.

To create a database using the Data Manager utility, follow these steps:

1. From the Add-ins menu, choose Data Manager.

2. Click on No if a dialog box appears that asks whether you want to "Add SYSTEM.MDA (Jet Security File) to INI File?" For this example, you do not need file security. The Data Manager utility starts, and the Data Manager window is displayed.

3. From the Data Manager's File menu, choose New Database. The New Database dialog box appears.

4. Type *Bday* in the dialog box to name the file, and click on Save. The filename extension MDB is automatically added to the filename. The Database window appears. At this point, the database exists, but it contains no table or field definitions.

5. Click on the New button in the Database window to add a new table. The Add Table dialog box appears.

6. Type *Birthdays* in the Name text box. This is the name of our one and only table.

7. Type *Name* in the Field Name text box to define the first field of the table.

8. Choose Text from the Data Type drop-down list box to define the type of data contained in the field.

9. Type *30* in the Size text box to define the maximum number of characters that can be contained in the field.

10. Click on the > button to add the field definition to the list of fields in the current table. You can now enter the definitions for the second field.

11. Type *Birthday* in the Field Name text box, select Date/Time from the Data Type drop-down list box, and click on the > button to define the second field and add the field definition to the list of fields.

12. Click on OK to close the New Table dialog box, and then choose Exit from the File menu to close the Data Manager and return to Visual Basic.

Now we have properly defined the database, although it contains no valid records yet.

Create the User Interface

Our database now needs a user interface. Start with a new form, and draw three controls on Form1: a text box named txtName, a second text box named txtBirthday, and a Data control named datBDay. The completed form, containing some sample data, is shown in Figure 19-1.

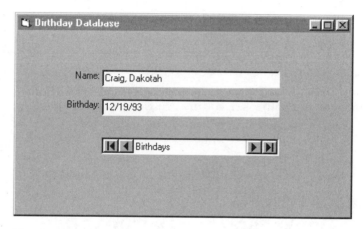

Figure 19-1.
A simple birthday database application using a Data control.

The key to using the Data control and associated data-bound controls is to set the properties correctly. Always start with the Data control by setting its DatabaseName property to the name of the database file to be connected. In this case, set DatabaseName to *Bday.mdb*, the file we just created with the Data Manager. Set the Data control's RecordSource property to *Birthdays*, the name of the table in the database that this Data control is to reference. Generally speaking, one Data control is associated with one table in a database.

In this example, we have one other property to set on the Data control. We need to be able to add new records when the application runs. Set the EOFAction property to *2 - Add New*. Now, when the user scrolls to the blank record at the end of the database and fills in a new name and birthdate, the database is automatically updated to contain the new record.

The Data control doesn't do much by itself. What we need to do is to associate other controls with the Data control. When they are associated, or data-bound, the controls become tools for working with the database. In our example, we use the DataSource and DataField properties of the text boxes to make these controls data-bound to the datBDay Data control. Set the Data-Source property of each text box to *datBDay*, the name of the Data control; and set the DataField property of each text box to the name of the field it's to

217

be associated with. Set txtName's DataField to *Name* and txtBirthday's to *Birthday*. These database-related properties often provide a pull-down list of available tables and fields after the Data control connection has been made, making it easier to set these properties.

Run the Application

That's it! You don't need to write any code to work with the database. Run the application, enter a new name and birth date, and click on the Data control's next record scrollbar arrow. You'll probably want to add some code and modify some of the properties to customize the application.

This simple example doesn't let you delete records or search for specific names or dates in the database. To turn this into a real application, you'd need to add code to provide capabilities along these lines.

Dear John, How Do I...

Use Data Access Objects to Connect an Application to a Database?

Objects are everywhere in Visual Basic 4, and one of the areas in which they've enhanced the language the most is data access. Let's use these objects, without touching a Data control at all, to build another simple database application. But first let's chart out the data access objects in Visual Basic 4.

Data Access Objects

One of the best ways to understand the organization of objects in Visual Basic is to study a chart that shows the hierarchy of these objects. The hierarchy of data access objects is shown in Figure 19-2. As I learned about data objects, this chart helped me see where collections and objects fit into the scheme of things, and with its help I was able to get the syntax down pat for accessing these nested objects.

I've put *(s)* on object names that can also be names of collections of objects. For example, there's a Workspace object, and then there's the Workspaces collection, of which Workspaces(0) is the first Workspace object. All object names follow this same scheme: the pluralizing *s* is added to the name of a type of object to name the collection. Notice in Figure 19-2 that the only data access object that is not part of a collection is DBEngine. There's only one DBEngine.

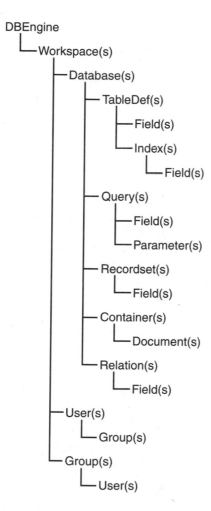

Figure 19-2.
The structure of data access objects in Visual Basic 4.

The sample code presented in this topic provides examples that declare and use these objects. Compare the notation I've used to access these objects with the structure shown in Figure 19-2. If any of this notation seems confusing, be sure to search the online help for these object names and study the examples and explanations you'll find there.

Creating a Database

The following short program creates a telephone number database from scratch, using only data access objects (no Data control). I've made this database similar to the birthday database we created earlier so that you can easily compare the two. In this case, two text fields are created: one for a name and one for its associated telephone number (or any other text you want to enter, such as an email address).

To create this example, start with a new form and add one command button named cmdCreate. Set the button's Caption property to *Create*. Be sure that you have the DAO library as a reference or you will get an error. If it is not referenced, choose References from the Tools menu and turn on the Microsoft DAO 3.0 Object Library check box. Add the following code to this button's Click event routine. Be sure to change the database file path and filename as desired if you don't want the new database to appear in the root directory of your C drive.

```
Option Explicit

Private Sub cmdCreate_Click()
    'Create data access object variables
    Dim dbWorkspace As Workspace
    Dim dbDatabase As Database
    Dim dbTableDef As TableDef
    Dim dbName As Field
    Dim dbNumber As Field
    'Create data access objects
    Set dbWorkspace = DBEngine.Workspaces(0)
    Set dbDatabase = dbWorkspace.CreateDatabase( _
        "C:\Phones.mdb", dbLangGeneral)
    Set dbTableDef = dbDatabase.CreateTableDef("Phones")
    Set dbName = dbTableDef.CreateField("Name", dbText)
    Set dbNumber = dbTableDef.CreateField("Number", dbText)
    'Set field properties
    dbName.Size = 30
    dbNumber.Size = 30
    'Append each field object to its table object
    dbTableDef.Fields.Append dbName
    dbTableDef.Fields.Append dbNumber
    'Append each table to its database
    dbDatabase.TableDefs.Append dbTableDef
    Close completed database
    dbDatabase.Close
    MsgBox "Database Created"
End Sub
```

Figure 19-3 shows this short program in action. All you have to do is click on the button once to create the new database. I've put a lot of comments in the code to describe the action, but the overall design of the routine is as follows: First all object variables are declared, and then objects are created and set to be referenced by these variable names. That describes roughly the first half of the preceding code. These new objects have properties and methods, and the rest of the code deals with these. The Size property of the two text fields is set, and then the various objects are linked to each other using the *Append* method of each. This completes the creation of the structure of the new database.

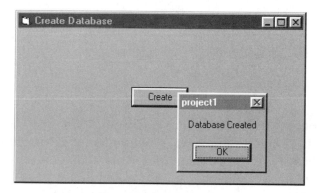

Figure 19-3.
Creating a database with the click of a button.

Note that although the new Phones database contains no valid data, the internal structure is complete and ready to go. We've created one table, Phones, and two text fields in this table, Name and Number. These two text fields are fixed to a maximum length of 30 characters.

NOTE: If, in the course of your experimentation, you want to start all over with the Phones database, simply delete the Phones .mdb file and rerun this program.

Accessing the Database

Now let's create a simple program to access the Phones database, again without using a Data control. I've kept this demonstration simple: the following application lets you move forward and backward through the table's records, append new records, and type any text (up to 30 characters) to change the records as desired. To enhance this application, you'd probably want to add code to delete records, search and sort, and so on.

Start with a new project and add two buttons. Name the buttons cmdPrevious and cmdNext, and set their caption properties to *Previous* and *Next*. Then add two text boxes and name them txtName and txtNumber. Figure 19-4 on the following page shows how I placed and sized these controls.

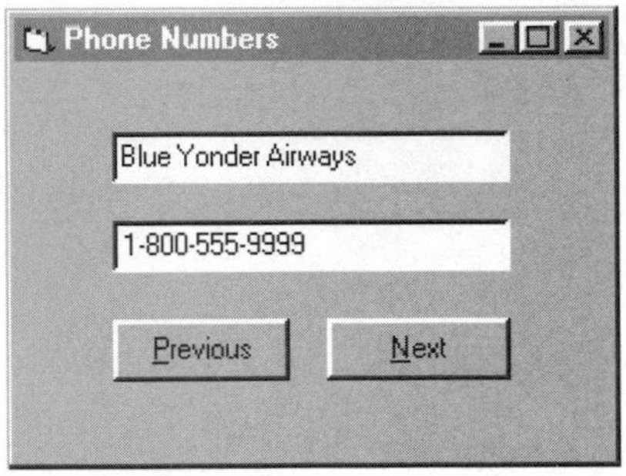

Figure 19-4.
The simple phone number database program in action.

The following code completes the demonstration. Add it to your form, and when you run it you'll have a working, albeit simple, database editor. Be sure to check the database file's pathname and filename to ensure that they match the location of the Phones database we created in the previous short program and that your project references the Microsoft DAO 3.0 Object Library. If it is not referenced, choose References from the Tools menu and turn on the Microsoft DAO 3.0 Object Library check box.

```
Option Explicit

'Create new data access object variables
Private dbWorkspace As Workspace
Private dbDatabase As Database
Private dbTable As Recordset
Private dbName As Field
Private dbNumber As Field

Private Sub cmdNext_Click()
    'Move only if current record isn't a blank one
    If txtName.Text <> " " And txtNumber.Text <> " " Then
        'Save any changes to current record
        UpdateRecord
        'Move to next record
        dbTable.MoveNext
        'Prepare new record if at end of table
        If dbTable.EOF Then NewRecord
        'Display data from record
        DisplayFields
```

(continued)

```
        End If
        'Keep focus on text boxes
        txtName.SetFocus
    End Sub

    Private Sub cmdPrevious_Click()
        'Save any changes to current record
        UpdateRecord
        'Step back one record
        dbTable.MovePrevious
        'Don't go past first record
        If dbTable.BOF Then dbTable.MoveNext
        'Display data from record
        DisplayFields
        'Keep focus on text boxes
        txtName.SetFocus
    End Sub

    Private Sub Form_Load()
        'Create data access objects
        Set dbWorkspace = DBEngine.Workspaces(0)
        'Change database path if neccessary
        Set dbDatabase = dbWorkspace.OpenDatabase("C:\Phones.mdb")
        Set dbTable = dbDatabase.OpenRecordset("Phones", dbOpenTable)
        'Use special handling if new database
        If dbTable.BOF And dbTable.EOF Then NewRecord
        'Start on first record
        dbTable.MoveFirst
        'Display data from record
        DisplayFields
    End Sub

    Private Sub NewRecord()
        'Add new record
        dbTable.AddNew
        'Install a space in each field
        dbTable!Name = " "
        dbTable!Number = " "
        'Update database
        dbTable.Update
        'Move to new record
        dbTable.MoveLast
    End Sub
```

(continued)

```
Private Sub UpdateRecord()
    'Prepare table for editing
    dbTable.Edit
    'Copy text box contents into record fields
    dbTable!Name = txtName.Text
    dbTable!Number = txtNumber.Text
    'Update database
    dbTable.Update
End Sub

Private Sub DisplayFields()
    'Display fields in the text boxes
    txtName.Text = dbTable!Name
    txtNumber.Text = dbTable!Number
End Sub
```

To make things simple, I've set up this code so that it automatically updates the current record whenever you click on the Previous or Next button. Notice that because we're not using data-bound text controls, it's entirely up to the program's code to coordinate what appears in the text boxes with what's in the fields of the current record. This takes a little more coding than a program using a Data control would require, but it is a lot more flexible.

For example, I've chosen to update the current record as the user moves to the next or the previous record. But it would be easy to update the record whenever any change occurs in either text box or to add an Update button and change the record if and only if this button is clicked. Data access object programming is much more flexible than using Data controls, although it requires a little more effort up front.

CHAPTER TWENTY

OLE Automation

OLE is an important part of Microsoft's vision for Windows and programming for Windows. Central to the overall OLE picture is OLE Automation, the technology that enables objects to be easily shared between applications. More and more applications will begin to provide OLE Automation objects to the external world, and Visual Basic will be able to immediately take advantage of those objects. As shown in the earlier chapter on object-oriented programming, Visual Basic 4 itself now lets you create class modules that define OLE Automation objects for use by external applications. The inclusion of OLE Automation capabilities makes Visual Basic a logical choice for software development in the Windows family of operating systems.

This chapter presents a sampling of common and useful tasks that are simplified by the OLE Automation technology provided in Microsoft Excel and Microsoft Word.

Dear John, How Do I...

Use OLE Automation to Do Spell Checking?

Microsoft Word and Microsoft Excel are two applications that support OLE Automation. Each exposes programmable objects that programmers can easily tap into. Let's see how we can use OLE Automation from Visual Basic to access the spell checker available in each of these applications and return the corrected spelling to our Visual Basic application.

Microsoft Word Spell Checking

The following code creates a WordBasic object and manipulates a few of the object's properties and methods to perform spell checking on a string from within a Visual Basic application. The WordBasic object provides direct access to over 900 WordBasic statements and functions. I've added many comments to the code to help you follow the action, but here's the basic scenario: The WordBasic object is instructed to create a new document, the text is inserted into it, and the spell checker engine is activated for this document. The results are copied into a document variable, from which they are accessed to replace the original text. This code will work with Word version 6 or 7.

```
Option Explicit

Private Sub cmdSpell_Click()
    On Error Resume Next
    Dim wb As Object
    'Use OLE Automation to create a Word object
    Set wb = CreateObject("Word.Basic")
    'Open a new document in Word
    wb.FileNewDefault
    'Copy text into document
    wb.Insert txtTest.Text
    'Run the spell checker
    wb.ToolsSpelling
    'Select all text in document
    wb.EditSelectAll
    'Transfer selection to a document variable
    wb.SetDocumentVar "MyVar", wb.Selection
    'Transfer document variable to a text box
    txtTest.Text = wb.GetDocumentVar("MyVar")
    'Close the Word document
    wb.FileClose 2
    'Remove the WordBasic object from memory
    Set wb = Nothing
End Sub
```

To try this example, create a new Visual Basic application. Add a command button named cmdSpell and a text box named txtTest. The code all goes into the cmdSpell button's Click event. Figure 20-1 shows some incorrectly spelled text just before the Spelling button is clicked, and Figure 20-2 shows Word's spell checker dialog box in action. Figure 20-3 shows the results of running Word's spell checker on the text.

This simple code works fine as long as Word is not already running. If you run the code when another file is already loaded in Word, you will have to manually switch to Word to respond to the Spelling dialog box. Because Word is already serving a file, it will remain running, and you will need to switch back to your Visual Basic application when the spell check is completed. For a complete application, you might want to check to see whether Word is already loaded before running the commands, or you might want to use Word macros to improve the operations of the program.

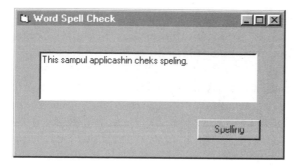

Figure 20-1.
Text as it appears before Word's spell checker is invoked.

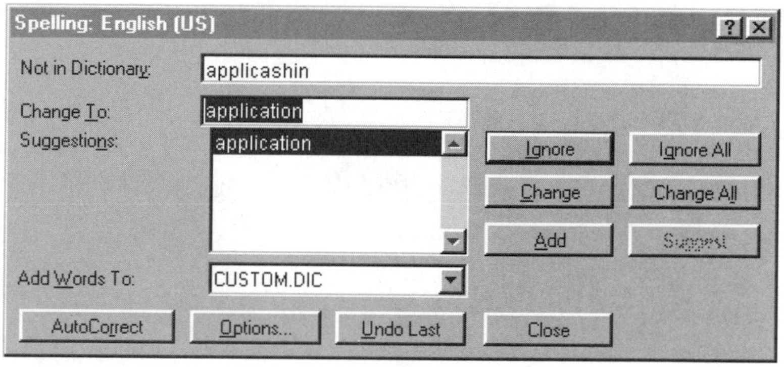

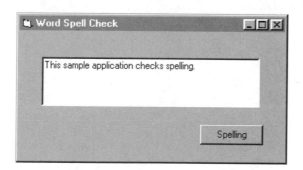

Figure 20-2.
Changing the spelling of the text using Word's spell checker.

Figure 20-3.
Results of invoking Word's spell checker.

Microsoft Excel Spell Checking

Programming through OLE Automation to access the spell checker engine in Excel is similar to the Word example. The code for this example accomplishes the same results, as shown in Figures 20-4 and 20-5. One noticeable difference between the Excel and Word versions of this example is the appearance of the external application. When WordBasic objects are created, Word loads itself into memory and displays itself, whereas Excel, by default, remains invisible while it does its work. For this reason, I prefer the Excel spell checker operation to the Word version. This code is designed to work with Microsoft Excel version 5 or 7.

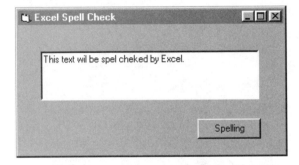

Figure 20-4.
Text as it appears before Excel's spell checker is invoked.

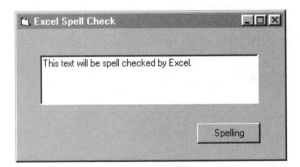

Figure 20-5.
Results of invoking Excel's spell checker.

In this code, an Excel Sheet object is created, the Visual Basic text string is loaded into a single cell of the sheet object, Excel's spell checker is invoked, and the cell's contents are copied back to the Visual Basic text box.

```
Option Explicit

Private Sub cmdSpell_Click()
    Dim xl As Object
    'Use OLE Automation to create an Excel object
    Set xl = CreateObject("Excel.Sheet")
    'Copy from text box to sheet
    xl.Range("A1").Value = txtTest.Text
    'Check spelling
    xl.CheckSpelling
    'Copy back to text box
    txtTest.Text = xl.Range("A1").Value
    'Remove object from memory
    Set xl = Nothing
End Sub
```

To run this code, create a new form containing a command button named cmdSpell and a text box named txtTest. Add the code to the cmdSpell button's Click event, and give it a try.

If this program is run when Excel is already loaded, Excel will stay active when the spell checking is completed. To prevent this problem, you can check whether Excel is running before using these commands, or you can use an Excel macro to return to the Visual Basic application.

Dear John, How Do I...

Use OLE Automation to Count Words?

Let's take a look at one more example of OLE Automation with Word, this time to count the words in a string. In this example, access to Word is achieved through the WordBasic object, as was shown before in the spell checking example. A second object variable (*dlg*) is created to access and hold the settings of Word's ToolWordCount dialog box. I've added a lot of comments to the following code so that you can see how the properties of this dialog box are accessed.

```
Option Explicit

Private Sub cmdWords_Click()
    On Error Resume Next
    Dim wb As Object, dlg As Object
    'Use OLE Automation to create a Word object
    Set wb = CreateObject("Word.Basic")
```

(continued)

```
'Open a new document in Word
wb.FileNewDefault
'Copy text into Word document
wb.Insert txtTest.Text
'Count words and characters
wb.ToolsWordCount
'Create an object to hold dialog box settings
Set dlg = wb.curvalues.ToolsWordCount
'Display results in a label control
lblWords.Caption = Str$(dlg.words) & " words   " _
    & Str$(dlg.Characters) & " characters"
'Close the Word document
wb.FileClose 2
'Remove the objects from memory
Set dlg = Nothing
Set wb = Nothing
End Sub
```

In this example, I've grabbed the number of words and the number of characters from the object holding the dialog box settings, but there are other properties you can access if you want. Search Word's WordBasic Help for the ToolsWordCount statement to learn more about the contents of this dialog box. Figure 20-6 shows the word and character count for a small sample of text.

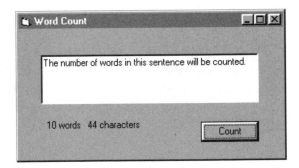

Figure 20-6.
Counting words and characters using Word's Word Count feature.

To run this example, start with a new form and add a command button named cmdWords, a text box named txtTest, and a label named lblWords to display the results. At runtime, type several words of text into the text box before clicking on the command button.

230

Dear John, How Do I...
Use Microsoft Excel's Advanced Math Functions?

Microsoft Excel contains a number of math functions that are not available in Visual Basic. The following routine uses OLE Automation to create an Excel Sheet object and then access one of Excel's functions to perform a calculation on a value passed to the object from the Visual Basic program. More important, this example shows how you can use Excel to create bigger and better Visual Basic programs.

In this example, I'm using two cells in the Excel Sheet object for input and two other cells for reading back the results of the calculation performed on the values placed in the first two cells. Excel's *ATAN2* function is used to calculate the angle between the positive *x* axis and a line drawn from the origin to the point represented by these two data values. The angle is returned in radians, which can easily be converted to degrees. Unlike Visual Basic's *atn()* function, which uses the ratio of two sides of a triangle to return a value of –pi/2 to pi/2 radians, Excel's *ATAN2* function uses the coordinates of the point to return a value between –pi and pi radians. In this way, the return value of *ATAN2* is correctly calculated for the quadrant that the given point is in.

The following code creates an Excel Sheet object, places the coordinates for the point into two cells of the Excel Sheet object, has Excel calculate the arctangent using the *ATAN2* function, and returns the value to the Visual Basic application.

```
Option Explicit

Private Sub cmdAngle_Click()
    Dim xl As Object
    'Use OLE Automation to create an Excel object
    Set xl = CreateObject("Excel.Sheet")
    'Set known values in cells
    xl.Range("A1").Value = txtX.Text
    xl.Range("A2").Value = txtY.Text
    'Calculate third cell
    xl.Range("A3").Formula = "=ATAN2(A1,A2)"
    xl.Range("A4").Formula = "=A3*180/PI()"
    'Display result in a label control
    lblRadians.Caption = xl.Range("A3").Value
    lblDegrees.Caption = xl.Range("A4").Value
    'Remove object from memory
    Set xl = Nothing
End Sub
```

To try this example, create a new form and add to it two text boxes named txtX and txtY, two labels named lblRadians and lblDegrees, and a command button named cmdAngle. As shown in Figure 20-7, an *x-y* coordinate pair entered into the text boxes is processed when the button is clicked to calculate the angle from the *x* axis to the given point. I've set up two calculations, the first to find the angle in radians and the second to convert this measurement to degrees. The results of these two Excel calculations are copied back to the labels for display. I've also added labels to the form to clarify the identity of the input text boxes and output labels.

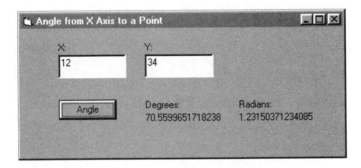

Figure 20-7.
An advanced Excel math function called from Visual Basic.

This technique of using an Excel Sheet object can be adapted to work with varying amounts of data, types of calculations, and levels of complexity, and the final result of all the number crunching can be copied back to your Visual Basic program. You'll find that using an Excel object for some types of data manipulations and calculations is easier and more efficient than trying to code the entire process in Visual Basic.

Screen Savers

It's actually fairly easy to create a screen saver using Visual Basic 4. In this chapter, I cover how to create a basic screen saver. But I also go further into the subject, showing you how to enhance the screen saver and have it work with the Windows 95 screen saver controls. The enhancements include making sure that only one instance of the program is run, turning off the mouse cursor, speeding up the graphics, detecting different user actions to terminate the screen saver, and using the current screen contents as part of a screen saver. I also look at how to use Windows controls to preview the screen saver and let the user set options.

Dear John, How Do I...

Create a Screen Saver?

Screen savers were originally created to protect screens from the "burn-in" that can be caused by pixels that don't change very often. Perhaps screen savers are now used more for entertainment than for screen protection, but the underlying principle of toggling all pixel locations through a variety of colors over time is still the foundation of their design. For this reason, a screen saver should display some sort of graphics that always move and change.

Any Visual Basic application can run as a screen saver. Of course, some programs will work better than others for this purpose. A basic screen saver is quite simple: a form that takes up the entire screen, code to create moving and changing graphics, and code to terminate the program when the user executes some action. This process creates a simple screen saver, and you will probably want to use the enhancements discussed in the topics following this one to improve the operation of your application.

To make your application function as a screen saver in the Windows environment, you need to compile the program as a screen saver. To do this, select Make EXE File from the File menu, and make the following changes in the Make EXE File dialog box: Instead of creating an executable file with the extension EXE, change the extension to SCR. Just type over EXE in the File Name field. Also, click on the Options button to bring up the EXE Options dialog box. Then type *SCRNSAVE:* in front of the application's title in the Title field. For example, you would enter *SCRNSAVE:ssaver1* for the example created in this section. Click on the OK buttons in these two dialog boxes to finish building the executable screen saver module. Finally, copy the resulting SCR file into your Windows folder so that it can be located and installed from the Display application in the Control Panel.

> **NOTE:** When you create the SCR file, Windows will reset the filename in all lowercase letters. Although this seems a bit peculiar, it actually helps you avoid a problem because Windows 95 is case-sensitive when dealing with filenames for screen savers that start with the letters *ss*. If you rename your screen saver application, be sure that the first *s* or the second *s* (or both) is lowercase. If you use two uppercase *S*'s, Windows will remove them and SSaver1.scr will be listed as "aver1" in the Display Options dialog box.

The following listing presents a simple screen saver application. The application does not handle some of the more complex features that are normally integrated into a screen saver. To act as a proper screen saver, your application should end when the mouse is moved or clicked, or when a key is pressed. It should also not allow multiple instances of itself to run, and in Windows 95, it should gracefully handle the Settings, Preview, and Password options that are accessed from the Screen Saver tab of the Display Options dialog box.

In this application, the screen saver does not respond to the options in the Display Options dialog box (other than the Wait period, which is handled by the system). The screen saver ends when you press a key, but it does not respond to any mouse actions. Adding all these features to the application is discussed in the topics following this one.

To create this project, add a timer named tmrExitNotify to a new form. Set the timer's Interval property to *1* and its Enabled property to *False*. Set the form's BorderStyle property to *0 - None* and its WindowState property to *2 - Maximized*, and add the following code:

```
'Ssaver1
Option Explicit

'Declare module-level variables
Dim QuitFlag As Boolean
```

(continued)

```
Private Sub Form_Click()
    'Quit if mouse is clicked
    QuitFlag = True
End Sub

Private Sub Form_KeyDown(KeyCode As Integer, Shift As Integer)
    'Quit if any key is pressed
    QuitFlag = True
End Sub

Private Sub Form_Load()
Dim x As Long

    'Proceed based on command line
    Select Case UCase$(Left$(Command$, 2))

    'Put the show on the road
    Case "/S"
        'Display full size
        Show

        'Display different graphics every time
        Randomize

        'Initialize graphics parameters
        Scale (0, 0)-(1, 1)
        BackColor = vbBlack

        'Loop to create graphics
        Do
            'Occasionally change line color and width
            If Rnd < 0.01 Then
                ForeColor = QBColor(Int(Rnd * 16))
                DrawWidth = Int(Rnd * 9 + 1)
            End If

            'Draw line
            Line (Rnd, Rnd)-(Rnd, Rnd)

            'Yield execution
            DoEvents

        Loop Until QuitFlag = True

        'Can't quit in this context; let timer do it
        tmrExitNotify.Enabled = True
```

(continued)

```
    Case Else
        Unload Me
        Exit Sub

    End Select

End Sub

Private Sub tmrExitNotify_Timer()
    'Time to quit
    Unload Me
End Sub
```

Create an SCR file from the project, as described earlier, and place it in your Windows folder. Right-click on the desktop, select Properties, and click on the Screen Saver tab of the Display Properties dialog box, from which you can try this example.

When activated, this screen saver draws random lines of varying thickness and color over a black background, as shown in Figure 21-1.

Figure 21-1.
The Ssaver1 screen saver program in action.

See Also...

- The other topics in this chapter for the details about enhancements to this screen saver

- The Ssaver application in Chapter 25 (Part III) for a good example of a more complete screen saver application

Dear John, How Do I...

Prevent Two Instances of a Screen Saver from Running at the Same Time?

Visual Basic provides an App object that has a PrevInstance property that is set to *True* if a previous instance of the current Visual Basic application is already running. This handy property makes it easy to bail out of an application quickly, during the form load event, to avoid running multiple instances of a screen saver simultaneously. The following code snippet shows how App.PrevInstance is typically implemented in a screen saver application:

```
'Don't allow multiple instances of program
If App.PrevInstance = True Then
    Unload Me
    Exit Sub
End If
```

I've described the use of the PrevInstance property because that is how most Visual Basic screen saver authors have handled the situation in the past. However, there is a better way to prevent a second instance of an active screen saver from being activated. I use a Windows 95 API function that informs the operating system that a screen saver is active. This puts the burden back on the operating system, where this responsibility should be.

The function is *SystemParametersInfo*, and its declaration is as follows:

```
Private Declare Function SystemParametersInfo _
Lib "user32" Alias "SystemParametersInfoA" ( _
    ByVal uAction As Long, _
    ByVal uParam As Long, _
    ByVal lpvParam As Any, _
    ByVal fuWinIni As Long _
) As Long
```

I call this function once at the start of the form load routine and again during the form unload event. The first call notifies the operating system that a screen saver is currently active, and the form unload version of the function call indicates that the screen saver is no longer operational. These two calls must be paired, and they must both be called during the execution of the screen saver. Here is the call to this function in the form load event:

```
x = SystemParametersInfo(17, 0, ByVal 0&, 0)
```

And here is the call in the form unload event:

```
x = SystemParametersInfo(17, 1, ByVal 0&, 0)
```

Note that the only difference is in the number passed as the second parameter (0 or 1).

Dear John, How Do I...

Hide the Mouse Pointer in a Screen Saver?

The *ShowCursor* API function allows you to hide or show the mouse pointer in a Visual Basic application. Windows keeps track of the mouse pointer's visibility by updating a count in a variable it maintains. Each call to *ShowCursor* with the parameter value *True* causes this count to increment, and each call that passes the value *False* causes it to decrement. If the count reaches 0 or lower, the mouse pointer is automatically hidden.

In a screen saver application, I declare the *ShowCursor* function and call it where appropriate to hide or temporarily reshow the mouse pointer.

> **NOTE:** In Visual Basic, we refer to the mouse *pointer,* but in Visual C++ it's called the mouse *cursor.* This is why the function name is *ShowCursor* instead of *ShowPointer,* which would be more logical to us Visual Basic types.

Here is the declaration for the API function *ShowCursor*:

```
Private Declare Function ShowCursor _
Lib "user32" ( _
    ByVal bShow As Long _
) As Long
```

Here are two examples of the use of the *ShowCursor* function, one that hides and one that shows the mouse pointer:

```
'Hide mouse pointer
x = ShowCursor(False)

'Show mouse pointer
x = ShowCursor(True)
```

Be sure to pair these functions so that the mouse pointer is restored at the termination of the program.

Dear John, How Do I...

Speed Up the Graphics in a Screen Saver?

The first time I created a screen saver using Visual Basic, I put each iteration of the graphics into a timer event, with the timer's Interval property set to the fastest possible value, 1 millisecond. This worked well, but there's an even faster technique. Here's the basic outline to follow:

```
Private Sub Form_Load()
    Show
    Do
        '(Display graphics here)
        DoEvents     'Yield execution to the system
    Loop
End Sub
```

The execution of the program actually stays in the Form_Load event until the program is terminated. The *DoEvents* command lets the system perform housekeeping tasks, such as checking for keypresses and mouse activity, but control is returned to the graphics generating loop as soon as possible.

You'll need to add code to allow the execution to exit from this loop when mouse or keyboard activity is detected, and you'll need to add code to prepare the graphics display. Take a look at the screen saver listing in the first topic to see how a keypress causes the execution to exit the loop. The concept to grasp here is that the tight looping lets the graphics updating proceed as fast as the system will allow while still letting the system monitor for keyboard and mouse activity.

NOTE: Visual Basic's online help suggests that you use the API function *Sleep* instead of the *DoEvents* function for 32-bit programming. I chose not to use *Sleep* for my screen savers for two reasons: First, it's slower, even when your execution is sleeping for only 1 millisecond at a time. Also, although the *Sleep* function is suggested because it handles 32-bit application interactions and multitasking better than *DoEvents* does, the screen saver application is designed to hog the whole system anyway. The advantages of *Sleep* over *DoEvents* are lost under these circumstances.

Dear John, How Do I...

Detect Mouse Movement or a Mouse Click to Terminate a Screen Saver?

The most obvious place to detect mouse movement is in the MouseMove event, but this presents a problem. The MouseMove event is triggered once when the application starts, even if the mouse doesn't physically move. The workaround for this problem is to detect the first mouse move event and to stop the screen saver only if the mouse actually moves from its starting position. Here's the code that accomplishes this technique:

```
Private Sub Form_MouseMove(Button As Integer, Shift As Integer, _
X As Single, Y As Single)
    Static Xlast, Ylast
    Dim Xnow As Single
    Dim Ynow As Single

    'Get current position
    Xnow = X
    Ynow = Y

    'On first move, simply record position
    If Xlast = 0 And Ylast = 0 Then
        Xlast = Xnow
        Ylast = Ynow
        Exit Sub
    End If

    'Quit only if mouse actually changes position
    If Xnow <> Xlast Or Ynow <> Ylast Then
        QuitFlag = True
    End If
End Sub
```

The static variables *Xlast* and *Ylast* keep track of the starting position of the mouse pointer. The program terminates if and only if the MouseMove event occurs and the mouse is no longer at the starting location. It's assumed that the mouse is always at a nonzero location to begin with, but even if the mouse is at the location 0,0 when the screen saver starts, the program will still terminate correctly when the mouse starts to move.

Mouse clicks are easier to detect. Any Form_Click event causes the screen saver to terminate, as shown in the following code:

```
Private Sub Form_Click()
    'Quit if mouse is clicked
    QuitFlag = True
End Sub
```

> NOTE: If your screen saver contains other controls on its main form, you'll probably want to catch mouse clicks on those objects too. Simply add the above code snippet to the Click event routine for each of the objects.

Dear John, How Do I...

Detect a Keypress to Terminate a Screen Saver?

The Form_KeyPress event can be used to detect keyboard activity, but this doesn't actually catch all keyboard activity. For example, pressing and releasing a shift key does not cause the Form_KeyPress event to fire. Instead, I chose to watch for keyboard activity in the Form_KeyDown event. This stops the screen saver the moment any key, including one of the shift keys, is pressed:

```
Private Sub Form_KeyDown(KeyCode As Integer, Shift As Integer)
    'Quit if any key is pressed
    QuitFlag = True
End Sub
```

Dear John, How Do I...

Use an Image of the Screen as a Screen Saver?

A lot of nifty screen savers act on the current display without permanently affecting any running applications. Perhaps you've seen those screen savers that cause the display to melt and drip away, or to swirl down a drain. By using a few API functions, you can easily copy the current display into a full screen form in which you can do whatever you want to the pixels without actually affecting the "real" display.

Below is the listing for a screen saver that demonstrates this effect. This program is similar to Ssaver1, which was introduced in the first topic of this chapter. The main difference is the addition of the API functions used to grab the screen contents and some enhancements based on some of the other topics in this chapter. Notice the declarations at the top of the listing for the API functions *BitBlt, GetDesktopWindow, GetDC,* and *ReleaseDC,* which are all required to copy the screen onto the form. These functions are called in the Form_Load event to display a copy of the screen on the main form. I've named this screen saver example Ssaver2.

Follow the same directions as in the first topic to compile this application to an executable file in the Windows directory with the extension SCR. Also, for proper operation, be sure to set several important properties of the form: Set AutoRedraw to *True,* BorderStyle to *0 - None,* ControlBox to *False,* KeyPreview to *True,* MaxButton and MinButton to *False,* and the WindowState to *2 - Maximized.* Finally, the tmrExitNotify.Enabled property must also be set to *False* in the design environment for this screen saver to work properly.

Here's the code:

```
'Ssaver2
Option Explicit

'Declare API to inform system whether screen saver is active
Private Declare Function SystemParametersInfo _
Lib "user32" Alias "SystemParametersInfoA" ( _
    ByVal uAction As Long, _
    ByVal uParam As Long, _
    ByVal lpvParam As Any, _
    ByVal fuWinIni As Long _
) As Long

'Declare API to hide or show mouse pointer
Private Declare Function ShowCursor _
Lib "user32" ( _
    ByVal bShow As Long _
) As Long

'Declare API to get a copy of entire screen
Private Declare Function BitBlt _
Lib "gdi32" ( _
    ByVal hDestDC As Long, _
    ByVal x As Long, ByVal y As Long, _
    ByVal nWidth As Long, _
    ByVal nHeight As Long, _
    ByVal hSrcDC As Long, _
    ByVal XSrc As Long, ByVal YSrc As Long, _
    ByVal dwRop As Long _
) As Long

'Declare API to get handle to screen
```

(continued)

```
Private Declare Function GetDesktopWindow _
Lib "user32" () As Long

'Declare API to convert handle to device context
Private Declare Function GetDC _
Lib "user32" ( _
    ByVal hwnd As Long _
) As Long

'Declare API to release device context
Private Declare Function ReleaseDC _
Lib "user32" ( _
    ByVal hwnd As Long, _
    ByVal hdc As Long _
) As Long

'Define constants
Const SPI_SETSCREENSAVEACTIVE = 17

'Define module-level variables
Dim QuitFlag As Boolean

Private Sub Form_Click()
    'Quit if mouse is clicked
    QuitFlag = True
End Sub

Private Sub Form_KeyDown(KeyCode As Integer, Shift As Integer)
    'Quit if any key is pressed
    QuitFlag = True
End Sub

Private Sub Form_Load()
Dim x As Long, y As Long
Dim XSrc As Long, YSrc As Long
Dim dwRop As Long, hwndSrc As Long, hSrcDC As Long
Dim Res As Long
Dim PowerOfTwo
Dim m1, m2
Dim n1, n2
Dim PixelColor, PixelCount

    'Tell system that application is active now
    x = SystemParametersInfo( _
        SPI_SETSCREENSAVEACTIVE, 0, ByVal 0&, 0)
```

(continued)

```
'Hide mouse pointer
x = ShowCursor(False)

'Proceed based on command line
Select Case UCase$(Left$(Command$, 2))

'Put the show on the road
Case "/S"

    'Display different graphics every time
    Randomize

    'Copy entire desktop screen into picture box
    ScaleMode = vbPixels
    Move 0, 0, Screen.Width + 1, Screen.Height + 1
    dwRop = &HCC0020
    hwndSrc = GetDesktopWindow()
    hSrcDC = GetDC(hwndSrc)
    Res = BitBlt(hdc, 0, 0, ScaleWidth, _
        ScaleHeight, hSrcDC, 0, 0, dwRop)
    Res = ReleaseDC(hwndSrc, hSrcDC)

    'Display full size
    Show

    'First time use high power of 2
    PowerOfTwo = 128

    'Graphics loop
    Do
        'Map screen into rectangular blocks
        Scale (0, 0)-(PowerOfTwo, PowerOfTwo)

        'Set a random solid color
        PixelColor = (PixelColor * 9 + 7) Mod 16
        PixelCount = 0

        'Algorithm to hit each location on screen
        m1 = Int(Rnd * (PowerOfTwo \ 4)) * 4 + 1
        m2 = Int(Rnd * (PowerOfTwo \ 4)) * 4 + 1
        n1 = Int(Rnd * (PowerOfTwo \ 2)) * 2 + 1
        n2 = Int(Rnd * (PowerOfTwo \ 2)) * 2 + 1
        Do
            'Jump to next coordinate
            x = (x * m1 + n1) Mod PowerOfTwo
            If x <> 0 Then
                y = (y * m2 + n2) Mod PowerOfTwo
```

(continued)

```
        Else
            'Let system do its thing
            DoEvents
        End If

        'Fill rectangular block with solid color
        Line (x, y)-(x + 1, y + 1), QBColor(PixelColor), BF
        PixelCount = PixelCount + 1

        'Exit this loop only to quit screen saver
        If QuitFlag = True Then Exit Do
    Loop Until PixelCount = PowerOfTwo * PowerOfTwo
    PowerOfTwo = 2 ^ (Int(Rnd * 5) + 2)
  Loop Until QuitFlag = True

    'Can't quit in this context; let timer do it
    tmrExitNotify.Enabled = True

Case Else
    Unload Me
    Exit Sub

End Select

End Sub

Private Sub Form_MouseMove(Button As Integer, _
Shift As Integer, X As Single, Y As Single)
Static Xlast, Ylast
Dim Xnow As Single
Dim Ynow As Single

    'Get current position
    Xnow = X
    Ynow = Y

    'On first move, simply record position
    If Xlast = 0 And Ylast = 0 Then
        Xlast = Xnow
        Ylast = Ynow
        Exit Sub
    End If

    'Quit only if mouse actually changes position
    If Xnow <> Xlast Or Ynow <> Ylast Then
        QuitFlag = True
    End If
```

(continued)

```
End Sub

Private Sub tmrExitNotify_Timer()
    'Time to quit
    Unload Me
End Sub

Private Sub Form_Unload(Cancel As Integer)
Dim x

    'Inform system that screen saver is now inactive
    x = SystemParametersInfo( _
        SPI_SETSCREENSAVEACTIVE, 1, ByVal 0&, 0)

    'Show mouse pointer
    x = ShowCursor(True)
End Sub
```

The graphics update loop in the Form_Load routine draws solid rectangular blocks of color, causing the display to gradually dissolve to the given color. Figure 21-2 shows the effect, with the original display dissolving to a solid gray.

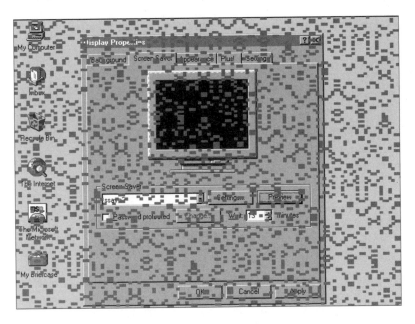

Figure 21-2.
The dissolving-display screen saver in action.

See Also...

- The Ssaver application in Chapter 25 (Part III) for additional creative screen saver effects

Dear John, How Do I...

Add Password and Setup Capabilities to a Screen Saver?

Windows automatically passes a command line parameter to the screen saver when it starts it up, based on how, and in what mode, the program is started. These command parameters and their descriptions are as follows:

/a   The password box is checked in the Display Options dialog box.

/p   A preview is shown in the Display Options dialog box whenever the Screen Saver tab is activated.

/c   The Settings button has been clicked in the Display Options dialog box.

/s   The Preview button has been clicked in the Display Options dialog box, or the application was started normally by the system.

I check for these parameters in the Form_Load event and take appropriate action based on the way the screen saver was started. In the two sample screen savers already presented in this chapter, I check only for the /s command parameter and terminate the program whenever any other parameter is used. This could be approached in a more user-friendly way by looking for some of the other command parameters and showing a message about the options, as shown here:

```
'Configuration command
    Case "/C"
        'Temporarily show mouse pointer
        x = ShowCursor(True)

        'Do any user interaction
        MsgBox "No setup options for this screen saver"

        'Hide mouse pointer
        x = ShowCursor(False)
```

(continued)

```
                'Configuration is completed
                Unload Me
                Exit Sub

        'Password setting command
        Case "/A"

                'Temporarily show mouse pointer
                x = ShowCursor(True)

                'Get and record new password here
                MsgBox "No password for this screen saver"

                'Hide mouse pointer
                x = ShowCursor(False)

                'Setting of new password is completed
                Unload Me
                Exit Sub
```

I've created a third screen saver, Ssaver3, which demonstrates the addition of a configuration setup form. Adding password capabilities can be done in a way similar to making the configuration settings except that you use a form to create and verify a password when the application is started with the /a command parameter and another form to enter the password when the user tries to terminate the program after it has been started with the /s command parameter.

This program displays stars randomly on the screen and lets the user select the number of points for the stars. Very different effects are created when you set different numbers of star points, as you'll discover if you try settings such as 3, 7, 17, and 97 points.

To create this screen saver, start with a new form and add a timer to it named tmrExitNotify. Set the timer's Interval property to *1* and its Enabled property to *False*. Also, set the form's BorderStyle property to *0 - None* and its WindowState property to *2 - Maximized*.

The number of points the user specifies is saved and retrieved from the Registry using the *SaveSetting* and *GetSetting* functions. These functions are described in Chapter 12, "The Registry." Here is the complete listing for Ssaver3:

```
'Ssaver3
Option Explicit
```

(continued)

```
'Declare API to inform system whether a screen saver is active
Private Declare Function SystemParametersInfo _
Lib "user32" Alias "SystemParametersInfoA" ( _
    ByVal uAction As Long, _
    ByVal uParam As Long, _
    ByVal lpvParam As Any, _
    ByVal fuWinIni As Long _
) As Long

'Declare API to hide or show mouse pointer
Private Declare Function ShowCursor _
Lib "user32" ( _
    ByVal bShow As Long _
) As Long

'Define data structure for Polygon API function
Private Type POINTAPI
    x As Long
    y As Long
End Type

'Declare API to draw polygonal "stars"
Private Declare Function Polygon _
Lib "gdi32" ( _
    ByVal hdc As Long, _
    lpPoint As POINTAPI, _
    ByVal nCount As Long _
) As Long

'Declare constants
Const SPI_SETSCREENSAVEACTIVE = 17

'Declare module-level variables
Dim QuitFlag As Boolean

Private Sub Form_Click()
    'Quit if mouse is clicked
    QuitFlag = True
End Sub

Private Sub Form_KeyDown(KeyCode As Integer, Shift As Integer)
    'Quit if any key is pressed
    QuitFlag = True
End Sub
```

(continued)

```
Private Sub Form_Load()
Dim i As Integer, j As Integer
Dim x As Long
Dim nPoints As Long
Dim xCenter As Long, yCenter As Long
Dim Radius As Single, Angle As Single

    'Tell system that application is now active
    x = SystemParametersInfo( _
        SPI_SETSCREENSAVEACTIVE, 0, ByVal 0&, 0)

    'Hide mouse pointer
    x = ShowCursor(False)

    'Proceed based on command line
    Select Case UCase$(Left$(Command$, 2))

    'Screen saver dialog quick preview mode
    Case "/P"
        Unload Me
        Exit Sub

    'Configuration command
    Case "/C"
        'Temporarily show mouse pointer
        x = ShowCursor(True)

        'Do any user interaction
        SS3Setup.Show vbModal

        'Hide mouse pointer
        x = ShowCursor(False)

        'Configuration is completed
        Unload Me
        Exit Sub

    'Password setting command
    Case "/A"
        'Temporarily show mouse pointer
        x = ShowCursor(True)

        'Get and record new password here
        MsgBox "Password is not available for this screen saver"
```

(continued)

```
        'Hide mouse pointer
        x = ShowCursor(False)

        'Setting of new password is completed
        Unload Me
        Exit Sub

'Put the show on the road
Case "/S"
        'Display full size
        Show

        'Display different graphics every time
        Randomize

        'Get current setting from the Registry
        nPoints = Val(GetSetting("Ssaver3", _
            "Startup", "Points", "5"))

        'Size array for number of star points
        ReDim P(nPoints) As POINTAPI

        'Initialize graphics parameters
        Scale (0, 0)-(1, 1)
        BackColor = vbBlack
        ScaleMode = vbPixels
        FillStyle = vbSolid

        'Loop to create graphics
        Do
            'Generate a somewhat random radius
            Radius = (1 + Rnd) * ScaleWidth / 20

            'Generate random center of star
            xCenter = Rnd * ScaleWidth
            yCenter = Rnd * ScaleHeight

            'Build array of polygon coordinates
            For i = 0 To nPoints - 1
                j = (j + nPoints \ 2) Mod nPoints
                Angle = j * 6.2831853 / nPoints
                P(i).x = xCenter + Radius * Cos(Angle)
                P(i).y = yCenter + Radius * Sin(Angle)
            Next i
```

(continued)

```
                'Create unique fill color each time
                FillColor = RGB(Rnd * 256, Rnd * 256, Rnd * 256)

                'Draw polygon, filling the interior
                x = Polygon(hdc, P(0), UBound(P))

                'Yield execution
                DoEvents

            Loop Until QuitFlag = True

            'Can't quit in this context; let timer do it
            tmrExitNotify.Enabled = True

        Case Else
            Unload Me
            Exit Sub

        End Select

End Sub

Private Sub Form_MouseMove(Button As Integer, _
Shift As Integer, X As Single, Y As Single)
Static Xlast, Ylast
Dim Xnow As Single
Dim Ynow As Single

    'Get current position
    Xnow = X
    Ynow = Y

    'On first move, simply record position
    If Xlast = 0 And Ylast = 0 Then
        Xlast = Xnow
        Ylast = Ynow
        Exit Sub
    End If

    'Quit only if mouse actually changes position
    If Xnow <> Xlast Or Ynow <> Ylast Then
        QuitFlag = True
    End If
End Sub

Private Sub tmrExitNotify_Timer()
    'Time to quit
```

(continued)

```
        Unload Me
End Sub

Private Sub Form_Unload(Cancel As Integer)
Dim x

    'Inform system that screen saver is now inactive
    x = SystemParametersInfo( _
        SPI_SETSCREENSAVEACTIVE, 1, ByVal 0&, 0)

    'Show mouse pointer
    x = ShowCursor(True)
End Sub
```

The dialog box used to make the configuration settings is a form named SS3Setup, which is activated from the main form when the command line contains the /c parameter. To create this dialog box, start with a new form and add a label, a text box named txtPoints, and a command button named cmdOK, as shown in Figure 21-3.

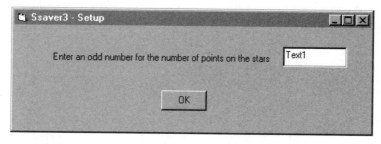

Figure 21-3.
The SS3Setup form at design time.

Add the following code to handle the maintenance of the number-of-points setting:

```
'SS3Setup
Option Explicit

Private Sub Form_Load()
    'Center this form
    Left = (Screen.Width - Width) \ 2
    Top = (Screen.Height - Height) \ 2
    'Get current setting from the Registry
    txtPoints.Text = GetSetting("Ssaver3", _
        "Startup", "Points", "5")
End Sub
```

(continued)

```
Private Sub cmdOK_Click()
    Dim nPoints As Integer
    'Get user input value
    nPoints = Val(txtPoints.Text)
    'Make sure it's odd and greater than 1
    If ((nPoints And 1) = 0) Or (nPoints < 3) Then
        Beep
        MsgBox "Must enter an odd number greater than 1", _
            vbExclamation, "Ssaver3"
        Exit Sub
    End If
    'Save the setting
    SaveSetting "Ssaver3", _
        "Startup", "Points", txtPoints.Text
    Unload Me
End Sub
```

Figure 21-4 shows the settings dialog box as it appears when the user is selecting this screen saver from Windows 95's Display application. Figure 21-5 shows the screen saver as it appears when it has been given a setting of 17, which creates 17-point stars on the display in random colors and at random locations.

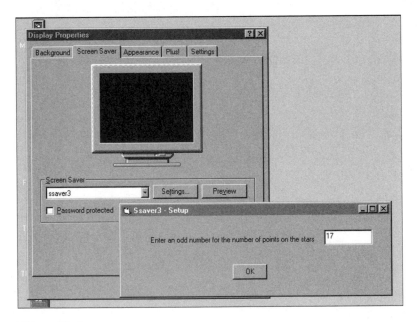

Figure 21-4.
The Ssaver3 settings dialog box.

Figure 21-5.
The Ssaver3 screen saver in action, showing 17-point stars.

CHAPTER TWENTY-TWO

Project Development

This chapter presents a few tricks I've picked up along the way that are useful for overall project development. The first topic shows you a very simple but often overlooked technique for grabbing images of your running application so that they can be added to your help file. (Help files, which are an important part of any complete application, are covered more fully in Chapter 13.)

The second topic in this chapter introduces some of Visual Basic 4's new techniques for internationalizing applications. The techniques discussed here will give you a great start on building applications for users around the world.

Dear John, How Do I...

Grab a Running Form and Save It as a Bitmap?

Here's a simple technique for grabbing all or part of the display to convert it to a bitmap (BMP) file, a technique that you might already know: simply press the Print Screen key to copy the entire screen to the clipboard. You can do this at any time while Windows is running. (If you want to copy only the form that currently has the focus, press Alt–Print Screen.) You won't hear a beep or notice anything other than perhaps a slight delay in the current program's operation, but the screen's contents (or the form's contents) will quickly be copied to the system's clipboard. Most of the forms shown in this book were grabbed using the Alt–Print Screen technique.

Pasting the Graphic into Paint

To process the clipboard's graphic contents, run Windows 95's Paint application and paste the clipboard's contents into it. You should see the upper-left corner of the captured display in Paint's workspace, as shown in Figure 22-1. With Paint's scrollbars, you can view any part of the image, and you can use its tools to make editing changes.

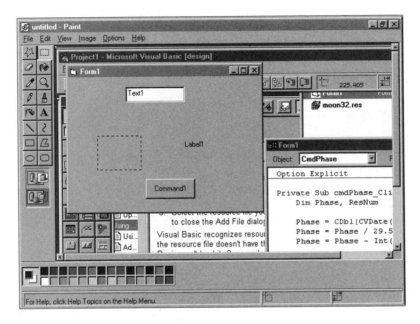

Figure 22-1.
A portion of a captured display, as shown in Paint.

Save As vs. Copy To

Select Save As from the File menu to save the image of the entire screen as a BMP file. To save a smaller region of the image, select part of the image using the selection rectangle tool, and then choose Copy To from Paint's Edit menu. This menu option prompts for a filename. Unlike the Save As choice, the Copy To option saves only the area of the image within the selection rectangle. Figure 22-2 shows the selection rectangle delineating a small part of the entire original screen image, and Figure 22-3 shows this small image after it has been reloaded into Paint from the BMP file it was written to.

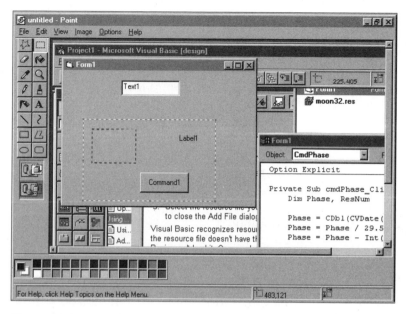

Figure 22-2.
A selection rectangle delineating a portion of a larger image.

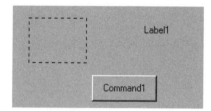

Figure 22-3.
The selected image loaded into Paint.

Dear John, How Do I...

Use Resource Files?

Resource file capability was added to Visual Basic 4 primarily to make it easier to internationalize applications. Before resource files were available, you had to edit all the captions, labels, and other strings for an application within the

Visual Basic project itself if you wanted your application to appear in another language. (I'm referring to spoken languages here, of course, not computer programming languages.) But now you can isolate all of your application's strings in a resource file, making it much easier to edit the strings for a second language. I've also found another useful feature of resource files: they allow you to easily include numerous graphic bitmap and icon files directly in your project. These images can then be loaded and manipulated from resource files much faster than from individual external files.

You can load one, and only one, resource file into your Visual Basic 4 project. But you can stuff a lot of strings, icons, bitmaps, sound files, and even video clips into a single resource file. In the following pages, I demonstrate the process of building a small resource file and then provide an example application that uses its contents.

Creating a Resource File

Start by creating an RC file using any text editor, such as Notepad. For this example, type in the following short file, which defines a collection of eight icons and eight strings for our resource file:

```
// Moon.rc - Resource file for moon phases example
//
// D:\tools\resource\rc32\rc /r /fo moon32.res moon.rc

// Icons
2  ICON  "C:\\VB4\\icons\\elements\\Moon01.ico"
3  ICON  "C:\\VB4\\icons\\elements\\Moon02.ico"
4  ICON  "C:\\VB4\\icons\\elements\\Moon03.ico"
5  ICON  "C:\\VB4\\icons\\elements\\Moon04.ico"
6  ICON  "C:\\VB4\\icons\\elements\\Moon05.ico"
7  ICON  "C:\\VB4\\icons\\elements\\Moon06.ico"
8  ICON  "C:\\VB4\\icons\\elements\\Moon07.ico"
9  ICON  "C:\\VB4\\icons\\elements\\Moon08.ico"

// Strings
STRINGTABLE
BEGIN
  2  "New"
  3  "Waxing, one quarter"
  4  "Waxing, half"
  5  "Waxing, three quarters"
  6  "Full"
  7  "Waning, three quarters"
  8  "Waning, half"
  9  "Waning, one quarter"
END
```

There are several details to note about this resource file listing:

- Comment lines begin with two slashes and are ignored during compilation.

- I've stayed away from using the resource number 1 because Visual Basic reserves this resource number for your application's internally stored icon.

- The backslash character separators in the full paths to the icons are doubled. Wherever there's normally a single backslash in your file paths, double it, as shown in my listing. This is a quirk of the C language that we just have to live with. A single backslash in a path will cause the character following the backslash to disappear, a detail that becomes apparent when you run the compiler and it stops with a message such as:

```
file not found: C:B4conslementsoon01.ico
```

- Strings are defined in one or more string tables in your resource file. In my listing, you'll see one such table. It starts with a STRING-TABLE declaration, and all strings are defined in a block between BEGIN and END lines.

- You include binary resources indirectly, by listing the full paths to the files the data resides in. At compile time the contents of each file will be pulled into the final RES file. My listing includes the eight phase-of-the-moon icons from my Visual Basic 4 installation. (You might need to change these paths slightly if you installed Visual Basic 4 in a different directory.) Binary file types you might find useful in resource files include bitmaps (BMP files), sound clips (WAV files), video clips (AVI files), and others. Refer to the Visual Basic 4 help, under the *LoadResData* function, for more information.

If your application has a large resource file that is likely to be used frequently, you should be aware of some further details of resource files. There are options that control when each resource is actually loaded into memory behind the scenes and when a resource can be discarded. Also, resources with resource numbers in the same block of 16 numbers (that is, those for which the most significant 12 bits of their 16-bit integer resource numbers are identical) will be loaded by the system simultaneously whenever any one of the resources is loaded by Visual Basic. You will probably want to work with this feature instead of against it, especially if your resources are large chunks of binary data and speed is your goal.

Notice that I've typed the compiler command line into a comment line at the top of my listing. This helps me remember exactly how to run the resource compiler. (For more information about using the resource compiler, check the Windows Software Development Kit or the Microsoft Developer Network CD, or look for a file named Resource.txt on your Visual Basic 4 CD-ROM in the Tools\Resource directory.) This command line runs the Rc.exe program directly from the Visual Basic CD-ROM disc. (Be sure you have your Visual Basic CD-ROM in the drive before running this command.) If your Rc.exe program is in a different location, be sure you modify this command line appropriately.

When the file has been successfully compiled, a sample resource file named Moon.res will be created. Use this file in the next step of our example.

Using a Resource File in Your Application

I designed this simple resource file to demonstrate the loading of strings and one type of binary data file (the Moon icons). The sample program I describe here loads these resources as required to show a very approximate phase-of-the-moon report for any given date. Start with a new project and add a text box named txtDate, a label named lblString, an Image control named imgMoon, and a command button named cmdPhase. Refer to Figure 22-4 for the placement and appearance of these controls. If you want, you can add a prompting label next to the text box and change the form's caption to spruce up the form a little. Figure 22-5 shows the program in action, displaying and describing the approximate phase of the moon for July 4, 1998.

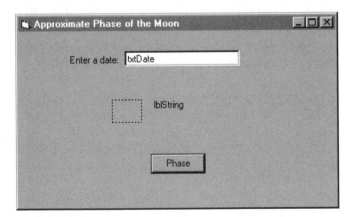

Figure 22-4.
The phase-of-the-moon form under construction.

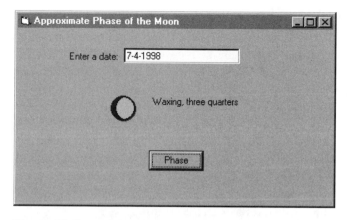

Figure 22-5.
The phase-of-the-moon program in action.

Add the following code to the form:

```
Option Explicit

Private Sub cmdPhase_Click()
    Dim Phase, ResNum
    'Calculate phase
    Phase = CDbl(CVDate(txtDate.Text))
    Phase = Phase / 29.530589 + 0.9291176
    Phase = Phase - Int(Phase)
    'Calculate resource number
    ResNum = 2 + Int(Phase * 8 + 0.5)
    If ResNum = 10 Then ResNum = 2
    'Load bitmap and string
    imgMoon.Picture = LoadResPicture(ResNum, vbResIcon)
    lblString.Caption = LoadResString(ResNum)

End Sub

Private Sub Form_Load()
    txtDate.Text = Date$
    cmdPhase_Click
End Sub
```

Most of this code is used for the calculation of the approximate phase of the moon for any given date. Once the phase is determined, a corresponding image and a string description are loaded from the project's resource file. The *LoadResPicture* and *LoadResString* functions do the loading. Before you run this program, be sure to add the Moon.res file to your project, just as you would add any other form, code, or class module.

When to Use a Resource File

The original motivation behind Microsoft's decision to add resource file capabilities to Visual Basic 4 was to make it easier for applications to be internationalized. In a form's load event, for example, you can easily load string resources into the caption properties of command buttons, forms, and label controls. Menus, sounds, pictures, text boxes—you name it—can all be modified at runtime to reflect the language of the user. The big advantage of this approach is that the task of reconstructing an application for one or more foreign languages is reduced to the single task of duplicating and editing an external ASCII resource file. You can then turn the resource file over to a skilled translator, who can create a new ASCII resource file without any working knowledge of Visual Basic programming.

In addition to making it easier to internationalize, resource files provide a few other advantages worth mentioning: For one thing, application speed is improved—graphics images load faster as resources than from external files. A second advantage is that multiple images are easier to manipulate. With earlier versions of Visual Basic, a common technique for manipulating multiple images was to load them into multiple controls. The moon icons, for example, can be loaded into separate Image or PictureBox controls, and these controls can then be manipulated to display one moon image at a time. In Visual Basic 4, however, you can store the bitmaps in a resource file and then load each bitmap into a single control as needed, thus avoiding the complexity and processing time of manipulating multiple controls.

CHAPTER TWENTY-THREE

Advanced Programming Techniques

With Visual Basic 4, it's easy to streamline and extend the capabilities of your applications. This chapter presents a few advanced programming techniques that will help you make your Visual Basic 4 applications more efficient and robust.

First, I show you how to use Dynamic Data Exchange (DDE) to share data among running applications. Although DDE is in the process of being replaced by OLE technology, it is still useful in some situations. The example in this section shows you how to set up a link between two Visual Basic 4 applications. The second and third topics in this chapter show you how to create a dynamic link library (DLL), which is a great way to speed up the execution of critical sections of your Visual Basic 4 applications. In the past, the only way you could create a DLL was by using another programming language, such as C. For speed-critical routines C is still a good choice, but you can also now use Visual Basic itself to create DLL modules using the new in-process OLE server technology. I'll show you examples of both DLL creation techniques. The final topic introduces another feature of Visual Basic 4: the ability to create add-ins for Visual Basic's integrated development environment (IDE). In this section, you will learn how to create a simple add-in, once again using Visual Basic itself.

Dear John, How Do I...

Use DDE (Dynamic Data Exchange) to Share Data Among Applications?

Visual Basic 4 makes it easy to pass data to or retrieve data from any Windows-based application that supports DDE. The applications presented in this topic are simple working examples designed to help demonstrate the process. You'll create two applications, VBsource and VBdest, that demonstrate how to set various properties for both the sending and the receiving of data between two applications.

NOTE: The future of interapplication communication is OLE technology, rather than DDE. Microsoft recommends using OLE techniques instead of DDE to maintain compatibility with future products whenever possible. In other words, be aware that DDE is slowly on its way out, and OLE is here to stay!

The VBsource Application

An application that supplies data to another application through a DDE link is called a *source,* and an application that requests and receives this data is called a *destination.* The VBsource application that you will create here will be set up as a source that can provide a date-and-time string to any destination applications that request it.

VBsource is a relatively simple application that requires only a Timer control and a Label control. Once every 1000 milliseconds (1 second), the code in the timer's subprogram reads the system clock and updates the label with the current date and time. To create the VBsource application, start with a blank form and add a timer named tmrDateTime and a Label control named lblDateTime, as shown in Figure 23-1.

Figure 23-1.
The VBsource form during development.

You'll need to add one line of code to update the date and time displayed in the Label control. Add the following code to tmrDateTime's Timer event:

```
Private Sub tmrDateTime_Timer()
    lblDateTime.Caption = Date$ & Space$(2) & Time$
End Sub
```

To make any application a source, you must set two properties of its source form accordingly: LinkMode must be set to *1 - Source*, and a meaningful name must be entered for the LinkTopic property. (In VBsource, Link-Topic is set to *DateTime*.) That's all there is to it! Destination applications can then request the contents of any text boxes, labels, or picture boxes on the source form.

VBsource can run by itself; it will display the current date and time as shown in Figure 23-2 until it is stopped. However, the real magic happens when you build the next application, VBdest, and establish a DDE link between the two applications.

Figure 23-2.
The VBsource program displaying the date and time.

Before you start building VBdest, compile VBsource to an executable module and run the compiled version of VBsource. Move the form off to a corner of the screen and leave it running while you take the next step, which is to build VBdest.

The VBdest Application

The VBdest application establishes a DDE link to VBsource, requesting that the data in VBsource's Label control be copied to a text box in VBdest whenever that data changes.

To establish a DDE link from a Visual Basic destination application to a source application during design time, you must have the source application

267

running while the destination application is being built. This is why you should leave the compiled version of VBsource running off in a corner somewhere while you build VBdest. The date and time will change continuously in the VBsource window while you create VBdest.

VBdest is also a simple application. It contains a single text box in which data received across the DDE link is displayed. To create VBdest, start a new project and add a text box named txtDateTime to a blank form.

As previously mentioned, to create a source application you change two link-related properties of the source form: LinkMode and LinkTopic. To create a destination application you change three link-related properties of the receiving control: LinkTopic, LinkItem, and LinkMode. In this example, the txtDateTime control will receive data, so you should set its three link-related properties as described in the following paragraphs.

Set LinkTopic to *VBsource/DateTime*. This string is made up of two parts, which are separated by a vertical bar (pipe) character. The first part, *VBsource*, is the name of the source application. The second part, *DateTime*, is the value of the source form's LinkTopic property. This can be any convenient (and preferably meaningful) name that describes the group of items to be requested from the source form.

Set LinkItem to *lblDateTime*. LinkItem is the name of the text box, label, or picture box on the source form from which data will be accessed. The lblDateTime control in VBsource contains the continually updated date and time. The LinkItem property can be set to any text box, label, or picture box on the indicated source form, and your program can even switch from one item to another while the application is running.

Set LinkMode to *1 - Automatic*. When you complete this setting, the VBdest text box will start to display the same date and time information that's displayed in VBsource. The DDE link works even while you are still working on the VBdest form—even before you run the VBdest program. Setting LinkMode to *2 - Manual* is another viable option; this causes data to transfer across the established link only when the VBdest application explicitly requests it by using the *LinkRequest* method. We'll use the automatic link for this example.

Note that VBdest requires no program code; the DDE link properties of the text box do it all. Figure 23-3 shows the VBdest form during design, with the text box's contents showing the current date and time, and Figure 23-4 shows VBdest at runtime.

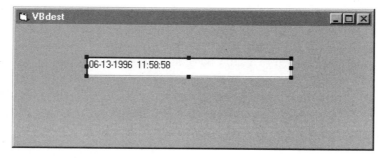

Figure 23-3.
VBdest during development.

Figure 23-4.
VBdest at runtime.

To properly establish the DDE link between a source and a destination, always run the source before the destination. Otherwise, the destination will try—and fail—to establish the DDE link, and a message to that effect will pop up. This is true whether the destination is compiled and run as an executable program or whether it's simply opened for editing in Visual Basic for Windows.

Dear John, How Do I...

Use Visual Basic to Create a DLL?

You can now use Visual Basic to create DLLs for 32-bit Windows-based applications. Visual Basic uses in-process OLE servers to accomplish this. A DLL created in this manner is a real DLL, complete with the filename extension

DLL. The main difference between an in-process OLE server DLL and a conventional DLL for previous versions of Windows is the way that calling programs interface with the provided routines. For example, you create and access an object that was created in Visual Basic and defined in a DLL by declaring a variable of the object's type, and then you use that object's properties and methods to achieve the desired results. With the old DLL calling convention, you use the *Declare* statement to define functions within the DLL, which is not possible with the new type of DLL.

The Fraction Object

In this example, you will create a simple in-process OLE server DLL, step by step, to see how this works. For complete information on all the technical details and guidelines for creating DLLs of this type, see the documentation that comes with your Visual Basic package. However, if you follow all the steps listed here, you should be able to create this example DLL with no complications. You'll create an in-process OLE server DLL that provides a Fraction class, which will let a calling program perform simple math operations with fractions. The Fraction object will provide two public properties, Num and Den, and four methods for performing addition, subtraction, multiplication, and division of fractions. One private method within the Fraction class will assist in reducing fractions to lowest terms.

Start with a new project, and add a code module and a class module. You can remove the default form module from the project because this DLL will not contain any forms. Save the code module as Math.bas and the class module as Math.cls. Add the following code to the Math.bas module:

```
Option Explicit

Sub Main()
    'No initialization required
End Sub
```

Every in-process OLE server project must have a Sub Main procedure as a starting point instead of a form because modeless forms are not allowed, and any startup form is by definition modeless. The Sub Main procedure is the best place to add initialization code to your project. In our simple example we don't need to do any initialization, so our Math.bas module is pretty skimpy. Nevertheless, this module serves the important purpose of adding the required Sub Main procedure to our sample in-process OLE server DLL.

The Math.cls Class Module

The Math.cls class module defines the single Fraction object contained in our DLL. Add the following code to Math.cls:

```
Option Explicit

Public Num
Public Den

Public Sub Add(Num2, Den2)
    Num = Num * Den2 + Den * Num2
    Den = Den * Den2
    Reduce
End Sub

Public Sub Sbt(Num2, Den2)
    Num = Num * Den2 - Den * Num2
    Den = Den * Den2
    Reduce
End Sub

Public Sub Mul(Num2, Den2)
    Num = Num * Num2
    Den = Den * Den2
    Reduce
End Sub

Public Sub Div(Num2, Den2)
    Mul Den2, Num2
End Sub

Private Sub Reduce()
Dim s, t, u
    s = Num
    t = Den
    If t = 0 Then Exit Sub
    Do
        u = (s \ t) * t
        u = s - u
        s = t
        t = u
    Loop While u > 0
    Num = Num \ s
    Den = Den \ s
End Sub
```

The Public properties Num and Den let a calling application set and read values that define a fraction. The four methods *Add*, *Sbt*, *Mul*, and *Div* perform fraction math on the Num and Den properties using a second fraction that is passed as parameters. (Notice that I couldn't use the more logical "Sub" abbreviation to name the subtract routine, because this is reserved by Visual Basic for naming subprograms.) The *Reduce* method is private and is used internally by the DLL to reduce all fraction results to lowest terms.

You must set this class module's three properties properly to successfully create an in-process OLE server DLL. Set the Instancing property to *Createable Multiuse*, the Public property to *True*, and the Name property to *Fraction*.

The Project Settings

Before you run or compile this project, you must set some of its properties to let Visual Basic know that this project is supposed to end up as an in-process OLE server DLL instead of a regular application. From the Tools menu select Options, and click on the Project tab. Set the Startup Form to *Sub Main*, the Project Name to *Math*, and the Application Description to *Fraction Math*, and click on the OLE Server option for the StartMode setting. To better trap errors while testing in the Visual Basic development environment, click on the Advanced tab and select the Use OLE DLL Restrictions option.

Testing in the Development Environment

Before you compile your new DLL as a separate file, you can test it within the development environment. Well, sort of. What happens is that you run the application, minimize Visual Basic to get it out of the way, and then start a second instance of Visual Basic (something you couldn't do in previous versions of Visual Basic). When you run the in-process OLE server within the development environment, Visual Basic temporarily registers it with the system, allowing it to be referenced and used from any other application that creates objects of the defined type.

In the second instance of Visual Basic, create a test application to exercise the Fraction object provided by the Math in-process OLE server. Add six text boxes and four buttons to Form1 in a layout similar to that shown in Figure 23-5. As shown in this figure, I added a few line controls and some labels to improve the appearance a little, but these are just extras you can add if you want to.

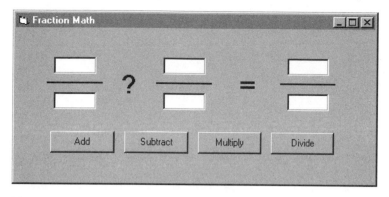

Figure 23-5.
A form for testing the new Fraction object.

Name the text controls txtN1, txtD1, txtN2, txtD2, txtN3, and txtD3 to represent the numerators and denominators for three fractions as viewed from left to right. Name the command buttons cmdAdd, cmdSubtract, cmdMultiply, and cmdDivide. Change their captions to match their functions. Finally, add the following code to the form to complete the application:

```
Option Explicit

Public Frac As New Math.Fraction

Private Sub cmdAdd_Click()
    Frac.Num = txtN1.Text
    Frac.Den = txtD1.Text
    Frac.Add txtN2.Text, txtD2.Text
    txtN3.Text = Frac.Num
    txtD3.Text = Frac.Den
End Sub

Private Sub cmdDivide_Click()
    Frac.Num = txtN1.Text
    Frac.Den = txtD1.Text
    Frac.Div txtN2.Text, txtD2.Text
    txtN3.Text = Frac.Num
    txtD3.Text = Frac.Den
End Sub
```

(continued)

```
Private Sub cmdMultiply_Click()
    Frac.Num = txtN1.Text
    Frac.Den = txtD1.Text
    Frac.Mul txtN2.Text, txtD2.Text
    txtN3.Text = Frac.Num
    txtD3.Text = Frac.Den
End Sub

Private Sub cmdSubtract_Click()
    Frac.Num = txtN1.Text
    Frac.Den = txtD1.Text
    Frac.Sbt txtN2.Text, txtD2.Text
    txtN3.Text = Frac.Num
    txtD3.Text = Frac.Den
End Sub
```

At the form level, I've declared the variable *Frac* to be an object reference of type Fraction, as defined in the Math DLL. The Frac object is defined at the module level, but it's not actually created until the first time you click on any of the four command buttons. The Frac object is destroyed automatically when its reference goes out of scope—that is, when the form unloads.

Referencing the Math DLL

Before running this application to test your new DLL, you must first add a reference to it in the project. From the Tools menu, select References. Scroll down to find the Fraction Math entry, and click on it. Now Visual Basic will know what to do when it encounters the object declaration in the test application. Notice that you can use the Object Browser to explore the properties and methods provided by any referenced object. In this relatively simple example, the methods and properties are fairly straightforward, but when you need to access the objects, properties, and methods within Microsoft Excel, for example, the Browser can help tremendously as you try to decipher the maze of information.

At this point, you're ready to run the test application and let it create and use a Fraction object as defined in the Math DLL, which is currently running in the first instance of Visual Basic. Enter numbers for the numerators and denominators of the two fractions on the left side of the dialog box, and click on the four buttons, one at a time, to perform the fraction math. The result, as displayed on the right, should always be a fraction reduced to its lowest terms. Figure 23-6 shows the result of multiplying ¾ by ⅚.

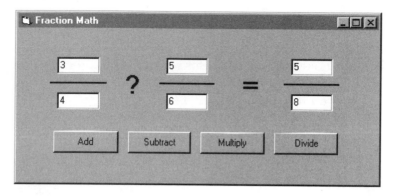

Figure 23-6.
The Fraction Math test in action.

Creating the Final DLL Module

Once your DLL has been debugged and is ready to roll, you'll want to compile your in-process OLE server to create a shippable DLL module. All you have to do to achieve this is select Make OLE DLL File from the File menu. It's that simple. When your DLL is in the hands of an end user, it must be registered with the user's system before it will show up in the list of references, or before any external application will be able to load the DLL into its running space so that it can use the objects the DLL defines. The simplest way to get a DLL registered with your user's system is to use the Setup Wizard to create an installation disk. The registration of a DLL is set up automatically by the Setup Wizard.

Dear John, How Do I...

Use C to Create a DLL?

Visual Basic's great strength is in the speed with which it allows you to produce applications for Windows; it's hard to beat the Visual Basic programming environment on the productivity score. On the other hand, Visual Basic is relatively slow when crunching numbers and performing other low-level computations. You can avoid this sluggishness, though, by isolating the speed-critical sections of your Visual Basic code and rewriting them in C as a DLL.

With the latest Visual C++ compilers, creating a DLL is easier than ever. Because this book focuses on using Microsoft tools to create applications for the 32-bit Windows 95 environment, I've streamlined the following example DLL code. This should make it easier for you to focus on the essential points of the DLL creation task. (If you need to program for the 16-bit Windows environment, or if you're using a version of C other than Microsoft Visual C++ version 2.2 or later, you'll need to make adjustments to the listings.) For the best in-depth explanation of every aspect of DLL creation, refer to the documentation that comes with your compiler.

The Two C Files

The following two listings are for the only two files you'll need in your Visual C++ project. Start a new project in the 32-bit version of Visual C++, and select Dynamic Link Library as the type of project to be built. Create a DEF file as part of your project, enter the following few lines, and name this file Mydll.def:

```
; Mydll.def
LIBRARY Mydll

CODE PRELOAD MOVEABLE DISCARDABLE
DATA PRELOAD MOVEABLE

EXPORTS
     TestByte            @1
     TestInteger         @2
     TestLong            @3
     TestSingle          @4
     TestDouble          @5
     ReverseString       @6
```

The DEF file tells the outside world the names of exported functions. In other words, this file provides the list of functions you can call from your Visual Basic applications.

This DLL project has just one C source code file. Enter the following lines into a file, save it as Mydll.c, and make sure it's included in your Visual C++ project.

```
#include <windows.h>
#include <ole2.h>

BYTE _stdcall TestByte( BYTE a, LPBYTE b )
```

(continued)

```
{
    *b = a + a;
    return( *b + a );
}

short _stdcall TestInteger( short a, short far * b )
{
    *b = a + a;
    return( *b + a );
}

LONG _stdcall TestLong( LONG a, LPLONG b )
{
    *b = a + a;
    return( *b + a );
}

float _stdcall TestSingle( float a, float far * b )
{
    *b = a + a;
    return( *b + a );
}

double _stdcall TestDouble( double a, double far * b )
{
    *b = a + a;
    return( *b + a );
}

void _stdcall ReverseString( BSTR a )
{
    int i, iLen;
    BSTR b;
    LPSTR pA, pB;

    iLen = strlen( (LPCSTR)a );
    b = SysAllocStringLen( NULL, iLen );

    pA = (LPSTR)a;
    pB = (LPSTR)b + iLen -1;

    for ( i = 0; i < iLen; i++ )
        *pB-- = *pA++;

    pA = (LPSTR)a;
    pB = (LPSTR)b;
```

(continued)

```
    for ( i = 0; i < iLen; i++ )
        *pA++ = *pB++;

    SysFreeString( b );
}
```

Click on the Build All button in the Visual C++ environment to compile and link the two files in your project and create a small DLL module named Mydll.dll. Move or copy Mydll.dll to your Windows System folder so that your Visual Basic *Declare* statements will be able to locate the DLL file automatically.

Testing the DLL

It's easy to try out the functions in your new DLL file from Visual Basic. To test the six functions in Mydll.dll, I started a new Visual Basic project and added the following code to a form containing a single command button named cmdGo:

```
Option Explicit

Private Declare Function TestByte _
Lib "mydll.dll" ( _
    ByVal a As Byte, _
    ByRef b As Byte _
) As Byte

Private Declare Function TestInteger _
Lib "mydll.dll" ( _
    ByVal a As Integer, _
    ByRef b As Integer _
) As Integer

Private Declare Function TestLong _
Lib "mydll.dll" ( _
    ByVal a As Long, _
    ByRef b As Long _
) As Long

Private Declare Function TestSingle _
Lib "mydll.dll" ( _
    ByVal a As Single, _
    ByRef b As Single _
) As Single

Private Declare Function TestDouble _
Lib "mydll.dll" ( _
```

(continued)

```
        ByVal a As Double, _
        ByRef b As Double _
    ) As Double

    Private Declare Sub ReverseString _
    Lib "mydll.dll" ( _
        ByVal a As String _
    )

    Private Sub cmdGo_Click()
        Dim bytA As Byte
        Dim bytB As Byte
        Dim bytC As Byte
        Dim intA As Integer
        Dim intB As Integer
        Dim intC As Integer
        Dim lngA As Long
        Dim lngB As Long
        Dim lngC As Long
        Dim sngA As Single
        Dim sngB As Single
        Dim sngC As Single
        Dim dblA As Double
        Dim dblB As Double
        Dim dblC As Double
        Dim strA As String

        bytA = 17
        bytC = TestByte(bytA, bytB)
        Print bytA, bytB, bytC

        intA = 17
        intC = TestInteger(intA, intB)
        Print intA, intB, intC

        lngA = 17
        lngC = TestLong(lngA, lngB)
        Print lngA, lngB, lngC

        sngA = 17
        sngC = TestSingle(sngA, sngB)
        Print sngA, sngB, sngC

        dblA = 17
        dblC = TestDouble(dblA, dblB)
        Print dblA, dblB, dblC
```

(continued)

279

```
strA = "This string will be reversed"
Print strA
ReverseString (strA)
Print strA
```

End Sub

When you run this program and click on the Go button, each of the new DLL functions will be called and the results will be printed to the form, as shown in Figure 23-7.

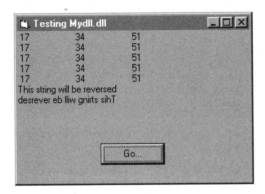

Figure 23-7.
The results of testing the functions in Mydll.dll.

A few words of explanation about this simple DLL are in order. Each of the five numeric functions demonstrates the passing of one data type in two ways. The first parameter is passed using *ByVal*, and the second is passed using *ByRef*. Parameters passed with *ByVal* can't be changed by the DLL function, but parameters passed with *ByRef* can be. In my test program, each function is passed a numeric value of 17 in the first parameter, which the DLL function doubles and stores in the second. Each of the numeric functions also returns a value of the same data type, and the value returned by the DLL to the Visual Basic test program is simply the sum of the two parameters. The results displayed in Figure 23-7 show how these values are modified by the DLL functions. In the Visual Basic declarations of the test program, I explicitly declared the *ByRef* parameters using that keyword, but because this is the default for all parameter passing in Visual Basic, you can drop the *ByRef* if you want to. The *ByVal* keyword is not optional, however, and I find it less confusing if I go ahead and explicitly declare both types of parameters. This is a matter of style, and you might prefer to drop all the *ByRef* keywords in your declarations.

You might have noticed in the source code that I didn't use C's int data type in the function that expects Visual Basic's Integer parameters, but instead I used the keyword *short*. This is because in 32-bit Microsoft C an int is actually a 32-bit integer, rather than the 16-bit size that Visual Basic's Integer declaration refers to. Fortunately, if you use *short* you're guaranteed a 16-bit integer in all versions of Microsoft C.

Strings are now handled internally as BSTR types, both in C code, if they are declared as such, and automatically in Visual Basic 4. In this example, I used a Visual Basic *ByVal* declaration to pass a string to the *ReverseString* function in Mydll.dll. You can pass a string using *ByRef*, but because BSTR strings are passed around by address anyway, a string passed with *ByVal* can be altered, as shown in this example, and little is gained by passing a string *ByRef*.

In the *ReverseString* function, you'll notice the use of the functions *SysAllocStringLen* and *SysFreeString*. These are just two of several API functions that can be used to manipulate BSTR strings, all of which make it easier than ever to manipulate Visual Basic strings within a C-language DLL. The long list of things you can do with strings in your DLLs is beyond the scope of this book, so I refer you to the Visual C++ documentation for all the details. The simple example functions I've provided here can help you get your feet wet.

See Also...

- The BitPack application in Chapter 30 (Part III) for a demonstration of the creation and use of another DLL

Dear John, How Do I...

Create an Add-In for the Visual Basic Development Environment?

A Visual Basic add-in is a special program that can be attached to the Visual Basic development environment to add extra or customized functionality to the environment. For example, you could use an add-in to add some capabilities to the environment in the form of new menu items on Visual Basic's menus, or to perform housekeeping chores whenever you load or save forms or code modules. One obviously useful type of add-in is a source code librarian, such as the Microsoft Visual SourceSafe product that ships with the Enterprise Edition of Visual Basic 4.

Three sample add-in applications, Datawiz, Spy, and Align, are included in Visual Basic's Samples folder, but I found these samples to be somewhat confusing at first because of their complex use of the Visual Basic IDE object model. Here I present a streamlined example to help you better understand the mechanics of creating and running an add-in program. After you have followed my example and have a clear understanding of it, you'll find the examples provided in the Visual Basic package much easier to master.

Basic Concepts

A Visual Basic add-in is simply a specially constructed Visual Basic program. The example program presented here will start in the subprogram Main, which is located in a code module (BAS file). This portion of the routine will do nothing more than make sure that the appropriate entry is made in VB.ini and in the system Registry. This entry enables Windows 95 to find and load the add-in when you want it. Registering an add-in is a one-time-only process that is best accomplished by simply running the add-in program once during the installation of the add-in. Because you're creating your own add-in instead of installing a commercial product, you'll run the program once manually, after you have built it.

When you select Add-In Manager from the Visual Basic Add-Ins menu, all registered add-ins will be available for either loading into or unloading out of the currently running instance of the Visual Basic development environment. For this example, you'll create special routines within the add-in program that will be activated when the add-in is loaded or unloaded, and it is in these routines that you'll program the steps required to add menu items and to connect to events of the Visual Basic environment to run your code.

Connecting to an event, such as a click on one of the new menu items your add-in will install, requires the passing of an object to a special *Connect-Events* method. The best way to approach this is to create class modules that define the required objects. This is why you'll see one or more class modules in the three add-in sample programs as well as this one. Once the add-in is connected, special methods within your class objects will fire when Visual Basic events dictate. For example, you'll add some code to an *AfterClick* method within your class module that will be activated when the user clicks on the new menu item.

The really cool work is accomplished in the *AfterClick* method or in other event-driven routines provided in the add-in. In this example, you'll use a small subset of the Visual Basic object hierarchy to locate and resize all command buttons on the currently active form within the Visual Basic environment. This is a small example of what can be accomplished with an add-in, yet I find it quite useful. I'm always tweaking my command buttons to make them all the same size in a project, and this little add-in lets me instantly resize all my command buttons to a fixed, standard size.

Building an Add-In

The following paragraphs provide a recipe-style series of steps to show you how to build your relatively simple add-in. When I was building my first add-in, I stumbled over several not-so-obvious details, mostly because I had to wade around in the Microsoft documentation to determine what I had done wrong. The steps presented here should help you breeze over these details.

Start with a new project, and insert two class modules and one code module. Name the code module Myaddin, and name the class modules Connect and Sizer. You'll need to make some important property settings in the Connect module, and in the project itself, before you try to run the add-in, but you should enter all the source code first and take care of the property settings when you have finished.

Add the following code to Myaddin. Note that the only task performed by the subprogram Main is to get this add-in registered with Windows 95. The Main code runs quickly, and the program terminates almost immediately, with no activity visible to the outside world:

```
Option Explicit

'Declare API to write to INI file
Declare Function WritePrivateProfileString _
Lib "Kernel32" _
Alias "WritePrivateProfileStringA" ( _
    ByVal AppName$, _
    ByVal KeyName$, _
    ByVal keydefault$, _
    ByVal FileName$ _
) As Long

'Declare API to read from INI file
Declare Function GetPrivateProfileString _
Lib "Kernel32" _
Alias "GetPrivateProfileStringA" ( _
    ByVal AppName$, _
    ByVal KeyName$, _
    ByVal keydefault$, _
    ByVal ReturnString$, _
    ByVal NumBytes As Long, _
    ByVal FileName$ _
) As Long
```

(continued)

```
Sub Main()
Dim ReturnString As String
Dim Section As String

    'Make sure you are in the VB.INI file
    Section = "Add-Ins32"
    ReturnString = String$(255, Chr$(0))
    GetPrivateProfileString Section, _
        "cmdSizer.Connect", "NotFound", _
        ReturnString, Len(ReturnString) + 1, "VB.INI"
    If InStr(ReturnString, "NotFound") Then
        WritePrivateProfileString Section, _
            "cmdSizer.Connect", "0", "VB.INI"
    End If
End Sub
```

The Connect class module provides the special *ConnectAddIn* and *DisconnectAddIn* methods that Visual Basic will automatically call when the user loads or unloads this add-in into or out of the Visual Basic environment. It's enlightening to realize that the previously mentioned Main subprogram will run *once per installation* of this add-in, whereas the subprograms provided in the Connect class module will run *once per load or unload* of this add-in. Continuing this pattern, the routines in the other class module will run *once per menu click*. Mentally partitioning this activity will help you understand better what's going on here. Add this code to the Connect class module:

```
Option Explicit

Dim VBInstance As VBIDE.Application
Dim mnuSize As VBIDE.MenuLine
Dim SizerHandler As Sizer
Dim ConnectID As Long

'Set these constants as desired
Const CMDBTNWIDTH = 1200
Const CMDBTNHEIGHT = 400

Sub ConnectAddIn(VBDriverInstance As VBIDE.Application)

    'Save this instance of Visual Basic so you can refer to it later
    Set VBInstance = VBDriverInstance

    'Add menu item to Visual Basic's Add-Ins menu
    Set mnuSize = VBInstance.AddInMenu.MenuItems.Add _
        ("&Size Command Buttons")
```

(continued)

```
'Create Sizer object from class definition
Set SizerHandler = New Sizer

'Save connection ID
ConnectID = mnuSize.ConnectEvents(SizerHandler)

'Pass VBInstance to child objects
Set SizerHandler.VBInstance = VBInstance

'Set command button sizing properties
SizerHandler.ButtonWidth = CMDBTNWIDTH
SizerHandler.ButtonHeight = CMDBTNHEIGHT

End Sub

Sub DisconnectAddIn(Mode As Integer)

'Remove menu event connection
mnuSize.DisconnectEvents ConnectID

'Remove menu item you installed
VBInstance.AddInMenu.MenuItems.Remove mnuSize

End Sub
```

Notice that I've defined two constants in this module, CMDBTN-WIDTH and CMDBTNHEIGHT, which define the size to which all command buttons processed by this add-in will be set. Feel free to change these constants if you want. Better yet, if you feel energetic, you might consider adding a dialog box to this add-in to let the user enter the desired sizing constants on the fly. I decided to keep this example simple by just using constants, which works well for almost all of my command buttons anyway.

The VBInstance object helps you stay in control if the user runs multiple copies of Visual Basic simultaneously. There'll be only one instance of your add-in in memory at a time, even if multiple copies of Visual Basic are running. By storing the VBIDE.Application object passed by Visual Basic to the *ConnectAddIn* method, you can refer only to the forms and controls in that particular instance of Visual Basic when a user clicks on the new menu item.

The other class module, Sizer, contains the code to be activated when the user clicks on the new menu item. This module contains one method, *AfterClick*, which is automatically called by the system when its containing object is connected to that menu. Add the source code on the following page to the Sizer class module.

```
Option Explicit

'Sizer object properties
Public ButtonWidth As Long
Public ButtonHeight As Long
Public VBInstance As VBIDE.Application

Public Sub AfterClick()
Dim AllControls As VBIDE.ControlTemplates
Dim Control As Object

Set AllControls = _
    VBInstance.ActiveProject.ActiveForm.ControlTemplates
    For Each Control In AllControls
        If Control.ClassName = "VB.CommandButton" Then
            With Control.Properties
                .Item("Width") = ButtonWidth
                .Item("Height") = ButtonHeight
            End With
        End If
    Next Control

End Sub
```

When the user clicks on the new menu item, this subprogram wades through all the controls on the currently selected form within the user's Visual Basic project. If a control is a command button, its Width and Height properties are set to the predetermined constant values. Later on, when you try out this add-in, you'll see all the command buttons on your current form snap to a fixed size.

Before you run this program as an add-in, you need to set some important properties. Select Options from the Tools menu, and click on the Project tab of the dialog box that appears. Set the Startup Form to *Sub Main* so that the correct routine will run when this program is executed for the first time. Type *cmdSizer* into the Project Name field. This name must be the same as the first part of the string *cmdSizer.Connect*, used in the system registration process executed in the Main subprogram. If the two don't match, you won't be able to load this add-in using Visual Basic's Add-In Manager tool. This is one of those fine points that tripped me up the first time. Click on OLE Server in the StartMode options. An add-in executable contains OLE code to be activated from an external application; in this case, the Visual Basic environment uses OLE technology to connect to the various objects within our add-in program. Type *Command button sizer add-in* in the Application Description field. This text appears in the Object Browser and helps identify the exposed objects. Finally, click on OK in the dialog box to set your options.

Another trip-up detail is remembering to enable the VBIDE object on which this whole add-in application depends so heavily. Select References from the Tools menu, and turn on the Microsoft Visual Basic 4.0 Development Environment item in the Available References list and then click on OK. If you forget to enable this reference, Visual Basic will assume that the VBIDE is supposed to be a user-defined type, and an error message will pop up when you try to run the program.

The Connect class module has two properties that must be set correctly: set its Instancing property to *2 - Creatable Multiuse*, and set its Public property to *True*. The Instancing setting allows this add-in to be loaded into multiple concurrent instances of Visual Basic. These two settings can be left as *0 - Not Creatable* and *False*, respectively, in the Sizer class module.

Running the Add-In for the First Time

Your new add-in must be run once to be registered with Windows 95. While you are debugging you can run an add-in from within the Visual Basic environment, and once it has been compiled to an EXE file it can be run from the Run command on Windows 95's Start menu. The system will load the EXE file and make its OLE objects available normally, but these objects can still be accessed during debugging if the program is left in the run state. To try this, click on the Run button and minimize the entire Visual Basic environment while your add-in is still running. Start a second instance of Visual Basic, and try loading your new add-in using the Add-In Manager item on the Add-Ins menu. If everything has gone smoothly, you'll see where you can click to activate your new add-in from the Add-In Manager dialog box.

The other approach is to go ahead and make an EXE file for the add-in. When compilation is successful, exit Visual Basic, run the new Myaddin.exe file once, noticing that nothing much appears to happen while it quickly registers itself with the system, and then start up Visual Basic again to see whether you can then load the new add-in. Remember that you need to run the add-in's EXE file only once, to let it register and effectively install itself into the Windows 95 system.

Using the Add-In

To test this add-in, start up Visual Basic and select Add-In Manager from the Add-Ins menu. Click to select the cmdSizer.Connect option, and click on OK. As shown in Figure 23-8, a new menu item, Size Command Buttons, should become available at the bottom of the Add-Ins menu.

Figure 23-8.
The new menu item installed by the add-in.

Throw a handful of odd-sized command buttons onto a form and give this new menu choice a try. You should see all command buttons quickly snap to the same size. Figure 23-9 shows one of my forms before command button resizing, and Figure 23-10 shows the form after I have clicked on the new menu item.

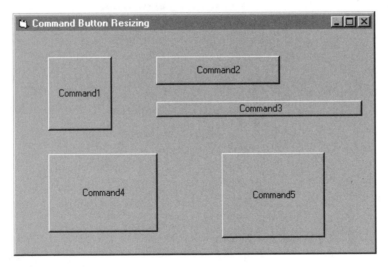

Figure 23-9.
Command buttons ready to be resized.

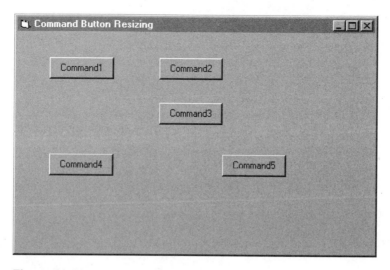

Figure 23-10.
Command buttons resized by the add-in.

CHAPTER TWENTY - FOUR

Miscellaneous Techniques

In this chapter, I cover a few odds and ends that don't quite fit anywhere else but that are still valuable tricks for the Visual Basic programmer to know.

One of the complaints I've heard in the past about the Basic language in general is its lack of pointers and data structures, features that a competent C programmer wouldn't know what to do without. Earlier in this book, I show how Variants allow great flexibility in the creation of structured data, and in the first topic in this chapter I show you how the new Collection object lets you create dynamic data structures that support very sophisticated data manipulation techniques. As a simple example, in the first topic I create the equivalent of a linked list.

Another technique that's useful to know is how to programmatically reboot the computer. You might want to do this, for example, as part of a setup or initialization application, or perhaps as a security measure when your program discovers that someone or something has been tampering with the system. The second topic shows you how to reboot from within a running Visual Basic application.

The third topic shows you how your application can dial a phone by sending commands to the modem through the serial port. This is a common programming task, and it turns out to be quite simple to accomplish.

Finally, error trapping capabilities have been greatly enhanced with this edition of Visual Basic. The last topic shows a generalized technique for inline error trapping that has advantages over the old *On Error GoTo Label* technique of the past.

Dear John, How Do I...

Create a Linked List?

Using a linked list to create, manage, and reorder a sequential series of data has long been a powerful C programming tool. When you create a linked list of data structures in C, you must rely on pointer variables to hold the addresses of linked members in the list. Visual Basic doesn't have explicit pointer variables, but it does provide several of its own techniques to handle references to objects and variables. Behind the scenes, Visual Basic does keep track of pointers, but you don't have to worry about those details. You can focus instead on the new, higher-level data handling concepts.

In this example, you will create the equivalent of a linked list of strings, in which you can insert strings as new members of the list while maintaining alphabetic order. The new Collection object is a powerful tool for accomplishing this task efficiently. In a new project, add a command button named cmdBuildList to a blank form and add the following lines of code:

```
Option Explicit

Private colWords As New Collection

Sub Insert(V As Variant)
    Dim i, j, k
    'Determine whether this is the first item to add
    If colWords.Count = 0 Then
        colWords.Add V
        Exit Sub
    End If
    'Get the range of the collection
    i = 1
    j = colWords.Count
    'Determine whether this should be inserted before first item
    If V <= colWords.Item(i) Then
        colWords.Add V, before:=i
        Exit Sub
    End If
    'Determine whether this should be inserted after last item
    If V >= colWords.Item(j) Then
        colWords.Add V, after:=j
        Exit Sub
    End If
    'Conduct binary search for insertion point
    Do Until j - i <= 1
```

(continued)

```
            k = (i + j) \ 2
            If colWords.Item(k) < V Then
                i = k
            Else
                j = k
            End If
        Loop
        'Insert item where it belongs
        colWords.Add V, before:=j
End Sub

Private Sub cmdBuildList_Click()
    Dim i
    Insert "One"
    Insert "Two"
    Insert "Three"
    Insert "Four"
    Insert "Five"
    Insert "Six"
    Insert "Seven"
    Insert "Eight"
    Insert "Nine"
    Insert "Ten"
    For i = 1 To colWords.Count
        Print colWords.Item(i)
    Next i
End Sub
```

I've declared the colWords Collection object at the module level to ensure that it exists for the duration of this program. As with other local variables, if you declare a Collection object within a subprogram, it is automatically removed from memory when that subprogram ends. When you declare a Collection object at the module level, it exists as long as the form is loaded. Also, it's common to create several routines that process the same collection, and this technique allows all the routines to share the same module-level Collection object.

Collection objects can contain two types of members: Objects and Variants. Of course, a Variant-type variable can contain a wide variety of data types, so a Collection object can actually contain just about anything you want it to contain. In this example, strings are passed and handled as Variants for insertion into the list. The online help explains in detail how to wrap a Collection object within a class module to better control the type of data that can be added to a collection. This would be important, for instance, if you were to use a Collection object within an OLE server application that you plan to distribute commercially, in which you might want the Collection object to contain only one type of data. In my example code, for instance, there's nothing to prevent me from passing something other than a string to the Insert routine, even though that would not make sense in the context of what my program is trying to accomplish.

Collection members can be directly accessed via a key string or an index number representing the member's position within the list. In my example, I use the index number to control the order in which the members are accessed. A Collection object's index allows you to insert, delete, and generally perform the same kinds of manipulations that a true linked list requires. A Collection object is like a linked list (and unlike an array) in that the insertion and deletion of members from anywhere within the Collection object is handled by Visual Basic efficiently, automatically, and with no wasted memory.

The Collection object's *Add* method is used to insert each string. Two named arguments of the *Add* method, before and after, allow you to add a new string just before or just after an indexed location in the object. I use both of these named arguments to insert each string into the object based on alphabetic order. This way the list of strings, when accessed sequentially through the Collection object's index, returns the strings in alphabetic order without requiring any further processing. Figure 24-1 shows the results of printing the Collection object's sorted contents on the form.

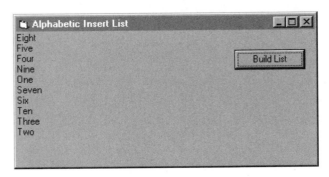

Figure 24-1.
Results of using an insertion sort in a linked list collection.

Be sure to study the online help for more information about the Collection object. This powerful and flexible construct, when combined with the flexibility of Variant data types and class module objects, frees you from many of the constraints that were imposed by the Basic language in the past, allowing you to program in ways never before possible.

Dear John, How Do I...

Exit and Restart Windows?

Rebooting Windows 95 from your application is not something you're likely to do frequently, but there are times when the ability to reboot can be useful. A detected security violation, for instance, can be counteracted with a programmatic reboot of the system. Some specialized application installation and setup procedures require a reboot to update current paths and Registry settings. It's easy to reboot from your code; just be sure you save any open files, including this project, before you try the following code!

Try this example by adding a command button named cmdReboot to a form, adding this code, saving it, and then running it and clicking on the command button:

```
Option Explicit

Private Declare Function ExitWindowsEx _
Lib "user32" ( _
    ByVal uFlags As Long, _
    ByVal dwReserved As Long _
) As Long

Private Sub cmdReboot_Click()
    ExitWindowsEx &H43, 0
End Sub
```

Once you have clicked on the command button, there's no turning back—the system will shut down and begin the reboot process.

Dear John, How Do I...

Dial a Phone from My Application?

The Microsoft Comm custom control is a complete, powerful, and easy-to-use control for handling all your serial communications requirements. One of the most common communication programming tasks is simply dialing a telephone. The NISTTime application in Part III of this book provides an example of a more sophisticated use of the Comm custom control, but here I provide the few lines of code required for a quick dial of the phone.

To make this example more useful, I've assumed that the phone number has been copied to the clipboard. This way, you can mark and copy a telephone number from just about anywhere and use it to dial the phone. To try this out, start a new project. If the custom control MSComm is not available, choose Custom Controls from the Tools menu and turn on the Microsoft Comm Control check box in the Custom Control dialog box. To a blank form, add an MSComm control named comOne and a command button named cmdDial. Then add the following code:

```
Private Sub cmdDial_Click()
    Dim A$
    A$ = Clipboard.GetText(vbCFText)
    If A$ = "" Then
        MsgBox "Mark and copy a number first"
        Exit Sub
    End If
    comOne.CommPort = 1
    comOne.Settings = "9600,N,8,1"
    comOne.PortOpen = True
    comOne.Output = "ATDT" & A$ & vbCr
    MsgBox "Dialing " & A$ & vbCrLf & "Pick up the phone...", _
        vbOKOnly, "Dial-A-Phone"
    comOne.PortOpen = False
End Sub
```

Figure 24-2 shows the program in action.

You will need to change the CommPort property setting to *2* if your modem is installed on COM2 instead of COM1, and in rare cases you might need to change some of the other properties for your hardware. In the vast majority of situations, though, the above property settings will work fine.

Figure 24-2.
The phone dialing program waiting for the user to pick up the phone.

The *MsgBox* command delays the program just before the PortOpen property is set to *False*. As soon as the user clicks on the OK button in the message box, the phone is hung up by the MSComm control. This gives the user time to pick up the phone before the program proceeds and disconnects the line at the modem.

See Also...

- The NISTTime application in Chapter 27 (Part III) for a demonstration of a more sophisticated use of the Comm custom control

Dear John, How Do I...

Use Inline Error Trapping?

The most commonly suggested way to set up error trapping code in a Visual Basic program is to add a labeled section of code with an automatic *On Error GoTo Label* branch set up at the beginning of the procedure. Here's a simple example of this type of error trapping:

```
Private Sub cmdTest_Click()

    On Error GoTo ErrorTrap
    Print 17 / 0   '(math error)
    Exit Sub

ErrorTrap:
    Print "Illegal to divide by zero"
    Resume Next

End Sub
```

There are several reasons why you might prefer a more inline approach to error trapping, though. First, the error trap label above is reminiscent of the old GOTO labels of ancient spaghetti coding days. Modern structured programming techniques, like those used for much of Visual Basic, have gotten us away from code containing discontinuous jumps and branches, a style that can be identified by the presence of a GOTO command. True, a simple error trapping *GoTo* is not as confusing as a lot of old Basic code I've seen in the past, but the action is still not as clear as it is when using other techniques. Even more discouraging, especially when you are dealing with objects in your code, is the confusion you might experience when you are using this method and would like to know exactly where the error occurred and what in your routine triggered the error. Although the old *Err* variable is now an enhanced object with properties of its own, the Err object provides limited information, especially in larger subprograms.

Inline Error Trapping

The error-trapping approach taken in C programming is to check for returned error information immediately after each function call. The best example of this technique is the way you check for errors in Visual Basic after calling an API function. For example, immediately after calling the *mciExecute* API function to play a sound file, you can check the returned value to see whether the call was successful:

```
x = mciExecute("Play c:\windows\tada.wav")
If x = 0 Then MsgBox "There was a problem"
```

There is a way to set up generalized error trapping in your Visual Basic code to check for errors immediately after they occur. I like this technique much better than the standard error trapping method, and Microsoft's documentation does suggest using this technique when you are working with objects. The trick is to use an *On Error Resume Next* statement at the start of your procedure and to check for possible errors immediately after the lines of code in which errors might occur. The following subprogram demonstrates this technique:

```
Option Explicit

Private Sub cmdTest_Click()
    Dim X, Y
    For X = -3 To 3
        Y = Reciprocal(X)
        Print "Reciprocal of "; X; " is "; Y; ""
        If IsError(Y) Then Print Err.Description
    Next X
End Sub

Function Reciprocal(X)
    Dim Y
    On Error Resume Next
    Y = 1 / X
    If Err.Number = 0 Then
        Reciprocal = Y
    Else
        Reciprocal = CVErr(Err.Number)
    End If
End Function
```

Here I've taken advantage of the fact that a Variant can actually be set to a value of type *Error* using the *CVErr* conversion function, which is an excellent way to signal back to a calling routine that an error has occurred. You can, of course, return a value from your functions to indicate an error, but the advantage of signaling an error implicitly through the returned data type is that the error can be indicated even if your function can theoretically return any numeric value.

Figure 24-3 shows the results of running this sample code in a small form. Notice that I print the contents of the returned Variant Y even in the case of an error. Because the returned value is a Variant, an error message instead of a number is returned.

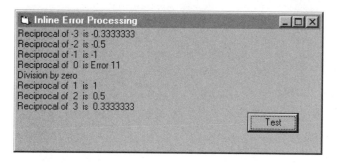

Figure 24-3.

Inline error trapping detecting and reporting a divide-by-zero condition.

I've briefly hinted at the many changes to error trapping provided by Microsoft in this release of Visual Basic. The new Err object provides several new properties and methods that greatly enhance what you can do, so be sure to review Visual Basic's documentation to learn about all the newest error handling features.

SAMPLE
APPLICATIONS

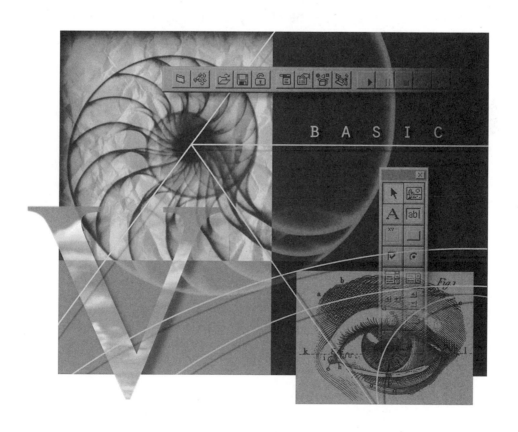

The applications in this part of the book are complete, stand-alone applications that demonstrate many of the solutions described in the previous chapters, and they demonstrate some other tricks and techniques I've picked up during my programming experiences. Some of these applications are useful utilities, some are informative, and some are just for fun. As you follow along and learn how each of these programs works, I hope you'll find some new and creative approaches that you can use in your own applications in Visual Basic 4. I've tried to include a variety of types of applications, but no matter what your field of interest might be, I think you'll find several interesting applications here. All the forms and source code for each application in this part of the book are included on the Companion CD.

CHAPTER TWENTY-FIVE

Graphics

This chapter contains a handful of fun applications that demonstrate some of the graphics techniques and features discussed in Part II of this book. The RGBHSV application is a handy utility for selecting colors. The Animate application demonstrates a few ways to create simple animated graphics on your Visual Basic forms. The Lottery application might not guarantee that you'll win a million dollars, but it will at least provide some fun graphics experimentation, and the Ssaver application provides a full-blown screen saver that includes multiple options.

The RGBHSV Application

The RGBHSV application is a simple utility to help you select any shade of color using either the RGB (red, green, blue) system or the HSV (hue, saturation, value) system of color definition. This application calls the *RgbToHsv* and *HsvToRgb* functions that were presented in Chapter 10 (Part II) of this book to make the necessary conversions between the two color systems. To keep them isolated and to make them easily portable to your own applications, I've kept these two functions in a separate code module named RGBHSV.bas.

Like many of the programs in this part of the book, this program includes menu items. Some of the items are not enabled and are grayed out, waiting for you to add code to give them purpose. All the items on the Help menu, however, are enabled, giving you access to my standard About dialog box and a help file created for this collection of programs. Use of the About dialog box is described in Chapter 8. Notice in the source code that the path to the help file is a relative path. By starting with the application's path and then working up a couple of folders and then down to the Help folder, you can locate the help file regardless of the drive you use for your CD or even if you copied the contents of the CD into a folder on your hard drive without changing the basic folder structure. If, however, you are using the Setup program to install your application, you will probably want to omit the path and specify only the filename, letting Setup take care of placing the help file where it can be found by the application.

One line of code might cause you to do a double take. The hexadecimal value of the currently selected color value is displayed in a label named lblColor, just above the picture box that displays the color itself. To create the standard Visual Basic notation for a hexadecimal number, I added an ampersand and an uppercase *H* prefix to the displayed hexadecimal value. Notice, however, that the string in my program line contains two ampersands in a row:

```
lblColor = "Color = " & "&&H" & Hex$(RGBColor)
```

A single ampersand just before the *H* causes the label to display an underlined *H*, a handy feature when you want it, but a nuisance when you want to actually display an ampersand. When you put two ampersands in a row, Visual Basic knows to display a single ampersand instead of an underlined character.

Figures 25-1 through 25-3 show runtime and development-time details of the RGBHSV application. Figure 25-1 shows the RGBHSV application in action. As each slider is moved, RGBHSV displays the color within the picture box to match the slider position and all other slider controls are adjusted programmatically. Figure 25-2 shows the contents of the project window, which provides a list of all forms and modules comprising this application. Figure 25-3 shows the RGBHSV form during the development process. The numbers

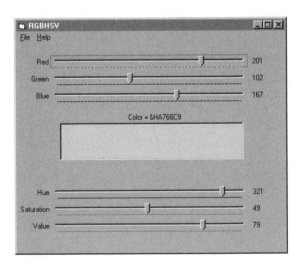

Figure 25-1.
The RGBHSV application in action.

Figure 25-2.
The RGBHSV project list.

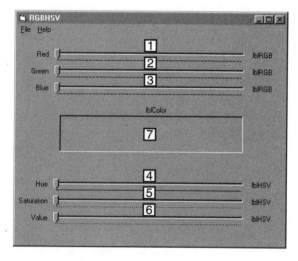

Figure 25-3.
RGBHSV.frm during development.

on the form identify the form's objects, as listed in the Object and Property
Settings table that follows.

To create this application, use the following tables and source code to
add the appropriate controls, set any nondefault properties as indicated, and
type in the source code lines as shown. Refer to Chapter 8 for a description of
the About form.

RGBHSV.frm Menu Design Window Entries

Caption	Name	Indentation	Enabled
&File	mnuFile	0	True
&New	mnuNew	1	False
&Open...	mnuOpen	1	False
&Save	mnuSave	1	False
Save &As...	mnuSaveAs	1	False
-	mnuFileDash1	1	True
E&xit	mnuExit	1	True
&Help	mnuHelp	0	True
&Contents	mnuContents	1	True
&Search for Help on...	mnuSearch	1	True
-	mnuHelpDash1	1	True
&About...	mnuAbout	1	True

RGBHSV.frm Objects and Property Settings

ID No.*	Property	Value
Slider		
1	Name	sliRGB
	Index	0
	Max	255
	LargeChange	10
Slider		
2	Name	sliRGB
	Index	1
	Max	255
	LargeChange	10
Slider		
3	Name	sliRGB
	Index	2
	Max	255
	LargeChange	10

* The number in the ID No. column corresponds to the number in Figure 25-3 that identifies the location of the object on the form.

(continued)

RGBHSV.frm Objects and Property Settings *continued*

ID No.	Property	Value
Slider		
4	Name	sliHSV
	Index	0
	Max	359
Slider		
5	Name	sliHSV
	Index	1
	Max	100
Slider		
6	Name	sliHSV
	Index	2
	Max	100
Label		
	Name	Label1
	Index	0
	Caption	Red
Label		
	Name	Label1
	Index	1
	Caption	Green
Label		
	Name	Label1
	Index	2
	Caption	Blue
Label		
	Name	Label2
	Index	0
	Caption	Hue
Label		
	Name	Label2
	Index	1
	Caption	Saturation

(continued)

RGBHSV.frm Objects and Property Settings *continued*

ID No.	Property	Value
Label		
	Name	Label2
	Index	2
	Caption	Value
Label		
	Name	lblRGB
	Index	0
Label		
	Name	lblRGB
	Index	1
Label		
	Name	lblRGB
	Index	2
Label		
	Name	lblHSV
	Index	0
Label		
	Name	lblHSV
	Index	1
Label		
	Name	lblHSV
	Index	2
Label		
	Name	lblColor
Picture		
7	Name	picColor

Source Code for RGBHSV.frm

```
Option Explicit

Private Declare Function WinHelp _
Lib "user32" Alias "WinHelpA" ( _
    ByVal hwnd As Long, _
```

(continued)

Source Code for RGBHSV.frm *continued*

```
        ByVal lpHelpFile As String, _
        ByVal wCommand As Long, _
        ByVal dwData As Long _
) As Long

Const TOHSV = 1
Const TORGB = 2

Dim RGBColor
Dim R, G, B, H, S, V

Private Sub Form_Load()
    Dim i
    'Set a random starting color
    Randomize
    R = Int(Rnd * 256)
    G = Int(Rnd * 256)
    B = Int(Rnd * 256)
    Update TOHSV
    Update TORGB
End Sub

Private Sub mnuAbout_Click()
    'Set properties of About form
    About.Application = "RGBHSV"
    About.Heading = "Microsoft Visual Basic 4.0 Developer's Workshop"
    About.Copyright = "1996 John Clark Craig"
    'Call a method
    About.Display
End Sub

Private Sub mnuContents_Click()
    'Display help contents
    WinHelp hwnd, App.Path & "\..\..\Help\Mvbdw.hlp", _
        cdlHelpContents, 0
End Sub

Private Sub mnuExit_Click()
    Unload Me
End Sub

Private Sub mnuSearch_Click()
    'Display Help's Search dialog box
```

(continued)

Source Code for RGBHSV.frm *continued*

```
    WinHelp hwnd, App.Path & "\..\..\Help\Mvbdw.hlp", _
        cdlHelpPartialKey, 0
End Sub
Private Sub sliHSV_Change(Index As Integer)
    H = sliHSV(0).Value
    S = sliHSV(1).Value
    V = sliHSV(2).Value
    Update TORGB
End Sub

Private Sub sliRGB_Change(Index As Integer)
    R = sliRGB(0).Value
    G = sliRGB(1).Value
    B = sliRGB(2).Value
    Update TOHSV
End Sub

Sub Update(Direction)
    Dim i
    Select Case Direction
    Case TOHSV
        RgbToHsv R, G, B, H, S, V
        sliHSV(0).Value = H
        sliHSV(1).Value = S
        sliHSV(2).Value = V
    Case TORGB
        HsvToRgb H, S, V, R, G, B
        sliRGB(0).Value = R
        sliRGB(1).Value = G
        sliRGB(2).Value = B
    End Select
    'Update RGB color labels
    lblRGB(0).Caption = Format$(R, "##0")
    lblRGB(1).Caption = Format$(G, "##0")
    lblRGB(2).Caption = Format$(B, "##0")
    'Update HSV color labels
    lblHSV(0).Caption = Format$(H, "##0")
    lblHSV(1).Caption = Format$(S, "##0")
    lblHSV(2).Caption = Format$(V, "##0")
    'Update displayed color
    RGBColor = RGB(R, G, B)
    picColor.BackColor = RGBColor
    'Update color's number
    lblColor = "Color = " & "&&H" & Hex$(RGBColor)
End Sub
```

(continued)

Source Code for RGBHSV.frm *continued*

```
Private Sub sliRGB_Scroll(Index As Integer)
    sliRGB_Change (Index)
End Sub

Private Sub sliHSV_Scroll(Index As Integer)
    sliHSV_Change (Index)
End Sub
```

Source Code for RGBHSV.bas

```
Option Explicit

Sub RgbToHsv(R, G, B, H, S, V)
    'Convert RGB to HSV values
    Dim vRed, vGreen, vBlue
    Dim Mx, Mn, Va, Sa, rc, gc, bc

    vRed = R / 255
    vGreen = G / 255
    vBlue = B / 255

    Mx = vRed
    If vGreen > Mx Then Mx = vGreen
    If vBlue > Mx Then Mx = vBlue

    Mn = vRed
    If vGreen < Mn Then Mn = vGreen
    If vBlue < Mn Then Mn = vBlue

    Va = Mx
    If Mx Then
        Sa = (Mx - Mn) / Mx
    Else
        Sa = 0
    End If
    If Sa = 0 Then
        H = 0
    Else
        rc = (Mx - vRed) / (Mx - Mn)
        gc = (Mx - vGreen) / (Mx - Mn)
        bc = (Mx - vBlue) / (Mx - Mn)
        Select Case Mx
        Case vRed
            H = bc - gc
```

(continued)

Source Code for RGBHSV.bas *continued*

```
        Case vGreen
            H = 2 + rc - bc
        Case vBlue
            H = 4 + gc - rc
        End Select
        H = H * 60
        If H < 0 Then H = H + 360
    End If

    S = Sa * 100
    V = Va * 100
End Sub

Sub HsvToRgb(H, S, V, R, G, B)
    'Convert HSV to RGB values
    Dim Sa, Va, Hue, i, f, p, q, t

    Sa = S / 100
    Va = V / 100
    If S = 0 Then
        R = Va
        G = Va
        B = Va
    Else
        Hue = H / 60
        If Hue = 6 Then Hue = 0
        i = Int(Hue)
        f = Hue - i
        p = Va * (1 - Sa)
        q = Va * (1 - (Sa * f))
        t = Va * (1 - (Sa * (1 - f)))
        Select Case i
        Case 0
            R = Va
            G = t
            B = p
        Case 1
            R = q
            G = Va
            B = p
        Case 2
            R = p
            G = Va
            B = t
```

(continued)

Source Code for RGBHSV.bas *continued*

```
        Case 3
            R = p
            G = q
            B = Va
        Case 4
            R = t
            G = p
            B = Va
        Case 5
            R = Va
            G = p
            B = q
        End Select
    End If

    R = Int(255.9999 * R)
    G = Int(255.9999 * G)
    B = Int(255.9999 * B)
End Sub
```

The Animate Application

The Animate application demonstrates a couple of graphics techniques you
might find useful in designing your own applications. In the code module
Animate.bas, Sub Main displays two forms, each demonstrating a unique
graphics technique. First, let's take a look at the source code for the entire
code module, and then we'll dive right into the two forms in this project.

Source Code for Animate.bas

```
Option Explicit
DefDbl A-Z

Public Const PI = 3.14159265358979
Public Const RADPERDEG = PI / 180

Sub Main()
    App.HelpFile = App.Path & "\..\..\Help\Mvbdw.hlp"
    frmClock.Show vbModeless
    frmGlobe.Show vbModeless
End Sub
```

(continued)

313

Source Code for Animate.bas *continued*

```basic
Sub RotateX(X, Y, Z, Angle)
    Dim Radians, Ca, Sa, Ty
    Radians = Angle * RADPERDEG
    Ca = Cos(Radians)
    Sa = Sin(Radians)
    Ty = Y * Ca - Z * Sa
    Z = Z * Ca + Y * Sa
    Y = Ty
End Sub

Sub RotateY(X, Y, Z, Angle)
    Dim Radians, Ca, Sa, Tx
    Radians = Angle * RADPERDEG
    Ca = Cos(Radians)
    Sa = Sin(Radians)
    Tx = X * Ca + Z * Sa
    Z = Z * Ca - X * Sa
    X = Tx
End Sub

Sub RotateZ(X, Y, Z, Angle)
    Dim Radians, Ca, Sa, Tx
    Radians = Angle * RADPERDEG
    Ca = Cos(Radians)
    Sa = Sin(Radians)
    Tx = X * Ca - Y * Sa
    Y = Y * Ca + X * Sa
    X = Tx
End Sub

Sub PolToRec(Radius, Angle, X, Y)
    Dim Radians
    Radians = Angle * RADPERDEG
    X = Radius * Cos(Radians)
    Y = Radius * Sin(Radians)
End Sub

Sub RecToPol(X, Y, Radius, Angle)
    Dim Radians
    Radius = Sqr(X * X + Y * Y)
    If X = 0 Then
        Select Case Y
        Case Is > 0
            Angle = 90
```

(continued)

Source Code for Animate.bas *continued*

```
        Case Is < 0
            Angle = -90
        Case Else
            Angle = 0
        End Select
    ElseIf Y = 0 Then
        Select Case X
        Case Is < 0
            Angle = 180
        Case Else
            Angle = 0
        End Select
    Else
        If X < 0 Then
            If Y > 0 Then
                Radians = Atn(Y / X) + PI
            Else
                Radians = Atn(Y / X) - PI
            End If
        Else
            Radians = Atn(Y / X)
        End If
        Angle = Radians / RADPERDEG
    End If
End Sub
```

Notice that I've used the *Defdbl A-Z* statement in all of the forms and modules of this project to cause all variables to default to double-precision floating-point values. This program will run just fine if you delete these statements and let all variables default to variants, but operation is slightly quicker if all variables are defined to be Double as shown.

Unlike most of the applications in this part of the book, these graphics demonstration forms don't have menus; hence, they have no menu selections to access the help file. However, this is a convenient place to demonstrate how to connect the F1 key to this application's help file so that the user can activate the help system at any time by pressing the F1 key. I simply set the application's HelpFile property in Sub Main to the path and filename of my help file.

An alternative to defining the HelpFile property in your code is to set the filename and optionally the full path of the help file in your project file. To do this, select Options from the Tools menu and click on the Project tab. In the Help File field, enter the name of the help file and leave the Help-ContextID field set to *0*, which calls up the Contents topic in the help file.

I set the program to start with Sub Main instead of one of the forms. To do this, I opened the Options dialog box as described earlier, and on the Project tab, I set the Startup Form field to Sub Main. The Sub Main code block is very short; its purpose is to show both of the animation demonstration forms and set the application's HelpFile property. The rest of the code in this module is a collection of handy routines for rotating Cartesian coordinates around each of the three axes and for converting coordinates between rectangular and polar. These routines are useful for three-dimensional graphics computations, such as the ones I use to display a spinning globe. We get into that in more detail later, but first let's look at the animated clock form.

AniClock.frm

This form creates a real-time clock using only a single Line control and a Timer control. Figure 25-4 shows these two controls on the form at design time, and Figure 25-5 shows the clock at runtime.

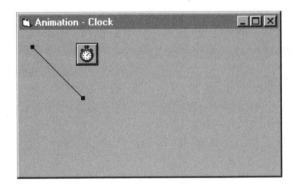

Figure 25-4.
The clock form, with only two controls.

You might be wondering how in the world all the straight-line elements of the clock face are drawn. The trick is to make 14 copies of the original Line control using the *Load* command, with the endpoint-coordinate properties of each instance of this control array set to properly place each line on the clock face. Most of these copies are placed once, and three of the Line controls are updated each second to give the illusion of movement of the hands of the clock.

Notice that no *Line* methods were used to create this clock and that no lines are ever erased directly by our application code. All the technical work of erasing and redrawing each hand as it moves is taken care of by Visual Basic

Figure 25-5.
The clock form at runtime.

when we update the endpoints of each Line control. Sometimes you don't need fancy graphics statements and commands—even a simple Line control can do amazing things.

You can change the appearance of the clock by adjusting property settings in the code. For example, you can create thinner or fatter lines by changing the setting of each Line control's BorderWidth property. To create this application, use the following table to add the appropriate controls and set any nondefault properties as indicated.

AniClock.frm Objects and Property Settings

Property	Value
Form	
Name	frmClock
Caption	Animation - Clock
MinButton	False
Timer	
Name	tmrClock
Interval	100
Line	
Name	linClock
Index	0

Notice that I set the timer's Interval property to 100, which is $1/10$ of a second. It might seem that logic would dictate a setting of 1000 milliseconds, or once per second, as ideal for updating the hands of the clock. However, this timing interval is not precise because Visual Basic's timers are designed to provide a delay that is at least as long as the specified interval, but there is no guarantee that every delay will be of exactly the same duration. Because of the slight variability in delay intervals, occasionally the second hand will "miss a beat," causing a noticeably jerky cycle in the movement of the second hand. To solve this timing unpredictability, I chose to check at the rate of ten times per second to see whether a new second has arrived. This results in an error of approximately $1/10$ of a second in the precision of each movement of the second hand, which is well within the tolerance of smooth operation for visual perception. About 9 out of 10 times that the timer event runs, it bails out immediately because the current second hasn't changed, wasting very little of the system's time.

Much of the work of the *tmrClock*'s Timer event is in recalculating and resetting the endpoint-coordinate properties X1, Y1, X2, and Y2. The source code for this form is shown here:

Source Code for AniClock.frm

```
Option Explicit
DefDbl A-Z

Private Sub Form_Load()
    Width = 4000
    Height = 4000
    Left = Screen.Width \ 2 - 4100
    Top = (Screen.Height - Height) \ 2
End Sub

Private Sub Form_Resize()
    Dim i, Angle
    Static Flag As Boolean
    If Flag = False Then
        Flag = True
        For i = 0 To 14
            If i > 0 Then Load linClock(i)
            linClock(i).Visible = True
            linClock(i).BorderWidth = 5
            linClock(i).BorderColor = RGB(0, 128, 0)
        Next i
    End If
```

(continued)

Source Code for AniClock.frm *continued*

```
    For i = 0 To 14
        Scale (-1, 1)-(1, -1)
        Angle = i * 2 * Atn(1) / 3
        linClock(i).x1 = 0.9 * Cos(Angle)
        linClock(i).y1 = 0.9 * Sin(Angle)
        linClock(i).x2 = Cos(Angle)
        linClock(i).y2 = Sin(Angle)
    Next i
End Sub

Private Sub tmrClock_Timer()
    Const HourHand = 0
    Const MinuteHand = 13
    Const SecondHand = 14
    Dim Angle
    Static LastSecond
    'Position hands only on the second
    If Second(Now) = LastSecond Then Exit Sub
    LastSecond = Second(Now)
    'Position hour hand
    Angle = 0.5236 * (15 - (Hour(Now) + Minute(Now) / 60))
    linClock(HourHand).x1 = 0
    linClock(HourHand).y1 = 0
    linClock(HourHand).x2 = 0.3 * Cos(Angle)
    linClock(HourHand).y2 = 0.3 * Sin(Angle)
    'Position minute hand
    Angle = 0.1047 * (75 - (Minute(Now) + Second(Now) / 60))
    linClock(MinuteHand).x1 = 0
    linClock(MinuteHand).y1 = 0
    linClock(MinuteHand).x2 = 0.7 * Cos(Angle)
    linClock(MinuteHand).y2 = 0.7 * Sin(Angle)
    'Position second hand
    Angle = 0.1047 * (75 - Second(Now))
    linClock(SecondHand).x1 = 0
    linClock(SecondHand).y1 = 0
    linClock(SecondHand).x2 = 0.8 * Cos(Angle)
    linClock(SecondHand).y2 = 0.8 * Sin(Angle)
End Sub
```

AniGlobe.frm

This form displays sequential images of a sphere's lines of latitude and longitude, creating the illusion of a spinning globe. The technique used here is an ImageList control that stores the sequential images and provides them for quick, animated copying to a PictureBox control. Figure 25-6 on the next page

319

shows the form during development, with the PictureBox, ImageList, and Timer controls for creating the animation effect.

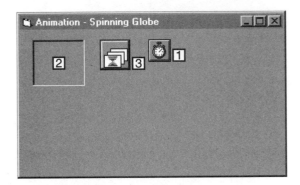

Figure 25-6.
The AniGlobe form at development time.

This form updates itself each time its tmrGlobe timer event fires. The first 15 times the routine runs, a new image is drawn, using the various 3–D graphics subprograms you'll find in the Animate.bas module. As each image is drawn, it is quickly saved to an ImageList control declared at the module level. After all 15 images have been tucked away for safekeeping, the routine begins to display them sequentially by updating the PictureBox's Picture property to refer to each image, as shown in Figure 25-7. This image transfer operation is fast and smooth, providing a great general technique for creating animated sequences.

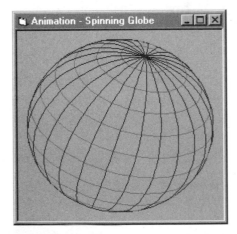

Figure 25-7.
The AniGlobe form in action.

This routine uses the following settings.

AniGlobe.frm Objects and Property Settings

ID No.*	Property	Value
Form		
	Name	frmGlobe
	Caption	Animation - Spinning Globe
Timer		
1	Name	tmrGlobe
	Interval	1
PictureBox		
2	Name	picGlobe
	AutoRedraw	True
ImageList		
3	Name	imlGlobe

* The number in the ID No. column corresponds to the number in Figure 25-6 that identifies the location of the object on the form.

In the source code below, I've isolated constants that define the forward and sideways tilt angles of the globe. Try changing the TILTSOUTH and TILT-EAST constants to see the dramatic changes to the appearance of the spinning globe.

The ImageList control is especially useful when associated with other controls, such as the new ListView, ToolBar, TabStrip, and TreeView controls. For more information on this powerful image manipulation tool, see the Visual Basic documentation.

The source code for this form is shown here:

Source Code for AniGlobe.frm

```
Option Explicit
DefDbl A-Z

Const TILTSOUTH = 37
Const TILTEAST = 27
```

(continued)

Source Code for AniGlobe.frm *continued*

```
Private Sub Form_Load()
    Width = 4000
    Height = 4000
    Left = Screen.Width \ 2 + 100
    Top = (Screen.Height - Height) \ 2
End Sub

Private Sub tmrGlobe_Timer()
    Dim Lat, Lon, Radians
    Dim R, A, i
    Dim x1, y1, x2, y2
    Dim Xc(72), Yc(72), Zc(72)
    Dim imgX As ListImage
    Static ImageIndex, ImageNum

    Select Case ImageNum

    'Pump next image to display
    Case -1
        ImageIndex = (ImageIndex Mod 15) + 1
        Set picGlobe.Picture = imlGlobe.ListImages(ImageIndex).Picture
        Exit Sub

    'Initialize PictureBox control
    Case 0
        picGlobe.Move 0, 0, ScaleWidth, ScaleHeight
        picGlobe.Scale (-1.1, 1.1)-(1.1, -1.1)
        Caption = "Animation ... PREPARATION"
        ImageNum = ImageNum + 1
        Exit Sub

    'Flag that last image has been drawn and saved in image list
    Case 16
        Caption = "Animation - Spinning Globe"
        ImageNum = -1
        Exit Sub
    End Select

    'Erase any previous picture in PictureBox control
    Set picGlobe.Picture = Nothing

    'Draw edge of globe
    picGlobe.ForeColor = vbBlue
```

(continued)

Source Code for AniGlobe.frm *continued*

```
For i = 0 To 72
    PolToRec 1, i * 5, Xc(i), Yc(i)
Next i
For i = 1 To 72
    picGlobe.Line (Xc(i - 1), Yc(i - 1))-(Xc(i), Yc(i))
Next i

'Calculate and draw latitude lines
picGlobe.ForeColor = vbRed
For Lat = -75 To 75 Step 15

    'Convert latitude to Radians
    Radians = Lat * RADPERDEG

    'Draw circle size based on latitude
    For i = 0 To 72
        PolToRec Cos(Radians), i * 5, Xc(i), Zc(i)
        Yc(i) = Sin(Radians)

        'Tilt globe's north pole toward us
        RotateX Xc(i), Yc(i), Zc(i), TILTSOUTH

        'Tilt globe's north pole toward the right
        RotateY Xc(i), Yc(i), Zc(i), TILTEAST
    Next i

    'Draw front half of rotated circle
    For i = 1 To 72
        If Zc(i) >= 0 Then
            picGlobe.Line (Xc(i - 1), Yc(i - 1))-(Xc(i), Yc(i))
        End If
    Next i
Next Lat

'Calculate and draw longitude lines
picGlobe.ForeColor = vbBlue
For Lon = 0 To 165 Step 15

    'Start with X-Y plane circle
    For A = 0 To 72
        PolToRec 1, A * 5, Xc(A), Yc(A)
        Zc(A) = 0
    Next A
```

(continued)

Source Code for AniGlobe.frm *continued*

```
        'Rotate points for current line of longitude
        For i = 0 To 72
            RotateY Xc(i), Yc(i), Zc(i), Lon + ImageNum

            'Tilt globe's north pole toward us
            RotateX Xc(i), Yc(i), Zc(i), TILTSOUTH

            'Tilt globe's north pole toward the right
            RotateY Xc(i), Yc(i), Zc(i), TILTEAST
        Next i

        'Draw front half of rotated circle
        For i = 1 To 72
            If Zc(i) >= 0 Then
                picGlobe.Line (Xc(i - 1), Yc(i - 1))-(Xc(i), Yc(i))
            End If
        Next i
    Next Lon

    'Update PictureBox control's state
    picGlobe.Refresh
    picGlobe.Picture = picGlobe.Image

    'Add this image to image list
    Set imgX = imlGlobe.ListImages.Add(, , picGlobe.Picture)

    'Prepare to draw next image
    ImageNum = ImageNum + 1

End Sub
```

The Lottery Application

The Lottery application is modeled after the Colorado lottery, in which a basket tumbles numbered Ping-Pong balls. With minor modifications, this application can model other similar games of chance. The concept is fairly simple—42 Ping-Pong balls, numbered 1 through 42, are tossed into a cylindrical basket and jumbled. Six balls are then selected, one at a time in a random manner. The six numbers drawn from the set of numbers 1 through 42 represent the winning ticket. The prize money can be a huge amount, but the chance of hitting all six numbers is extremely small, so the state wins big on the average. In the application, each time you click on the Next ball command button, one of the balls is selected and placed at the bottom of the screen. Figure 25-8 shows the application in action, after two of the numbers have been selected. After you've finished selecting six balls, you can see how lucky you are—I've added an option to simulate the purchase of a thousand lottery tickets so that you can see how hard it is to hit the jackpot even if you buy a lot of tickets. As you'll discover, it's very rare that you'll match even five out of the six numbers.

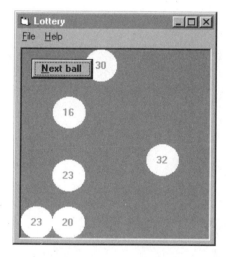

Figure 25-8.
The Lottery program in action.

This application demonstrates a Random object I've created that generates random numbers with a much greater sequence length than the generator built into Visual Basic. The application also demonstrates one of the simplest methods of animation, which is simply to redraw a picture repeatedly with enough speed to make it appear that the action is continuous.

In addition to the main Lottery form, which displays the tumbling Ping-Pong balls, this project contains a class module named Random.cls and the standard About form that I described in Chapter 8. Figure 25-9 on the following page shows the Lottery project list.

Figure 25-9.
The Lottery application's project list.

Lottery.frm

Lottery.frm is the main startup form for this application. The picTumble picture box displays the tumbling balls and the selected balls, the two command buttons control the action, and the tmrPingPong Timer control triggers each update of the action. Figure 25-10 shows this form during development, and the following tables and source code listing define the form's design.

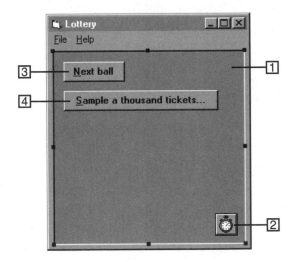

Figure 25-10.
The Lottery.frm form during development.

Lottery.frm Menu Design Window Entries

Caption	Name	Indentation	Enabled
&File	mnuFile	0	True
&New	mnuNew	1	False
&Open...	mnuOpen	1	False
&Save	mnuSave	1	False
Save &As...	mnuSaveAs	1	False
-	mnuFileDash1	1	True
E&xit	mnuExit	1	True
&Help	mnuHelp	0	True
&Contents	mnuContents	1	True
&Search for Help on...	mnuSearch	1	True
-	mnuHelpDash1	1	True
&About...	mnuAbout	1	True

Lottery.frm Objects and Property Settings

ID No.*	Property	Value
Form		
	Name	frmLottery
	Caption	Lottery
PictureBox		
1	Name	picTumble
	Autoredraw	True
	Backcolor	&H00FF0000&
	Height	3600
	Width	3600
Timer		
2	Name	tmrPingPong
	Interval	50
CommandButton		
3	Name	cmdNextBall
	Caption	&Next ball

* The number in the ID No. column corresponds to the number in Figure 25-10 that identifies the location of the object on the form.

(continued)

Lottery.frm Objects and Property Settings *continued*

ID No.	Property	Value
CommandButton		
4	Name	cmdSample
	Caption	&Sample a thousand tickets...

Source Code for Lottery.frm

```
Option Explicit
DefLng A-Z

Private Declare Function WinHelp _
Lib "user32" Alias "WinHelpA" ( _
    ByVal hwnd As Long, _
    ByVal lpHelpFile As String, _
    ByVal wCommand As Long, _
    ByVal dwData As Long _
) As Long

Const MAXNUM = 42

Dim PPBall(6)
Dim R As New Random

Private Sub cmdNextBall_Click()
    Dim i, j

    'Set command button caption
    cmdNextBall.Caption = "&Next ball"
    cmdSample.Visible = False

    'Get current count of selected balls
    i = PPBall(0)

    'If all were grabbed, start over
    If i = 6 Then
        For i = 0 To 6
            PPBall(i) = 0
        Next i
        Exit Sub
    End If
```

(continued)

Source Code for Lottery.frm *continued*

```
    'Select next unique Ping-Pong ball
    GrabNext PPBall()

    'Change command button caption
    'and show sample command button
    If PPBall(0) = 6 Then
        cmdNextBall.Caption = "Start &over"
        cmdSample.Visible = True
    End If
End Sub

Private Sub cmdSample_Click()
    Dim i, j, k, n
    Dim Ticket(6)
    Dim Hits(6)
    Dim Msg$

    'Display hourglass mouse pointer
    MousePointer = vbHourglass

    'Now simulate a thousand "quick pick" tickets
    For i = 1 To 1000

        'Generate a ticket
        Ticket(0) = 0
        For j = 1 To 6
            GrabNext Ticket()
        Next j

        'Tally the hits
        n = 0
        For j = 1 To 6
            For k = 1 To 6
                If Ticket(j) = PPBall(k) Then
                    n = n + 1
                End If
            Next k
        Next j

        'Update the statistics
        Hits(n) = Hits(n) + 1

    Next i
```

(continued)

Source Code for Lottery.frm *continued*

```
        'Display default mouse pointer
        MousePointer = vbDefault

        'Display summarized statistics
        Msg$ = "Sample of 1000 tickets..." & vbCrLf & vbCrLf
        Msg$ = Msg$ & Space$(10) & "Hits    Tally" & vbCrLf
        For i = 0 To 6
            Msg$ = Msg$ & Space$(12) & Format$(i) & Space$(6)
            Msg$ = Msg$ & Format$(Hits(i)) & vbCrLf
        Next i
        MsgBox Msg$, , "Lottery"

End Sub

Private Sub Form_Load()
        'Seed new random numbers
        Randomize
        R.Shuffle Rnd

        'Set range of random integers
        R.MinInt = 1
        R.MaxInt = MAXNUM

        'Center form
        Left = (Screen.Width - Width) \ 2
        Top = (Screen.Height - Height) \ 2

        'Hide sample command button for now
        cmdSample.Visible = False

        'Prepare tumble animation
        picTumble.Scale (0, 12)-(12, 0)
        picTumble.FillStyle = vbSolid
        picTumble.FillColor = vbWhite
        picTumble.ForeColor = vbRed
End Sub

Private Sub picTumble_Paint()
        Dim i, x, y, n$

        'Erase previous tumble animation
        picTumble.Cls
        For i = 1 To 6
```

(continued)

Source Code for Lottery.frm *continued*

```
        'Determine whether ball has been selected
        If PPBall(i) > 0 Then
            x = i * 2 - 1
            y = 1
            n$ = Format$(PPBall(i))

        Else
            x = Rnd * 10 + 1
            y = Rnd * 8 + 3
            n$ = Format$(R.RandomInt)
        End If

        'Draw each Ping-Pong ball
        picTumble.Circle (x, y), 1, vbWhite
        picTumble.CurrentX = x - picTumble.TextWidth(n$) / 2
        picTumble.CurrentY = y - picTumble.TextHeight(n$) / 2

        'Label each Ping-Pong ball
        picTumble.Print n$
    Next i
End Sub

Private Sub tmrPingPong_Timer()
    picTumble_Paint
End Sub

Private Sub mnuAbout_Click()
    'Set properties
    About.Application = "Lottery"
    About.Heading = "Microsoft Visual Basic 4.0 Developer's Workshop"
    About.Copyright = "1996 John Clark Craig"
    About.Display
End Sub

Private Sub mnuExit_Click()
    Unload Me
End Sub

Private Sub mnuContents_Click()
    WinHelp hwnd, App.Path & "\..\..\Help\Mvbdw.hlp", _
        cdlHelpContents, 0
End Sub
```

(continued)

Source Code for Lottery.frm *continued*

```
Private Sub mnuSearch_Click()
    WinHelp hwnd, App.Path & "\..\..\Help\Mvbdw.hlp", _
        cdlHelpPartialKey, 0
End Sub

Sub GrabNext(Ary())
Dim i, j

    'Store index in first array element
    Ary(0) = Ary(0) + 1
    i = Ary(0)

    'Get next unique Ping-Pong ball number
    Do
        Ary(i) = R.RandomInt
        If i > 1 Then
            For j = 1 To i - 1
                If Ary(i) = Ary(j) Then
                    Ary(i) = 0
                End If
            Next j
        End If
    Loop Until Ary(i)

End Sub
```

Notes About the Lottery.frm Source Code

Long integers are the most common type of variable in this application, so I simplified the declarations of my variables by adding the *DefLng A-Z* statement at the module level.

The *WinHelp* API function is used to activate the help file when the appropriate menu items are clicked. In some of the applications in this section of the book, I'll add a CommonDialog control to the project to provide the connection to the help file, even in cases in which the menu is identical to the menu shown here. Both techniques produce identical results, and it's largely a matter of personal preference as to the method you choose.

Notice in the Form_Load event routine that I've created an object of type Random. This type of object is defined by the Random.cls module, which I'll describe next.

Random.cls

The Random class module provides the template for creating objects of type Random. At the core of the Random objects is a technique that greatly expands the sequence length of the random-number generator built into Visual Basic. I've used an array of type Double to add a shuffling and mixing action to the generation of the random numbers.

Random.cls Public Properties

The following public properties are defined in Random.cls:

- **MinInt** The minimum value for the range of generated random integers

- **MaxInt** The maximum value for the range of generated random integers

- **Random** A random double number in the range 0 through 1

- **RandomInt** A random integer in the range defined by MinInt and MaxInt

Random.cls Public Methods

The one public method defined in Random.cls is *Shuffle*, which initializes the random-number sequence.

The random-number generator in Visual Basic is very good, but I've heard of some concerns. First, it's not at all clear how to initialize Visual Basic's random-number generator to a repeatable sequence. Okay, I'll let you in on a little secret—there is a simple, albeit tricky, way to reinitialize Visual Basic's random-number generator to a repeatable sequence. You need to call Randomize immediately after passing a negative value to the *Rnd* function, as in the following:

```
Randomize Rnd(-7)
```

Every time you pass −7 to these two functions, as shown, you'll initialize Visual Basic's random numbers to the same sequence. I've used this technique, modified slightly, in the *Shuffle* method of my Random object to initialize the object's sequence. For flexibility, if you pass a negative value to *Shuffle*, a repeatable sequence is initialized. A positive or 0 value results in a completely unpredictable sequence.

Another concern I've heard, especially from cryptographers, is that the random numbers generated by Visual Basic don't take into account such phenomena as subtle patterns and entropy, reducing the value of the generated sequences for high-quality cryptography work. My Random objects maintain an array of double-precision numbers that effectively shuffle and randomize Visual Basic's sequence by many orders of magnitude, while maintaining a good distribution of numbers in the range 0 through 1. Study the Random public property routine to see how this is accomplished.

The RandomInt property routine modifies a value returned by the Random routine to provide an integer in the range defined by the user-set properties MinInt and MaxInt. The distribution of these pseudorandom integers is as good as the distribution of the values returned by Random.

There are two private subprograms in the Random class module. The Zap subprogram initializes the array and its indexes to a known state during the initialization performed by the *Shuffle* method. The *Stir* private method helps warm up the generator.

Source Code for Random.cls

```
Option Explicit

Const SIZE = 17

Private Seed(SIZE - 1) As Double
Private p1 As Integer
Private p2 As Integer

Public MinInt As Long
Public MaxInt As Long

Public Sub Shuffle(x As Double)
    Dim n$
    Dim i As Integer
    Zap
    n$ = Str$(x)
    For i = 1 To Len(n$)
        Stir 1 / Asc(Mid$(n$, i, 1))
    Next i
    Randomize Rnd(Seed(p1) * Sgn(x))
    For i = 1 To SIZE * 2.7
        Stir Rnd
    Next i
End Sub

Property Get Random() As Double
    p1 = (p1 + 1) Mod SIZE
```

(continued)

Source Code for Random.cls *continued*

```
        p2 = (p2 + 1) Mod SIZE
        Seed(p1) = Seed(p1) + Seed(p2) + Rnd
        Seed(p1) = Seed(p1) - Int(Seed(p1))
        Random = Seed(p1)
End Property

Property Get RandomInt() As Long
        RandomInt = Int(Random() * (MaxInt - MinInt + 1)) + MinInt
End Property

Private Sub Zap()
    Dim i As Integer
    For i = 1 To SIZE - 1
        Seed(i) = 1 / i
    Next i
    p1 = SIZE \ 2
    p2 = SIZE \ 3
    If p1 = p2 Then
        p1 = p1 + 1
    End If
End Sub

Private Sub Stir(x As Double)
    p1 = (p1 + 1) Mod SIZE
    p2 = (p2 + 1) Mod SIZE
    Seed(p1) = Seed(p1) + Seed(p2) + x
    Seed(p1) = Seed(p1) - Int(Seed(p1))
End Sub
```

The Ssaver Application

The Ssaver application expands on the screen saver examples presented in Chapter 21. I've added a larger set of graphics options that let the user set a wide variety of effects without a lot of additional code. Figure 25-11 on the following page shows this screen saver in action, although you should try the many combinations of settings to get the full effect of its many graphics variations.

As shown in Figure 25-12, also on the following page, this project contains only two form modules. Ssaver.frm is the main startup form, and Ssetup-.frm is activated when the user clicks on the Setup button in the Screen Saver dialog box on the Windows 95 desktop.

Figure 25-11.
The Ssaver application in action.

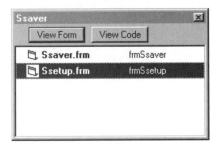

Figure 25-12.
The Ssaver project list.

Ssaver.frm

The Ssaver.frm form is where all the graphical screen saver action takes place. Notice that I set the form's WindowState property to *2 - Maximized* and turn off all visible parts of the form, such as setting the MinButton and MaxButton properties to *False*. This lets the form provide a drawing surface covering the entire screen.

The only control on this form, as shown in Figure 25-13, is a timer. The graphics update happens in a continuous loop during the form's Load event. Visual Basic generates an error if your program tries to unload itself from within the Load event, so the timer is a tricky way to allow the form to unload quickly after exiting from the graphics loop within the Load event routine. I wouldn't normally suggest structuring a program to continuously loop within the Load event in this way, but I did it this way because it's slightly faster than letting a timer trigger each update of the graphics and because the system doesn't interact with the user while a screen saver is running.

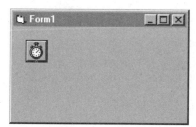

Figure 25-13.
Ssaver.frm during development.

The following table and source code listing define the form's design.

Ssaver.frm Objects and Property Settings

Property	Value
Form	
Name	frmSsaver
BorderStyle	0 - None
ControlBox	False
MaxButton	False
MinButton	False
WindowState	2 - Maximized
Timer	
Name	tmrExitNotify
Interval	1
Enabled	False

Source Code for Ssaver.frm

```
Option Explicit
DefLng A-Z

'Declare API to inform system a screen saver is active
Private Declare Function SystemParametersInfo _
Lib "user32" Alias "SystemParametersInfoA" ( _
    ByVal uAction As Long, _
    ByVal uParam As Long, _
    ByVal lpvParam As Any, _
    ByVal fuWinIni As Long _
) As Long

'Declare API to hide and reshow mouse pointer
Private Declare Function ShowCursor _
Lib "user32" ( _
    ByVal bShow As Long _
) As Long

'Declare Constants
Const SPI_SETSCREENSAVEACTIVE = 17

'Declare module-level variables
Dim Xai As Double, Yai As Double
Dim Xbi As Double, Ybi As Double
Dim LineCount
Dim LineWidth
Dim ActionType
Dim Xmax, Ymax
Dim Inc
Dim ColorNum()
Dim Dx1() As Double, Dx2() As Double
Dim Dy1() As Double, Dy2() As Double
Dim Xa(), Xb()
Dim Ya(), Yb()
Dim QuitFlag As Boolean

Private Sub Form_Click()
    'Quit if mouse is clicked
    QuitFlag = True
End Sub

Private Sub Form_KeyDown(KeyCode As Integer, Shift As Integer)
    'Quit if any key is pressed
    QuitFlag = True
End Sub
```

(continued)

Source Code for Ssaver.frm *continued*

```
Private Sub Form_Load()
    Dim x, Action$

    'Tell system screen saver is active now
    x = SystemParametersInfo( _
        SPI_SETSCREENSAVEACTIVE, 0, ByVal 0&, 0)

    'Proceed based on command line
    Select Case UCase$(Left$(Command$, 2))

    'Show quick preview
    Case "/P"
        Unload Me
        Exit Sub

    'Configure screen saver
    Case "/C"
        'Do any user interaction
        frmSsetup.Show vbModal

        'Continue after configuring screen saver
        Unload Me
        Exit Sub

    'Set password
    Case "/A"
        'Get and record new password here
        MsgBox "No password for this screen saver"

        'Continue after setting new password
        Unload Me
        Exit Sub

    'Put the show on the road
    Case "/S"
        'Create different display each time
        Randomize

        'Display full size
        Show

        'Set control values
        Inc = 5
        Xmax = 300
        Ymax = 300
```

(continued)

Source Code for Ssaver.frm *continued*

```
'Get current user settings from Registry
ActionType = Val(GetSetting("Ssaver", "Options", _
    "Action", "1"))
LineCount = Val(GetSetting("Ssaver", "Options", _
    "LineCount", "1"))
LineWidth = Val(GetSetting("Ssaver", "Options", _
    "LineWidth", "1"))

'Initialize graphics
BackColor = vbBlack
DrawWidth = LineWidth
Scale (-Xmax, -Ymax)-(Xmax, Ymax)

'Size arrays
ReDim ColorNum(0 To LineCount)
ReDim Xa(1 To LineCount), Xb(1 To LineCount)
ReDim Ya(1 To LineCount), Yb(1 To LineCount)

'Handle action types above 4 a little differently
If ActionType < 5 Then
    ReDim Dx1(1 To LineCount), Dx2(1 To LineCount)
    ReDim Dy1(1 To LineCount), Dy2(1 To LineCount)
Else
    ReDim Dx1(0), Dx2(0)
    ReDim Dy1(0), Dy2(0)
    Dx1(0) = Rnd * Inc
    Dx2(0) = Rnd * Inc
    Dy1(0) = Rnd * Inc
    Dy2(0) = Rnd * Inc
End If

'Hide mouse pointer
x = ShowCursor(False)

'Do main processing as a loop
Do
    'Update the display
    DoGraphics

    'Yield execution
    DoEvents

Loop Until QuitFlag = True
```

(continued)

Source Code for Ssaver.frm *continued*

```
        'Show mouse pointer
        x = ShowCursor(True)

        'Can't quit in this context; let timer do it
        tmrExitNotify.Enabled = True

    Case Else
        Unload Me
        Exit Sub

    End Select
End Sub

Private Sub Form_MouseMove(Button As Integer, Shift As Integer, _
    x As Single, y As Single)
    Static Xlast, Ylast
    Dim Xnow
    Dim Ynow

    'Get current position
    Xnow = x
    Ynow = y

    'On first move, simply record position
    If Xlast = 0 And Ylast = 0 Then
        Xlast = Xnow
        Ylast = Ynow
        Exit Sub
    End If

    'Quit only if mouse actually changes position
    If Xnow <> Xlast Or Ynow <> Ylast Then
        QuitFlag = True
    End If
End Sub

Private Sub tmrExitNotify_Timer()
    'Time to quit
    Unload Me
End Sub

Private Sub Form_Unload(Cancel As Integer)
    Dim x
```

(continued)

Source Code for Ssaver.frm *continued*

```
    'Must inform system screen saver is now inactive
    x = SystemParametersInfo( _
        SPI_SETSCREENSAVEACTIVE, 1, ByVal 0&, 0)
End Sub

Sub ColorReset()
    Dim i

    'Randomize set of colors
    If ActionType <= 4 Then
        For i = 1 To LineCount
            ColorNum(i) = RGB(Rnd * 256, Rnd * 256, Rnd * 256)
        Next i

    'Use bright colors for action types 5 or 6
    Else
        ColorNum(0) = QBColor(Int(8 * Rnd) + 8)
    End If
End Sub

Sub DoGraphics()
    Dim i
    Static ColorTime As Double

    'Shuffle line colors every so often
    If Timer > ColorTime Then
        ColorReset
        If LineCount < 5 Then
            ColorTime = Timer + LineCount * Rnd + 0.3
        Else
            ColorTime = Timer + 5 * Rnd + 0.3
        End If
    End If

    'Process based on count of lines
    For i = 1 To LineCount

        'Handle action types above 4 with special procedures
        If ActionType < 5 Then

            'Keep ends of lines in bounds
            If Xa(i) <= 0 Then
                Dx1(i) = Inc * Rnd
            End If
```

(continued)

Source Code for Ssaver.frm *continued*

```
        If Xb(i) <= 0 Then
            Dx2(i) = Inc * Rnd
        End If

        If Ya(i) <= 0 Then
            Dy1(i) = Inc * Rnd
        End If

        If Yb(i) <= 0 Then
            Dy2(i) = Inc * Rnd
        End If

        If Xa(i) >= Xmax Then
            Dx1(i) = -Inc * Rnd
        End If

        If Xb(i) >= Xmax Then
            Dx2(i) = -Inc * Rnd
        End If

        If Ya(i) >= Ymax Then
            Dy1(i) = -Inc * Rnd
        End If

        If Yb(i) >= Ymax Then
            Dy2(i) = -Inc * Rnd
        End If

        'Increment position of line ends
        Xa(i) = Xa(i) + Dx1(i)
        Xb(i) = Xb(i) + Dx2(i)
        Ya(i) = Ya(i) + Dy1(i)
        Yb(i) = Yb(i) + Dy2(i)

        'Set each line with a unique color
        ForeColor = ColorNum(i)
    Else

        'Set action types 5 and 6 with the same color
        ForeColor = ColorNum(0)
    End If

    'Draw lines based on action type
    Select Case ActionType
```

(continued)

Source Code for Ssaver.frm *continued*

```
Case 1
    Line (Xa(i), Ya(i))-(Xb(i), Yb(i))
    Line (-Xa(i), -Ya(i))-(-Xb(i), -Yb(i))
    Line (-Xa(i), Ya(i))-(-Xb(i), Yb(i))
    Line (Xa(i), -Ya(i))-(Xb(i), -Yb(i))
Case 2
    Line (Xa(i), Ya(i))-(Xb(i), Yb(i)), , B
    Line (-Xa(i), -Ya(i))-(-Xb(i), -Yb(i)), , B
    Line (-Xa(i), Ya(i))-(-Xb(i), Yb(i)), , B
    Line (Xa(i), -Ya(i))-(Xb(i), -Yb(i)), , B
Case 3
    Circle (Xa(i), Ya(i)), Xb(i)
    Circle (-Xa(i), -Ya(i)), Xb(i)
    Circle (-Xa(i), Ya(i)), Xb(i)
    Circle (Xa(i), -Ya(i)), Xb(i)
Case 4
    Line (Xa(i), Ya(i))-(Xb(i), -Yb(i))
    Line -(-Xa(i), -Ya(i))
    Line -(-Xb(i), Yb(i))
    Line -(Xa(i), Ya(i))

'Handle action types above 4 a little differently
Case 5, 6
    If ActionType = 5 Then
        Line (Xa(i), Ya(i))-(Xb(i), Yb(i)), BackColor
    Else
        Line (Xa(i), Ya(i))-(Xb(i), Yb(i)), BackColor, B
    End If

    If Xai <= -Xmax Then
        Dx1(0) = Inc * Rnd + 1
    End If

    If Xbi <= -Xmax Then
        Dx2(0) = Inc * Rnd + 1
    End If

    If Yai <= -Ymax Then
        Dy1(0) = Inc * Rnd + 1
    End If

    If Ybi <= -Ymax Then
        Dy2(0) = Inc * Rnd + 1
    End If
```

(continued)

Source Code for Ssaver.frm *continued*

```
                If Xai >= Xmax Then
                    Dx1(0) = -Inc * Rnd + 1
                End If

                If Xbi >= Xmax Then
                    Dx2(0) = -Inc * Rnd + 1
                End If

                If Yai >= Ymax Then
                    Dy1(0) = -Inc * Rnd + 1
                End If

                If Ybi >= Ymax Then
                    Dy2(0) = -Inc * Rnd + 1
                End If

                Xai = Xai + Dx1(0)
                Xbi = Xbi + Dx2(0)
                Yai = Yai + Dy1(0)
                Ybi = Ybi + Dy2(0)

                Xa(i) = Xai
                Xb(i) = Xbi
                Ya(i) = Yai
                Yb(i) = Ybi

                If ActionType = 5 Then
                    Line (Xa(i), Ya(i))-(Xb(i), Yb(i))
                Else
                    Line (Xa(i), Ya(i))-(Xb(i), Yb(i)), , B
                End If
        End Select
    Next i
End Sub
```

This code acts on the standard command line parameters that the system passes to any screen saver. In particular, the /C parameter causes the display of the Ssetup form, and the /S parameter activates the main graphics display loop. For more explanation of the way screen savers interact with the system, refer to Chapter 21.

I've set up six unique types of graphics animations, with variations on the number of lines and the thickness of each line in pixels. Much of the code is only slightly different for these different modes, although the effects can be dramatically different. For example, by simply adding the B parameter to the Line method, you can cause the same command to draw a series of boxes instead of diagonal lines.

Ssetup.frm

As mentioned earlier, the Ssetup form is activated when the user clicks on the Setup button while selecting this screen saver. Recall that you can select a screen saver by right-clicking on the Windows 95 desktop, selecting Properties, and then clicking on the Screen Saver tab in the Display Properties dialog box that appears.

Ssetup.frm is a dialog box that lets you select one of six types of graphics displays and lets you modify each of these by selecting the number of lines and the thickness in pixels of each line. These settings are read from and written to the system Registry using the *GetSetting* and *SaveSetting* statements. The dialog box always displays the current settings when it opens. Figure 25-14 shows the Ssetup form during the development process.

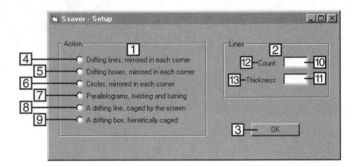

Figure 25-14.
Ssetup.frm during development.

The following table and source code listing define the form:

Ssetup.frm Objects and Property Settings

ID No.*	Property	Value
Form		
	Name	frmSsetup
	BorderStyle	3 - Fixed Dialog
	Caption	Ssaver - Setup
	ScaleMode	3 - Pixel

*   The number in the ID No. column corresponds to the number in Figure 25-14 that identifies the location of the object on the form.

(continued)

346

Ssetup.frm Objects and Property Settings *continued*

ID No.	Property	Value
Frame		
1	Name	Frame1
	Caption	Action
Frame		
2	Name	Frame2
	Caption	Lines
CommandButton		
3	Name	cmdOK
	Caption	OK
OptionButton		
4	Name	optAction
	Index	0
	Caption	Drifting lines, mirrored in each corner
OptionButton		
5	Name	optAction
	Index	1
	Caption	Drifting boxes, mirrored in each corner
OptionButton		
6	Name	optAction
	Index	2
	Caption	Circles, mirrored in each corner
OptionButton		
7	Name	optAction
	Index	3
	Caption	Parallelograms, twisting and turning
OptionButton		
8	Name	optAction
	Index	4
	Caption	A drifting line, caged by the screen

(continued)

Ssetup.frm Objects and Property Settings *continued*

ID No.	Property	Value
OptionButton		
9	Name	optAction
	Index	5
	Caption	A drifting box, frenetically caged
TextBox		
10	Name	txtLineCount
TextBox		
11	Name	txtLineWidth
Label		
12	Name	Label1
	Caption	Count:
Label		
13	Name	label2
	Caption	Thickness:

Source Code for Ssetup.frm

```
Option Explicit

Dim Action$

Private Sub Form_Load()
    'Center this form
    Left = (Screen.Width - Width) \ 2
    Top = (Screen.Height - Height) \ 2

    'Get current settings from Registry
    Action$ = GetSetting("Ssaver", "Options", "Action", "1")
    optAction(Val(Action$) - 1).Value = True

    txtLineCount.Text = GetSetting("Ssaver", "Options", _
        "LineCount", "5")

    txtLineWidth.Text = GetSetting("Ssaver", "Options", _
        "LineWidth", "1")
End Sub
```

(continued)

Source Code for Ssetup.frm *continued*

```
Private Sub cmdOK_Click()
    Dim n

    'Check line count option
    n = Val(txtLineCount.Text)
    If n < 1 Or n > 1000 Then
        MsgBox "Line count should be a small positive integer", _
            vbExclamation, "Ssaver"
        Exit Sub
    End If

    'Check line thickness option
    n = Val(txtLineWidth.Text)
    If n < 1 Or n > 100 Then
        MsgBox "Line thickness should be a small positive integer", _
            vbExclamation, "Ssaver"
        Exit Sub
    End If

    'Save the settings
    SaveSetting "Ssaver", "Options", "Action", Action$
    SaveSetting "Ssaver", "Options", "LineCount", txtLineCount.Text
    SaveSetting "Ssaver", "Options", "LineWidth", txtLineWidth.Text

    'Close Setup dialog box
    Unload Me
End Sub

Private Sub optAction_Click(Index As Integer)
    Action$ = Format$(Index + 1)
End Sub
```

Most of the code in this form is used to read and write settings to and from the Registry. I used defaults in the *GetSetting* statements to guarantee a valid setting even if the setting doesn't yet exist in the Registry.

The screen saver works only after being compiled, using special settings to create a screen saver. For details on properly compiling this application to create the required Ssaver.scr file in the Windows directory, see the instructions in Chapter 21.

CHAPTER TWENTY-SIX

Development Tools

This chapter contains three applications that have to do with your Visual Basic programming environment. The ColorBar application helps you adjust your monitor so that you can see all the color characteristics your users will see. The APIAddin application is an add-in to the Visual Basic development environment that helps you locate, copy, and paste constants, types, and declarations for Windows 32-bit API functions. The Metric application demonstrates one way to extend your set of application development tools—in this case by putting much of the functionality of the application in the help file and using Visual Basic to do the tasks it does best.

The ColorBar Application

The ColorBar application is quite simple, but I've found it very useful for adjusting my monitor to balance the colors and brightness. It also demonstrates a couple of programming techniques you'll probably find useful elsewhere. Figure 26-1 on the following page shows the ColorBar application in action, and Figure 26-2 shows the short project list.

When you run ColorBar, you see a form filled with 16 rectangles, each containing one of the 16 primary colors defined by the *QBColor()* function. Make sure the yellow block doesn't look brown (I had a monitor like that a few years ago, and it drove me nuts!)—and make sure each color is distinct from all the others. For example, you should see three distinct shades of gray. Click with the left mouse button on the form to rotate the color blocks one way and with the right button to rotate them the other way. After 16 clicks in either direction, the blocks return to their original locations.

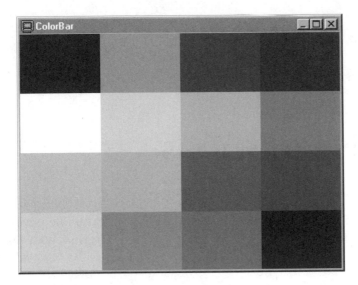

Figure 26-1.
The ColorBar application in action.

Figure 26-2.
The ColorBar project list.

ColorBar.frm

Take note of a couple of details about this form. The MinButton property is set to *False* to prevent an error condition. Each time the user resizes the form, the surface of the form is rescaled to simplify the drawing of the blocks. The *Scale* statement generates an error if the form is minimized to an icon. Because this utility serves little purpose in the minimized state, I decided to simply eliminate the MinButton option. As shown in Figure 26-1, the button is still visible even when the form's MinButton property is set to *False*. Notice, however, that the button is grayed and inactive.

The only control on the form is a timer, as shown in Figure 26-3. Originally I put the block drawing code in the form's Paint event routine, a technique that worked great as long as I stretched the form to a larger size at runtime, triggering a Paint event. But when I shrank the form a little, the Paint event was not called. To get around this result, I activated the timer at the various places in my program where I wanted to redraw the blocks of color. The timer is set up as a one-shot event, which means its code is activated once and then the timer shuts itself off. This one-shot action is triggered by setting the timer's Enabled property to *True* whenever the blocks are to be updated. By setting this property within the Resize event, I effectively enabled the program to redraw the blocks whenever the form is resized either larger or smaller. This also makes it easy to redraw the blocks when the mouse is clicked to rotate the order of the blocks.

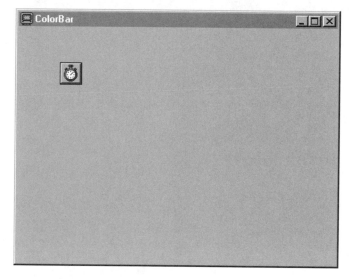

Figure 26-3.
The ColorBar form during development.

To create this application, use the following table and source code to add the appropriate control, set any nondefault properties as indicated, and type in the source code lines as shown.

ColorBar.frm Objects and Property Settings

Property	Value
Form	
Name	frmColorBar
Caption	ColorBar
MinButton	False
Icon	Monitr01.ico
Timer	
Name	trmDrawBars
Interval	1

Source Code for ColorBar.bas

```
Option Explicit
DefInt A-Z

Dim ColorShift

Private Sub Form_Load()
    'Center form on screen
    Left = (Screen.Width - Width) \ 2
    Top = (Screen.Height - Height) \ 2
End Sub

Private Sub Form_MouseDown(Button As Integer, _
Shift As Integer, X As Single, Y As Single)
    'Shift color bars based on mouse button
    ColorShift = (ColorShift - Button * 2 + 19) Mod 16
    'Activate timer to draw color bars
    tmrDrawBars.Enabled = True
End Sub

Private Sub Form_Resize()
    'Activate timer to draw color bars
    tmrDrawBars.Enabled = True
End Sub
```

(continued)

Source Code for ColorBar.bas *continued*

```
Private Sub tmrDrawBars_Timer()
    Dim X, Y
    'Scale form for convenience
    Scale (4, 4)-(0, 0)
    'Fill in colors
    For X = 0 To 3
        For Y = 0 To 3
            ColorShift = (ColorShift + 1) Mod 16
            Line (X, Y)-(X + 1, Y + 1), _
                QBColor(ColorShift), BF
        Next Y
    Next X
    'Deactivate timer so color bars are drawn only once
    tmrDrawBars.Enabled = False
End Sub
```

The APIAddin Application

The APIAddin application is an add-in to the Visual Basic development environment. I include it to provide a working example of an add-in, and because I like the way I've structured the API declarations better than the way this information is presented in Win32api.txt, a file you'll find in the Winapi subfolder of the Visual Basic 4.0 installation.

The new line continuation character makes it easy to format declarations in an easier-to-read, multiline layout. Throughout this book, I've taken advantage of this capability, and this application lets you easily add API functions to your applications in the same format. Figure 26-4 on the following page shows the APIAddin application in action. Notice that once the application is installed as an add-in, the dialog box that this application creates is accessed directly from the Visual Basic menu, letting you quickly and easily locate, copy, and paste API functions into your applications.

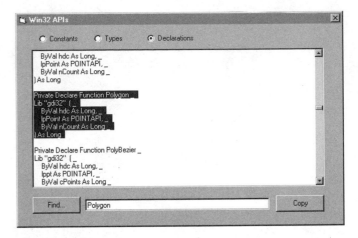

Figure 26-4.
The APIAddin application in action.

Preparation

Before I describe the APIAddin application itself, I want to make you aware that the original Win32api.txt file must be modified to provide three new working files that the APIAddin application loads at runtime. This conversion process is performed only once, and because I've provided the resulting files on the Companion CD with this book, you won't even need to run it once. However, I'll include the source code for the conversion process in case you might be interested in modifying the format even further or in case you receive a newer version of the Win32api.txt file and you want to perform an update conversion.

The following code can be plopped into a fresh, blank form. I've provided no controls or other modifications. Simply click once on the running form and wait until "Done" shows up on the form. (This demonstrates, by the way, a handy way to create a small utility program for your own use, when there's no need for a fancy user interface.) You'll need to either move the Win32api.txt file, normally located in your Visual Basic folder, to the folder containing your application or modify the path in the code so the program can find the file. I've included this code on the Companion CD in the project Cvtapitx.vbp.

Source Code for Converting Win32api.txt

```
Option Explicit

Private Sub Form_Click()
    Dim A$, t$, Flag, i, j, k, n
    Print "Working..."
    Open App.Path & "\Win32api.txt" For Input As #1
    Open App.Path & "\W32cons.txt" For Output As #2
    Open App.Path & "\W32type.txt" For Output As #3
    Open App.Path & "\W32decl.txt" For Output As #4
    Do Until EOF(1)
        Line Input #1, A$
        If InStr(A$, "Const ") Then Flag = 2
        If InStr(LTrim$(A$), "Type ") = 1 Then
            Flag = 3
        End If
        If InStr(LTrim$(A$), "Declare ") = 1 Then
            Flag = 4
        End If
        If Flag = 2 Then
            i = InStr(A$, "=")
            j = InStr(i, A$, "'")
            If j > i Then
                A$ = Trim$(Left$(A$, j - 1))
            End If
            Print #2, A$
        End If
        If Flag = 3 Then
            If Left$(A$, 1) = " " Then
                A$ = Space$(4) & Trim$(A$)
            End If
            j = InStr(A$, "'")
            If j > 0 Then
                A$ = RTrim$(Left$(A$, j - 1))
            End If
            Print #3, A$
        End If
        If Flag = 4 Then
            n = 2
            If Trim$(A$) = "" Then
                Print #4, ""
            Else
                'Lop off comments
                i = InStr(A$, ")")
```

(continued)

Source Code for Converting Win32api.txt *continued*

```
            j = InStr(i, A$, "'")
            If j > i Then A$ = Trim$(Left$(A$, j - 1))
            'Drop Alias if not different from original function
            i = InStr(A$, "Alias")
            If i Then
                j = InStr(i, A$, Chr$(34))
                k = InStr(j + 1, A$, Chr$(34))
                t$ = Mid$(A$, j + 1, k - j - 1)
                t$ = Space$(1) & t$ & Space$(1)
                If InStr(A$, t$) Then
                    A$ = Left$(A$, i - 1) & Mid$(A$, k + 1)
                End If
            End If
            'Locate "Lib"
            i = InStr(A$, " Lib")
            Print #4, "Private " & Left$(A$, i) & "_"
            A$ = Mid$(A$, i + 1)
            'Locate left parenthesis
            i = InStr(A$, "(")
            Print #4, Left$(A$, i) & " _"
            A$ = Mid$(A$, i + 1)
            'Locate each parameter
            Do
                i = InStr(A$, ", ")
                If i = 0 Then Exit Do
                If n < 9 Then
                    Print #4, Space$(4) & Left$(A$, i) & " _"
                Else
                    Print #4, Space$(4) & Left$(A$, i)
                End If
                n = n + 1
                A$ = Mid$(A$, i + 2)
            Loop
            'Locate right parenthesis
            i = InStr(A$, ")")
            If n < 9 Then
                Print #4, Space$(4) & Left$(A$, i - 1) & " _"
            Else
                Print #4, Space$(4) & Left$(A$, i - 1)
            End If
            Print #4, Mid$(A$, i)
        End If
```

(continued)

Source Code for Converting Win32api.txt *continued*

```
        End If
        If Flag = 2 Then Flag = 0
        If Flag = 3 And InStr(A$, "End Type") > 0 Then
            Flag = 0
            Print #3, ""
        End If
        If Flag = 4 Then
            Flag = 0
            Print #4, ""
        End If
    Loop
    Close #1
    Close #2
    Close #3
    Close #4
    Print "Done"
End Sub
```

When you run the preceding code, Win32api.txt is split into three files: W32cons.txt contains a list of all constants, W32type.txt contains all type structure definitions, and W32decl.txt contains all the declarations for all API functions. The program removes all extraneous comments and extra blank lines in order to keep the files small and quick to load. For explanations and descriptions of these functions, you'll need to look elsewhere. These trimmed-down files are designed to provide the declarations as efficiently as possible and not to explain their use.

I discovered an interesting fact about Visual Basic while creating these files. On one of the first iterations using these files, I left all Alias modifiers within the *Declare* statements. However, when you enter a *Declare* statement in which the aliased function name is identical to the original name, Visual Basic automatically deletes the Alias part. This is cool, except that it completely and automatically messed up the rest of the declaration when I attempted to copy and paste these declarations into my own applications. So my preparation program strips out the Alias modifiers when the original name is identical to the aliased name. Compare the contents of W32decl.txt and Win32api.txt to see the difference in the functions when this modification is performed.

One other "feature" I stumbled onto is that Visual Basic won't accept more than nine line continuation characters for a single line of source code. A few of the API functions have too many parameters for the structure I've created, and upon attempting to paste these declarations into an application,

Visual Basic generates an error and none of the pasted lines actually show up. I worked around this limitation by splitting the parameters into multiple lines and, after nine continued lines, dropping the underscores at the ends of the lines. This way, when you paste the declaration into your code, everything shows up, although the text is bright red (or whatever color you set for syntax error text in the editor), indicating a syntax error. It's up to you in these cases to condense the lines manually until the syntax is acceptable to Visual Basic.

One final note: Keep these three text files in the same directory as the APIAddin application's executable file. I've used the App.Path property to locate these files as they are needed, simplifying the housekeeping.

The APIAddin Application

In Chapter 23, I covered the details of creating an add-in, including special project property settings and techniques for debugging within the environment during development. If you plan to build the APIAddin application from scratch, refer to Chapter 23 for these details. To use the source code from this book's Companion CD, follow these directions:

Compile the project to create the file APIAddin.exe and then copy the files APIAddin.exe, W32const.txt, W32type.txt, and W32decl.txt to a single folder on your hard disk drive. After you copy these files, double-click on the icon in that folder to run APIAddin.exe once. Nothing much will appear to happen, but it's important that you run it once to allow the application to register itself with the system Registry. Then, from the running Visual Basic development environment, choose Add-In Manager from the Add-Ins menu. In the Add-In Manager dialog box, turn on the check box for APIAddin-.clsAPIAddin when you want the new Win32 APIs item to appear in Visual Basic's Add-Ins menu, or turn off the check box to remove it. Notice that this menu item will remain selected from run to run of Visual Basic.

Figure 26-5 shows the project list for the APIAddin application. The two class modules handle the connection to and activation of new objects with Visual Basic's Add-Ins menu. The BAS code module provides the Sub Main starting point for the application, which runs to register the add-in with the system Registry. The single form in this project displays the constants, types, and declarations and lets the user select and copy parts of this information. This form is what you'll see and interact with when the add-in is selected from Visual Basic's Add-Ins menu.

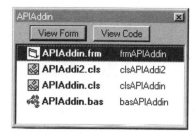

Figure 26-5.
The APIAddin project list.

APIAddin.frm

The APIAddin form displays one of three files in a RichTextBox control, depending on which option button is selected along the top of the form. For efficiency, each of the three files is loaded into a string variable only if it's requested by the user, and it's loaded only once per run of the application. When selected, the contents of the appropriate string are copied into the rich text box's Text property. Figure 26-6 shows the APIAddin form during the development process, and Figure 26-7 on the following page shows the form in action while the user is selecting from the list of constants.

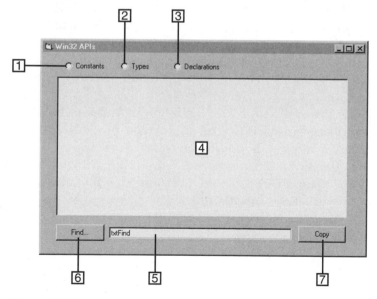

Figure 26-6.
The APIAddin form during development.

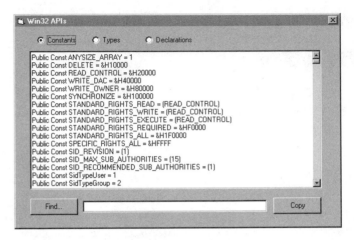

Figure 26-7.
The APIAddin form displaying the list of constants.

The rich text box turns out to be very easy to use for this application. Scrollbars allow manual scanning of the large amount of text, and the RichTextBox control provides its own *Find* method. I found that this *Find* method solved a lot of implementation details that would be complicated otherwise. For example, once a fragment of text is searched for and found, the rich text box automatically scrolls to the appropriate spot and highlights the text as the user would expect. Likewise, the special properties related to text selection simplify the task of identifying a block of text to be copied to the clipboard. See the descriptions of the SelStart, SelLength, and SelText properties in Visual Basic's online help for more information on text selection within a RichTextBox control.

To create this application, use the following table and source code to add the appropriate controls, set any nondefault properties for APIAddin.frm as indicated, and type in the source code lines as shown. Be sure to set the names of the modules as shown in Figure 26-5. Also, be sure that the Microsoft Visual Basic 4 Development Environment is included in your references, be sure you set the APIAddin.cls Instancing property to *2 - Createable MultiUse* and the Public property to *True*, and be sure you set *Sub Main* as the Startup Form.

APIAddin.frm Objects and Property Settings

ID No.*	Property	Value
Form		
	Name	frmAPIAddin
	Caption	Win32 APIs
	BorderStyle	3 - Fixed Dialog
Option Button		
1	Name	optAPI
	Caption	Constants
	Index	0
Option Button		
2	Name	optAPI
	Caption	Types
	Index	1
Option Button		
3	Name	optAPI
	Caption	Declarations
	Index	2
RichTextBox		
4	Name	rtfAPI
	HideSelection	False
	Scrollbars	3 - Both
TextBox		
5	Name	txtFind
CommandButton		
6	Name	cmdFind
	Caption	Find...
CommandButton		
7	Name	cmdCopy
	Caption	Copy

* The number in the ID No. column corresponds to the number in Figure 26-6 that identifies the location of the object on the form.

Source Code for APIAddin.frm

```
Option Explicit

Dim Con$, Typ$, Dec$

Private Sub cmdCopy_Click()
    'Copy to clipboard if anything is selected
    If rtfAPI.SelLength Then
        Clipboard.SetText rtfAPI.SelText
    End If
    'Return to user's project
    Unload Me
End Sub


Private Sub cmdFind_Click()
    Dim ptr As Long, F$
    'Put focus onto rich text box
    rtfAPI.SetFocus
    'Grab search string
    F$ = txtFind.Text
    If F$ = "" Then
        MsgBox "Please enter some text to be located"
        Exit Sub
    End If
    'Determine where to begin search
    If rtfAPI.SelLength Then
        ptr = rtfAPI.SelStart + rtfAPI.SelLength
    Else
        ptr = 0
    End If
    'Use rich text box's Find method
    ptr = rtfAPI.Find(F$, ptr)
    If ptr = -1 Then
        MsgBox "Search text not found"
    End If
End Sub


Private Sub Form_Load()
    'Start showing declarations
    optAPI(2).Value = True
    txtFind.Text = ""
    Me.Show
    Me.ZOrder
End Sub
```

(continued)

Source Code for APIAddin.frm *continued*

```
Private Sub optAPI_Click(Index As Integer)
    Select Case Index
    Case 0
        If Con$ = "" Then
            LoadUp Con$, "W32cons.txt"
        End If
        rtfAPI.Text = Con$
    Case 1
        If Typ$ = "" Then
            LoadUp Typ$, "W32type.txt"
        End If
        rtfAPI.Text = Typ$
    Case 2
        If Dec$ = "" Then
            LoadUp Dec$, "W32decl.txt"
        End If
        rtfAPI.Text = Dec$
    End Select
End Sub

Private Sub LoadUp(A$, Fil$)
    Open App.Path & "\" & Fil$ For Binary As #1
    A$ = Space$(LOF(1))
    Get #1, , A$
    DoEvents
    Close #1
End Sub

Private Sub rtfAPI_SelChange()
    If rtfAPI.SelLength Then
        cmdCopy.Caption = "Copy"
    Else
        cmdCopy.Caption = "Cancel"
    End If
End Sub
```

Source Code for APIAddin.bas

```
Option Explicit

Declare Function WritePrivateProfileString _
Lib "Kernel32" _
```

(continued)

Source Code for APIAddin.bas *continued*

```
Alias "WritePrivateProfileStringA" ( _
    ByVal AppName$, _
    ByVal KeyName$, _
    ByVal keydefault$, _
    ByVal FileName$ _
) As Long

Declare Function GetPrivateProfileString _
Lib "Kernel32" _
Alias "GetPrivateProfileStringA" ( _
    ByVal AppName$, _
    ByVal KeyName$, _
    ByVal keydefault$, _
    ByVal ReturnString$, _
    ByVal NumBytes As Long, _
    ByVal FileName$ _
) As Long

Sub Main()
    Dim ReturnString As String
    Dim Section$

    'Make sure we are in the VB.ini file
    Section$ = "Add-Ins32"
    ReturnString = String$(255, Chr$(0))
    GetPrivateProfileString Section$, "APIAddin.clsAPIAddin", _
        "NotFound", ReturnString, Len(ReturnString) + 1, "VB.INI"
    If InStr(ReturnString, "NotFound") Then
        WritePrivateProfileString Section$, _
            "APIAddin.clsAPIAddin", "0", "VB.INI"
    End If
End Sub
```

Source Code for APIAddin.cls

```
Option Explicit

Dim VBInstance As VBIDE.Application
Dim mnuAPI As VBIDE.MenuLine
Dim APIAddinHandler As clsAPIAddi2
Dim ConnectID As Long
```

(continued)

Source Code for APIAddin.cls *continued*

```
Sub ConnectAddIn(VBDriverInstance As VBIDE.Application)

    'Save this instance of Visual Basic so we can refer to it later
    Set VBInstance = VBDriverInstance

    'Add menu item to VB's Add-Ins menu
    Set mnuAPI = VBInstance.AddInMenu.MenuItems.Add("&Win32 APIs")

    'Create new object from class definition
    Set APIAddinHandler = New clsAPIAddi2

    'Save connection ID
    ConnectID = mnuAPI.ConnectEvents(APIAddinHandler)

    'Pass VBInstance to child objects
    Set APIAddinHandler.VBInstance = VBInstance

End Sub

Sub DisconnectAddIn(Mode As Integer)

    'Remove menu event connection
    mnuAPI.DisconnectEvents ConnectID

    'Remove menu item we installed
    VBInstance.AddInMenu.MenuItems.Remove mnuAPI

End Sub
```

Source Code for APIAddi2.cls

```
Option Explicit

'Sizer object properties
Public VBInstance As VBIDE.Application

Public Sub AfterClick()
    frmAPIAddin.Show
End Sub
```

The Metric Application

The Metric application is rather simple, but it demonstrates the powerful technique of combining a Visual Basic application with a help file to achieve a symbiotic relationship that incorporates the best features of each. I've created a very short example tutorial on the metric system of weights and measures using this technique. The Metric.hlp file displays easy-to-read text and has pop-up windows and hypertext jump hot spots; Metric.exe, the Visual Basic half of the team, plays sound files and video clips, performs metric conversions for the user, and displays a quiz to test the user's understanding. Help files in Windows 95 can do much more than help files in previous versions of Windows, but when you connect to Visual Basic the possibilities are virtually limitless.

When you run Metric.exe, it first checks to see whether you used any command line parameters. Assuming that you start the program by double-clicking on its name or icon, there won't be any parameters, and the program immediately runs the Metric.hlp help file. I've provided several buttons in the main topic of the help file that jump back into the Metric.exe program, each passing a different set of command line parameters. The Metric.exe program takes action based on these parameters and then terminates, allowing the user to interact once again with the help file.

Metric.exe effectively lets a help file play a sound file or a video clip, display a full-blown dialog box, perform mathematical computations, or do just about anything else you can imagine. The Metric application demonstrates each of these techniques. For example, when you click on the Video Clip button in the main topic of the help file, a short sample video clip plays. Likewise, when you click on the Quiz button, a dialog box full of quiz questions is displayed, as shown in Figure 26-8. Study the source code listings to see how easily this was accomplished. Note that both Metric.exe and Metric.hlp should be in the same directory at runtime.

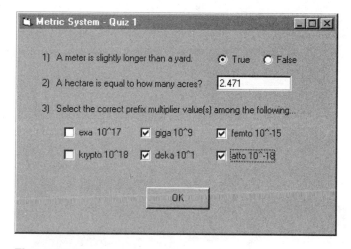

Figure 26-8.
The quiz activated from within the Metric.hlp help file.

Metric.exe Construction

The Visual Basic part of the Metric application consists of three files, as shown in the project list in Figure 26-9.

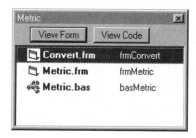

Figure 26-9.
The Metric project list.

The code module (Metric.bas) contains most of the code for this application, including the startup routine Sub Main, in which action decisions based on the command line parameters are made. The Metric.frm form module displays the sample quiz, and the Convert.frm form lets the user perform conversions from meters to feet and from centimeters to inches.

Metric.bas

The Metric.bas module contains the Sub Main startup point for the Visual Basic half of this application. Sub Main calls a useful subprogram titled GetParms, which analyzes and parses an application's command line parameters, returning an array of parameters that's often much easier to process than Visual Basic's *Command* function. The public dynamic array *Parm()* returns each parameter, and even in the case in which no command line parameters were given, *Parm(0)* returns the full pathname and filename of the executable file.

Based on the evaluated command line parameters, Sub Main plays a multimedia file, displays a quiz, or performs metric conversions. You can easily add other capabilities by modifying the *Select Case* statements to intercept and process command line parameters of your own design.

Source Code for Metric.bas

```
Option Explicit

Private Declare Function WinExec _
Lib "kernel32" ( _
    ByVal lpCmdLine As String, _
    ByVal nCmdShow As Long _
) As Long

Private Declare Function mciExecute _
Lib "winmm.dll" ( _
    ByVal lpstrCommand As String _
) As Long

Public Parm()

Sub Main()
    GetParms
    Select Case UBound(Parm)
    Case 0
        TakeAction
    Case 1
        TakeAction Parm(1)
    Case 2
        TakeAction Parm(1), Parm(2)
    End Select
End Sub

Private Sub TakeAction(Optional Cmd, Optional Fil)
    'If no parameters, start help file
    If IsMissing(Cmd) Then
```

(continued)

Source Code for Metric.bas *continued*

```
            WinExec "Winhelp.exe "& App.Path & "\Metric.hlp", 1
            Exit Sub
        End If
        'First parameter determines action to take
        Select Case UCase$(Cmd)
        'Display units conversion form
        Case "M2F", "C2I"
            frmConvert.Show
        'Play a sound file
        Case "WAV"
            Select Case Fil
            Case 1
                mciExecute "Play c:\windows\msremind.wav"
            End Select
        'Play a video clip
        Case "AVI"
            Select Case Fil
            Case 1
                mciExecute "Play c:\windows\help\dragdrop.avi"
            End Select
        'Display a quiz form
        Case "QUIZ"
            frmMetric.Show
        End Select
    End Sub

Private Sub GetParms()
    Dim p, n, Cmd$
    ReDim Parm(0)
    Cmd$ = Command$
    'Always return full path of this application
    If Right$(App.Path$, 1) <> "\" Then
        Parm(0) = App.Path & "\" & App.EXEName
    Else
        Parm(0) = App.Path & App.EXEName
    End If
    'Trim and add one space to command line
    Cmd$ = Trim$(Cmd$) + Space$(1)
    'Extract each parameter from command line
    Do
        p = InStr(Cmd$, Space$(1))
        If p <= 1 Then Exit Do
        n = n + 1
        ReDim Preserve Parm(n)
        Parm(n) = Left$(Cmd$, p - 1)
        Cmd$ = LTrim$(Mid$(Cmd$, p + 1))
    Loop
End Sub
```

Metric.bas uses two API functions—one to play the multimedia files and one to start the Metric.hlp file. Notice that I've used yet another technique to start up a help file. (See Chapter 13 for other ways to do this.) The *WinExec* API function lets your Visual Basic application start any Windows application—WinHelp, in this case. You could use this function to start the Calculator applet, for instance, which might be a handy addition to a tutorial.

The TakeAction subprogram demonstrates the use of optional parameters by accepting none, one, or two parameters.

Metric.frm

This form displays a sample quiz when the Quiz button in the help file is clicked. (Read on to see how the help file handles this button click.) To keep this sample application simple, I've created a nongraded quiz that displays one True/False, one fill-in-the-blank, and one multiple-choice question. It's a start, but I'm sure you'd want to enhance a real quiz dialog box beyond this simple example. Figure 26-10 shows the Metric form during development, and Figure 26-8 on page 369 shows it in action after it has been activated from within the help file.

To create this application, use the following table and source code to add the appropriate controls, set any nondefault properties as indicated, and type in the source code lines as shown.

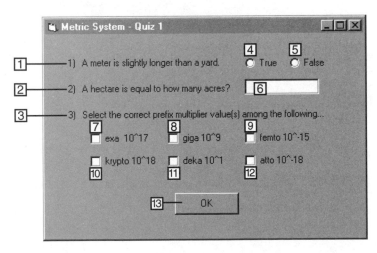

Figure 26-10.
The Metric.frm form during development.

Metric.frm Objects and Property Settings

ID No.*	Property	Value
Form		
	Name	frmMetric
	Caption	Metric System - Quiz 1
Label		
1	Name	Label 1
	Caption	1) A meter is slightly longer than a yard.
Label		
2	Name	Label 2
	Caption	2) A hectare is equal to how many acres?
Label		
3	Name	Label 3
	Caption	3) Select the correct prefix multiplier value(s) among the following...
Option1		
4	Caption	True
Option2		
5	Caption	False
Text1		
6	Text	(blank)
Check1		
7	Caption	exa 10^17
Check2		
8	Caption	giga 10^9
Check3		
9	Caption	femto 10^-15

* The number in the ID No. column corresponds to the number in Figure 26-10 that identifies the location of the object on the form.

(continued)

Metric.frm Objects and Property Settings *continued*

ID No.	Property	Value
Check4		
10	Caption	krypto 10^18
Check5		
11	Caption	deka 10^1
Check6		
12	Caption	atto 10^−18
CommandButton		
13	Name	cmdOK
	Caption	OK

Source Code for Metric.frm

```
Option Explicit

Private Sub cmdOK_Click()
    MsgBox "This example quiz is not graded."
    Unload Me
End Sub
```

Convert.frm

The Convert form displays a dialog box that lets the user perform mathematical calculations—in this case, conversions of meters to feet and centimeters to inches. Once again, this example is greatly simplified, and a full suite of conversions would probably be in order for a real application along these lines. I've included enough in this dialog box to get you started and to demonstrate the core technique of using Visual Basic to add computational abilities to a help file. Figure 26-11 shows the Convert.frm form during development, and Figure 26-12 shows the form at runtime, after the user has clicked on one of the buttons in the Conversions section of the help file.

To create this application, use the following table and source code to add the appropriate controls, set any nondefault properties as indicated, and type in the source code lines as shown.

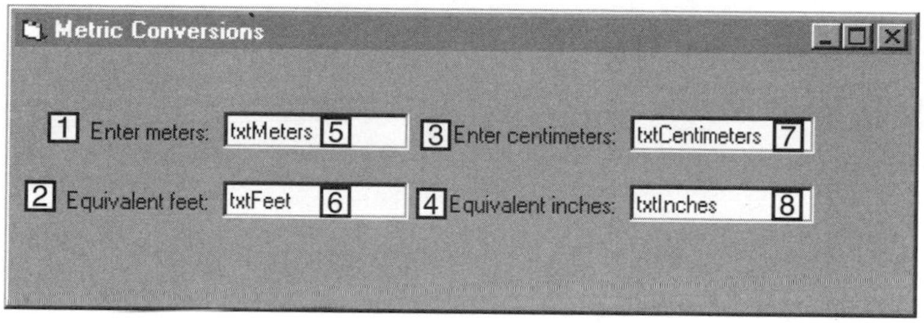

Figure 26-11.
The Convert.frm form during development.

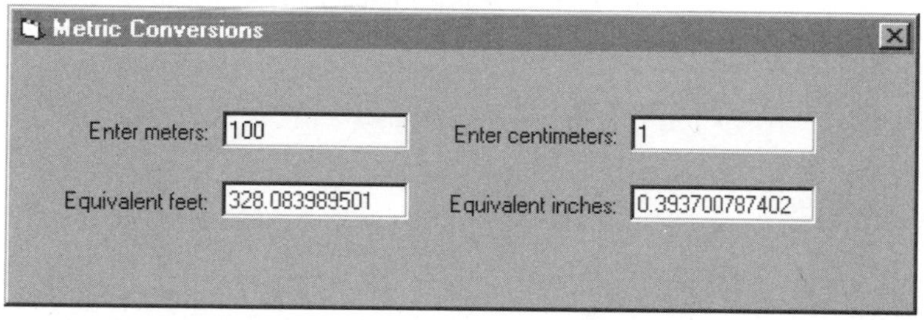

Figure 26-12.
The Metric Conversions dialog box when activated by a button in the Metric help file.

Convert.frm Objects and Property Settings

ID No.*	Property	Value
Form		
	Name	frmConvert
	Caption	Metric Conversions
	BorderStyle	3 - Fixed Dialog
Label		
1	Name	lblMeters
	Caption	Enter meters:
Label		
2	Name	lblFeet
	Caption	Equivalent feet:

   * The number in the ID No. column corresponds to the number in Figure 26-11 that identifies the location of the object on the form.

(continued)

Convert.frm Objects and Property Settings *continued*

ID No.	Property	Value
Label		
3	Name	lblCentimeters
	Caption	Enter centimeters:
Label		
4	Name	lblInches
	Caption	Equivalent inches:
TextBox		
5	Name	txtMeters
TextBox		
6	Name	txtFeet
	Enabled	False
TextBox		
7	Name	txtCentimeters
TextBox		
8	Name	txtInches
	Enabled	False

Source Code for Convert.frm

```
Option Explicit

Private Sub Form_Load()
    txtMeters.Text = "0"
    txtCentimeters = "0"
End Sub

Private Sub txtCentimeters_Change()
    txtInches.Text = Val(txtCentimeters.Text) * 0.393700787402
End Sub

Private Sub txtMeters_Change()
    txtFeet.Text = Val(txtMeters.Text) * 3.28083989501
End Sub
```

Metric.hlp

Perhaps you've been wondering how the Metric.exe application is activated, complete with a variety of command line parameters, from within the Metric-.hlp help file. It's beyond the scope of this book to go into all the details of building a help file, but I will describe this critical part of the process. I used RoboHelp 95, from Blue Sky Software, to create the Metric help file. (Robo-Help 95 is a great product for enhancing your 32-bit Visual Basic applications with full-blown 32-bit help files using all the latest techniques.) RoboHelp makes it easy to add macros to buttons or hot spots, and these macros are the key to activating an external application such as Metric.exe. You can also insert the buttons and macros using other help-building tools, such as the Microsoft Help Workshop that came with Visual Basic 4 (Hcw.exe), or you can even code everything directly. See the online help for the Microsoft Help Workshop for the button and macro syntax. For reference, here are the macros embedded in the Metric.rtf source code for the buttons that appear in the main topic of the help file:

Conversions:

{button Meters to feet,ExecProgram("Metric.exe M2F")}

{button Centimeters to inches,ExecProgram("Metric.exe C2I")}

To hear a {button Sound,ExecProgram("Metric.exe wav 1")} click on this button, and to see a sample {buttonVideoclip,ExecProgram("Metric.exe avi 1")} click here. When you're ready, click on this {button Quiz,ExecProgram("Metric.exe QUIZ 1")} button.

For each button, everything between the braces is processed by the help file compiler to create a button that activates an external application named Metric.exe, passing two command line parameters. Macros such as these are a standard feature of help files. RoboHelp explains the use of macros in detail, but no matter what tool you use to edit and compile help files, the documentation should provide an explanation of the inclusion of macros. Figure 26-13 on the following page shows this primary help topic in action. All the buttons providing macros leading back to the Metric.exe program are shown in this first topic.

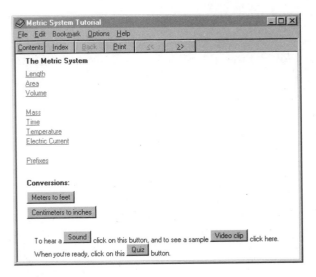

Figure 26-13.
The Metric.hlp file displaying the first topic.

CHAPTER TWENTY-SEVEN

Date and Time

This chapter provides several applications to handle date and time tasks: a calendar form (VBCal) that enhances the way users of your applications can select a date; a visually appealing analog clock (VBClock) that displays the current system time; and a utility that dials in to the National Institute of Standards and Technology (NIST) to set your computer's clock precisely.

The VBCal Application

A common task in many business applications is to let the user select a date. The easiest way to do this is to simply have the user type a date into a text box. This method, however, requires careful attention to validation of the entered date and to internationalization issues. (For example, does the string *3/5/97* indicate March 5 or May 3?) A better approach is to display a visual calendar sheet and let the user click on the date. The VBCal form lets the user select any date from January 1, 1000, to December 31, 9899.

> NOTE: The date functions in Visual Basic 4 are valid for dates from January 1, 100, to December 31, 9999. I've limited the range of VBCal's dates to a subset of this range to prevent complications and errors in my program at the limiting values.

It's a Wizard

I've designed this application as a simple wizard, which is a useful concept in itself. The wizard metaphor, first used by Microsoft in several products, is a convenient and standard way to perform interactions with the user in a linear, sequential manner. The VBCal form is the core calendar sheet form, and the rest of the forms in this project are used to step through the wizard action. The code module VBCalWiz.bas contains only two lines of code, which make the dates the user selected available to all the forms. These forms have some combination of the command buttons Date, Back, Next, Finish, and Cancel; a visual element in the left half of each form; and step-by-step instructions in the upper right. In general, most wizards are laid out the same way. Figures 27-1 through 27-5 show these wizard forms in action.

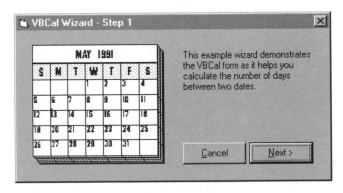

Figure 27-1.
Step 1 of the VBCal wizard.

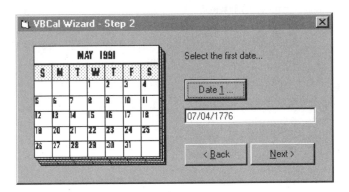

Figure 27-2.
Step 2 of the VBCal wizard, prompting for the first date.

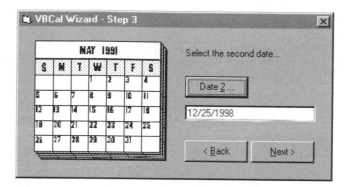

Figure 27-3.

Step 3 of the VBCal wizard, prompting for the second date.

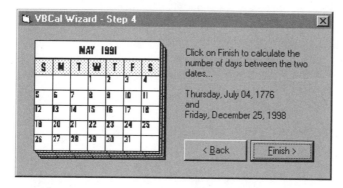

Figure 27-4.

Step 4 of the VBCal wizard, preparing for the final step.

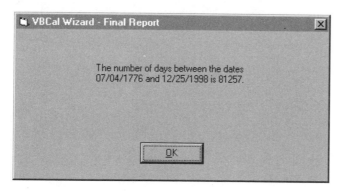

Figure 27-5.

The report display for the VBCal wizard, displaying the final results.

The VBCal Form

> NOTE: Microsoft Access 7 provides a calendar control that you can use in your applications if you have Access installed. VBCal provides a good alternative if you don't have Access.

When you click on the Date button in the wizard, the VBCal form is called. The VBCal form displays a one-month calendar sheet with scrollbars to efficiently flip through the months, years, and centuries. I've added a Today button to quickly jump back to the current day and month, and OK and Cancel buttons to accept the selection or to cancel it. To select a date, the user clicks on the day number on the calendar sheet and then clicks on the OK button. Figure 27-6 shows the VBCal form in action while the user selects the date July 4, 1776.

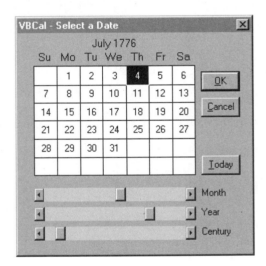

Figure 27-6.
The VBCal form in use.

The VBCal form interacts with a calling routine through two public variables. *DateSelectedFlag* is a Boolean variable that returns *True* if a date was selected by the user or *False* if the Cancel button was used to cancel the selection. *DateNum* is a Date variable that returns the selected date. The code for the Date1 button in the second step of the wizard shows how these two variables return the selected date to the calling routine:

```
Private Sub cmdDate1_Click()
    frmVBCal.Show vbModal
    If frmVBCal.DateSelectedFlag Then
        txtDate1.Text = Format(frmVBCal.DateNum, "mm/dd/yyyy")
    End If
End Sub
```

Figure 27-7 shows the project list for the VBCal application. The form frmVBCalWiz1 is set as the startup form. Most of the files in this project define the steps of the wizard action. The source code, tables, and illustrations on the following pages describe the construction of each of these forms.

Figure 27-7.
The VBCal project list.

VBCal.frm at Development Time

The VBCal form comprises two PictureBox controls, three scrollbars, three buttons, and three descriptive labels. To enhance performance and reduce the use of resources, I used a single PictureBox control instead of an array of Text or Label controls to display the days of the month. Figure 27-8 on the following page shows the VBCal form during development. To create this form, use the following table and source code to add the appropriate controls, set any nondefault properties as indicated, and type in the source code lines as shown.

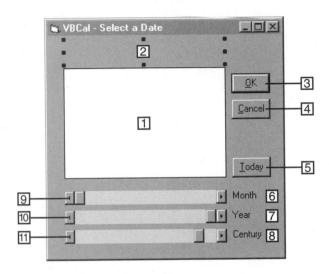

Figure 27-8.
The VBCal form during development.

VBCal.frm Objects and Property Settings

ID No.*	Property	Value
Form		
	Name	frmVBCal
	Caption	VBCal - Select a Date
	BorderStyle	3 - Fixed Dialog
PictureBox		
1	Name	picMonth
	Appearance	0 - Flat
PictureBox		
2	Name	picTitle
	Appearance	0 - Flat
	BackColor	&H00C0C0C0&
	BorderStyle	0 = None
CommandButton		
3	Name	cmdOK
	Default	True
	Caption	&OK

* The number in the ID No. column corresponds to the number in Figure 27-8 that identifies the location of the object on the form.

(continued)

VBCal.frm Objects and Property Settings *continued*

ID No.	Property	Value
CommandButton		
4	Name	cmdCancel
	Cancel	True
	Caption	&Cancel
CommandButton		
5	Name	cmdToday
	Caption	&Today
Label		
6	Name	lblMonth
	Caption	Month
	Appearance	0 = Flat
Label		
7	Name	lblYear
	Caption	Year
	Appearance	0 = Flat
Label		
8	Name	lblCentury
	Caption	Century
	Appearance	0 = Flat
HScrollBar		
9	Name	hsbMonth
	Min	1
	Max	12
HScrollBar		
10	Name	hsbYear
	Max	99
	LargeChange	10
HScrollBar		
11	Name	hsbCentury
	Min	10
	Max	98
	LargeChange	10

Source Code for VBCal.frm

```
Option Explicit
DefLng A-Z

Public DateNum As Date
Public DateSelectedFlag As Boolean

Dim CenturyNum
Dim YearNum
Dim MonthNum
Dim DayNum
Dim MarkedDay
Dim FirstTime
Dim MouseX As Single, MouseY As Single
Dim StartDate As Double

Private Sub cmdCancel_Click()
    'Signal that no date was selected
    DateSelectedFlag = False
    'All done
    Unload Me
End Sub

Private Sub cmdOK_Click()
    'Build serial date number for selected date
    DateNum = DateSerial(CenturyNum * 100 + YearNum, _
        MonthNum, DayNum)
    'Signal that date was selected
    DateSelectedFlag = True
    'All done
    Unload frmVBCal
End Sub

Private Sub cmdToday_Click()
    'Reset selected date to today
    DateNum = Now
    'Redraw calendar
    picTitle.Cls
    picMonth.Cls
    Form_Load
    Form_Paint
End Sub

Private Sub DrawLines()
    Dim x As Integer
    Dim y As Integer
```

(continued)

Source Code for VBCal.frm *continued*

```
    'Draw lines that separate days
    picMonth.Scale (0, 0)-(7, 6)
    picMonth.DrawMode = 13
    'Draw vertical lines
    For x = 1 To 6
        picMonth.Line (x, 0)-(x, 6)
    Next x
    'Draw horizontal lines
    For y = 1 To 5
        picMonth.Line (0, y)-(7, y)
    Next y
End Sub

Private Sub FillCal()
    Dim Serial1 As Double
    Dim Serial2 As Double
    Dim NumDays As Long
    Dim DayOffset As Integer
    Dim i As Integer
    'Get serial date number for first of current month
    Serial1 = DateSerial(CenturyNum * 100 + YearNum, _
        MonthNum, 1)
    'Get serial date number for first of next month
    Serial2 = DateSerial(CenturyNum * 100 + YearNum, _
        MonthNum + 1, 1)
    'Calculate number of days in month
    NumDays = Serial2 - Serial1
    'Skip over blank days at start of month
    DayOffset = WeekDay(Serial1) - 1
    For i = 1 To NumDays
        PutNum i + DayOffset, i
    Next i
End Sub

Private Sub Form_Load()
    'Center form
    Move (Screen.Width - Width) \ 2, _
        (Screen.Height - Height) \ 2
    'Default to no date selected
    DateSelectedFlag = False
    'Record starting date
    StartDate = DateNum
    'If no starting date, use current date
    If DateNum = 0 Then DateNum = Now
    'Keep track of marked day
```

(continued)

Source Code for VBCal.frm *continued*

```
        MarkedDay = 0
        'Extract date parts
        CenturyNum = Year(DateNum) \ 100
        YearNum = Year(DateNum) Mod 100
        MonthNum = Month(DateNum)
        DayNum = Day(DateNum)
        'Flag that this is first time through
        FirstTime = True
        'Initialize scrollbars
        hsbCentury.Value = CenturyNum
        hsbYear.Value = YearNum
        hsbMonth.Value = MonthNum
        'Flag first time setting scrollbars is done
        FirstTime = False
End Sub

Private Sub Form_Paint()
        'Display names of days at top
        WeekDayNames
        'Draw lines that form calendar
        DrawLines
        'Fill calendar with day numbers
        FillCal
        'Update month name
        UpdateTitle
        'Mark currently selected day
        MarkDay
End Sub

Private Sub hsbMonth_Change()
        'Get new month number
        MonthNum = hsbMonth.Value
        'Redraw calendar and mark the first day
        If FirstTime = False Then
            DayNum = 1
            Sketch
        End If
End Sub

Private Sub hsbYear_Change()
        'Get new year number
        YearNum = hsbYear.Value
        'Redraw calendar and mark the first day
        If FirstTime = False Then
            DayNum = 1
```

(continued)

Source Code for VBCal.frm *continued*

```
        Sketch
    End If
End Sub

Private Sub hsbCentury_Change()
    'Get new century number
    CenturyNum = hsbCentury.Value
    'Redraw calendar and mark first day
    If FirstTime = False Then
        DayNum = 1
        Sketch
    End If
End Sub


Private Sub MarkDay()
    Dim TheDay As Integer
    Dim i As Integer
    Dim Serial As Double
    Dim DayBox As Integer
    Dim x As Integer
    Dim y As Integer
    Dim x1 As Single
    Dim y1 As Single
    Dim x2 As Single
    Dim y2 As Single
    'Record day number
    TheDay = DayNum
    'Erase previous mark, then mark current day
    For i = 1 To 2
        'Calculate box number for day
        Serial = DateSerial(CenturyNum * 100 + YearNum, _
            MonthNum, 1)
        DayBox = WeekDay(Serial) + DayNum - 1
        'Calculate location of box number
        x = ((DayBox - 1) Mod 7) + 1
        y = ((DayBox - 1) \ 7) + 1
        'Get first corner location of box
        x1 = (x - 1) * picMonth.ScaleWidth / 7
        y1 = (y - 1) * picMonth.ScaleHeight / 6
        'Get second corner location of box
        x2 = x1 + picMonth.ScaleWidth / 7
        y2 = y1 + picMonth.ScaleHeight / 6
        'XOR box pixels
        picMonth.DrawMode = 7
```

(continued)

Source Code for VBCal.frm *continued*

```
            picMonth.Line (x1, y1)-(x2, y2), QBColor(15), BF
            'Quit if no previously marked day
            If MarkedDay = 0 Then
                Exit For
            'Prepare to mark currently selected day
            Else
                DayNum = MarkedDay
            End If
        Next i
        'Reset day number
        DayNum = TheDay
        'Record marked day for next trip through here
        MarkedDay = DayNum
    End Sub

    Private Sub picMonth_Click()
        Dim x As Integer
        Dim y As Integer
        Dim DayBox As Integer
        Dim LastDay As Integer
        Dim FirstDay As Integer
        Dim Serial As Double
        Dim NewDay As Integer
        'Get current location of mouse
        x = Int(MouseX) + 1
        y = Int(MouseY) + 1
        'Calculate which day-number box mouse is on
        DayBox = x + (y - 1) * 7
        'Get serial date number for first of month
        Serial = DateSerial(CenturyNum * 100 + YearNum, _
            MonthNum, 1)
        'Get last serial date number for month
        LastDay = DateSerial(CenturyNum * 100 + YearNum, _
            MonthNum + 1, 1) - Serial
        'Find day of week for first day
        FirstDay = WeekDay(Serial)
        'Determine day number selected
        NewDay = DayBox - FirstDay + 1
        'Handle selection of blank box before first day
        If DayBox < FirstDay Then
            Beep
            Exit Sub
        End If
        'Handle selection of blank box after end of month
        If DayBox - FirstDay + 1 > LastDay Then
```

(continued)

Source Code for VBCal.frm *continued*

```
            Beep
            Exit Sub
        End If
        'Continue if selection passed tests; new day selected
        DayNum = NewDay
        'Re-mark selected day
        MarkDay
    End Sub

    Private Sub picMonth_DblClick()
        'Get currently selected date
        DateNum = DateSerial(CenturyNum * 100 + YearNum, _
            MonthNum, DayNum)
        'Signal that a date was selected
        DateSelectedFlag = True
        'All done
        Unload frmVBCal
    End Sub

    Private Sub picMonth_MouseMove(Button As Integer, _
        Shift As Integer, x As Single, y As Single)
        'Keep track of mouse location when on calendar
        MouseX = x
        MouseY = y
    End Sub

    Private Sub PutNum(Square As Integer, Num As Integer)
        Dim n As String
        Dim x As Integer
        Dim y As Integer
        'Build string of day-number digits
        n = LTrim$(Str$(Num))
        'Calculate location of box
        x = ((Square - 1) Mod 7) + 1
        y = (Square - 1) \ 7 + 1
        'Set print position
        picMonth.CurrentX = x - 0.5 - picMonth.TextWidth(n) / 2
        picMonth.CurrentY = y - 0.5 - picMonth.TextHeight(n) / 2
        'Display day number
        picMonth.Print n
    End Sub

    Private Sub Sketch()
        'Clear out previous stuff
        picMonth.Cls
```

(continued)

Source Code for VBCal.frm *continued*

```
    picTitle.Cls
    frmVBCal.Cls
    'Redraw calendar
    MarkedDay = 0
    Form_Paint
End Sub

Private Sub UpdateTitle()
    Dim WorkDate As Double
    Dim Tmp As String
    Dim T1 As String
    'Build long date string for selected month
    WorkDate = DateSerial(CenturyNum * 100 + YearNum, _
        MonthNum, 1)
    Tmp = Format$(WorkDate, "long date")
    'Remove day of week
    Tmp = Mid$(Tmp$, InStr(Tmp, ",") + 2)
    'Remove day number from string
    T1 = Left$(Tmp, InStr(Tmp, " ") - 1)
    Tmp = T1 + Right$(Tmp, 5)
    'Display month and year at top
    picTitle.CurrentX = 3.5 - picTitle.TextWidth(Tmp) / 2
    picTitle.CurrentY = 0
    picTitle.Print Tmp
End Sub

Private Sub WeekDayNames()
    Dim i As Integer
    Dim D As String
    'Scale for displaying seven day names
    picTitle.Scale (0, 0)-(7, 1)
    'Display each weekday name
    For i = 0 To 6
        'Get three-letter abbreviation
        D = Format$(CDbl(i + 1), "ddd")
        'Use two characters if user's font is too wide
        If picTitle.TextWidth("Wed") > 1 Then
            D = Left$(D, 2)
        End If
        'Display each weekday name
        picTitle.CurrentX = i + 0.5 - _
            picTitle.TextWidth(D) / 2
        picTitle.CurrentY = 1 - picTitle.TextHeight(D)
        picTitle.Print D
    Next i
End Sub
```

To create the wizards for this application, use the following tables and source code to add the appropriate controls, set any nondefault properties as indicated, and type in the source code lines as shown.

VBCaWiz1.frm Objects and Property Settings

Property	Value
Form	
Name	frmVBCalWiz1
Caption	VBCal Wizard - Step 1
BorderStyle	3 - Fixed Dialog
Image	
Name	imgCal
Picture	Calendar.wmf
Stretch	True
Label	
Name	lblPrompt
CommandButton	
Name	cmdNext
Caption	&Next>
Default	True
CommandButton	
Name	cmdCancel
Cancel	True
Caption	&Cancel

Source Code for VBCaWiz1.frm

```
Option Explicit

Private Sub cmdCancel_Click()
    Unload Me
End Sub

Private Sub cmdNext_Click()
    frmVBCalWiz2.Show
    Unload Me
End Sub
```

(continued)

Source Code for VBCaWiz1.frm *continued*

```
Private Sub Form_Load()
    Dim T As String
    'Display the prompting text
    T = "This example wizard demonstrates "
    T = T & "the VBCal form as it helps you "
    T = T & "calculate the number of days "
    T = T & "between two dates."
    lblPrompt.Caption = T
    'Center form
    Move (Screen.Width - Width) \ 2, _
        (Screen.Height - Height) \ 2
    Show
    cmdNext.SetFocus
End Sub
```

VBCaWiz2.frm Objects and Property Settings

Property	Value
Form	
Name	frmVBCalWiz2
Caption	VBCal Wizard - Step 2
BorderStylel	3 - Fixed Dialog
Image	
Name	imgCal
Picture	Calendar.wmf
Stretch	True
Label	
Name	lblPrompt
Caption	Select the first date...
CommandButton	
Name	cmdNext
Caption	&Next>
Default	True
CommandButton	
Name	cmdBack
Caption	<&Back

(continued)

VBCaWiz2.frm Objects and Property Settings *continued*

Property	Value
CommandButton	
Name	cmdDate1
Caption	Date &1...
TextBox	
Name	txtDate1

Source Code for VBCaWiz2.frm

```
Option Explicit

Private Sub cmdBack_Click()
    frmVBCalWiz1.Show
    Unload Me
End Sub

Private Sub cmdDate1_Click()
    frmVBCal.Show vbModal
    If frmVBCal.DateSelectedFlag Then
        txtDate1.Text = Format(frmVBCal.DateNum, "mm/dd/yyyy")
    End If
End Sub

Private Sub cmdNext_Click()
    Date1 = txtDate1.Text
    frmVBCalWiz3.Show
    Unload Me
End Sub

Private Sub Form_Load()
    'Center form
    Move (Screen.Width - Width) \ 2, _
        (Screen.Height - Height) \ 2
    txtDate1.Text = Format(Date, "mm/dd/yyyy")
    Show
    cmdNext.SetFocus
End Sub
```

VBCaWiz3.frm Objects and Property Settings

Property	Value
Form	
Name	frmVBCalWiz3
Caption	VBCal Wizard - Step 3
BorderStyle	3 - Fixed Dialog
Image	
Name	imgCal
Picture	Calendar.wmf
Stretch	True
Label	
Name	lblPrompt
Caption	Select the second date…
CommandButton	
Name	cmdNext
Caption	&Next>
Default	True
CommandButton	
Name	cmdBack
Caption	<&Back
CommandButton	
Name	cmdDate2
Caption	Date &2…
TextBox	
Name	txtDate2

Source Code for VBCaWiz3.frm

```
Option Explicit

Private Sub cmdBack_Click()
    frmVBCalWiz2.Show
    Unload Me
End Sub
```

(continued)

Source Code for VBCaWiz3.frm *continued*

```
Private Sub cmdDate2_Click()
    frmVBCal.Show vbModal
    If frmVBCal.DateSelectedFlag Then
        txtDate2.Text = Format(frmVBCal.DateNum, "mm/dd/yyyy")
    End If
Fnd Sub

Private Sub cmdNext_Click()
    Date2 = txtDate2.Text
    frmVBCalWiz4.Show
    Unload Me
End Sub

Private Sub Form_Load()
    'Center form
    Move (Screen.Width - Width) \ 2, _
        (Screen.Height - Height) \ 2
    txtDate2.Text = Format(Date, "mm/dd/yyyy")
    Show
    cmdNext.SetFocus
End Sub
```

VBCaWiz4.frm Objects and Property Settings

Property	Value
Form	
Name	frmVBCalWiz4
Caption	VBCal Wizard - Step 4
BorderStyle	3 - Fixed Dialog
Image	
Name	imgCal
Picture	Calendar.wmf
Stretch	True
Label	
Name	lblPrompt

(continued)

VBCaWiz4.frm Objects and Property Settings *continued*

Property	Value
CommandButton	
Name	cmdFinish
Caption	&Finish>
Default	True
CommandButton	
Name	cmdBack
Caption	<&Back

Source Code for VBCaWiz4.frm

```
Option Explicit

Private Sub cmdBack_Click()
    frmVBCalWiz3.Show
    Unload Me
End Sub

Private Sub cmdFinish_Click()
    frmVBCalWiz5.Show
    Unload Me
End Sub

Private Sub Form_Load()
    Dim T As String
    T = "Click on Finish to calculate "
    T = T & "the number "
    T = T & "of days between the two dates..."
    T = T & vbCrLf & vbCrLf
    T = T & Format$(Date1, "long date")
    T = T & vbCrLf & "and " & vbCrLf
    T = T & Format$(Date2, "long date")
    lblPrompt.Caption = T$
    'Center form
    Move (Screen.Width - Width) \ 2, _
        (Screen.Height - Height) \ 2
End Sub
```

VBCaWiz5.frm Objects and Property Settings

Property	Value
Form	
Name	frmVBCalWiz5
Caption	VBCal Wizard - Final Report
BorderStyle	3 - Fixed Dialog
Label	
Name	lblReport
CommandButton	
Name	cmdOK
Caption	&OK

Source Code for VBCaWiz5.frm

```
Option Explicit

Private Sub cmdOK_Click()
    Unload Me
End Sub

Private Sub Form_Load()
    'Center form
    Move (Screen.Width - Width) \ 2, _
        (Screen.Height - Height) \ 2
    lblReport.Caption = "The number of days between the dates " _
    & Format$(Date1, "mm/dd/yyyy") & " and " _
    & Format$(Date2, "mm/dd/yyyy") & " is " _
    & Abs(Date1 - Date2) & "."
End Sub
```

Source Code for VBCaWiz.bas

```
Option Explicit

Public Date1 As Date
Public Date2 As Date
```

The VBClock Application

This application provides a visually appealing and fun analog clock showing the system time. The VBClock application also demonstrates several graphics techniques and an alternative approach to adding a generic About box to your applications. As shown in Figure 27-9, the VBClock form's background is a colorful bitmap graphic. I created mine using a public domain program that generates fractals based on the Mandelbrot set, but you can load any bitmap file into the picBackGround control to customize the clock.

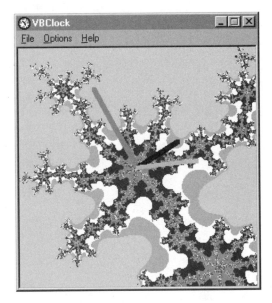

Figure 27-9.
The VBClock application in action.

The Options menu provides selections to manually set the time and to change the colors of the clock's hands. To set the time, I added a simple *Input-Box* function to the program. To change the hand colors, I used a dialog box form that demonstrates a useful "hot spot" graphics technique. The Help menu provides access to the Contents and Search entry points into the associated help file.

NOTE: A great way to update your system time is to use the NISTTime application, which is the next application described in this chapter. You can run NISTTime and VBClock simultaneously to see the clock adjustment in real time.

Figure 27-10 shows the project list for this application. Each of the three files is explained in more detail below.

Figure 27-10.
The VBClock project list.

VBClock.frm

The VBClock form displays the analog clock image and updates the clock's hands once a second. This form has only three controls: a PictureBox control to display the background and the clock hands, a timer to update the clock, and a CommonDialog control to provide the interface to the associated help file. You can load any bitmap image into the PictureBox control or change the startup hand colors to suit your taste. (One advantage of having the source code to an application is the ability to customize it as desired.) Figure 27-11 on the following page shows the VBClock form during development.

NOTE: AutoRedraw is an important property of the PictureBox control. It should be set to *True* so that the hands are drawn smoothly and crisply. If AutoRedraw is set to *False*, you'll probably see some flickering of the image as the hands are erased and redrawn.

To create this form, use the following tables and source code to add the appropriate controls, set any nondefault properties as indicated, and type in the source code lines as shown.

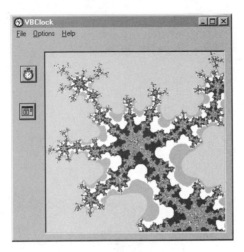

Figure 27-11.
The VBClock form during development.

VBClock.frm Menu Design Window Entries

Caption	Name	Indentation	Enabled
&File	mnuFile	0	True
&New	mnuNew	1	False
&Open...	mnuOpen	1	False
&Save	mnuSave	1	False
Save &As...	mnuSaveAs	1	False
-	mnuFileDash1	1	True
E&xit	mnuExit	1	True
&Options	mnuOption	0	True
&Set Time...	mnuSetTime	1	True
&Hand Colors...	mnuHandColors	1	True
&Help	mnuHelp	0	True
&Contents	mnuContents	1	True
&Search For Help On...	mnuSearch	1	True
-	mnuHelpDash1	1	True
&About...	mnuAbout	1	True

VBClock.frm Objects and Property Settings

Property	Value
Form	
Name	frmVBClock
Caption	VBClock
BorderStyle	3 - Fixed Dialog
Timer	
Name	tmrClock
Interval	100
CommonDialog	
Name	cdlOne
PictureBox	
Name	picBackGround
AutoRedraw	True
AutoSize	True
Picture	Mandel1.bmp

Source Code for VBClock.bas

```
Option Explicit

Dim Hnum As Integer
Dim Mnum As Integer
Dim Snum As Integer
Dim Hcolor As Long
Dim Mcolor As Long
Dim Scolor As Long
Dim Hlen As Single
Dim Mlen As Single
Dim Slen As Single
Dim Appname$, Section$, Key$, Setting$

Public HourHandColor As Integer
Public MinuteHandColor As Integer
Public SecondHandColor As Integer

Const Pi = 3.14159265358979
```

(continued)

403

Source Code for VBClock.bas *continued*

```
Const TwoPi = Pi + Pi
Const HalfPi = Pi / 2

Private Sub Form_Load()
    'Fill form exactly with background image
    picBackGround.Move 0, 0
    Width = picBackGround.Width + (Width - ScaleWidth)
    Height = picBackGround.Height + (Height - ScaleHeight)
    'Change the scaling of the clock face
    picBackGround.Scale (-2, -2)-(2, 2)
    'Center form
    Left = (Screen.Width - Width) \ 2
    Top = (Screen.Height - Height) \ 2
    'Set width of hands in pixels
    picBackGround.DrawWidth = 5
    'Set length of hands
    Hlen = 0.8
    Mlen = 1.5
    Slen = 1
    'Set colors of hands from Registry settings
    Appname$ = "VBClock"
    Section$ = "Hands"
    Key$ = "Hcolor"
    Setting$ = GetSetting(Appname$, Section$, Key$)
    HourHandColor = Val(Setting$)
    Key$ = "Mcolor"
    Setting$ = GetSetting(Appname$, Section$, Key$)
    MinuteHandColor = Val(Setting$)
    Key$ = "Scolor"
    Setting$ = GetSetting(Appname$, Section$, Key$)
    SecondHandColor = Val(Setting$)
End Sub

Private Sub Form_Unload(Cancel As Integer)
    'Save current hand colors
    Key$ = "Hcolor"
    Setting$ = Str$(HourHandColor)
    SaveSetting Appname$, Section$, Key$, Setting$
    Key$ = "Mcolor"
    Setting$ = Str$(MinuteHandColor)
    SaveSetting Appname$, Section$, Key$, Setting$
    Key$ = "Scolor"
    Setting$ = Str$(SecondHandColor)
    SaveSetting Appname$, Section$, Key$, Setting$
End Sub
```

(continued)

Source Code for VBClock.bas *continued*

```
Private Sub mnuAbout_Click()
    frmAbout2.Display
End Sub

Private Sub mnuExit_Click()
    Unload Me
End Sub

Private Sub mnuContents_Click()
    cdlOne.HelpFile = App.Path & "\..\..\Help\Mvbdw.hlp"
    cdlOne.HelpCommand = cdlHelpContents
    cdlOne.ShowHelp
End Sub

Private Sub mnuHandColors_Click()
    'Show form for selecting hand colors
    frmVBClock2.Show vbModal
End Sub

Private Sub mnuSearch_Click()
    cdlOne.HelpFile = App.Path & "\..\..\Help\Mvbdw.hlp"
    cdlOne.HelpCommand = cdlHelpPartialKey
    cdlOne.ShowHelp
End Sub

Private Sub tmrClock_Timer()
    Dim Hang As Double
    Dim Mang As Double
    Dim Sang As Double
    Dim Hx As Double
    Dim Hy As Double
    Dim Mx As Double
    Dim My As Double
    Dim Sx As Double
    Dim Sy As Double
    'Keep track of current second
    Static LastSecond
    'Check to see if new second
    If Second(Now) = LastSecond Then
        Exit Sub
    Else
        LastSecond = Second(Now)
    End If
```

(continued)

Source Code for VBClock.bas *continued*

```
        'Update time variables
        Hnum = Hour(Now)
        Mnum = Minute(Now)
        Snum = Second(Now)
        'Calculate hand angles
        Hang = TwoPi * (Hnum + Mnum / 60) / 12 - HalfPi
        Mang = TwoPi * (Mnum + Snum / 60) / 60 - HalfPi
        Sang = TwoPi * Snum / 60 - HalfPi
        'Calculate endpoints for each hand
        Hx = Hlen * Cos(Hang)
        Hy = Hlen * Sin(Hang)
        Mx = Mlen * Cos(Mang)
        My = Mlen * Sin(Mang)
        Sx = Slen * Cos(Sang)
        Sy = Slen * Sin(Sang)
        'Restore background image
        picBackGround.Cls
        'Draw new hands
        picBackGround.Line (0, 0)-(Mx, My), QBColor(MinuteHandColor)
        picBackGround.Line (0, 0)-(Hx, Hy), QBColor(HourHandColor)
        picBackGround.Line (0, 0)-(Sx, Sy), QBColor(SecondHandColor)
End Sub

Private Sub mnuSetTime_Click()
        Dim Prompt$, Title$, Default$
        Dim StartTime$, Tim$, Msg$
        'Ask user for new time
        Prompt$ = "Enter the time, using the format 00:00:00"
        Title$ = "VBClock"
        Default$ = Time$
        StartTime$ = Default$
        Tim$ = InputBox$(Prompt$, Title$, Default$)
        'Check whether user clicked on Cancel
        'or clicked on OK with no change to time
        If Tim$ = "" Or Tim$ = StartTime$ Then
            Exit Sub
        End If
        'Set new time
        On Error GoTo ErrorTrap
        Time$ = Tim$
        Exit Sub
ErrorTrap:
        Msg$ = "The time you entered is invalid... " + Tim$
        MsgBox Msg$, 48, "VBClock"
        Resume Next
End Sub
```

The Timer control's Interval property is set to 100 milliseconds (1/10 of a second) instead of 1000 (1 second). The hands need to be updated at the rate of once per second, but setting the timer to a rate of once per second causes intermittent jerkiness in the movement of the hands. The jerkiness occurs because a Visual Basic timer isn't based on an exact timing between activations. Instead, the timer activates after the indicated interval, as soon as the system can get back to the timer after that interval has transpired. This causes a slight, unpredictable variation in the actual activations of timer events. (Activations are probably more accurate in faster computers and less accurate in slower ones.) Every so often, this unpredictable delay can cause the VBClock hands to jump to the next second erratically.

To fix this problem, set the timer's Interval property to something less than half a second. I chose 100 milliseconds, or 1/10 of a second. The result is that the hands are updated much more accurately and are never off by more than about a tenth of a second. This updating action is smooth enough that the user won't notice any variation in the beat. The Timer event checks the system time against the previously updated second shown by the hands of the clock. If a new second has not yet arrived, the routine exits, causing very little delay to the overall system's speed.

Using the Registry

The user has the option of changing the color of the clock's hands. To maintain this information between sessions, the application uses the Registry to retrieve the last known color settings during the form's Load event and saves the current color settings during the form's Unload event. This simple example demonstrates the use of the Registry to save the state of an application. Using these same techniques, you can use the Registry to store any additional details about the state of the application that you may want to add.

VBClock2.frm

The VBClock2 form provides a graphical way to select the colors for the three hands of the clock. My goal here was to allow the user to select one of the 16 main colors for each of the hands, but I didn't want to complicate the form with a lot of verbal descriptions of the colors. The solution was to draw all 16 colors in each of three picture boxes and let the user select the colors visually. Figure 27-12 on the following page shows the VBClock2 form in action. This approach is simple and uncluttered, and the user sees exactly what color he or she is selecting. Besides, like they always say, a picture is worth two thousand bytes!

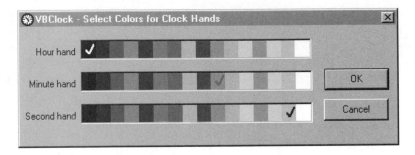

Figure 27-12.
The VBClock2 form, which lets the user select clock hand colors.

During the form's Load procedure I scaled the three picture boxes to divide them into 16 regions. The height of each picture box is scaled from 0 to 1, and the width from 0 to 16. Regardless of the actual size of the picture boxes, each one will display the 16 main colors in rectangular regions of equal size. Likewise, when the user clicks anywhere on a picture box, the *x* coordinate converts to a number from 0 to 15, indicating the selected color.

Image Hot Spots

The Click event doesn't provide the required information to determine exactly where in a picture box the mouse click happened. The best way to determine the location of the click is to maintain the last known position of the mouse pointer using a global variable. The picture box's MouseMove event does provide *x* and *y* pointer location information, so it's easy to update the global variables (which are *HourMouseX*, *MinuteMouseX*, and *SecondMouseX*, in this case) to keep track of the mouse. The values stored in these variables at the time of a Click event determine the color the user is selecting. This technique can be used to define hot spots on your graphics. In fact, by mathematically scrutinizing the current *x* and *y* coordinates of the mouse pointer, you can define hot spots in your graphics that are circular, polygonal, or whatever shape and size you want.

Figure 27-13 shows the VBClock2 form during the development process. To create this form, use the following table and source code to add the appropriate controls, set any nondefault properties as indicated, and type in the source code lines as shown.

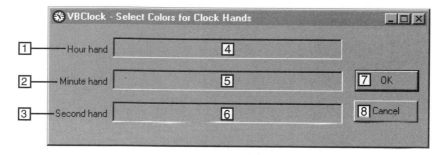

Figure 27-13.
The VBClock2 form during development.

VBClock2.frm Objects and Property Settings

ID No.*	Property	Value
Form		
	Name	frmVBClock2
	Caption	VBClock - Select Colors for Clock Hands
	BorderStyle	3 - Fixed Dialog
Label		
1	Name	lblHourHand
	Caption	Hour hand
	Alignment	1 - Right Justify
Label		
2	Name	lblMinuteHand
	Caption	Minute hand
	Alignment	1 - Right Justify
Label		
3	Name	lblSecondHand
	Caption	Second hand
	Alignment	1 - Right Justify
PictureBox		
4	Name	PicHourColor

* The number in the ID No. column corresponds to the number in Figure 27-13 that identifies the location of the object on the form.

(continued)

VBClock2.frm Objects and Property Settings *continued*

ID No.	Property	Value
PictureBox		
5	Name	picMinuteColor
PictureBox		
6	Name	picSecondColor
CommandButton		
7	Name	cmdOK
	Caption	OK
	Default	True
CommandButton		
8	Name	cmdCancel
	Caption	Cancel
	Cancel	True

Source Code for VBClock2.frm

```
Option Explicit

Dim HourMouseX As Integer
Dim MinuteMouseX As Integer
Dim SecondMouseX As Integer
Dim HourHand As Integer
Dim MinuteHand As Integer
Dim SecondHand As Integer

Private Sub cmdCancel_Click()
    'Cancel and don't change hand colors
    Unload Me
End Sub

Private Sub cmdOK_Click()
    'Reset hand colors
    frmVBClock.HourHandColor = HourHand
    frmVBClock.MinuteHandColor = MinuteHand
    frmVBClock.SecondHandColor = SecondHand
```

(continued)

Source Code for VBClock2.frm *continued*

```
     'Return to clock form
     Unload Me
 End Sub

 Private Sub Form_Load()
     'Get current hand colors
     HourHand = frmVBClock.HourHandColor
     MinuteHand = frmVBClock.MinuteHandColor
     SecondHand = frmVBClock.SecondHandColor
     'Scale picture boxes
     picHourColor.Scale (0, 0)-(16, 1)
     picMinuteColor.Scale (0, 0)-(16, 1)
     picSecondColor.Scale (0, 0)-(16, 1)
 End Sub

 Private Sub Form_Paint()
     Dim i As Integer
     'Draw the 16 colors in each picture "bar"
     For i = 0 To 15
         'Draw colored boxes
         picHourColor.Line (i, 0)-(i + 1, 1), QBColor(i), BF
         picMinuteColor.Line (i, 0)-(i + 1, 1), QBColor(i), BF
         picSecondColor.Line (i, 0)-(i + 1, 1), QBColor(i), BF
     Next i
     'Draw check marks for current colors
     picHourColor.DrawWidth = 2
     picHourColor.Line (HourHand + 0.3, 0.5) _
         -(HourHand + 0.5, 0.7), QBColor(HourHand Xor 15)
     picHourColor.Line (HourHand + 0.5, 0.7) _
         -(HourHand + 0.8, 0.2), QBColor(HourHand Xor 15)
     picMinuteColor.DrawWidth = 2
     picMinuteColor.Line (MinuteHand + 0.3, 0.5) _
         -(MinuteHand + 0.5, 0.7), QBColor(MinuteHand Xor 15)
     picMinuteColor.Line (MinuteHand + 0.5, 0.7) _
         -(MinuteHand + 0.8, 0.2), QBColor(MinuteHand Xor 15)
     picSecondColor.DrawWidth = 2
     picSecondColor.Line (SecondHand + 0.3, 0.5) _
         -(SecondHand + 0.5, 0.7), QBColor(SecondHand Xor 15)
     picSecondColor.Line (SecondHand + 0.5, 0.7) _
         -(SecondHand + 0.8, 0.2), QBColor(SecondHand Xor 15)
 End Sub

 Private Sub picHourColor_Click()
     'Determine selected hour hand color
     HourHand = HourMouseX
```

(continued)

Source Code for VBClock2.frm *continued*

```
    Form_Paint
End Sub

Private Sub picHourColor_MouseMove(Button As Integer, _
    Shift As Integer, X As Single, Y As Single)
    'Keep track of mouse location
    HourMouseX = Int(X)
End Sub

Private Sub picMinuteColor_Click()
    'Determine selected minute hand color
    MinuteHand = MinuteMouseX
    Form_Paint
End Sub

Private Sub picMinuteColor_MouseMove(Button As Integer, _
    Shift As Integer, X As Single, Y As Single)
    'Keep track of mouse location
    MinuteMouseX = Int(X)
End Sub

Private Sub picSecondColor_Click()
    'Determine selected second hand color
    SecondHand = SecondMouseX
    Form_Paint
End Sub

Private Sub picSecondColor_MouseMove(Button As Integer, _
    Shift As Integer, X As Single, Y As Single)
    'Keep track of mouse location
    SecondMouseX = Int(X)
End Sub
```

About2.frm

Earlier in this book, I provided a generic, fill-in-the-blanks About dialog box that you can easily plug into your own applications. To further demonstrate the new App properties and how they can automate the About dialog box even further, I created About2.frm. This form is completely generic in that all displayed data is modified by the calling application, yet the only line of source code required to activate this form is a call to the *frmAbout2.Display* method. Figure 27-14 shows the About2 form as displayed by the VBClock application.

Figure 27-14.

The About2 form as activated by VBClock.

So when, where, and how does the information displayed by the About2 form get set? The trick is to set properties of the App object during the development process. From the Visual Basic File menu select Make EXE File and click on the Options button to display the EXE Options dialog box, as shown in Figure 27-15.

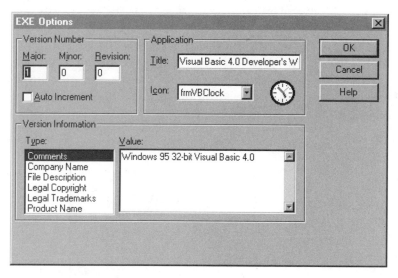

Figure 27-15.

The EXE Options dialog box, in which many of the App properties are set.

NOTE: After you fill in the various fields of the EXE Options dialog box and click on OK, you can click on the Cancel button in the Make EXE File dialog box to exit. The property settings will be retained, and you won't have to compile the application each time you activate this dialog box.

Visual Basic's App object now provides a long list of useful properties, many of which you can set using the EXE Options dialog box. The version numbers, title, and all six properties listed in the Version Information list can be set here, and they can be accessed programmatically by referring to properties of the application's App object.

The About2 form accesses four App properties to set the caption properties of four Label controls. Here's the code that loads these labels, which you'll find in the form's Load routine:

```
'Set labels using App properties
lblHeading.Caption = App.Title
lblApplication.Caption = App.ProductName
lblVB.Caption = App.Comments
lblCopyright.Caption = App.LegalCopyright
```

Feel free to modify the About2 form to display any other App properties you want. For example, you might want to display the version number information or the trademarks text. I chose only four of the properties to make this About box similar to the original About dialog box so that you can easily compare the two techniques. Figure 27-16 shows the About2 form during development. To create this form, use the following table and source code to add the appropriate controls, set any nondefault properties as indicated, and type in the source code lines as shown.

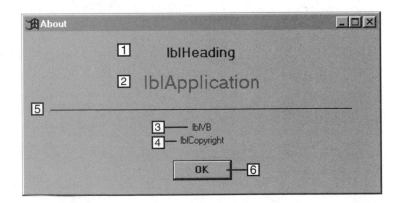

Figure 27-16.
The About2 form during development.

About2.frm Objects and Property Settings

ID No.*	Property	Value
Form		
	Name	frmAbout2
	Caption	About
	BorderStyle	3 - Fixed Dialog
Label		
1	Name	lblHeading
	Alignment	2 - Center
	Font	MS Sans Serif, Bold, 12
Label		
2	Name	lblApplication
	Alignment	2 - Center
	Font	MS Sans Serif, Bold, 18
	ForeColor	&H00008000&
Label		
3	Name	lblVB
	Alignment	2 - Center
Label		
4	Name	lblCopyright
	Alignment	2 - Center
Line		
5	Name	linSeparator
CommandButton		
6	Name	cmdOK
	Caption	OK

* The number in the ID No. column corresponds to the number in Figure 27-16 that identifies the location of the object on the form.

Source Code for About2.frm

```
Option Explicit

Private Sub cmdOK_Click()
    Unload Me
End Sub
```

(continued)

Source Code for About2.frm *continued*

```
Private Sub Form_Load()
    'Center form
    Left = (Screen.Width - Width) \ 2
    Top = (Screen.Height - Height) \ 2
    'Set labels using App properties
    lblHeading.Caption = App.Title
    lblApplication.Caption = App.ProductName
    lblVB.Caption = App.Comments
    lblCopyright.Caption = App.LegalCopyright
End Sub

Public Sub Display()
    'Display self as modal
    Me.Show vbModal
End Sub
```

The NISTTime Application

This little utility automatically dials up and connects with the National Institute of Standards and Technology (NIST) in Boulder, Colorado. You can use it to adjust your computer's clock to something better than 1-second accuracy. I say "something better" because various factors can limit the efficiency of the processing, such as modem throughput speed, the speed and efficiency of your computer at setting its clock, telephone line delays, and so on. The NIST time service does attempt to adjust for this delay by sending the "on mark" character 45 milliseconds before the actual time. As a result, the NISTTime application can set your clock's time far more accurately than you can set it manually.

How NISTTime Works

The NISTTime application uses the MSComm control to handle the modem connection over the telephone to the NIST facility. This control makes it simple to set up the correct baud rate, telephone number, and other modem parameters, as shown in the relevant lines of code in the form's Load event routine. Until recently, the baud rate for this service was limited to either 300 or 1200 baud, but NIST has now installed modems that adjust automatically to the baud rate of the modem making the call. As shown in the source code listing, I've set my modem speed to 14400 baud, which has worked fine for me. If you experience any line noise or inconsistent connections, try a lower baud rate.

Once connected, the service sends a header message, followed by a line of information repeated once per second. At the end of this line of data an asterisk is transmitted, marking the exact time. The NISTTime application reads and stores this data as it arrives, watching for two occurrences of the asterisk time marks. When the second asterisk arrives, the NISTTime application extracts minute and second information from the string of data and sets the system clock to these values.

The string of incoming data provides other useful information, such as the Modified Julian Date; the month, day, year, and hour numbers for Universal Coordinated Time; and even a number indicating a possible leap second adjustment at the end of the current month. All of this extra data is ignored in the NISTTime application because your clock is probably already close to the correct local time and only an adjustment for minutes and seconds will be necessary.

NOTE: To get a full accounting and description of the information broadcast by this service, dial in to the same number using a terminal program such as Hyperterminal. Once you are connected, type a question mark to receive several pages of detailed information.

The NISTTime form uses two timers to control the communications interaction: one timer's interval is set to 1 millisecond to process incoming bytes; the other control is set to trigger after 1 minute. Normally, the NIST-Time application makes the connection, sets your clock, and hangs up just a few seconds after dialing. However, if anything is amiss, the 1-minute timer disconnects the phone at the end of a minute. The service itself disconnects after roughly 1 minute of operation—all of which makes the chances of accidentally running up long distance bills highly unlikely. I added this second watchdog timer as a redundant safety mechanism.

As NISTTime runs, several short messages are displayed to indicate its progress. No interaction by the user is required, and the application unloads shortly after the clock is set. Figures 27-17 through 27-19 on the following page show the normal sequence of these messages during the few seconds of operation.

NOTE: To monitor your system's time, either run the VBClock program presented in the previous topic, or double-click on the time displayed in your Windows 95 desktop task bar to display the Date/Time Properties sheet.

Figure 27-17.
The NISTTime application as it dials in to NIST.

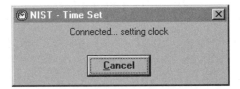

Figure 27-18.
The application receiving the data used to set the system clock.

Figure 27-19.
The NISTTime message displayed while disconnecting from NIST.

NISTTime.frm

The NISTTime form is small—just big enough to display progress messages in the upper-left corner of your display. The form contains two Timer controls, an MSComm control, and a Label control to display progress messages. Figure 27-20 shows the form during development. To create this form, use the following table and source code to add the appropriate controls, set any non-default properties as indicated, and type in the source code lines as shown.

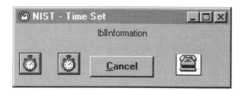

Figure 27-20.
The NISTTime form during development.

NISTTime.frm Objects and Property Settings

Property	Value
Form	
Name	frmNISTTime
Caption	NIST - Time Set
BorderStyle	3 - Fixed Dialog
Timer	
Name	tmrGetBytes
Interval	1
Enabled	False
Timer	
Name	tmrWatchDog
Interval	60000
Enabled	False
MSComm	
Name	comControl
Handshaking	2 = Request-to-send/clear-to-send handshaking.
CommandButton	
Name	cmdCancel
Caption	&Cancel
Label	
Name	lblInformation

Source Code for NISTTime.bas

```
Option Explicit
DefInt A-Z

Const PORT = 1
Const TELEPHONE = "1-303-494-4774"
Const BUFSIZ = 3000

Dim NistNdx
Dim NistBuf As String * BUFSIZ

Private Sub cmdCancel_Click()
    Unload Me
End Sub

Private Sub Form_Load()
Dim X
    'Locate form near upper-left corner
    Left = (Screen.Width - Width) * 0.1
    Top = (Screen.Height - Height) * 0.1
    'Display first informational message
    lblInformation.Caption = _
        "Dialing National Institute of Standards " & _
        "and Technology Telephone Time Service"
    'Show form and first message
    Show
    'Set up Communications control parameters
    comControl.CommPort = PORT
    comControl.Settings = "14400,N,8,1"
    'Set to read entire buffer
    comControl.InputLen = 0
    comControl.PortOpen = True
    'Send command to dial NIST
    comControl.Output = "ATDT" + TELEPHONE + vbCr
    'Activate timers
    tmrGetBytes.Enabled = True
    tmrWatchDog.Enabled = True
    'Enable Cancel button
    cmdCancel.Enabled = True
End Sub

Private Sub Form_Unload(Cancel As Integer)
```

(continued)

Source Code for NISTTime.bas *continued*

```
        'This usually hangs up phone
        comControl.DTREnable = False
        'The following also hangs up phone
        Pause 1500
        'Update message for user
        lblInformation.Caption = "Hanging up"
        Refresh
        'Send commands to control modem
        comControl.Output = "+++"
        Pause 1500
        comControl.Output = "ATH0" + vbCrLf
        'Close down communications
        comControl.PortOpen = False
End Sub

Private Sub Pause(millisec)
Dim EndOfPause As Double
Dim X
        'Determine end time of delay
        EndOfPause = Timer + millisec / 1000
        'Loop away time
        Do
        Loop While Timer < EndOfPause
End Sub

Private Sub SetTime(a$)
        Dim Ho, Mi, Se
        Dim TimeNow As Double
        'Extract current hour from system
        Ho = Hour(Now)
        'Extract minute and second from NIST string
        Mi = Val(Mid$(a$, 22, 2))
        Se = Val(Mid$(a$, 25, 2))
        'Construct new time
        TimeNow = TimeSerial(Ho, Mi, Se)
        'Set system clock
        Time$ = Format$(TimeNow, "hh:mm:ss")
End Sub

Private Sub tmrGetBytes_Timer()
        Static ConnectFlag As Boolean
        Dim Tmp$
```

(continued)

Source Code for NISTTime.bas *continued*

```
    Dim Bytes
    Dim p1, p2
    'Check for incoming bytes
    If comControl.InBufferCount = 0 Then
        Exit Sub
    Else
        Tmp$ = comControl.Input
        Bytes = Len(Tmp$)
        If Bytes + NistNdx >= BUFSIZ Then
            lblInformation.Caption = "Hanging Up"
            tmrGetBytes.Enabled = False
            tmrWatchDog.Enabled = False
            Unload Me
        Else
            Mid$(NistBuf, NistNdx + 1, Bytes) = Tmp$
            NistNdx = NistNdx + Bytes
        End If
    End If
    'Check for sign that we've connected
    If ConnectFlag = False Then
        If InStr(NistBuf, "*" & vbCrLf) Then
            lblInformation.Caption = "Connected... setting clock"
            ConnectFlag = True
        End If
    Else
        'Check for time marks
        p1 = InStr(NistBuf, "*")
        p2 = InStr(p1 + 1, NistBuf, "*")
        'Time received if two time marks found
        If p2 > p1 Then
            SetTime Mid$(NistBuf, p1, p2 - p1 + 1)
            Unload Me
        End If
    End If
End Sub

Private Sub tmrWatchDog_Timer()
    'Activate safety timeout if no connection
    Beep
    Unload Me
End Sub
```

Two constants are declared at the beginning of the code that you may need to change. The PORT constant indicates the COM port your modem is connected to. If your modem is at COM1, PORT should be set to *1*, as shown, but if your modem is at COM2, COM3, or COM4, change PORT to *2, 3*, or *4*.

If you happen to live in the Denver metropolitan area, you can remove the long-distance digits from the TELEPHONE constant. Similarly, if you need to dial 9 to get an outside line, you'll want to add this to the string constant, along with a comma for a half-second delay. For example, I'm lucky enough to live near Denver, so my NISTTime program's TELEPHONE constant is set to *494-4774*. A typical string that dials 9 first would be *9,1-303-494-4774*.

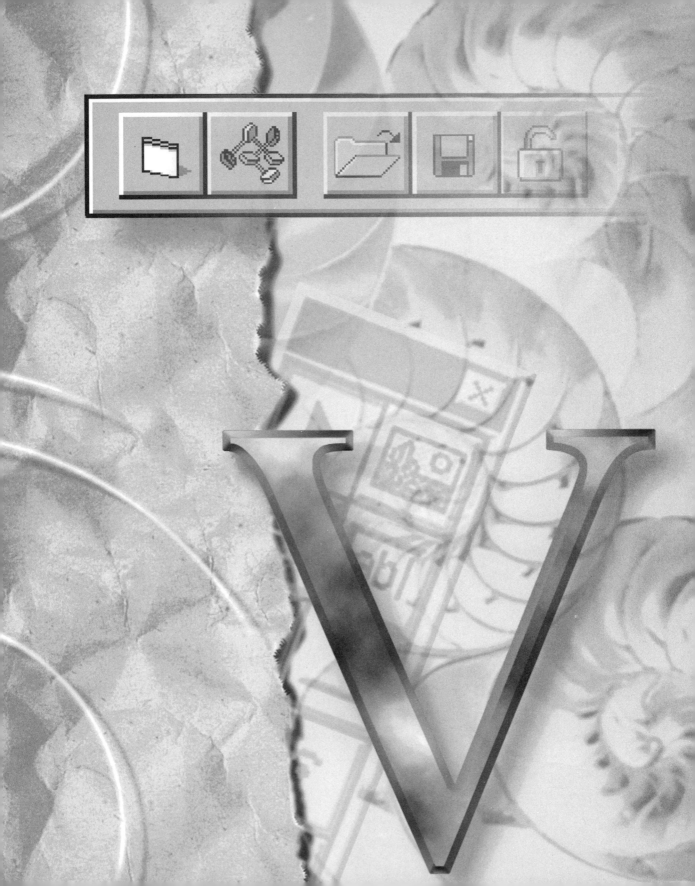

CHAPTER TWENTY-EIGHT

Databases

Visual Basic is playing an increasingly important role in the corporate environment, especially since its database capabilities have been enhanced to make it a powerful development and front-end tool. The three applications in this chapter—AreaCode, DataDump, and Jot—provide examples of just how easy it is to work with Microsoft Access or other databases using Visual Basic.

The AreaCode Application

The AreaCode application consists of two forms, AreaCode.frm and the generic About.frm. AreaCode.frm uses two Data controls to access the same database of telephone area codes in different ways. The first Data control, in the top half of the form, accesses a table of area codes in the database file AreaCode.mdb, which was created using Microsoft Access 7.0. The Data control in the bottom half of the form accesses a query in the same database file. The table tapped by the first Data control presents area code data in ascending (0 through 999) area code order. The query provides the same table of area code data in ascending state abbreviation order (A through Z). This application makes it easy to either look up where a call came from when all you know is the area code or to look up an area code for a known state.

The single form for the AreaCode application uses few database-related lines of code, because the Data control and several TextBox controls have properties that simplify the connection to the database. To create the form, I drew the controls and then set a handful of properties to make the connection to the database. I added few lines of code to handle minor details of the search process—and then I was done!

Connecting controls to a database in this way is a two-step process. First a Data control is connected to the database file by setting the DatabaseName property, and then it is connected to a specific table or query within that database by setting the RecordSource property. In general, each Data control connects to a single table or query. Many other types of controls, such as Label and ListBox controls, now have properties that make the final connection to the database by connecting to a specific Data control. In this case, I've used several TextBox controls. All I had to do was set each TextBox control's DataSource property to the name of one of the Data controls and then set each of their DataField properties to indicate the specific field within the table or query.

Although you can navigate the database table or query by clicking on the Data control, I've added some code to demonstrate another way to manipulate the database records. The txtAreaCode text box lets the user type in a three-digit area code. After the user enters the three digits, Visual Basic sets a bookmark at the current record (so that the current record can be displayed again if the search fails), and several RecordSet properties of the Data control are set to cause the txtAreaCode_Change subprogram to begin searching for a matching area code in the database immediately. Similarly, the second Data control searches for a state abbreviation and displays the first record for that state when the user types two characters into the txtStateAbbrev1 text box in the bottom half of the form. The user can then click on the next record button of the Data control to see the records with the additional area codes for that state. Figure 28-1 shows the AreaCode form after a successful search for the area code 303 in the top half and after a successful search for the state of Washington in the bottom half. Note how the top and bottom halves of the form work independently of each other, even though they access the same database.

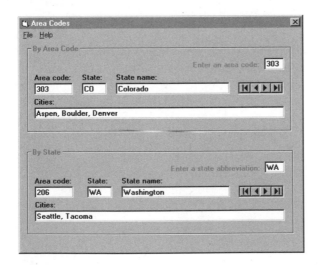

Figure 28-1.
The AreaCode form after locating area code 303 in the top half and an area code for Washington State in the bottom half.

AreaCode.frm

This form contains two nearly identical sets of controls, one set for the top half of the form and one set for the bottom half. Two Data controls connect to the same database, and several text boxes connect to fields through the associated Data control. To organize the TextBox controls, I've grouped them with some descriptive labels within Frame controls. A single CommonDialog control provides access to the associated help file using the control's *ShowHelp* method. I assigned the name of the database file to the Data controls' DataBaseName property in the Form Load subroutine so that I could use the App.Path property to identify the location of the database. If your database is in a location other than the folder containing the application, assign the full path to the database. Figure 28-2 shows the AreaCode form during development. To create this form, use the following tables and source code to add the appropriate controls, set any nondefault properties as indicated, and type in the source code lines as shown.

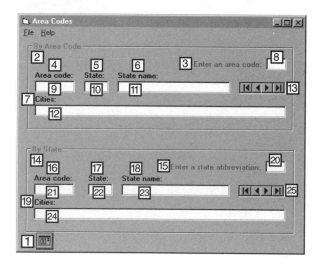

Figure 28-2.
The AreaCode form during development.

AreaCode.frm Menu Design Window Entries

Caption	Name	Indentation	Enabled
&File	mnuFile	0	True
&New	mnuNew	1	False
&Open...	mnuOpen	1	False
&Save	mnuSave	1	False
Save &As...	mnuSaveAs	1	False
-	mnuFileDash1	1	True
E&xit	mnuExit	1	True
&Help	mnuHelp	0	True
&Contents	mnuContents	1	True
&Search for Help on...	mnuSearch	1	True
-	mnuHelpDash1	1	True
&About...	mnuAbout	1	True

AreaCode.frm Objects and Property Settings

ID No.*	Property	Value
Form		
	Name	frmAreaCode
	Caption	Area Codes
	BorderStyle	3 - Fixed Dialog
CommonDialog		
1	Name	cdlOne
Frame		
2	Name	fraByAreaCode
	Caption	By Area Code
	ForeColor	&H000000FF&
Label		
3	Name	lblPrompt2
	Caption	Enter an area code:
	ForeColor	&H00FF0000&

* The number in the ID No. column corresponds to the number in Figure 28-2 that identifies the location of the object on the form.

(continued)

AreaCode.frm Objects and Property Settings *continued*

ID No.	Property	Value
Label		
4	Name	lblAreaCode2
	Caption	Area code:
Label		
5	Name	lblState2
	Caption	State:
Label		
6	Name	lblStateName2
	Caption	State name:
Label		
7	Name	lblCities2
	Caption	Cities:
TextBox		
8	Name	txtAreaCode
	Alignment	2 - Center
TextBox		
9	Name	txtAreaCode2
	DataSource	datAreaCode2
	DataField	Areacode
TextBox		
10	Name	txtState2
	DataSource	datAreaCode2
	DataField	State
TextBox		
11	Name	txtStateName2
	DataSource	datAreaCode2
	DataField	StateName
TextBox		
12	Name	txtCities2
	DataSource	datAreaCode2
	DataField	Cities

(continued)

AreaCode.frm Objects and Property Settings *continued*

ID No.	Property	Value
Data		
13	Name	datAreaCode2
	RecordSource	AreaCode
Frame		
14	Name	fraByState
	Caption	By State
	ForeColor	&H000000FF&
Label		
15	Name	lblPrompt1
	Caption	Enter a state abbreviation:
	ForeColor	&H00FF0000&
Label		
16	Name	lblAreaCode1
	Caption	Area code:
Label		
17	Name	lblState1
	Caption	State:
Label		
18	Name	lblStateName1
	Caption	State name:
Label		
19	Name	lblCities1
	Caption	Cities:
TextBox		
20	Name	txtStateAbbrev1
	Alignment	2 - Center
TextBox		
21	Name	txtAreaCode1
	DataSource	datAreaCode1
	DataField	Areacode

(continued)

AreaCode.frm Objects and Property Settings *continued*

ID No.	Property	Value
TextBox		
22	Name	txtState1
	DataSource	datAreaCode1
	DataField	State
TextBox		
23	Name	txtStateName1
	DataSource	datAreaCode1
	DataField	StateName
TextBox		
24	Name	txtCities1
	DataSource	datAreaCode1
	DataField	Cities
Data		
25	Name	datAreaCode1
	RecordSource	Bystate

Source Code for AreaCode.frm

```
Option Explicit

Private Sub Form_Load()
    'Center this form
    Left = (Screen.Width - Width) \ 2
    Top = (Screen.Height - Height) \ 2
    datAreaCode1.DatabaseName = App.Path & "\AreaCode.mdb"
    datAreaCode2.DatabaseName = App.Path & "\AreaCode.mdb"
End Sub

Private Sub txtAreaCode_Change()
    Dim Bookmark$
    Dim Criteria$
    'Wait for user to enter all three digits
    If Len(txtAreaCode.Text) = 3 Then
        'Record current record
        Bookmark$ = datAreaCode2.Recordset.Bookmark
```

(continued)

431

Source Code for AreaCode.frm *continued*

```
        'Search for first matching area code
        Criteria$ = "Areacode = " + txtAreaCode.Text
        datAreaCode2.Recordset.FindFirst Criteria$
        'Handle unmatched area code
        If datAreaCode2.Recordset.NoMatch Then
            Beep
            datAreaCode2.Recordset.Bookmark = Bookmark$
        End If
    End If
End Sub

Private Sub txtAreaCode_KeyPress(KeyAscii As Integer)
    If Len(txtAreaCode.Text) = 3 Then
        txtAreaCode.Text = ""
    End If
End Sub

Private Sub txtStateAbbrev1_Change()
    Dim Bookmark$
    Dim Criteria$
    'Wait for user to enter two-letter abbreviation
    If Len(txtStateAbbrev1.Text) = 2 Then
        'Record current record
        Bookmark$ = datAreaCode1.Recordset.Bookmark
        'Search for first matching state
        Criteria$ = "State = '" + txtStateAbbrev1.Text + "'"
        datAreaCode1.Recordset.FindFirst Criteria$
        'Handle unmatched state abbreviation
        If datAreaCode1.Recordset.NoMatch Then
            Beep
            datAreaCode1.Recordset.Bookmark = Bookmark$
        End If
    End If
End Sub

Private Sub txtStateAbbrev1_KeyPress(KeyAscii As Integer)
    KeyAscii = Asc(UCase$(Chr$(KeyAscii)))
    If Len(txtStateAbbrev1.Text) = 2 Then
        txtStateAbbrev1.Text = ""
    End If
End Sub

Private Sub mnuAbout_Click()
    'Set properties
    About.Application = "AreaCode"
```

(continued)

Source Code for AreaCode.frm *continued*

```
        About.Heading = "Microsoft Visual Basic 4.0 Developer's Workshop"
        About.Copyright = "1996 John Clark Craig"
        About.Display
End Sub

Private Sub mnuExit_Click()
    Unload Me
End Sub

Private Sub mnuContents_Click()
    cdlOne.HelpFile = App.Path & "\..\..\Help\Mvbdw.hlp"
    cdlOne.HelpCommand = cdlHelpContents
    cdlOne.ShowHelp
End Sub

Private Sub mnuSearch_Click()
    cdlOne.HelpFile = App.Path & "\..\..\Help\Mvbdw.hlp"
    cdlOne.HelpCommand = cdlHelpPartialKey
    cdlOne.ShowHelp
End Sub
```

This code relies on a query within the database to sort the AreaCode records by state, but there is a simple alternative to creating the query. We can set the Data control's RecordSource property to a SQL string, which provides a flexible and powerful tool for manipulating data. For example, you can add the following line of code to the form's Load event to produce the same result as setting the RecordSource property to the *Bystate* query.

```
datAreaCode1.RecordSource = "Select * from AREACODE order by State"
```

If you add this line to the program listing, you can delete the *Bystate* query from the database. Both Data controls now access the same database table: one using the default area code order of the records and the other using the SQL command to reorder the records by state.

The DataDump Application

With Visual Basic 4, it's easy to manipulate database files programmatically. The data access object (DAO) model provides a structured hierarchy of objects that let you access and modify any part of a database. (See Chapter 19 for more about the DAO model.) The DataDump application described here is a stream-lined utility that demonstrates how you can loop through the various parts of this hierarchy to determine the layout of any field in any table of any database.

433

Unlike the AreaCode application, this program contains no Data controls or other data-bound controls. This application contains only a TextBox control for displaying the analyzed internal structure of a user-selected database and a CommonDialog control for selecting a database file to analyze. All analysis of the database file contents is performed by looping through various objects within the DAO model.

This application provides a list of all tables within the database and all fields within each table. Each field is described by name, type, and data size in bytes. I've found this utility useful for quickly reviewing the contents of a database's tables without having to run Access. If you want, you can easily extend the current code to include a listing of any queries stored in the database in the analysis. The online help system for Visual Basic 4 provides a good explanation of the complete DAO hierarchy for those interested in digging into the subject even deeper.

At load time, the DataDump form prompts for a database filename using the CommonDialog control, as shown in Figure 28-3. It then proceeds to analyze the selected database, concatenating all the results into a single string variable. The database structure is traversed just once per run of the program, and the results string is displayed in the TextBox control whenever the form is

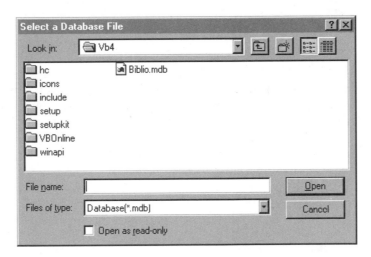

Figure 28-3.
The CommonDialog control that lets the user select a database file for analysis.

resized. To improve the readability of the output, I have formatted the string using vbCrLf constants and extra spaces for padding. The font of the text box is set to Courier New, which is a nonproportional font that provides consistent alignment of the indented text lines. The TextBox control has scrollbars that let you view the data no matter how long it gets, and the control adjusts automatically to fill the form whenever the form is resized. Figure 28-4 shows the structure of the Biblio.mdb sample file that ships with Visual Basic 4.

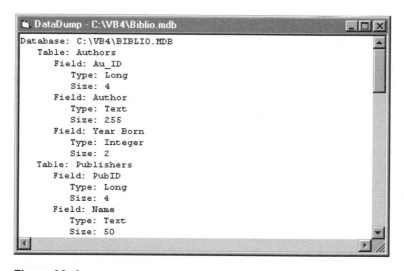

Figure 28-4.
The DataDump application in action, showing the tables and fields in Biblio.mdb.

DataDump.frm

Figure 28-5 on the following page shows the DataDump form during development. The TextBox control is smaller than the form but is resized at runtime to the size of the form. To create this form, use the following table and source code to add the appropriate controls, set any nondefault properties as indicated, and type in the source code lines as shown.

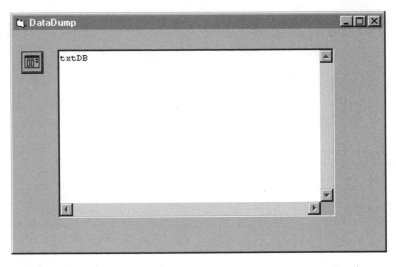

Figure 28-5.
The DataDump form during development.

DataDump.frm Objects and Property Settings

Property	Value
Form	
Name	frmDataDump
Caption	DataDump
CommonDialog	
Name	cdlOne
TextBox	
Name	txtDB
Font	Couricr New
MultiLine	True
Scrollbars	3 - Both

Source Code for DataDump.frm

```
Option Explicit

Dim DBFileName$
Dim dbs$
```

(continued)

Source Code for DataDump.frm *continued*

```
Private Sub Form_Load()
    'Center this form
    Left = (Screen.Width - Width) \ 2
    Top = (Screen.Height - Height) \ 2
    'Prompt user for database filename
    cdlOne.DialogTitle = "Select a Database File"
    cdlOne.Filter = "Database(*.mdb)|*.mdb"
    cdlOne.CancelError = True
    'Check for Cancel button click
    On Error Resume Next
    cdlOne.ShowOpen
    If Err = cdlCancel Then End
    'Prepare to analyze database
    DBFileName$ = cdlOne.filename
    Me.Caption = "DataDump - " & DBFileName$
    GetStructure
End Sub

Private Sub Form_Paint()
    'Size text box to fit form
    txtDB.Move 0, 0, ScaleWidth, ScaleHeight
    'Display analysis string in text box
    txtDB.Text = dbs$
End Sub

Private Sub GetStructure()
    'Looping variables
    Dim i, j
    'Database objects
    Dim db As Database
    Dim rs As Recordset
    Dim td As TableDef
    Dim fd As Field
    'Open the database
    Set db = Workspaces(0).OpenDatabase(DBFileName$)
    dbs$ = "Database: " & db.Name & vbCrLf
    'Process each table
    For i = 0 To db.TableDefs.Count - 1
        Set td = db.TableDefs(i)
        If Left$(td.Name, 4) <> "MSys" Then
            'Get table's name
            dbs$ = dbs$ & Space$(3) & "Table: "
            dbs$ = dbs$ & td.Name & vbCrLf
            'Process each field in each table
```

(continued)

Source Code for DataDump.frm *continued*

```
            For j = 0 To td.Fields.Count - 1
                Set fd = td.Fields(j)
                'Get field's name
                dbs$ = dbs$ & Space$(6) & "Field: "
                dbs$ = dbs$ & fd.Name & vbCrLf
                'Get field's data type
                dbs$ = dbs$ & Space$(9) & "Type: "
                Select Case fd.Type
                Case dbBoolean
                    dbs$ = dbs$ & "Boolean" & vbCrLf
                Case dbByte
                    dbs$ = dbs$ & "Byte" & vbCrLf
                Case dbInteger
                    dbs$ = dbs$ & "Integer" & vbCrLf
                Case dbLong
                    dbs$ = dbs$ & "Long" & vbCrLf
                Case dbCurrency
                    dbs$ = dbs$ & "Currency" & vbCrLf
                Case dbSingle
                    dbs$ = dbs$ & "Single" & vbCrLf
                Case dbDouble
                    dbs$ = dbs$ & "Double" & vbCrLf
                Case dbDate
                    dbs$ = dbs$ & "Date" & vbCrLf
                Case dbText
                    dbs$ = dbs$ & "Text" & vbCrLf
                Case dbLongBinary
                    dbs$ = dbs$ & "LongBinary" & vbCrLf
                Case dbMemo
                    dbs$ = dbs$ & "Memo" & vbCrLf
                Case Else
                    dbs$ = dbs$ & "(unknown) & vbCrLf"
                End Select
                'Get field's size in bytes
                If fd.Type <> dbLongBinary And _
                  fd.Type <> dbMemo Then
                    dbs$ = dbs$ & Space$(9) & "Size: "
                    dbs$ = dbs$ & fd.Size & vbCrLf
                End If
            Next j
        End If
    Next i
    'Close database
    db.Close
End Sub
```

The Jot Application

The Jot application uses a multiple document interface (MDI) form to pop up multiple note windows. To make this a commercial application, you'd probably want to add a lot of features and modify the design, but the application is fully functional as is and it demonstrates a number of useful Visual Basic programming features.

I've included features that demonstrate yet another way to add Tool-Tips to your toolbar buttons, how to create multiple copies of MDI child forms, how to use hot keys on an MDI form, how to create a database from scratch programmatically, and one way to center an image on an MDI form.

Figure 28-6 shows the Jot application at runtime. Buttons on the toolbar let you create new note windows and delete them when you're finished. Other buttons arrange the note windows and their icons. When you close Jot, all notes are saved in a database; when you run Jot the next time, these notes reappear.

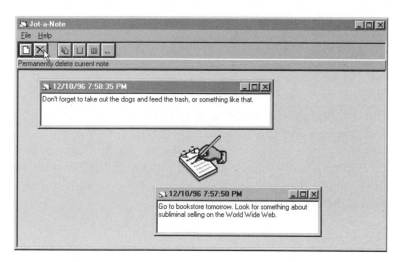

Figure 28-6.
The Jot application in action.

A Simple Type of ToolTip

As the mouse is moved over each button on the toolbar, a description of the button is displayed in the SSPanel control just below the toolbar. In Figure 28-6, for instance, positioning the mouse pointer over the big X button on the toolbar displays a message in the panel below the toolbar that describes the purpose of the button—to permanently delete the current note (the note window with the focus). This method provides an alternative to adding

ToolTips to your buttons, since the text description serves the same purpose. It's very easy to add this type of descriptive labeling to buttons or to just about any other control on your forms. You simply display text in response to a MouseMove event for the specified button or control. In this example, I placed an SSPanel control just under the toolbar and set its Caption property to display these descriptions. You may prefer to place the panel across the bottom of the form. Notice that MouseMove events for the form itself, and for the SSPanel containing the buttons, are used to set the panel's Caption property to an empty string. This setting erases the description as the user moves the mouse off each button.

Multiple Child Forms

The first button in the toolbar creates a new, blank note window: I created a single Note child form named frmNote at design time, and placed a call in the sscNewNote command button's Click event to a subprogram, MakeNew-Note, which creates a new copy of the Note form. If you look in the Make-NewNote routine, you'll see two lines of code that create and display each new copy of the Note form:

```
Dim newNote As New frmNote
newNote.Show
```

Each copy of this child form shares the same event-driven routines. To refer to the properties of the current copy of the child form (the Note form with the focus) in these routines I've used the *Me* prefix. For example, during the child form's Unload event its Caption property is saved in a field of the database. To record the caption of the child form currently unloading, the routine refers to Me.Caption.

MDI Form Hot Key

The Note form's KeyPreview property is set to *True* so that all keypresses are intercepted before they are processed further by the form or its controls. The only keypress the Note form intercepts is Ctrl-T, which updates the date and time displayed in the current Note form's caption to the current date and time. Normally the date and time of each note are fixed at the time the note is created. This hot key combination lets you update the caption when you want. Even if you assign your own hot key combinations, you can still use the standard Windows shortcut key combinations Ctrl-X, Ctrl-C, and Ctrl-V to cut, copy, and paste as you edit these notes. The Ctrl-T command works much like these built-in commands. You can easily add code to process any other keys, or combinations of keys, in the same KeyDown event routine. If you do process any key combinations, remember to set KeyAscii to *0* to prevent the form from further acting on the intercepted keys. Figures 28-7 and 28-8 show a Note form just before and just after Ctrl-T is pressed to update the date and time in the caption.

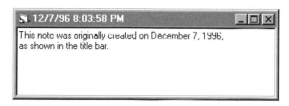

Figure 28-7.

A note originally created on December 7, 1996.

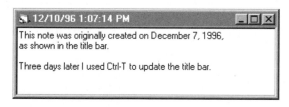

Figure 28-8.

The same note updated to the current date and time.

Creating a Database

When the Jot form loads, it attempts to open the Jot.mdb database file to load any previously saved notes. If this database file doesn't exist, which is true the first time you run the Jot application, the Jot form ignores the request. The database is not created until the first Note child form is unloaded. When a Note child form unloads and there is no database, a special block of code creates the database automatically. Understanding how these lines of code work provides concepts you'll find useful for understanding a lot of other database programming techniques. Here are the lines that create the new database (if the database doesn't already exist) in the form's Unload event:

```
'Create empty database
Set db = Workspaces(0).CreateDatabase("Jot.mdb", dbLangGeneral)
'Create table
Set td = db.CreateTableDef("JotTable")
'Create field
Set fd = td.CreateField("JotDateTime", dbDate)
```

(continued)

```
'Add new field to table's Fields collection
td.Fields.Append fd
'Create second field
Set fd = td.CreateField("JotNote", dbMemo)
'Add it to table
td.Fields.Append fd
'Add new table to TableDefs collection
db.TableDefs.Append td
'New database is now open
```

CreateDatabase, CreateTableDef, and *CreateField* are methods of the objects that will eventually contain the objects they create. However, these methods don't actually hook the created objects into their parent objects—they just allocate memory and create all the behind-the-scenes details of the database objects. It takes an explicit second step to connect each new object into the structure of the parent object that created it. The above code shows several *Append* methods used to hook the new objects into the structure of the containing collection. For example, the TableDef object contains a collection named Fields, which contains all Field objects in the defined table. The *Append* method of the Fields collection is called to hook the freshly created Field object into this collection. It's a two-step process: create an object and then append it to a collection to tie everything together. As shown in the code above, this same two-step process is used to create fields and tables, append fields to tables, and append tables to a database.

Centering an Image on an MDI Form

The types of controls that can be placed on an MDI form are limited. In general, only those controls with Align properties can be placed on an MDI form, and these controls will always be aligned at the top, bottom, left, or right of the form. An MDI form does have a Picture property, but any image loaded into this property is also aligned to the top-left corner of the form. So how did the Jot application end up with a bitmap image that always moves to the center of the MDI form as the form is resized? It's a useful trick to know.

You can move a child form to any relative position within the MDI parent form, including dead center, with a little bit of calculation. I've taken advantage of this by centering the Splash form in the Jot form's Resize event routine.

The Splash form doesn't display anything except a picture because its BorderStyle property has been set to *0 - None* and the form is sized to match that of the Image control it contains. As a result, when the Splash form is placed in the center of the MDI Jot form, the user sees only a centered bitmap picture. Figures 28-9 and 28-10 show the Jot form with the centered image before and after the form is resized.

Figure 28-9.
The Jot form with a centered image.

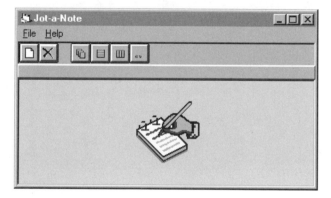

Figure 28-10.
The image staying centered as the Jot form is resized.

Jot.frm

As shown in the project window in Figure 28-11 on the following page, the Jot application contains five files. Jot.frm is the main MDI startup form, so we'll take a look at it first. Figure 28-12 shows the Jot form during development.

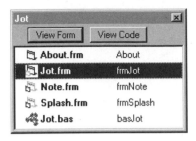

Figure 28-11.
The Jot application's project window.

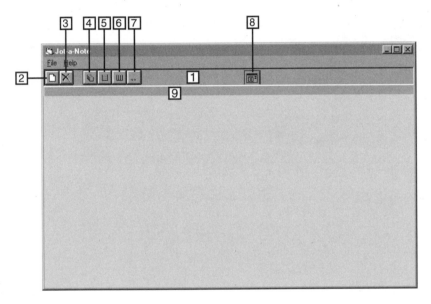

Figure 28-12.
The MDI Jot form during development.

Most controls cannot be drawn directly on an MDI form. In general, though, you can add any "illegal" controls to an MDI form by drawing them in a PictureBox control (one of the few controls that can be drawn on an MDI form), as I've done in this application. To create this form, use the following tables and source code to add the appropriate controls, set any nondefault properties, and type in the source code lines as shown.

Jot.frm Menu Design Window Entries

Caption	Name	Indentation	Enabled
&File	mnuFile	0	True
&New	mnuNew	1	False
&Open...	mnuOpen	1	Falsc
&Save	mnuSave	1	False
Save &As...	mnuSaveAs	1	False
-	mnuFileDash1	1	True
E&xit	mnuExit	1	Truc
&Help	mnuHelp	0	True
&Contents	mnuContents	1	True
&Search for Help on...	mnuSearch	1	True
-	mnuHelpDash1	1	True
&About...	mnuAbout	1	True

Jot.frm (MDI) Objects and Property Settings

ID No.*	Property	Value
Form		
	Name	frmJot
	Caption	Jot-a-Note
PictureBox		
1	Name	picToolBar
	Align	1 - Align Top
*SSCommand**		
2	Name	sscNewNote
	Picture	New.bmp
	Caption	(blank)

 * The number in the ID No. column corresponds to the number in Figure 28-12 that identifies the location of the object on the form.

 ** The first two SSCommand button pictures, New.bmp and Delete.bmp, are found in Visual Basic 4's Bitmaps\Tlbr_w95 folder. The Cascade.bmp, TileH.bmp, TileV.bmp, and ArngIcon.bmp bitmaps were created using the Paint utility and can be found on the Companion CD.

(continued)

Jot.frm (MDI) Objects and Property Settings *continued*

ID No.	Property	Value
*SSCommand***		
3	Name	sscDelete
	Picture	Delete.bmp
	Caption	(blank)
SSCommand		
4	Name	sscCascade
	Picture	Cascade.bmp
	Caption	(blank)
SSCommand		
5	Name	sscTileH
	Picture	TileH.bmp
	Caption	(blank)
SSCommand		
6	Name	sscTileV
	Picture	TileV.bmp
	Caption	(blank)
SSCommand		
7	Name	sscArrangeIcons
	Picture	ArngIcon.bmp
	Caption	(blank)
CommonDialog		
8	Name	cdlOne
SSPanel		
9	Name	sspTips
	Align	1 - Align Top
	Alignment	1 - Left Justify - MIDDLE

Source Code for Jot.frm

```
Option Explicit

Private Sub MDIForm_Load()
    'Center this form on-screen
    Move (Screen.Width - Width) \ 2, _
```

(continued)

Source Code for Jot.frm *continued*

```
        (Screen.Height - Height) \ 2
    'Load all previous notes from database
    LoadNotes
    'Display splash image
    frmSplash.Show
End Sub

Private Sub MDIForm_MouseMove(Button As Integer, _
    Shift As Integer, X As Single, Y As Single)
    sspTips.Caption = ""
End Sub

Private Sub MDIForm_Resize()
    'Move splash image to center of MDI form
    frmSplash.Move (Me.ScaleWidth - frmSplash.Width) \ 2, _
            (Me.ScaleHeight - frmSplash.Height) \ 2
End Sub

Private Sub mnuAbout_Click()
    'Set properties and display About form
    About.Application = "Jot"
    About.Heading = "Microsoft Visual Basic 4.0 Developer's Workshop"
    About.Copyright = "1996 John Clark Craig"
    About.Display
End Sub

Private Sub mnuExit_Click()
    Unload frmJot
End Sub

Private Sub mnuContents_Click()
    cdlOne.HelpFile = App.Path & "\..\..\Help\Mvbdw.hlp"
    cdlOne.HelpCommand = cdlHelpContents
    cdlOne.ShowHelp
End Sub

Private Sub mnuSearch_Click()
    cdlOne.HelpFile = App.Path & "\..\..\Help\Mvbdw.hlp"
    cdlOne.HelpCommand = cdlHelpPartialKey
    cdlOne.ShowHelp
End Sub

Private Sub Picture1_MouseMove(Button As Integer, _
    Shift As Integer, X As Single, Y As Single)
```

(continued)

Source Code for Jot.frm *continued*

```
        sspTips.Caption = ""
End Sub

Private Sub sscArrangeIcons_Click()
        frmJot.Arrange vbArrangeIcons
End Sub

Private Sub sscArrangeIcons_MouseMove(Button As Integer, _
        Shift As Integer, X As Single, Y As Single)
        sspTips.Caption = "Arrange icons"
End Sub

Private Sub sscCascade_Click()
        frmJot.Arrange vbCascade
End Sub

Private Sub sscCascade_MouseMove(Button As Integer, _
        Shift As Integer, X As Single, Y As Single)
        sspTips.Caption = "Cascade"
End Sub

Private Sub sscNewNote_Click()
        'Create new, blank note form
        MakeNewNote Format(Now, "General Date"), ""
End Sub

Private Sub sscNewNote_MouseMove(Button As Integer, _
        Shift As Integer, X As Single, Y As Single)
        sspTips.Caption = "Create a new note"
End Sub

Private Sub sscTileH_Click()
        frmJot.Arrange vbTileHorizontal
End Sub

Private Sub sscTileH_MouseMove(Button As Integer, _
        Shift As Integer, X As Single, Y As Single)
        sspTips.Caption = "Tile horizontally"
End Sub

Private Sub sscTileV_Click()
        frmJot.Arrange vbTileVertical
End Sub
```

(continued)

Source Code for Jot.frm *continued*

```
Private Sub LoadNotes()
    Dim db As Database
    Dim rs As Recordset
    'Open database of previous notes
    On Error Resume Next
    Set db = Workspaces(0).OpenDatabase("Jot.mdb")
    'If database doesn't exist, nothing to display
    If Err Then Exit Sub
    On Error GoTo 0
    'Open table of notes
    Set rs = db.OpenRecordset("JotTable")
    'RecordCount will be 1 if there are any records
    If rs.RecordCount Then
        'Create note window for each note
        Do Until rs.EOF
            MakeNewNote Format(rs!JotDateTime, _
                "General Date"), rs!JotNote
            rs.MoveNext
        Loop
    End If
    'Empty database table for now
    db.Execute "Delete * from JotTable"
    'Close recordset and database
    rs.Close
    db.Close
End Sub

Private Sub MakeNewNote(DateTime$, Note$)
    'Create new copy of note form
    Dim newNote As New frmNote
    'Set caption and note contents
    newNote.rtfNote.Text = Note$
    newNote.Caption = DateTime$
    'Display new note form
    newNote.Show
End Sub

Private Sub sscTileV_MouseMove(Button As Integer, _
    Shift As Integer, X As Single, Y As Single)
    sspTips.Caption = "Tile vertically"
End Sub
```

(continued)

Source Code for Jot.frm *continued*

```
Private Sub sscDelete_Click()
    'Set DropFlag so this note isn't saved
    DropFlag = True
    Unload ActiveForm
    DropFlag = False
End Sub

Private Sub sscDelete_MouseMove(Button As Integer, _
    Shift As Integer, X As Single, Y As Single)
    sspTips.Caption = "Permanently delete current note"
End Sub

Private Sub sspTips_MouseMove(Button As Integer, _
    Shift As Integer, X As Single, Y As Single)
    sspTips.Caption = ""
End Sub
```

Splash.frm

This borderless form displays the Jot logo in the center of the main Jot form, as explained previously. The form contains one Image control, which you can load at design time with the Jot.bmp bitmap image file (found on the Companion CD). Figure 28-13 shows the Splash form during development. Notice that the form's border is visible during development, even though the BorderStyle property is set to *0 - None.* At runtime the border is not visible.

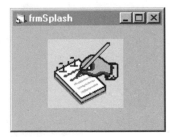

Figure 28-13.
The Splash form during development.

To create this form, place an Image control on a blank form and set the nondefault settings for the form and control as shown.

Splash.frm Objects and Property Settings

Property	Value
Form	
Name	frmSplash
BorderStyle	0 - Nonc
Caption	frmSplash
MDIChild	True
ShowOnTaskBar	False
Image	
Name	imgSplash
Picture	Jot.bmp

The code for this form is contained in the Form_Load routine. When the form loads, the Image control is moved to the upper-left corner of the form and the form is sized to the dimensions of the Image control.

Source Code for Splash.frm

```
Option Explicit

Private Sub Form_Load()
    'Move image to upper-left corner
    imgSplash.Move 0, 0
    'Size this form to size of splash image
    Width = imgSplash.Width
    Height = imgSplash.Height
End Sub
```

Note.frm

The Note form is created once during development and mass-produced as needed at runtime. Each copy of this form holds a single user-edited note. I chose to use a RichTextBox control for the actual note-editing control on the Note form, but a TextBox control would work well too. If you want to enhance the Jot application, the RichTextBox control offers more formatting capabilities and allows longer notes. Figure 28-14 on the following page shows the Note form during development with the single RichTextBox control.

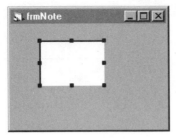

Figure 28-14.
The Note form during development.

To create this form, place a RichTextBox control on a blank form, set the nondefault settings for the form and control, and add the source code as shown.

Note.frm Objects and Property Settings

Property	Value
Form	
Name	frmNote
Caption	frmNote
KeyPreview	True
RichTextBox	
Name	rtfNote
ScrollBars	3 - Both

Source Code for Note.frm

```
Option Explicit

Private Sub Form_KeyDown(KeyCode As Integer, Shift As Integer)
    'Update date and time in caption with hot key Ctrl-T
    If KeyCode = 84 And Shift = 2 Then
        Me.Caption = Format(Now, "General Date")
    End If
End Sub

Private Sub Form_Resize()
    rtfNote.Move 0, 0, ScaleWidth, ScaleHeight
End Sub
```

(continued)

Source Code for Note.frm *continued*

```
Private Sub Form_Unload(Cancel As Integer)
    Dim db As Database
    Dim rs As Recordset
    Dim td As TableDef
    Dim fd As Field
    Dim ErrorNumber As Variant
    Dim DateTime As Date
    Dim Note As String
    'DropFlag means don't save this note
    If DropFlag = True Then Exit Sub
    'Open database to save this note
    On Error Resume Next
    Set db = Workspaces(0).OpenDatabase("Jot.mdb")
    ErrorNumber = Err
    On Error GoTo 0
    'Create database if it does not already exist
    If ErrorNumber Then
        'Create empty database
        Set db = Workspaces(0).CreateDatabase( _
            "Jot.mdb", dbLangGeneral)
        'Create table
        Set td = db.CreateTableDef("JotTable")
        'Create field
        Set fd = td.CreateField("JotDateTime", dbDate)
        'Add new field to table's Fields collection
        td.Fields.Append fd
        'Create second field
        Set fd = td.CreateField("JotNote", dbMemo)
        'Add it to the table
        td.Fields.Append fd
        'Add new table to TableDefs collection
        db.TableDefs.Append td
        'New database is now open
    End If
    'Get working recordset
    Set rs = db.OpenRecordset("JotTable", dbOpenTable)
    'Add new record
    rs.AddNew
    'Prepare data for placing in record
    DateTime = Me.Caption
    Note = Me.rtfNote.Text
    If Note = "" Then Note = " "
    'Load fields in new record
    rs!JotDateTime = DateTime
```

(continued)

Source Code for Note.frm *continued*

```
    rs!JotNote = Note
    'Make sure database gets updated
    rs.Update
    'Close recordset and database
    rs.Close
    db.Close
End Sub
```

The Jot.bas Module

Normally you can declare Public variables in Visual Basic 4. Public variables are shared by all forms and modules in an application and can be declared in any form or source code module. However, the MDI form is the exception to this rule. Public variables to be shared by an MDI module and other form or code modules must be declared in a code module. That's the only purpose of the very small Jot.bas module in this application:

Source Code for Jot.bas

```
Option Explicit

Public DropFlag As Boolean
```

CHAPTER TWENTY-NINE

Utilities

It can be extremely easy to create a very useful little utility in Visual Basic. Sometimes such utilities are useful tools that can help you during the development of other Visual Basic applications, and sometimes they're just good ways to learn more about Visual Basic programming in general. This chapter presents three utilities: one to let you experiment with the mouse pointer, one to allow you to quickly view or listen to multimedia files anywhere on your system, and even one to tell you today's windchill index.

The MousePtr Application

The MousePtr application is a handy utility you can use to quickly review any of the 16 standard mouse pointers and to load and view any icon file as a mouse pointer.

Figure 29-1 on the following page shows the MousePtr form at runtime. When you click on a mouse pointer option, the mouse pointer changes to reflect your choice. To use an icon as a mouse pointer, click on the last option, *99 - Custom Icon*. The first time you click on this option, the Select An Icon File dialog box appears. This dialog box allows you to choose the icon to be displayed. Subsequent clicks on the *99* option display the same custom icon. To change the icon that is displayed, click on the Select Icon button and choose a different icon in the Select An Icon File dialog box.

I've provided a TextBox control as a learning experience and memory aid. Setting the MousePointer property to *0 - Default* and to *1 - Arrow* appears to display the same standard arrow. You'll see the difference in the way these mouse pointers behave when you move them across the face of the TextBox control. The Default mouse pointer changes to an I-beam when it's located over editable text in a text box, whereas the Arrow mouse pointer stays fixed as an arrow no matter which controls it passes over.

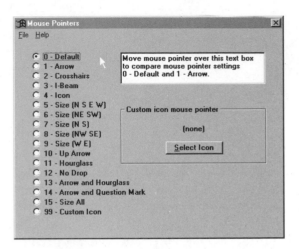

Figure 29-1.

The MousePtr form in action.

Figure 29-2 shows the Earth.ico icon as a mouse pointer. You'll find this icon and many others in your Visual Basic subfolders. If you plan to use several icon files as custom mouse pointers in an application, you might want to store them in a resource file, as described in Chapter 22.

This project contains two files, as shown in the project list in Figure 29-3. The About form displays the standard About dialog box for this application.

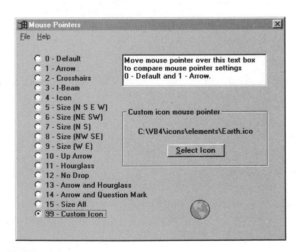

Figure 29-2.

Using the Earth.ico icon as an interesting mouse pointer.

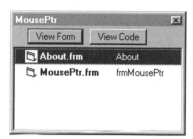

Figure 29-3.
The MousePtr project list.

MousePtr.frm

The MousePtr form displays an array of option buttons you can click on to select a mouse pointer. The Index property of each option button corresponds to the value assigned to the form's MousePointer property, which displays the type of mouse pointer. These numbers range from 0 through 15, with a big jump to 99 for the special case in which an icon file is loaded as a user-defined (custom) mouse pointer. If you build this form manually, be sure to set the last option button's Index property to *99*. Figure 29-4 shows the MousePtr form during development. To create this form, use the following tables and source code to add the appropriate controls, set any nondefault properties as indicated, and type in the source code lines as shown.

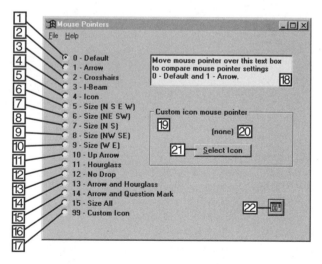

Figure 29-4.
The MousePtr form during development.

MousePtr.frm Menu Design Window Entries

Caption	Name	Indentation	Enabled
&File	mnuFile	0	True
&New	mnuNew	1	False
&Open...	mnuOpen	1	False
&Save	mnuSave	1	False
Save &As...	mnuSaveAs	1	False
-	mnuFileDash1	1	True
E&xit	mnuExit	1	True
&Help	mnuHelp	0	True
&Contents	mnuContents	1	True
&Search for Help on...	mnuSearch	1	True
-	mnuHelpDash1	1	True
&About...	mnuAbout	1	True

MousePtr.frm Objects and Property Settings

ID No.*	Property	Value
Form		
	Name	frmMousePtr
	Caption	Mouse Pointers
	BorderStyle	3 - Fixed Dialog
OptionButton		
1	Name	optMousePtr
	Caption	0 - Default
	Index	0
OptionButton		
2	Name	optMousePtr
	Caption	1 - Arrow
	Index	1

* The number in the ID No. column corresponds to the number in Figure 29-4 that identifies the location of the object on the form.

(continued)

MousePtr.frm Objects and Property Settings *continued*

ID No.	Property	Value
OptionButton		
3	Name	optMousePtr
	Caption	2 - Crosshairs
	Index	2
OptionButton		
4	Name	optMousePtr
	Caption	3 I Beam
	Index	3
OptionButton		
5	Name	optMousePtr
	Caption	4 - Icon
	Index	4
OptionButton		
6	Name	optMousePtr
	Caption	5 - Size (N S E W)
	Index	5
OptionButton		
7	Name	optMousePtr
	Caption	6 - Size (NE SW)
	Index	6
OptionButton		
8	Name	optMousePtr
	Caption	7 - Size (N S)
	Index	7
OptionButton		
9	Name	optMousePtr
	Caption	8 - Size (NW SE)
	Index	8
OptionButton		
10	Name	optMousePtr
	Caption	9 - Size (W E)
	Index	9

(continued)

MousePtr.frm Objects and Property Settings *continued*

ID No.	Property	Value
OptionButton		
11	Name	optMousePtr
	Caption	10 - Up Arrow
	Index	10
OptionButton		
12	Name	optMousePtr
	Caption	11 - Hourglass
	Index	11
OptionButton		
13	Name	optMousePtr
	Caption	12 - No Drop
	Index	12
OptionButton		
14	Name	optMousePtr
	Caption	13 - Arrow and Hourglass
	Index	13
OptionButton		
15	Name	optMousePtr
	Caption	14 - Arrow and
		Question Mark
	Index	14
OptionButton		
16	Name	optMousePtr
	Caption	15 - Size All
	Index	15
OptionButton		
17	Name	optMousePtr
	Caption	99 - Custom Icon
	Index	99

(continued)

MousePtr.frm Objects and Property Settings *continued*

ID No.	Property	Value
TextBox		
18	Name	txtTestArea
	Text	Move mouse pointer over this text box to compare mouse pointer settings 0 - Default and 1 - Arrow.
	Multiline	True
Frame		
19	Name	fraSelect
	Caption	Custom icon mouse pointer
Label		
20	Name	lblIcon
	Caption	(none)
CommandButton		
21	Name	cmdSelect
	Caption	&Select Icon
CommonDialog		
22	Name	cdlOne

Source Code for MousePtr.frm

```
Option Explicit

Private Sub cmdSelect_Click()
    'Prompt user for database filename
    cdlOne.DialogTitle = "Select an Icon File"
    cdlOne.Filter = "Icon(*.ico)|*.ico"
    cdlOne.CancelError = True
    'Check for Cancel button click
    On Error Resume Next
    cdlOne.ShowOpen
    If Err <> cdlCancel Then
        'Load icon as mouse pointer
        frmMousePtr.MouseIcon = LoadPicture(cdlOne.filename)
        'Display current icon path
```

(continued)

461

Source Code for MousePtr.frm *continued*

```
            lblIcon.Caption = cdlOne.filename
            'Select mouse pointer type 99
            optMousePtr(99).SetFocus
        End If
    End Sub

    Private Sub Form_Load()
        'Center this form
        Left = (Screen.Width - Width) \ 2
        Top = (Screen.Height - Height) \ 2
        'Move focus off text box and onto option buttons
        Show
        optMousePtr(0).SetFocus
    End Sub

    Private Sub optMousePtr_Click(Index As Integer)
        'Set selected mouse pointer
        frmMousePtr.MousePointer = Index
        'Open dialog box if no icon file previously specified
        If Index = 99 And lblIcon = "(none)" Then
            cmdSelect_Click
        End If
    End Sub

    Private Sub mnuAbout_Click()
        'Set properties
        About.Application = "MousePtr"
        About.Heading = "Microsoft Visual Basic 4.0 Developer's Workshop"
        About.Copyright = "1996 John Clark Craig"
        About.Display
    End Sub

    Private Sub mnuExit_Click()
        Unload Me
    End Sub

    Private Sub mnuContents_Click()
        cdlOne.HelpFile = App.Path & "\..\..\Help\Mvbdw.hlp"
        cdlOne.HelpCommand = cdlHelpContents
        cdlOne.ShowHelp
    End Sub

    Private Sub mnuSearch_Click()
        cdlOne.HelpFile = App.Path & "\..\..\Help\Mvbdw.hlp"
        cdlOne.HelpCommand = cdlHelpPartialKey
        cdlOne.ShowHelp
    End Sub
```

The ShowTell Application

The ShowTell application is simple in its design, yet it provides a handy utility for quickly reviewing any standard image files (bitmaps, icons, and Windows metafiles), listening to sound files, or viewing video clips.

The startup point of the program is Sub Main, and the first form you see at runtime is the CommonDialog control. Figure 29-5 shows the ShowTell application in action, prompting the user for a media file. The main interaction with the user is through this CommonDialog control. The frmShowTell form appears only when it's required to display a selected image file. Figure 29-6 on the following page shows the frmShowTell form as it displays the Buttrfly.wmf graphic from the Office 95 Clipart folder. The MMControl is used to play a sound file or display a video file. Figure 29-7 on the following page shows a video clip from the Windows\Help folder.

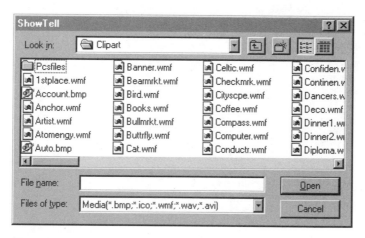

Figure 29-5.
The CommonDialog control as it appears when you run the ShowTell application.

Immediately after the user closes the form displaying a static graphic image, or when a sound or video clip finishes playing, the CommonDialog control returns, allowing the user to select a sequence of files. To close the application, click on the Cancel button instead of selecting a file.

As shown in Figure 29-8 on the following page, the ShowTell project consists of one form and one code module. The startup point is Sub Main in the code module, and I'll describe this very simple module first.

Figure 29-6.
The ShowTell application displaying a bitmap file.

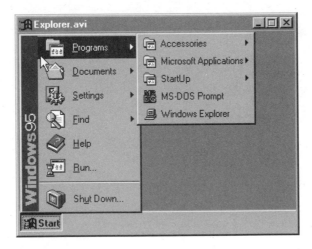

Figure 29-7.
An MMControl playing a video clip.

Figure 29-8.
The ShowTell project list.

ShowTell.bas

The ShowTell.bas module provides the Sub Main starting point for the ShowTell application. The only action Sub Main takes is to enable a timer on the ShowTell form. This timer event displays the CommonDialog control to prompt for a media file. I've enabled this timer from within Sub Main to prevent the ShowTell form from appearing until a graphic image file has been selected. If the ShowTell form was designated as the startup form, it would appear before we're ready for it.

Source Code for ShowTell.bas

```
Option Explicit

Sub Main()
    frmShowTell.tmrOne.Enabled = True
End Sub
```

ShowTell.frm

The ShowTell form does most of the work for this application, but frequently the work takes place when the form is not visible. A form can be loaded but not shown, and I've taken advantage of this capability by having the Sub Main startup routine load the ShowTell form using a Load command instead of the Show method. The ShowTell form displays a CommonDialog control to perform all interactions with the user, and then the form takes appropriate action based on the type of file the user selects. If the user selects only video clips or sound files, the ShowTell form is never displayed. If the user selects a bitmap file (BMP), an icon file (ICO), or a Windows metafile graphics file, the image is displayed on the ShowTell form.

Figure 29-9 on the following page shows the ShowTell form during development. This form contains four controls, only one of which is visible at runtime. The MMControl is used to play sound files and show video clips. At runtime this control is moved off-screen to be out of sight. The Timer control is enabled and disabled at various places in the program to trigger the appearance of the CommonDialog control, which prompts for the name of a media file. The Image control is used to load and display any of the three types of static graphic image files this application lets you view. To create this form, use the following table and source code to add the appropriate controls, set any nondefault properties as indicated, and type in the source code lines as shown.

Figure 29-9.
The ShowTell form during development.

ShowTell.frm Objects and Property Settings

Property	Value
Form	
Name	frmShowTell
Caption	ShowTell
Icon	Eye.icon
Timer	
Name	tmrOne
Interval	1
Enabled	False
Image	
Name	imgOne
Common Dialog	
Name	cdlOne
MMControl	
Name	mciOne

Source Code for ShowTell.frm

```
Option Explicit

Private Sub Form_Activate()
    'Move image to upper-left corner of form
    imgOne.Left = 0
    imgOne.Top = 0
```

(continued)

Source Code for ShowTell.frm *continued*

```
      'Set form to display image's full width
      Width = imgOne.Width + (Width - ScaleWidth)
      'Prevent form from being too narrow
      If Width < 2500 Then Width = 2500
      'Set form to display image's full height
      Height = imgOne.Height + (Height - ScaleHeight)
Fnd Sub

Private Sub Form_Load()
      'Move MMControl out of sight
      mciOne.Left = Screen.Width * 2
      'Place form's upper-left corner at 20% of screen's
      'height and width
      Move Screen.Width \ 5, Screen.Height \ 5, 1, 1
End Sub

Private Sub mciOne_Done(NotifyCode As Integer)
      'Close MMControl
      mciOne.Command = "Close"
      'Trigger CommonDialog to reappear
      tmrOne.Enabled = True
End Sub

Private Sub tmrOne_Timer()
      Dim cd As CommonDialog
      Set cd = frmShowTell.cdlOne
      'Prompt user for media file selection
      cd.DialogTitle = "ShowTell"
      cd.Flags = cdlOFNHideReadOnly
      cd.Filter = "Media(*.bmp;*.ico;*.wmf;*.wav;*.avi)" & _
          "|*.bmp;*.ico;*.wmf;*.wav;*.avi"
      cd.CancelError = True
      On Error Resume Next
      cd.ShowOpen
      'Quit if user canceled or closed dialog box
      If Err Then End
      On Error GoTo 0
      'Don't pop up CommonDialog right away
      tmrOne.Enabled = False
      'Display or play file
      Process cd.FileName
      Set cd = Nothing
End Sub
```

(continued)

Source Code for ShowTell.frm *continued*

```
Private Sub Process(FileName$)
    On Error Resume Next
    'Process graphic image file
    If InStr(".BMP.ICO.WMF", UCase$(Right$(FileName$, 4))) Then
        frmShowTell.imgOne.Picture = LoadPicture(FileName$)
        If Err Then
            MsgBox "Media file not found: " & FileName$, _
                vbExclamation, "ShowTell"
        Else
            frmShowTell.Show vbModal
        End If
        'Trigger CommonDialog to reappear
        tmrOne.Enabled = True
    'Process sound file or video file
    ElseIf InStr(".WAV.AVI", UCase$(Right$(FileName$, 4))) Then
        With frmShowTell.mciOne
            .FileName = FileName$
            .Command = "Open"
            .Command = "Play"
        End With
    End If
End Sub
```

You might wonder why I moved the MMControl off the screen and out of sight by setting its Left property to twice the width of the screen, instead of just setting its Visible property to *False*. When an MMControl's Visible property is set to *False*, notification of completion via the control's Done event doesn't work as expected. I wanted to delay the reappearance of the CommonDialog control until the selected video clip was finished playing. With Visible set to *False*, however, the CommonDialog control reappears immediately, covering the video clip as it plays. The workaround is to leave the MMControl visible so the Done event fires as expected, and set the control's Left property to remove it from sight. I set Left to twice the width of the screen, which in the mind of your computer moves it about an arm's length to the right of your monitor.

The WindChil Application

The WindChil application uses the same equation the National Weather Service uses to calculate the effective windchill given the actual air temperature and the wind speed. (If the scientific and technical aspects defining the windchill factor interest you, search on the keywords "wind chill" on the World Wide Web. I've found several sites with excellent explanations.)

This application demonstrates the new Slider control, which I've set up to let the user select the current air temperature and wind speed. Figure 29-10 shows the WindChil form in action: the two sliders are set to a temperature of 32 degrees Fahrenheit and a wind speed of 25 miles per hour.

This application has some advantages over the standard charts you'll find posted on the World Wide Web and elsewhere. In my application, the temperature and wind speed can be set to any values in the ranges provided by the slider controls, whereas the charts round off values to the nearest 5 or 10 degrees or miles per hour. The biggest advantage, however, is that with the addition of a few option buttons I've made it easy to use metric values if you want. You have your choice of temperature scales (Fahrenheit or Celsius) and your choice of wind speed units (miles per hour or kilometers per hour). When you click on an option button, the current settings of the sliders are retained and the numbers are converted to the alternate units. Figure 29-11 on the following page shows the same settings as in Figure 29-10, but converted to metric units.

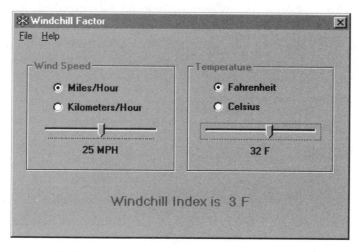

Figure 29-10.
The WindChil form in action.

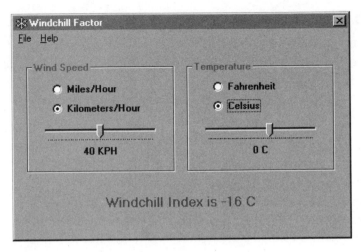

Figure 29-11.
The WindChil form showing values in metric units.

WindChil.frm

The Min and Max properties of the two sliders are set to the full range of accuracy for the windchill equation: 5 through 50 miles per hour for wind speed and −50 through 90 degrees Fahrenheit for temperature. Values outside these ranges are invalid. The use of sliders, instead of text box data entry fields, simplifies the process of validating the numbers a user enters. If you use a slider control, there's no way a user can enter an invalid wind speed or temperature value and no code is needed to check and enforce the entered values. In the WindChil.frm Objects and Property Settings table on page 472, notice that the LargeChange property of the slider controls is set to *1*. This allows the user to click on the slider at either side of the slider's knob and adjust the setting by 1 degree or 1 unit of wind speed. This technique works well for the range of values selected.

Figure 29-12 shows the WindChil form during development. I've set the ForeColor property of some of the text labels to red and blue to brighten the appearance of the form. You may prefer the default black ForeColor setting for your labels. You can experiment with the appearance of this form without affecting its calculations. To create this form, use the following tables and source code to add the appropriate controls, set any nondefault properties as indicated, and type in the source code lines as shown.

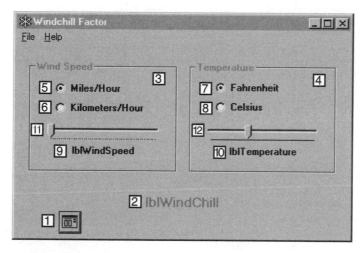

Figure 29-12.
The WindChil form during development.

WindChil.frm Menu Design Window Entries

Caption	Name	Indentation	Enabled
&File	mnuFile	0	True
&New	mnuNew	1	False
&Open...	mnuOpen	1	False
&Save	mnuSave	1	False
Save &As...	mnuSaveAs	1	False
-	mnuFileDash1	1	True
E&xit	mnuExit	1	True
&Help	mnuHelp	0	True
&Contents	mnuContents	1	True
&Search for Help on...	mnuSearch	1	True
-	mnuHelpDash1	1	True
&About...	mnuAbout	1	True

WindChil.frm Objects and Property Settings

ID No.*	Property	Value
Form		
	Name	frmWindChill
	Caption	Windchill Factor
	BorderStyle	3 - Fixed Dialog
	Icon	Snow.ico
CommonDialog		
1	Name	cdlOne
Label		
2	Name	lblWindChill
	Alignment	2 - Center
	Font	MS Sans Serif Bold 12
	ForeColor	&H00FF0000&
Frame		
3	Name	fraWindSpeed
	Caption	Wind Speed
	ForeColor	&H000000FF&
Frame		
4	Name	fraTemperature
	Caption	Temperature
	ForeColor	&H000000FF&
OptionButton		
5	Name	optMPH
	Caption	Miles/Hour
	Value	True
OptionButton		
6	Name	optKPH
	Caption	Kilometers/Hour
OptionButton		
7	Name	optFahrenheit
	Caption	Fahrenheit
	Value	True

* The number in the ID No. column corresponds to the number in Figure 29-12 that identifies the location of the object on the form.

(continued)

WindChil.frm Objects and Property Settings *continued*

ID No.	Property	Value
OptionButton		
8	Name	optCelsius
	Caption	Celsius
Label		
9	Name	lblWindSpeed
	Alignment	2 - Center
Label		
10	Name	lblTemperature
	Alignment	2 - Center
Slider		
11	Name	hslWindSpeed
	LargeChange	1
	Max	50
	Min	5
Slider		
12	Name	hslTemperature
	LargeChange	1
	Max	90
	Min	−50

Source Code for WindChil.frm

```
Option Explicit

Private Sub mnuAbout_Click()
    'Set properties
    About.Application = "WindChil"
    About.Heading = "Microsoft Visual Basic 4.0 Developer's Workshop"
    About.Copyright = "1996 John Clark Craig"
    About.Display
End Sub

Private Sub mnuExit_Click()
    Unload Me
End Sub
```

(continued)

Source Code for WindChil.frm *continued*

```
Private Sub mnuContents_Click()
    cdlOne.HelpFile = App.Path & "\..\..\Help\Mvbdw.hlp"
    cdlOne.HelpCommand = cdlHelpContents
    cdlOne.ShowHelp
End Sub

Private Sub mnuSearch_Click()
    cdlOne.HelpFile = App.Path & "\..\..\Help\Mvbdw.hlp"
    cdlOne.HelpCommand = cdlHelpPartialKey
    cdlOne.ShowHelp
End Sub

Private Function Celsius(F)
    'Convert Fahrenheit to Celsius
    Celsius = (F + 40) * 5 / 9 - 40
End Function

Private Sub ChillOut()
    Dim Wind
    Dim Temp
    Dim Chill
    Dim Y As String

    'Get working values from scrollbars
    Wind = hslWindSpeed.Value
    Temp = hslTemperature.Value

    'Convert to MPH if KPH selected
    If optKPH.Value = True Then
        Wind = Mph(Wind)
    End If

    'Convert to Fahrenheit if Celsius selected
    If optCelsius.Value = True Then
        Temp = Fahrenheit(Temp)
    End If

    'Calculate windchill index
    Chill = Int(0.0817 * (Sqr(Wind) * 3.71 + _
        5.81 - 0.25 * Wind) * (Temp - 91.4) + 91.4)

    'Convert back to Celsius if selected
    If optCelsius.Value = True Then
        Chill = Celsius(Chill)
    End If
```

(continued)

Source Code for WindChil.frm *continued*

```
    'Display windchill index
    Y = "Windchill Index is " & Str$(CInt(Chill))
    If optFahrenheit.Value = True Then
        lblWindChill.Caption = Y & " F"
    Else
        lblWindChill.Caption = Y & " C"
    End If
End Sub

Private Sub cmdCancel_Click()
    'End if Cancel button clicked
    Unload frmWindChill
End Sub

Private Function Fahrenheit(C)
    'Convert Celsius to Fahrenheit
    Fahrenheit = (C + 40) * 9 / 5 - 40
End Function

Private Sub Form_Load()
    'Force scrollbars to update
    hslWindSpeed_Change
    hslTemperature_Change
End Sub

Private Sub hslTemperature_Change()
    Dim Tmp As Variant

    'Get temperature
    Tmp = hslTemperature.Value

    'Display using selected units
    If optCelsius.Value = True Then
        lblTemperature.Caption = Tmp & " C"
    Else
        lblTemperature.Caption = Tmp & " F"
    End If

    'Calculate windchill index
    ChillOut
End Sub

Private Sub hslTemperature_Scroll()
    'Update when scroll box moves
```

(continued)

Source Code for WindChil.frm *continued*

```
    hslTemperature_Change
End Sub

Private Sub hslWindSpeed_Change()
    Dim Tmp

    'Get wind speed
    Tmp = hslWindSpeed.Value

    'Display using selected units
    If optKPH.Value = True Then
        lblWindSpeed.Caption = Tmp & " KPH"
    Else
        lblWindSpeed.Caption = Tmp & " MPH"
    End If

    'Calculate windchill index
    ChillOut
End Sub

Private Sub hslWindSpeed_Scroll()
    'Update when scroll box moves
    hslWindSpeed_Change
End Sub

Private Function Kph(M)
    'Convert MPH to KPH
    Kph = M * 1.609344
End Function

Private Function Mph(K)
    'Convert KPH to MPH
    Mph = K / 1.609344
End Function

Private Sub optCelsius_Click()
    Dim X As Integer

    'Convert current temperature to Celsius
    X = Celsius(hslTemperature.Value)
    If X < -45 Then X = -45

    'Reset scrollbar for Celsius
    hslTemperature.Min = -45
    hslTemperature.Max = 32
```

(continued)

Source Code for WindChil.frm *continued*

```
    hslTemperature.Value = X
    hslTemperature_Change
End Sub

Private Sub optFahrenheit_Click()
    Dim X

    'Convert current temperature to Fahrenheit
    X = Fahrenheit(hslTemperature.Value)
    If X < -50 Then X = -50

    'Reset scrollbar for Fahrenheit
    hslTemperature.Min = -50
    hslTemperature.Max = 90
    hslTemperature.Value = CInt(X)
    hslTemperature_Change
End Sub

Private Sub optKPH_Click()
    Dim X

    'Convert current wind speed to KPH
    X = Kph(hslWindSpeed.Value)

    'Reset scrollbar for KPH
    hslWindSpeed.Min = 8
    hslWindSpeed.Max = 80
    hslWindSpeed.Value = X
    hslWindSpeed_Change
End Sub

Private Sub optMPH_Click()
    Dim X

    'Convert current wind speed to MPH
    X = Mph(hslWindSpeed.Value)

    'Reset scrollbar for MPH
    hslWindSpeed.Min = 5
    hslWindSpeed.Max = 50
    hslWindSpeed.Value = X
    hslWindSpeed_Change
End Sub
```

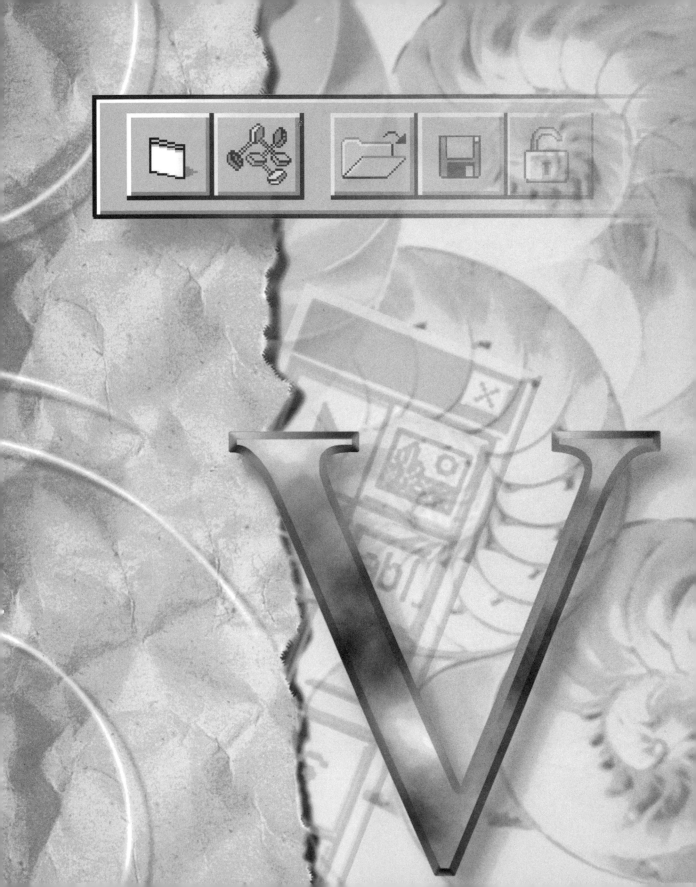

CHAPTER THIRTY

Advanced Techniques

This chapter covers a few advanced programming techniques that can enhance your Visual Basic development productivity. The Messages application demonstrates one way you can use commands embedded in an externally edited text file to control an application's behavior. The Secret application pieces together several forms and techniques presented earlier in this book to create a file enciphering program. BitPack provides a working demonstration of a C-language DLL that enhances speed and utility, and the Dialogs application demonstrates several creative techniques that can enhance your Visual Basic forms.

The Messages Application

You can create your own programming, or scripting, language to perform specific tasks. I've created the Messages application as a simple example. This application displays a series of text boxes containing messages on the screen. It accomplishes this by declaring and using Msg objects. The Msg objects are defined by the class module Msg.cls and its associated Msg.frm file.

A Msg object has a FileName property, which is set to the name of a specially formatted text file with the extension MES (a message file). (I describe the syntax of these message files below.) The Msg.cls and Msg.frm files work together to display messages from the message file. I've set up two special commands that can be typed into the message files to control the appearance and behavior of the displayed messages. I've kept these commands simple, but it would be easy to expand on the concept presented here if you want more creative control over the messages displayed.

Message File Syntax

Each message file contains blocks of text to be displayed. Three tilde characters (~~~) mark the start of each text block, and a message file can contain as many text blocks as you want. All messages in the selected message file are displayed sequentially. You can control the display of each message somewhat by including commands on the same line as each block separator.

An example message file helps clarify how this works. Here's the sample Message.mes file I've provided with this sample application on the CD-ROM included with this book:

```
Message.mes

This message file provides a sampling of the
features demonstrated in the Messages application.

Note that all of these lines appearing before
the first text block header will be ignored.


~~~
This is the first text block in the Message.mes file.
Notice that the display window sizes automatically for
the dimensions of the message.

Close this display window to proceed to the next text
block in this file. Click on the Close button in the
upper-right corner of this message.
~~~ P 10
This message should automatically disappear in 10 seconds.
You may close it manually before then if you want.
~~~ F 2
This message should be in a flashing window, with the
flash rate set to 2 per second.
~~~ F 5
This message should be in a flashing window, with the
flash rate set to 5 per second.
~~~ P 20 F 1
This is the last message in this file. The flash rate
is 1 per second, and it will disappear automatically
in 20 seconds if you don't close it manually before then.
```

This file defines five messages to be displayed sequentially by the Msg object when it is activated in the Messages application. The first message is displayed in a nonflashing window and stays displayed until the user closes the window. The second text block's header contains the *P* command, which indicates that the message is to disappear after being displayed for the specified number of seconds. In this case, the second message disappears (and the next message appears) after a delay of 10 seconds. The third message is controlled by the *F* command, which sets a flash rate for the display window. The number after the *F* is the toggle rate for the flashing, in this case twice per second. Notice that in the final message of the file both commands are given; this message will be displayed for 20 seconds, with a flash rate of once per second.

I've provided only the *P* and *F* commands, but it would be easy to add others. For example, you might want to add a *C* command to control the color of the message text. By studying the way the two commands work, you can easily add other commands on your own.

Figure 30-1 shows the first message as it's displayed, and Figure 30-2 shows the third message.

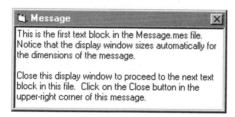

Figure 30-1.

A message as displayed by the Messages application.

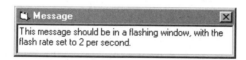

Figure 30-2.

The message window that flashes to catch the user's attention.

Why Use Message Files?

It would be fairly straightforward to embed the messages shown directly in an application's source code. Using external ASCII text files has some advantages, however. For example, to change the displayed messages you simply edit the message file using Notepad, WordPad, or any other text editor. Also, creating multiline text messages in Visual Basic code requires you to concatenate the lines with the vbCrLf constant, and making changes to these somewhat messy lines in your application can be tedious. An external message file has the same advantage as a resource file if you're creating applications to distribute internationally. Instead of editing and recompiling the application's source code for each foreign language, you need only change the message file's contents.

Figure 30-3 shows the project list for the Messages application. To add the messaging capabilities to your own applications, add the Msg.cls and Msg.frm files and activation code similar to that found in the Messages.frm demonstration form.

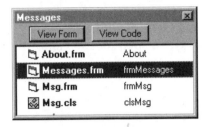

Figure 30-3.
The Messages project list.

Messages.frm

Messages.frm is the main startup form for the Messages application. In the source code for this application, you'll notice that a single instance of a Msg object, msgOne, is declared and manipulated by this form. To sequentially display all messages defined in the Message.mes file, this form sets the declared Msg object's FileName property to the selected file's path and name and then calls the object's *Display* method. The rest of the control over the displayed message's appearance is provided by commands embedded within the message file itself.

I've added a CommonDialog control and a Command button to this form so that you can select any other message file or files you might want to create for experimentation purposes. Figure 30-4 shows the Messages form during development, where you can see these CommonDialog and command button controls on the form.

Figure 30-4.
The Messages form during development.

To create this form, use the following tables and source code to add the appropriate controls, set any nondefault properties as indicated, and type in the source code lines as shown.

Messages.frm Menu Design Window Entries

Caption	Name	Indentation	Enabled
&File	mnuFile	0	True
&New	mnuNew	1	False
&Open...	mnuOpen	1	False
&Save	mnuSave	1	False
Save &As...	mnuSaveAs	1	False
-	mnuFileDash1	1	True
E&xit	mnuExit	1	True
&Help	mnuHelp	0	True
&Contents	mnuContents	1	True
&Search for Help on...	mnuSearch	1	True
-	mnuHelpDash1	1	True
&About...	mnuAbout	1	True

Messages.frm Objects and Property Settings

Property	Value
Form	
Name	frmMessages
BorderStyle	3 = Fixed Dialog
Caption	Display a Message File...
CommandButton	
Name	cmdMessages
Caption	&File...
CommonDialog	
Name	cdlOne

Source Code for Messages.frm

```
Option Explicit

Private Sub cmdMessages_Click()
    'Declare a new clsMsg object
    Dim msgOne As New clsMsg
    'Prompt user for message file (*.mes)
    cdlOne.DialogTitle = "Message Files"
    cdlOne.Flags = cdlOFNHideReadOnly
    cdlOne.Filter = "Messages(*.mes)|*.mes"
    cdlOne.CancelError = True
    On Error Resume Next
    cdlOne.ShowOpen
    'Quit if user canceled or closed dialog box
    If Err Then Exit Sub
    On Error GoTo 0
    'Display message file
    With msgOne
        .FileName = cdlOne.FileName
        .Display
    End With
End Sub

Private Sub Form_Load()
    'Center this form
    Left = (Screen.Width - Width) \ 2
    Top = (Screen.Height - Height) \ 2
End Sub

Private Sub mnuAbout_Click()
    'Set properties
    About.Application = "Messages"
    About.Heading = "Microsoft Visual Basic 4.0 Developer's Workshop"
    About.Copyright = "1996 John Clark Craig"
    About.Display
End Sub

Private Sub mnuExit_Click()
    Unload Me
End Sub

Private Sub mnuContents_Click()
    cdlOne.HelpFile = App.Path & "\..\..\Help\Mvbdw.hlp"
```

(continued)

Source Code for Messages.frm *continued*

```
        cdlOne.HelpCommand = cdlHelpContents
        cdlOne.ShowHelp
    End Sub

    Private Sub mnuSearch_Click()
        cdlOne.HelpFile = App.Path & "\..\..\Help\Mvbdw.hlp"
        cdlOne.HelpCommand = cdlHelpPartialKey
        cdlOne.ShowHelp
    End Sub
```

Msg.cls

The Msg.cls class module is the blueprint used to create Msg objects. This particular class module requires an associated Msg.frm file that provides the visual elements of the Msg object. If you want to add Msg objects to your applications, be sure to add both of these files.

Each Msg object provides one property, FileName, which the calling application must set in order to display messages. Set the FileName property to the full path and name of a selected message file. The only method provided by each Msg object is *Display*, which starts the sequential display of all messages contained in the indicated message file.

There are quite a few lines of code in the *Display* method. This code interacts with, and controls, the properties and methods of the associated Msg form. Commands embedded within the given message file are interpreted in the *Display* method, and the Msg form is controlled from here to provide the indicated operation.

Source Code for Msg.cls

```
Option Explicit
DefLng A-Z

'Property that defines message file to be displayed
Public FileName As String

'Method to display the message file
Public Sub Display()
    Dim h$, j$, a$, b$, c$
    Dim FilNum As Integer
    Dim ndx, FlashRate, PauseTime
    Dim Th, Tw, TwTest
```

(continued)

Source Code for Msg.cls *continued*

```
'Get next available file I/O number
FilNum = FreeFile
'Trap error if filename is invalid
On Error Resume Next
Open FileName For Input As #FilNum
If Err Then
    MsgBox "File not found: " & FileName
    Exit Sub
End If
On Error GoTo 0
'Find start of first text block
Do Until EOF(FilNum)
    Line Input #FilNum, h$
    'Skip lines until three tilde characters found
    If InStr(h$, "~~~") = 1 Then
        j$ = UCase$(h$)
        Exit Do
    End If
Loop
'Loop through all text blocks
Do Until EOF(FilNum)
    b$ = ""
    h$ = j$
    Tw = 0
    Th = 0
    'Load all of the current text block
    Do Until EOF(FilNum)
        Line Input #FilNum, a$
        'End of block is at start of next one
        If InStr(a$, "~~~") = 1 Then
            j$ = UCase$(a$)
            Exit Do
        End If
        'Keep track of widest line of text
        TwTest = frmMsg.TextWidth(a$ & "XX")
        If TwTest > Tw Then Tw = TwTest
        'Keep track of total height of all lines
        Th = Th + 1
        'Accumulate block of text lines
        If Th > 1 Then
            b$ = b$ & vbCrLf & a$
        Else
            b$ = a$
        End If
    End If
```

(continued)

Source Code for Msg.cls *continued*

```
        Loop
        'Check for flash rate in block header
        ndx = InStr(h$, "F")
        If ndx Then
            FlashRate = Val(Mid$(h$, ndx + 1))
        Else
            FlashRate = 0
        End If
        'Check for pause time in block header
        ndx = InStr(h$, "P")
        If ndx Then
            PauseTime = Val(Mid$(h$, ndx + 1))
        Else
            PauseTime = 0
        End If
        'Prepare message form's text box
        With frmMsg.txtMsg
            .Text = b$
            .Left = 0
            .Top = 0
            .Width = Tw
            .Height = (Th + 1) * frmMsg.TextHeight("X")
        End With
        'Prepare message form
        With frmMsg
            .Width = .txtMsg.Width + (.Width - .ScaleWidth)
            .Height = .txtMsg.Height + (.Height - .ScaleHeight)
            .Left = (Screen.Width - .Width) \ 2
            .Top = (Screen.Height - .Height) \ 2
            'Set flash and pause properties if given
            If PauseTime > 0 Then .Pause = PauseTime
            If FlashRate > 0 Then .Flash = FlashRate
        End With
        'Show message and wait until it closes
        frmMsg.Show vbModal
    Loop
End Sub
```

Msg.frm

The Msg form is the working partner of the Msg.cls class module. Together they form the blueprint for a Msg object. Notice that Msg.frm interacts only with the Msg.cls module. The main Messages form does not directly set any of the Msg form's properties, call any of its methods, or in any way directly interact with it. In this way, the Msg form becomes an integral part of the Msg objects defined by the Msg.cls class module.

487

Msg.frm has several controls: two timers, a TextBox control to display the messages, and a dummy command button, which will be explained shortly. Figure 30-5 shows Msg.frm during the development process.

Figure 30-5.
The Msg form during development.

To create this form, use the following table and source code to add the appropriate controls, set any nondefault properties as indicated, and type in the source code lines as shown.

Msg.frm Objects and Property Settings

Property	Value
Form	
Name	frmMsg
Caption	Message
BorderStyle	3 - Fixed Dialog
Text Box	
Name	txtMsg
ForeColor	&H00FF0000&
MultiLine	True
Locked	True
Timer	
Name	tmrTerminate
Timer	
Name	tmrFlash
CommandButton	
Name	cmdDummy
Default	True
Caption	Dummy

Source Code for Msg.frm

```
Option Explicit

Private Declare Function FlashWindow _
Lib "user32" ( _
    ByVal hwnd As Long, _
    ByVal bInvert As Long _
) As Long

Private Sub Form_Paint()
    'Remove focus from text box
    cmdDummy.left = Screen.Width * 2
    cmdDummy.SetFocus
End Sub

Private Sub tmrTerminate_Timer()
    Unload Me
End Sub

Private Sub tmrFlash_Timer()
    'Toggle form flashing
    FlashWindow hwnd, CLng(True)
End Sub

Property Let Flash(PerSecond As Integer)
    'Set and activate form flashing rate
    tmrFlash.Interval = 1000 / PerSecond
    tmrFlash.Enabled = True
End Property

Property Let Pause(Seconds As Double)
    'Set and activate auto-unload timing
    tmrTerminate.Interval = 1000 * Seconds
    tmrTerminate.Enabled = True
End Property
```

The *FlashWindow* API function is called from the tmrFlash_Timer event to toggle the flashing of the Msg.frm form. The Interval property of this timer determines the flash rate.

The Dummy command button's only purpose is to get the focus, and the flashing cursor, out of the text box while the message is displayed. As this form is painted, the Dummy command button's Left property is set to twice the width of the screen, guaranteeing that it will be out of sight. By setting the button's Default property to *True*, you ensure that the focus goes with it.

The Flash and Pause properties are not set directly by a calling application. Instead, these properties are set by the Msg.cls module to control the form's behavior.

The Secret Application

There's a lot of talk about privacy and security nowadays, particularly in reference to the transfer of financial transactions or other proprietary information over the Internet. The Secret application shouldn't be used for critical security situations, but it does provide a modest level of personal privacy for your email, or for any file that you'd rather not have others view indiscriminately.

> NOTE: The level of security provided by this application is not foolproof, and determined attackers, as the experts call them, could crack messages enciphered with this program. Realistically, though, your messages and files will be secure from the prying eyes of 99 percent of the population.

To keep this application very simple, and very legal for exporting overseas, I've used a private key technique rather than the sophisticated but slightly messy public key technology that's currently all the rage. If you use this application to encipher email, both you and the party at the other end must agree on a password phrase in advance. Any password phrase of reasonable length can be used as the private key, but the password string is hashed down by the program to 36 bits of unique key data—well within the 40 bits allowed by the authorities. I've also used a linear congruential generator at the heart of the cipher algorithm, which is generally avoided for really secure ciphers. Even so, someone would have to be highly motivated to go to the effort of cracking your Secret messages and files. If you need an extremely secure cipher, go with one of the commercial products on the market. If you just want a tool that will provide reasonable privacy and that's very easy to use, the Secret application will do the trick.

How Does the Secret Application Work?

Here's how it works. You can select any file to encipher or decipher. A small header line is inserted at the beginning of enciphered files, to allow Secret to detect whether a selected file is currently enciphered. When you click on either the Encipher or the Decipher button, a password dialog box appears.

The same password should be used to both decipher and encipher a file—so don't forget the password! I've set up the Password dialog box to provide two text boxes for entering the same password twice. This is a commonly used method that requires the user to type the password correctly in each box, thus preventing typographical errors from creeping in. Any mistyping of the password, during either enciphering or deciphering, will prevent the file from being deciphered. The file contents are enciphered or deciphered using the password as the key source. Rather than processing all bytes in a file, the Secret application modifies only readable and printable ASCII characters. This means an enciphered text file can still be viewed and printed, although the words will appear unreadable. It also means you won't need to do anything special to transfer enciphered text in an email message.

Figure 30-6 shows the Secret application just after a text file named Test.txt has been selected. Because this file is not yet enciphered, the Encipher button is enabled and the Decipher button is not. Figure 30-7 on the following page shows the interface after the Encipher button was clicked and the password dialog box popped up. The user has entered the password phrase *gray alien* in both text boxes. To complete the sequence of events, Figure 30-8 on the following page shows the main Secret form after the file has been enciphered. Notice that the Decipher button is now enabled and the Encipher button is not.

Figure 30-9 on the following page shows the sample Test.txt file before it's enciphered, and Figure 30-10 on page 493 shows its contents in the enciphered state. Notice that the readable and printable characters are the only bytes modified in the file. The enciphered file retains the same layout as the unenciphered file.

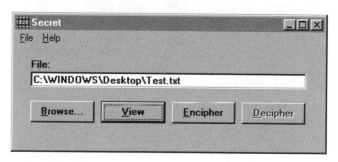

Figure 30-6.
The Test.txt file selected to be enciphered by the Secret application.

Figure 30-7.
The cipher key password entered twice to prevent typing errors.

Figure 30-8.
The dialog box displaying the name of an enciphered file.

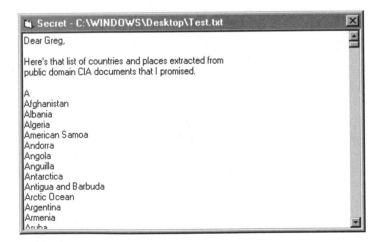

Figure 30-9.
The Test.txt file containing typical readable text.

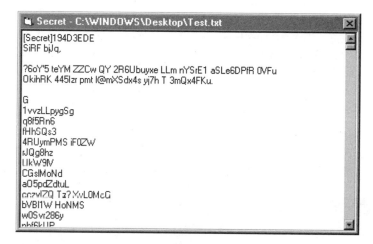

Figure 30-10.
Test.txt after encryption.

The Secret project comprises five files, as shown in the project list window in Figure 30-11. The Secret.bas code module contains the same cipher subprogram presented in Chapter 14 and also includes a *Hash* function that converts any string to a repeatable but unpredictable sequence of 8 hexadecimal characters. This hash value is used to verify a user's password before a file is deciphered. The View form is a simple file-contents viewer that displays the contents of a selected file, ciphered or not, to let the user review the file in read-only mode.

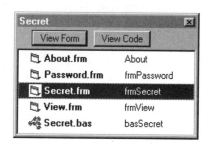

Figure 30-11.
The project list for the Secret application.

Secret.frm

Secret.frm is the main startup form for the Secret application. As shown in Figure 30-12, the form contains one text box for selecting a file to be processed and four command buttons that control all operations on the file. The CommonDialog control is used during the file selection process.

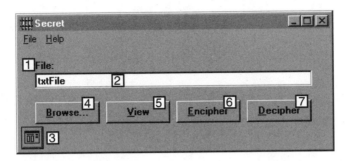

Figure 30-12.
The Secret form during development.

To create this form, use the following tables and source code to add the appropriate contents, set any nondefault properties as indicated, and type in the source code lines as shown.

Secret.frm Menu Design Window Entries

Caption	Name	Indentation	Enabled
&File	mnuFile	0	True
&New	mnuNew	1	False
&Open...	mnuOpen	1	False
&Save	mnuSave	1	False
Save &As...	mnuSaveAs	1	False
-	mnuFileDash1	1	True
E&xit	mnuExit	1	True
&Help	mnuHelp	0	True
&Contents	mnuContents	1	True
&Search for Help on...	mnuSearch	1	True
-	mnuHelpDash1	1	True
&About...	mnuAbout	1	True

Secret.frm Objects and Property Settings

ID No.*	Property	Value
Form		
	Name	frmSecret
	Caption	Secret
	Icon	Secur03.ico
Label		
1	Name	lblFile
	Caption	File:
	Font	MS Sans Serif Bold
TextBox		
2	Name	txtFile
	Font	MS Sans Serif Bold
CommonDialog		
3	Name	cdlOne
CommandButton		
4	Name	cmdBrowse
	Caption	&Browse...
	Font	MS Sans Serif Bold
CommandButton		
5	Name	cmdView
	Caption	&View
	Font	MS Sans Serif Bold
CommandButton		
6	Name	cmdEncipher
	Caption	&Encipher
	Font	MS Sans Serif Bold
CommandButton		
7	Name	cmdDecipher
	Caption	&Decipher
	Font	MS Sans Serif Bold

* The number in the ID No. column corresponds to the number in Figure 30-12 that identifies the location of the object on the form.

Source Code for Secret.frm

```
Option Explicit
DefLng A-Z

Private Sub cmdBrowse_Click()
    'Prompt user for filename
    cdlOne.DialogTitle = "Secret"
    cdlOne.Flags = cdlOFNHideReadOnly
    cdlOne.Filter = "All files (*.*)|*.*"
    cdlOne.CancelError = True
    On Error Resume Next
    cdlOne.ShowOpen
    'Grab filename
    If Err = 0 Then
        txtFile.Text = cdlOne.filename
    End If
    On Error GoTo 0
End Sub

Private Sub cmdDecipher_Click()
    'Check password
    frmPassword.Show vbModal
    If Password$ = "" Then Exit Sub
    'Decipher file if password is valid
    If InStr(Head$, Hash$(Password$)) = 9 Then
        MousePointer = vbHourglass
        cmdEncipher.Enabled = False
        cmdDecipher.Enabled = False
        cmdView.Enabled = False
        cmdBrowse.Enabled = False
        Refresh
        Decipher
        txtFile_Change
        cmdBrowse.Enabled = True
        MousePointer = vbDefault
    Else
        MsgBox "Sorry - password incorrect for this file.", _
            48, "Secret"
    End If
End Sub

Private Sub cmdEncipher_Click()
    'Check password
    frmPassword.Show vbModal
    If Password$ = "" Then Exit Sub
```

(continued)

Source Code for Secret.frm *continued*

```
    'Encipher file
    MousePointer = vbHourglass
    cmdEncipher.Enabled = False
    cmdDecipher.Enabled = False
    cmdView.Enabled = False
    cmdBrowse.Enabled = False
    Refresh
    Encipher
    txtFile_Change
    cmdBrowse.Enabled = True
    MousePointer = vbDefault
End Sub

Private Sub cmdView_Click()
    Dim A$
    Dim i, ndx
    MousePointer = vbHourglass
    'Get file contents
    Open txtFile.Text For Binary As #1
    A$ = Space$(LOF(1))
    Get #1, , A$
    Close #1
    Do
        ndx = InStr(A$, Chr$(0))
        If ndx = 0 Or ndx > 5000 Then Exit Do
        Mid$(A$, ndx, 1) = Chr$(1)
    Loop
    'Display file contents
    MousePointer = vbDefault
    frmView.rtfView.Text = A$
    frmView.Caption = "Secret - " & txtFile.Text
    frmView.Show vbModal
End Sub

Private Sub Form_Load()
    'Center this form
    Left = (Screen.Width - Width) \ 2
    Top = (Screen.Height - Height) \ 2
    'Disable most command buttons
    cmdEncipher.Enabled = False
    cmdDecipher.Enabled = False
    cmdView.Enabled = False
```

(continued)

Source Code for Secret.frm *continued*

```
        'Initialize filename field
        txtFile.Text = ""
End Sub

Private Sub mnuAbout_Click()
        'Set properties
        About.Application = "Secret"
        About.Heading = "Microsoft Visual Basic 4.0 Developer's Workshop"
        About.Copyright = "1996 John Clark Craig"
        About.Display
End Sub

Private Sub mnuExit_Click()
        Unload Me
End Sub

Private Sub mnuContents_Click()
        cdlOne.HelpFile = App.Path & "\..\..\Help\Mvbdw.hlp"
        cdlOne.HelpCommand = cdlHelpContents
        cdlOne.ShowHelp
End Sub

Private Sub mnuSearch_Click()
        cdlOne.HelpFile = App.Path & "\..\..\Help\Mvbdw.hlp"
        cdlOne.HelpCommand = cdlHelpPartialKey
        cdlOne.ShowHelp
End Sub

Private Sub txtFile_Change()
        Dim FileLen
        'Check to see whether file exists
        On Error Resume Next
        FileLen = Len(Dir$(txtFile.Text))
        'Disable buttons if filename isn't valid
        If Err <> 0 Or FileLen = 0 Or Len(txtFile.Text) = 0 Then
            cmdEncipher.Enabled = False
            cmdDecipher.Enabled = False
            cmdView.Enabled = False
            Exit Sub
        End If
        'Get first 16 bytes of selected file
        Open txtFile.Text For Binary As #1
        Head$ = Space$(16)
        Get #1, , Head$
        Close #1
```

(continued)

Source Code for Secret.frm *continued*

```
        'Check to see whether file is already enciphered
        If InStr(Head$, "[Secret]") = 1 Then
            cmdEncipher.Enabled = False
            cmdDecipher.Enabled = True
        Else
            cmdEncipher.Enabled = True
            cmdDecipher.Enabled = False
        End If
        cmdView.Enabled = True
    End Sub

    Sub Encipher()
        Open txtFile.Text For Binary As #1
        Dim A$, H$
        'Load entire file into A$
        A$ = Space$(LOF(1))
        Get #1, , A$
        'Prepare header string
        H$ = "[Secret]" & Hash$(Password$) & vbCrLf
        'Do the actual encryption
        Process A$
        'Write header
        Put #1, 1, H$
        'Write enciphered data
        Put #1, , A$
        Close #1
    End Sub

    Sub Decipher()
        Open txtFile.Text For Binary As #1
        Dim A$, H$
        'Get header (first 18 bytes of enciphered file)
        H$ = Space$(18)
        'Get file contents (all remaining bytes in file)
        A$ = Space$(LOF(1) - 18)
        'Load header bytes
        Get #1, , H$
        'Load all the rest
        Get #1, , A$
        Close #1
        'Decipher file contents
        Process A$
        'Replace file with deciphered version
        Kill txtFile.Text
        Open txtFile.Text For Binary As #1
```

(continued)

Source Code for Secret.frm *continued*

```
    Put #1, , A$
    Close #1
End Sub

Sub Process(A$)
    Dim n1, n2, n3
    Dim i
    'Form control numbers from password
    For i = 1 To Len(Password$)
        n1 = n1 + Asc(Mid$(Password$, i, 1))
        n1 = (n1 * 367 + 331) Mod &HFFF
        n2 = ((n2 + n1) * 743 + 599) Mod &HFFF
        n3 = ((n3 + n2) * 563 + 787) Mod &HFFF
    Next i
    'Do the XOR cipher
    Cipher A$, n1, n2, n3
End Sub
```

Password.frm

Figure 30-13 shows the Password form during development. Two text boxes are provided for the user to type a password in twice. If the two passwords are not identical, a message box pops up and the user gets to try again. This technique helps prevent accidental typographical errors from clobbering the password, especially when the user sees only asterisks as the password phrase is typed.

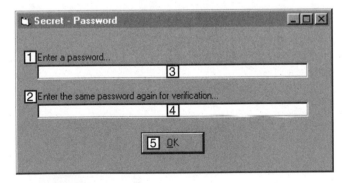

Figure 30-13.
The Password form during development.

To create this form, use the following table and source code to add the appropriate controls, set any nondefault properties as indicated, and type in the source code lines as shown.

Password.frm Objects and Property Settings

ID No.*	Property	Value
Form		
	Name	frmPassword
	BorderStyle	3 - Fixed Dialog
	Caption	Secret - Password
Label		
1	Name	lblPassword
	Caption	Enter a Password...
Label		
2	Name	lblPassCheck
	Caption	Enter the same password again for verification...
TextBox		
3	Name	txtPassword
	Font	Terminal
	PasswordChar	*
TextBox		
4	Name	txtPassCheck
	Font	Terminal
	PasswordChar	*
CommandButton		
5	Name	cmdOK
	Caption	&OK

* The number in the ID No. column corresponds to the number in Figure 30-13 that identifies the location of the object on the form.

Source Code for Password.frm

```
Option Explicit

Private Sub cmdOK_Click()
    'Make sure both passwords match exactly
    If txtPassword.Text <> txtPassCheck.Text Then
        MsgBox "The two passwords are not the same!", _
            vbExclamation, "Secret"
```

(continued)

501

Source Code for Password.frm *continued*

```
    Else
        Password$ = txtPassword.Text
        Unload Me
    End If
End Sub

Private Sub Form_Load()
    Password$ = ""
    'Center this form
    Left = (Screen.Width - Width) \ 2
    Top = (Screen.Height - Height) \ 2
End Sub
```

View.frm

This relatively simple form provides a read-only file viewer window for the Secret application. Figure 30-14 shows the View form during development. The only control this form contains is a RichTextBox control to display the selected file.

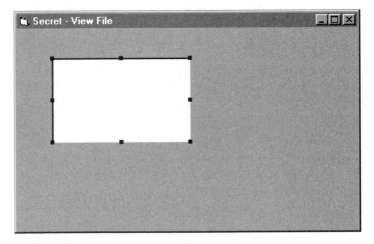

Figure 30-14.
The View form during development.

To create this form, use the following table and source code to add the appropriate control, set any nondefault properties as indicated, and type in the source code lines as shown.

View.frm Objects and Property Settings

Property	Value
Form	
Name	frmView
Caption	Secret - View File
MaxButton	False
MinButton	False
RichTextBox	
Name	rtfView
Scrollbars	3 - Both
Locked	True

Source Code for View.frm

```
Option Explicit

Private Sub Form_Resize()
    'Center this form
    Left = (Screen.Width - Width) \ 2
    Top = (Screen.Height - Height) \ 2
    'Size RichTextBox to fill form
    rtfView.Move 0, 0, ScaleWidth, ScaleHeight
End Sub
```

Secret.bas

This source code module provides two encryption routines that are at the heart of the Secret application. The Cipher subprogram is described in Chapter 14. The *Hash* function returns an 8-character hexadecimal number string for any string you pass to it. I use this function to compare a password entered for decryption with the hash string stored in the deciphered file's header line. If the two blocks of hexadecimal characters don't match, the user entered the wrong password and there's no need to continue the deciphering procedure.

A one-way hash doesn't tell an attacker what the password is. By definition, a one-way hash converts a variable-length input string to a fixed-length output string, with no easy conversion back the other way. It's easy to generate a hash value from a string, but it's much harder to figure out what the password is from the hash value. Its only use is to verify to a high degree of probability that the current password matches the original one.

To create this module, add a new module to your project and type in the source code lines as shown.

503

Source Code for Secret.bas

```
Option Explicit

Public Password$
Public Head$

Sub Cipher(Txt$, Optional Rvalue, Optional A, _
    Optional B)
    Static R As Long
    Static M As Long
    Static N As Long
    Const BigNum As Long = 32768
    Dim i As Long, c As Long, d As Long
    If IsMissing(Rvalue) = False Then
        R = Rvalue
    End If
    If IsMissing(A) Then
        If M = 0 Then M = 69
    Else
        M = (A * 4 + 1) Mod BigNum
    End If
    If IsMissing(B) Then
        If N = 0 Then N = 47
    Else
        N = (B * 2 + 1) Mod BigNum
    End If
    For i = 1 To Len(Txt$)
        c = Asc(Mid$(Txt$, i, 1))
        Select Case c
        Case 48 To 57
            d = c - 48
        Case 63 To 90
            d = c - 53
        Case 97 To 122
            d = c - 59
        Case Else
            d = -1
        End Select
        If d >= 0 Then
            R = (R * M + N) Mod BigNum
            d = (R And 63) Xor d
            Select Case d
            Case 0 To 9
                c = d + 48
            Case 10 To 37
                c = d + 53
```

(continued)

Source Code for Secret.bas *continued*

```
            Case 38 To 63
                c = d + 59
            End Select
            Mid$(Txt$, i, 1) = Chr$(c)
        End If
    Next i
End Sub

Function Hash$(A$)
    Dim i As Long, N As Long
    Dim H$
    For i = 1 To Len(A$)
        N = N + Asc(Mid$(A$, i, 1))
        N = (N * 1717 + 1717) Mod 1048576
    Next i
    For i = 1 To 7
        N = (N * 997 + 997) Mod 1048576
    Next i
    H$ = Right$("0000" & Hex$(N), 4)
    For i = 1 To Len(A$)
        N = N + Asc(Mid$(A$, i, 1))
        N = (N * 997 + 997) Mod 1048576
    Next i
    For i = 1 To 7
        N = (N * 1717 + 1717) Mod 1048576
    Next i
    Hash$ = H$ & Right$("0000" & Hex$(N), 4)
End Function
```

The BitPack Application

I created the BitPack application while experimenting with C-language DLLs to see how much extra speed I could squeeze out of Visual Basic. For certain types of problems, a C DLL can make a real difference in the speed-critical sections of your applications. The BitPack application demonstrates this well.

I created BitPack.dll to manipulate individual bits in a byte array, which is a task that Visual Basic is not particularly well suited for. This DLL provides three functions: *BitGet*, to return the current state of a bit; *BitSet*, to set the bit at the given location to 1; and *BitClr*, to set the bit to 0. You pass a byte array to these functions, along with a bit number, and the C code does the rest. For example, to retrieve bit number 542 from a byte array, the C code in the *BitGet* routine efficiently locates bit number 6 from byte number 67 in the array, extracts the bit, and returns 1 if that bit is set or 0 if it isn't. Byte arrays can be huge in 32-bit Visual Basic, so a practically unlimited store of bits can be accessed by these routines, all stored in a single byte array.

The Sieve of Eratosthenes (Generating a Table of Prime Numbers)

A practical use for these functions is in the field of data acquisition and process control. The state of thousands of switches, contact closures, and the like can be maintained in a byte array using only the three functions in the BitPack application (*BitGet*, *BitSet*, and *BitClr*). For this book, though, I created a small program to generate a table of prime numbers using the famous sieve of Eratosthenes. Each bit in the byte array represents an odd integer. Using a couple of nested loops, it's easy to toggle all bits representing nonprime numbers to 1s, leaving all primes as 0s. Because of the DLL's speed, we can generate a table of primes in the range 1 through 1,000,000, for example, in just a few seconds. When you realize how many times the *BitSet* and *BitGet* functions are called to generate this table, you begin to get a sense of how much the C-language DLL functions can speed up some types of code!

BitPack DLL Project Files

Before creating the Visual Basic application to generate the prime numbers table, you must create the DLL that is at the core of its operation. I covered the mechanics of creating a C-language DLL in Chapter 23, so I'll just present the source code for the two files that compose the Visual C++ project here. The BitPack.def file is quite short:

```
;BitPack.def
LIBRARY BitPack

CODE PRELOAD MOVEABLE DISCARDABLE
DATA PRELOAD MOVEABLE

EXPORTS
      BitGet        @1
      BitSet        @2
      BitClr        @3
```

The BitPack.c source code file is another short file. The efficient single-line functions perform all the addressing, masking, and other bit manipulations required to access or process a single bit anywhere in a huge byte array:

```
#include <windows.h>
#include <ole2.h>
```

(continued)

```
BYTE _stdcall BitGet( LPBYTE bytes, LONG bitpos )
{
    return( bytes[bitpos >> 3] & ( 1 << ( bitpos % 8 )) ? 1 : 0 );
}

BYTE _stdcall BitSet( LPBYTE bytes, LONG bitpos )
{
    return( bytes[bitpos >> 3] |= ( 1 << ( bitpos % 8 )));
}

BYTE _stdcall BitClr( LPBYTE bytes, LONG bitpos )
{
    return( bytes[bitpos >> 3] &= ~( 1 << ( bitpos % 8 )));
}
```

After you successfully create BitPack.dll, be sure you copy it into your Windows directory. Its three functions can then be declared and called from a Visual Basic program located anywhere in your system.

BitPack.frm

This form prompts the user for the largest desired prime number. It then calls the functions within the BitPack DLL to generate a table of prime numbers represented by bits in a byte array and creates an output file of the results. I've added a progress indicator bar to the form so you can monitor the speed of the prime number calculations. On my computer, the generation of the prime numbers table is faster than the creation of the output file! Figure 30-15 shows the form in action, as it calculates all prime numbers up to 1,000,000.

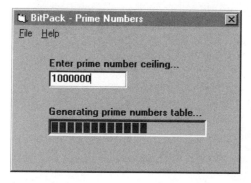

Figure 30-15.
The BitPack application as it generates prime numbers.

The output file of prime numbers is written to the file C:\Windows\ Desktop\Primes.txt, but you can change the location or the filename. The path and filename string is isolated for easy maintenance in a constant named FileName, near the top of the BitPack.frm source code. If you elect to generate a large table of prime numbers, this file can get to be fairly large. To roughly predict the size of the output file, cut the largest prime number value in half. For example, the generation of prime numbers up to 200,000 creates a Primes.txt file of just a little over 100,000 bytes in size. Figure 30-16 shows the contents of Primes.txt after the BitPack application has generated prime numbers up to 500.

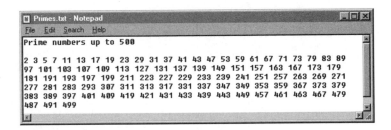

Figure 30-16.
The file Primes.txt listing the generated prime numbers.

This BitPack form provides a working example of the ProgressBar control. It monitors the progress of the application as it creates the prime numbers table, and also while it creates the Primes.txt output file. I've toggled the Visible properties of the ProgressBar and CommandButton controls so you'll always see one or the other, but not both at the same time. Figure 30-17 shows the BitPack form during development.

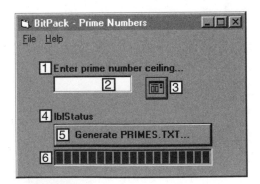

Figure 30-17.
The BitPack form during development.

To create this form, use the following tables and source code to add the appropriate controls, set any nondefault properties as indicated, and type in the source code lines as shown.

BitPack.frm Menu Design Window Entries

Caption	Name	Indentation	Enabled
&File	mnuFile	0	True
&New	mnuNew	1	False
&Open...	mnuOpen	1	False
&Save	mnuSave	1	False
Save &As...	mnuSaveAs	1	False
-	mnuFileDash1	1	True
E&xit	mnuExit	1	True
&Help	mnuHelp	0	True
&Contents	mnuContents	1	True
&Search for Help on...	mnuSearch	1	True
-	mnuHelpDash1	1	True
&About...	mnuAbout	1	True

BitPack.frm Objects and Property Settings

ID No.*	Property	Value
Form		
	Name	frmBitPack
	BorderStyle	3 - Fixed Dialog
	Caption	BitPack - Prime Numbers
Label		
1	Name	lblPrompt
	Caption	Enter prime number ceiling...
TextBox		
2	Name	txtMaxPrime

* The number in the ID No. column corresponds to the number in Figure 30-17 that identifies the location of the object on the form.

(continued)

509

BitPack.frm Objects and Property Settings *continued*

ID No.	Property	Value
CommonDialog		
3	Name	cdlOne
Label		
4	Name	lblStatus
CommandButton		
5	Name	cmdPrimes
	Caption	Generate PRIMES.TXT...
ProgressBar		
6	Name	prgOne

Source Code for BitPack.frm

```
Option Explicit
DefLng A-Z

Private Declare Function BitGet _
Lib "BitPack.dll" ( _
    ByRef b As Byte, _
    ByVal n As Long _
) As Byte

Private Declare Function BitSet _
Lib "BitPack.dll" ( _
    ByRef b As Byte, _
    ByVal n As Long _
) As Byte

Private Declare Function BitClr _
Lib "BitPack.dll" ( _
    ByRef b As Byte, _
    ByVal n As Long _
) As Byte

'Change output path or filename here
Const FileName = "C:\Windows\Desktop\Primes.txt"
```

(continued)

Source Code for BitPack.frm *continued*

```
Private Sub cmdPrimes_Click()
    Dim n, i, j, k
    Dim NextVal, LastVal
    Dim b() As Byte
    Dim p$
    MousePointer = vbHourglass
    cmdPrimes.Visible = False
    prgOne.Top = cmdPrimes.Top
    prgOne.Visible = True
    prgOne.Value = 0
    'Get largest prime number specified
    n = Abs(Val(txtMaxPrime.Text))
    'Match only odd numbers to bits in byte array
    ReDim b(n \ 16)
    'Keep user informed of progress
    lblStatus.Caption = "Generating prime numbers table..."
    Refresh
    'Process byte array.  0 bits represent prime numbers.
    k = (n - 3) \ 2
    For i = 0 To k
        'If next number is prime...
        If BitGet(b(0), i) = 0 Then
            '...set bits that are multiples
            For j = 3 * i + 3 To k Step 2 * i + 3
                BitSet b(0), j
            Next j
            'Update progress bar, but not too often
            NextVal = Int(100 * i / k)
            If NextVal <> LastVal Then
                LastVal = NextVal
                prgOne.Value = NextVal
            End If
        End If
    Next i
    'Keep user informed
    lblStatus.Caption = "Writing prime numbers file..."
    LastVal = 0
    prgOne.Value = 0
    Refresh
    'Write primes to file on desktop
    Open FileName For Output As #1
    'Bit table starts at 3, so output 2 as prime
    Print #1, "Prime numbers up to" & Str$(n) & vbCrLf
    p$ = "2"
```

(continued)

Source Code for BitPack.frm *continued*

```
    For i = 0 To k
        'If prime number...
        If BitGet(b(0), i) = 0 Then
            'Concatenate number with string for output
            p$ = p$ & Str$(i + i + 3)
            'If string is long enough...
            If Len(p$) > 65 Then
                'Output string to file
                Print #1, LTrim$(p$)
                'Prepare for next line of output
                p$ = ""
                'Update progress bar, but not too often
                NextVal = Int(100 * i / k)
                If NextVal > LastVal Then
                    LastVal = NextVal
                    prgOne.Value = NextVal
                End If
            End If
        End If
    Next i
    'Print any last-line primes
    Print #1, LTrim$(p$)
    Close #1
    'Set form to original visible state
    lblStatus.Caption = ""
    cmdPrimes.Visible = True
    prgOne.Visible = False
    MousePointer = vbDefault
End Sub

Private Sub Form_Load()
    txtMaxPrime.Text = ""
    lblStatus.Caption = ""
End Sub

Private Sub mnuAbout_Click()
    'Set properties
    About.Application = "BitPack"
    About.Heading = "Microsoft Visual Basic 4.0 Developer's Workshop"
    About.Copyright = "1996 John Clark Craig"
    About.Display
End Sub

Private Sub mnuExit_Click()
    Unload Me
End Sub
```

(continued)

Source Code for BitPack.frm *continued*

```
Private Sub mnuContents_Click()
    cdlOne.HelpFile = App.Path & "\..\..\Help\Mvbdw.hlp"
    cdlOne.HelpCommand = cdlHelpContents
    cdlOne.ShowHelp
End Sub

Private Sub mnuSearch_Click()
    cdlOne.HelpFile = App.Path & "\..\..\Help\Mvbdw.hlp"
    cdlOne.HelpCommand = cdlHelpPartialKey
    cdlOne.ShowHelp
End Sub
```

In the BitPack form, all calls to the bit manipulation functions in Bit-Pack.dll pass the first member of the byte array *b()*. You can also pass a single nonarray byte variable to these functions, in which case the BitPos parameter should stay in the range 0 through 7. For maximum speed, I elected not to include range-checking code within the DLL, so it's up to you to develop the code to prevent your application from passing BitPos values outside the range of a byte value or of a byte array. Because there are 8 bits per byte-array element, an array dimensioned with the value 100, for example, has a range of legal BitPos values from 0 through 807.

To compute prime numbers using the sieve of Eratosthenes, I mapped the odd integers 3, 5, 7,… to the bits 0, 1, 2,… in the byte array. This allows a range of 16 integers to be covered in each 8-bit byte element. Because Visual Basic 4 supports huge byte arrays, you can theoretically compute primes up to a huge value using this program.

The Dialogs Application

The CommonDialog control provides many powerful options for interacting with users in a standard way. The Dialogs application illustrates the five common dialog boxes provided by this one control. I've set up five buttons in a toolbar to activate the Open, Save As, Color, Font, and Print dialog boxes. The user's choices in each dialog box are displayed for verification, but no files or settings are affected. You can select any file on your system while the Save As dialog box is displayed, for instance, but the file is left unaffected.

On the following pages, Figure 30-18 shows the Dialogs application at runtime and Figures 30-19 through 30-23 show the dialog boxes that appear when you click the associated buttons in the toolbar.

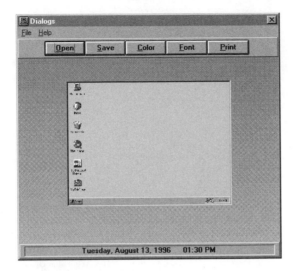

Figure 30-18.
The Dialogs application in action.

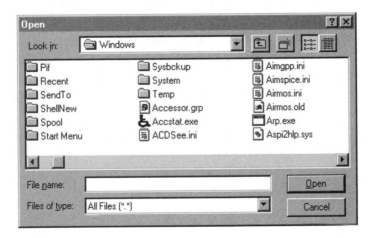

Figure 30-19.
The CommonDialog control's Open dialog box.

Figure 30-20.
The CommonDialog control's Save As dialog box.

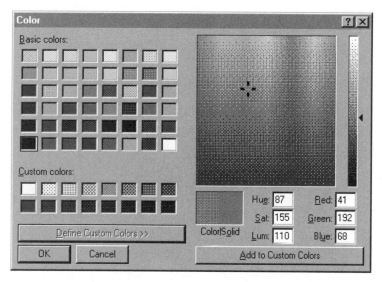

Figure 30-21.
The CommonDialog control's Color dialog box.

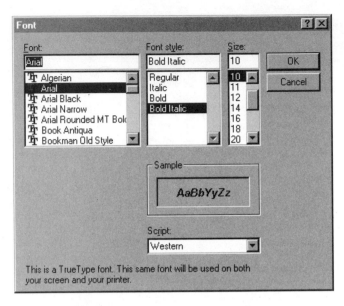

Figure 30-22.
The CommonDialog control's Font dialog box.

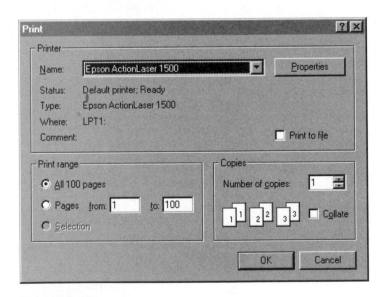

Figure 30-23.
The CommonDialog control's Print dialog box.

I like to keep this application handy while working on new applications. When I need to set up a color selection feature in my new application, for example, I simply copy the relevant code from the Dialogs application, add a CommonDialog control, and modify the code for any unique requirements of the new application. Often this method saves me time compared to searching the online help to recall how to set up the CommonDialog control.

Some Special Features

The Dialogs application contains several unique features that demonstrate some handy techniques.

About and About2

Two types of About dialog boxes are shown by this program. The Help menu has both an About item and an About2 item. The About dialog box is the one I've used in many of the applications throughout this book, and the About2 dialog box provides the alternative About dialog box I presented in the VBClock application in Chapter 27. Although both forms create similar About dialog boxes in the application, they are created using different techniques. I've included both of them here so you can do a direct comparison of the two techniques.

The Sunset Background

There are a few other interesting twists to this application. By a simple modification of the blue-to-black fade algorithm presented in Chapter 10, this form's background fades from red to yellow, like a colorful sunset. It's easy to tweak this code to fade from any color to another color that you specify. A more subtle color gradation would probably be more appropriate for many forms, but I liked the bright colors for this demonstration application.

The Hidden Message

I've also added a hidden message to this application, along the lines of the Easter egg presented in Chapter 14. Hidden messages, such as author credits, can be activated in a nearly infinite number of ways. In this application, I keep track of the locations of the last four mouse clicks on the main form. When the correct sequence of clicks occurs near each of the corners of the picture box in the middle of the form, a borderless, full-screen message window pops up for 10 seconds. Try clicking just outside the picture box, near the upper-left corner, then near the upper-right corner, the lower-right corner, and finally near the lower-left corner. If the order and locations of these four clicks are correct, you'll see a bright yellow full-screen message. Figure 30-24 shows the 10-second message that appears immediately after the last click.

This "Egg" (hidden message)
will disappear in 10 seconds.

Figure 30-24.
The hidden message.

Form Position

Throughout this book, I've centered most forms on the screen during each form's load event. A slight modification of this technique allows you to position a form at any location on the screen. To see how this works, click anywhere on the screen graphic in the middle of the Dialog application's main form. If you click one-quarter of the way across the image of the screen, and three-quarters of the way down from its top, the entire form will jump to the same relative position on the real screen. After a short delay of 2 seconds, the form relocates to the center of the screen again, so you can experiment further. Take a look at the picScreen_Click event routine in the source code to see how the form's center is moved temporarily to the relative position indicated by the mouse click in the picture box. Figure 30-25 shows the mouse at roughly the position described above, and Figure 30-26 shows the form's new, temporary location on my screen.

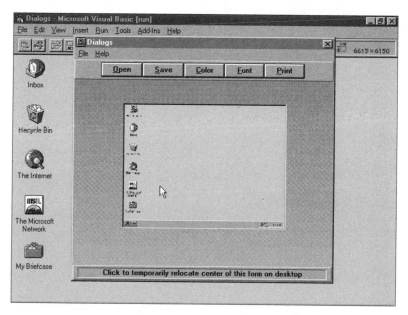

Figure 30-25.
Clicking in the picture box to cause the application to temporarily relocate.

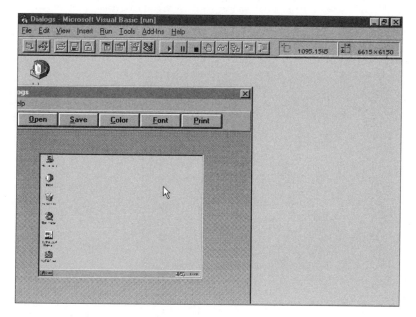

Figure 30-26.
The entire application temporarily located in the indicated position on the screen.

The Application Files

The Dialogs project contains four files. In addition to the main Dialogs form, two types of About dialog forms and a special hidden messages form are part of the project. Figure 30-27 shows the project list window.

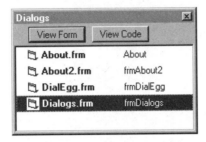

Figure 30-27.
The Dialogs application project list.

Dialogs.frm

The Dialogs form displays what looks like the Windows 95 desktop within a form. Actually, a picture box in the middle of the form displays a small image of the Windows 95 desktop. (As described in the previous section, a click any-where in this image causes the form to temporarily jump to the same relative position on the real desktop.) Figure 30-28 shows the Dialogs form during development.

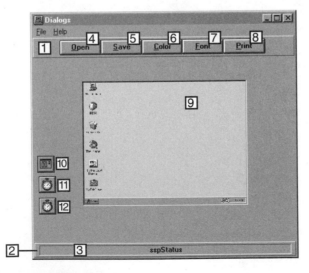

Figure 30-28.
The Dialogs form during development.

I've used several SSPanel and SSCommand controls to set up the tool-bar, status bar, and command buttons. These controls provide a lot of appearance options, and I encourage you to experiment with them freely. If I can get away with drawing a sunset in the background, just imagine what other possibilities there must be!

To create this form, use the following tables and source code to add the appropriate controls, set any nondefault properties as indicated, and type in the source code lines as shown.

Dialogs.frm Menu Design Window Entries

Caption	Name	Indentation	Enabled
&File	mnuFile	0	True
&New	mnuNew	1	False
&Open...	mnuOpen	1	False
&Save	mnuSave	1	False
Save &As...	mnuSaveAs	1	False
-	mnuFileDash1	1	True
E&xit	mnuExit	1	True
&Help	mnuHelp	0	True
&Contents	mnuContents	1	True
&Search for Help on...	mnuSearch	1	True
-	mnuHelpDash1	1	True
&About...	mnuAbout	1	True
About&2...	mnuAbout2	1	True

Dialogs.frm Objects and Property Settings

ID No.*	Property	Value
Form		
	Name	frmDialogs
	Caption	Dialogs
	BorderStyle	3 - Fixed Dialog
	Icon	Pc01.ico

* The number in the ID No. column corresponds to the number in Figure 30-28 that identifies the location of the object on the form.

(continued)

Dialogs.frm Objects and Property Settings *continued*

ID No.	Property	Value
SSPanel		
1	Name	sspTop
	Align	1 - Align Top
SSPanel		
2	Name	sspBottom
	Align	2 - Align Bottom
SSPanel		
3	Name	sspStatus
	BevelOuter	1 - Inset
SSCommand		
4	Name	sscOpen
	Caption	&Open
SSCommand		
5	Name	sscSave
	Caption	&Save
SSCommand		
6	Name	sscColor
	Caption	&Color
SSCommand		
7	Name	sscFont
	Caption	&Font
SSCommand		
8	Name	sscPrint
	Caption	&Print
PictureBox		
9	Name	picScreen
	AutoSize	True
	Picture	Desktop.bmp

(continued)

Dialogs.frm Objects and Property Settings *continued*

ID No.	Property	Value
CommonDialog		
10	Name	cdlOne
Timer		
11	Name	tmrClock
	Interval	100
Timer		
12	Name	tmrRelocate
	Enabled	False
	Interval	2000

Source Code for Dialogs.frm

```
Option Explicit

Dim mX, mY
Dim LastSec
Dim EggX(1 To 4), EggY(1 To 4)

Private Sub Form_Click()
    Dim i As Integer
    'Keep track of last four clicks on form
    For i = 1 To 3
        EggX(i) = EggX(i + 1)
        EggY(i) = EggY(i + 1)
    Next i
    EggX(4) = mX
    EggY(4) = mY
    'Check for correct sequence and position
    If Abs(EggX(1) - 70) < 15 And _
    Abs(EggY(1) - 60) < 15 And _
    Abs(EggX(2) - 360) < 15 And _
    Abs(EggY(2) - 60) < 15 And _
    Abs(EggX(3) - 360) < 15 And _
    Abs(EggY(3) - 290) < 15 And _
    Abs(EggX(4) - 70) < 15 And _
    Abs(EggY(4) - 290) < 15 Then
```

(continued)

Source Code for Dialogs.frm *continued*

```vb
            'Display hidden message
            frmDialEgg.Show vbModal
        End If
    End Sub

    Private Sub Form_Load()
        'Center this form
        Left = (Screen.Width - Width) \ 2
        Top = (Screen.Height - Height) \ 2
    End Sub

    Private Sub Form_MouseMove(Button As Integer, _
        Shift As Integer, X As Single, Y As Single)
        'Signal timer to update status bar
        LastSec = -1
        'Keep track of mouse location
        mX = X
        mY = Y
    End Sub

    Private Sub Form_Paint()
        Dim i As Long
        ScaleMode = vbPixels
        DrawStyle = 5 'Transparent
        DrawWidth = 1
        'Draw sunset background (fade from red to yellow)
        For i = 0 To ScaleHeight Step ScaleHeight \ 16
            Line (-1, i - 1)-(ScaleWidth, i + ScaleHeight \ 16), _
                RGB(255, i * 255 \ ScaleHeight, 0), BF
        Next i
    End Sub

    Private Sub mnuAbout_Click()
        'Set properties for the About dialog box
        About.Application = "Dialogs"
        About.Heading = "Microsoft Visual Basic 4.0 Developer's Workshop"
        About.Copyright = "1996 John Clark Craig"
        About.Display
    End Sub

    Private Sub mnuAbout2_Click()
        'Display the About2 dialog box
        frmAbout2.Display
    End Sub
```

(continued)

Source Code for Dialogs.frm *continued*

```vb
Private Sub mnuExit_Click()
    Unload Me
End Sub

Private Sub mnuContents_Click()
    cdlOne.HelpFile = App.Path & "\..\..\Help\Mvbdw.hlp"
    cdlOne.HelpCommand = cdlHelpContents
    cdlOne.ShowHelp
End Sub

Private Sub mnuSearch_Click()
    cdlOne.HelpFile = App.Path & "\..\..\Help\Mvbdw.hlp"
    cdlOne.HelpCommand = cdlHelpPartialKey
    cdlOne.ShowHelp
End Sub

Private Sub picScreen_Click()
    Dim Xpct, Ypct
    'Determine mouse's relative position in picture
    Xpct = 100 * mX \ picScreen.ScaleWidth
    Ypct = 100 * mY \ picScreen.ScaleHeight
    'Move form's center to same relative position on screen
    Left = Screen.Width * Xpct \ 100 - Width \ 2
    Top = Screen.Height * Ypct \ 100 - Height \ 2
    'Set timer to move form back later
    tmrRelocate.Enabled = True
End Sub

Private Sub picScreen_MouseMove(Button As Integer, _
    Shift As Integer, X As Single, Y As Single)
    'Keep track of mouse location
    mX = X
    mY = Y
    'Update status message at bottom of form
    sspStatus = "Click to temporarily relocate center " & _
        "of this form on desktop"
    'Signal timer not to display date and time in status bar
    LastSec = -2
End Sub

Private Sub sscColor_Click()
    'Set flags for Color dialog box
    cdlOne.Flags = cdlCCRGBInit
```

(continued)

Source Code for Dialogs.frm *continued*

```
    'Show Color dialog box
    cdlOne.ShowColor
    'Display selected color value
    MsgBox "&H" & Hex$(cdlOne.Color), , _
        "Selected color..."
End Sub

Private Sub sscFont_Click()
    Dim Tab2 As String
    Tab2 = vbTab & vbTab
    'Set flags for Font dialog box
    cdlOne.Flags = cdlCFWYSIWYG + cdlCFBoth + cdlCFScalableOnly
    'Show Font dialog box
    cdlOne.ShowFont
    'Display selected font values
    MsgBox _
        "Font Name:" & vbTab & cdlOne.FontName & vbCrLf & _
        "Font Size:" & Tab2 & cdlOne.FontSize & vbCrLf & _
        "Bold:" & Tab2 & cdlOne.FontBold & vbCrLf & _
        "Italic:" & Tab2 & cdlOne.FontItalic, , _
        "Selected font..."
End Sub

Private Sub sscOpen_Click()
    'Set up sample filter for Open dialog box
    Dim Bat$, Txt$, All$
    Bat$ = "Batch Files (*.bat)|*.bat"
    Txt$ = "Text Files (*.txt)|*.txt"
    All$ = "All Files (*.*)|*.*"
    cdlOne.Filter = Bat$ & "|" & Txt$ & "|" & All$
    'Set default filter to third one listed
    cdlOne.FilterIndex = 3
    'Hide "ReadOnly" check box
    cdlOne.Flags = cdlOFNHideReadOnly
    'Deselect previously selected file, if any
    cdlOne.filename = ""
    'Show Open dialog box
    cdlOne.ShowOpen
    'Display selected filename
    If cdlOne.filename = "" Then Exit Sub
    MsgBox cdlOne.filename, , "Selected file..."
End Sub
```

(continued)

Source Code for Dialogs.frm *continued*

```
Private Sub sscPrint_Click()
    Dim PrintToFile$
    'Set flags for Print dialog box
    cdlOne.Flags = cdlPDAllPages + cdlPDNoSelection
    'Set imaginary page range
    cdlOne.Min = 1
    cdlOne.Max = 100
    cdlOne.FromPage = 1
    cdlOne.ToPage = 100
    'Show Print dialog box
    cdlOne.ShowPrinter
    'Extract some printer data
    If cdlOne.Flags And cdlPDPrintToFile Then
        PrintToFile$ = "Yes"
    Else
        PrintToFile$ = "No"
    End If
    'Display selected print values
    MsgBox _
        "Begin Page:" & vbTab & cdlOne.FromPage & vbCrLf & _
        "End Page:" & vbTab & cdlOne.ToPage & vbCrLf & _
        "No. Copies:" & vbTab & cdlOne.Copies & vbCrLf & _
        "Print to file:" & vbTab & PrintToFile$ _
        , , "Selected print information..."
End Sub

Private Sub sscSave_Click()
    'Set up filter for Save As dialog box
    Dim Bat$, Txt$, All$
    Bat$ = "Batch Files (*.bat)|*.bat"
    Txt$ = "Text Files (*.txt)|*.txt"
    All$ = "All Files (*.*)|*.*"
    cdlOne.Filter = Bat$ & "|" & Txt$ & "|" & All$
    'Set default filter to third one listed
    cdlOne.FilterIndex = 3
    'Hide ReadOnly check box
    cdlOne.Flags = cdlOFNHideReadOnly
    'Deselect previously selected file, if any
    cdlOne.filename = ""
    'Show Save As dialog box
    cdlOne.ShowSave
```

(continued)

Source Code for Dialogs.frm *continued*

```
        'Display selected file
        If cdlOne.filename = "" Then Exit Sub
        MsgBox cdlOne.filename, , "'Save As' file..."
    End Sub

    Private Sub tmrRelocate_Timer()
        'Relocate form once per move
        tmrRelocate.Enabled = False
        'Center this form
        Left = (Screen.Width - Width) \ 2
        Top = (Screen.Height - Height) \ 2
    End Sub

    Private Sub tmrClock_Timer()
        Dim Sec
        Sec = Second(Now)
        If Sec = LastSec Then Exit Sub
        If LastSec = -2 Then Exit Sub
        LastSec = Sec
        'Update date and time in status bar
        sspStatus = Format(Date, "Long Date") & _
            Space$(5) & Format(Time, "hh:mm AMPM")
    End Sub
```

DialEgg.frm

DialEgg.frm is a borderless, full-screen form that displays the secret message when the user clicks in the specified locations in the correct sequence. A timer causes the form to unload itself after a 10-second delay, although you could easily modify this form to unload when the user clicks anywhere on the form. Feel free to change the message or enhance the form as you want. Figure 30-29 shows the form during development. Notice that at runtime the border of the form is not visible and the form is displayed in its maximized state so it covers the entire screen. Code in the load event moves the message to the center of the screen.

To create this form, use the following table and source code to add the appropriate controls, set any nondefault properties as indicated, and type in the source code lines as shown.

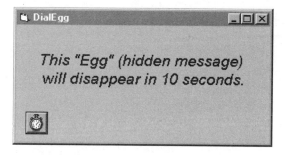

Figure 30-29.
The DialEgg form during development.

DialEgg.frm Objects and Property Settings

Property	Value
Form	
Name	frmDialEgg
Caption	DialEgg
BackColor	&H0000FFFF&
BorderStyle	0 - None
ControlBox	False
MaxButton	False
MinButton	False
WindowState	2 - Maximized
Label	
Name	lblEgg
Alignment	2 - Center
Caption	This "Egg" (hidden message) will disappear in 10 seconds.
Font	Arial - Italic - 14
BackColor	&H0000FFFF&
Timer	
Name	tmrQuit
Enabled	True
Interval	10000

Source Code for DialEgg.frm

```
Option Explicit

Private Sub Form_Load()
    lblEgg.Move (Screen.Width - lblEgg.Width) \ 2, _
        (Screen.Height - lblEgg.Height) \ 2
End Sub

Private Sub tmrQuit_Timer()
    Unload Me
End Sub
```

INDEX

Note: *Italicized* page references indicate figures, tables, or program listings.

John Clark Craig

Since 1980, John Clark Craig has written more than a dozen books on computer programming, including *Microsoft Visual Basic Workshop, Windows Edition* (Microsoft Press, 1993), *The Microsoft Visual Basic for MS-DOS Workshop* (Microsoft Press, 1993), *Microsoft QuickC Programmer's Toolbox* (Microsoft Press, 1990), and *Microsoft QuickBASIC Programmer's Toolbox* (Microsoft Press, 1988). He also made substantial contributions to the first and second editions of *Microsoft Mouse Programmer's Reference* (Microsoft Press, 1989, 1991), *Microsoft Windows 3.1 Developer's Workshop* (Microsoft Press, 1993), and *Microsoft Word Developer's Kit* (Microsoft Press, 1994). Craig lives with his family in Castle Rock, Colorado.

The manuscript for this book was prepared and submitted to Microsoft Press in electronic form. Text files were prepared using Microsoft Word 6.0 for Windows. Pages were composed by Microsoft Press using Aldus PageMaker 5.0 for Windows, with text in New Baskerville and display type in Helvetica Bold. Composed pages were delivered to the printer as electronic prepress files.

Cover Graphic Designer
Greg Erickson

Cover Illustrator
Glenn Mitsui

Interior Graphic Designer
Kim Eggleston

Interior Graphic Artist
Michael Victor

Principal Compositor
Barb Runyan

Principal Proofreader/Copy Editor
Shawn Peck

Indexer
Foxon-Maddocks Associates

Register Today!

Return this

Microsoft® Visual Basic® 4.0 Developer's Workshop

registration card for a Microsoft Press® catalog

U.S. and Canada addresses only. Fill in information below and mail postage-free. Please mail only the bottom half of this page.

1-55615-664-2A   *Microsoft® Visual Basic® 4.0 Developer's Workshop*   *Owner Registration Card*

_____
NAME

_____
INSTITUTION OR COMPANY NAME

_____
ADDRESS

_____

_____
CITY   STATE   ZIP

Microsoft®*Press*
Quality Computer Books

**For a free catalog of
Microsoft Press® products, call
1-800-MSPRESS**